The Third World in Perspective

The Third World in Perspective

H.A. Reitsma and J.M.G. Kleinpenning

With a foreword by Stanley Brunn

Rowman & Allanheld, 1985

Library of Congress Cataloging-in-Publication Data

Reitsma, H.A.

The third world in perspective.

Includes bibliographical references and indexes.
1. Developing countries – Economic conditions. 2. Developing countries – Economic policy.
3. Economic development. I. Kleinpenning, J.M.G. II. Title.
HC59.7.R43 1985 330.9172'4 85-14507
ISBN 0-8476-7450-9

Photo Credits
Photo 10, Girls in Benin. Janny Groen; Photo 11, Settler's home in Ecuador. Matthijs de Vreede; Photo 13, Granaries in Mali. G.J. Wijchers; Photo 15, Terraced rice fields in Bali. Roel Burgler; Photo 19, Rice production in Sierra Leone. A.W. Haas; Photo 20, Rural market in Gambia. Jan Zwart; Photo 23, Textile mill in Mexico. Michel Pellanders; Photo 29, Drying laundry in Karachi. Ron Giling; Photo 30, Garbage dump in Honduras. Hans Spruyt; Photo 31, Urban scene in Morocco. Janny Poley; Photo 33, Residential neighborhood in Benin City. Hans Spruyt; Photo 35, Squatter settlement in Jakarta. Ron Giling; Photo 37, Nomads in Ethiopia. Sipke van der Land; Photo 39, Railroad construction in India. Marcel Minnée; Photo 40, Road construction in India. Marcel Minnée; Photo 41, Chopping kindling in India. Marcel Minnée; Photo 42, Bathing in India. Marcel Minnée; Photo 44, Crop production in Taiwan. Kuang Hua Film Syndicate; Photo 45, Air-conditioned dormitory in Taiwan. Kuang Hua Film Syndicate; Photo 46, Shopping street in downtown Taipei. Kuang Hua Film Syndicate; Photo 47, Urban development in Taipei. Kuang Hua Film Syndicate.
    All other photos were provided by Voorlichtingsdienst Ontwikkelingssamenwerking (VDO), Ministerie van Buitenlandse Zaken, The Hague, Netherlands.

Printed in The Netherlands by Van Gorcum, Assen

The more general a fact, the more precious it is. Those which serve many times are better than those which have little chance of coming up again.

How then choose the interesting fact, the one that begins again and again? . . . It's proper to begin with the regular facts, but after a rule is established beyond all doubt, the facts in conformity with it become dull because they no longer teach us anything new. Then it's the exception that becomes important. We seek not resemblances but differences, choose the most accentuated differences because they're the most striking and also the most instructive . . . But what we ought to aim at is less the ascertainment of resemblances and differences than the recognition of likenesses hidden under apparent divergences.

Robert M. Pirsig, Zen and the Art of Motorcycle Maintenance.

Foreword

Within the past decade, Third World countries and regions have achieved their proper status in the international economic, political, and cultural communities. This international emergence has been accompanied by swelling populations, frequent changes in political leadership, persistent economic woes, and exposure to pervasive natural and technological hazards. For the developed nations to understand the variety and diversity of countries and regions lumped together as the 'Third World,' we need to examine in detail their economic, demographic, and social geographies. Equally vital to our comprehension of these regions is why they are underdeveloped. Critical assessments of the accuracy, utility, and validity of the theories of colonialism, imperialism, dependency, and Marxism will help to answer the whys and wherefores of development.

Reitsma and Kleinpenning provide a timely, comprehensive, and scholarly examination of the human geographies of the Third World, in which they identify salient features and patterns of agricultural, industrial, and service economies. They also examine the problems of urban squatters, land reform, poverty, health care, refugees, overpopulation, and cultural conflict endemic to the Third World. The authors point out that many countries are making deliberate and effective progress in solving these and other problems. Reitsma and Kleinpenning's examinations of the reasons for underdevelopment, and their case studies of Ethiopia, India, Cuba, and Taiwan will be especially valuable for use in intermediate and advanced geography classes, where their parallels to underdevelopment in other Latin American, African, and Asian countries can be utilized.

The authors present a readable, well-written, and relatively bias-free geography and enrich our thinking about Third World theories and their utility in examining current economic, social, and political problems. To university students, this book will demonstrate the importance of our continuing to study the historical, current, and future geographies of Third World countries and regions. It will elevate our awareness of the Third World and is appropriate for a growing number of classes devoted to these regions.

Stanley D. Brunn
University of Kentucky

Preface

The number of poor countries far exceeds the number of rich countries. More than twice as many people live in the Third World as in the First and Second Worlds combined. Notwithstanding these facts, Western geographers generally have paid relatively little attention to the low-income countries of Africa, Asia and Latin America. Although interest in the Third World has been growing in recent years, there was prior to 1982 not one English-language geography text that dealt specifically with the problems of underdevelopment.

Because an excellent introductory text, written in Dutch, has been available since 1978, it seemed only logical to translate this book, *Profiel van de Derde Wereld (Profile of the Third World)* into English. The result is the book lying before you. In addition to a change in title, the present text differs from its predecessor in several respects. A number of chapters in *Profiel* have been deleted, while others have been rewritten and updated. A new introductory chapter, four case studies of individual countries, and a new Epilogue have been added.

When writing a textbook, authors are constantly faced with difficult questions. What should be included and what should not? How detailed should the selected topics be discussed? How much attention must be given to theory; how much to empirical studies? What should be treated first and what later? The answers to such questions depend above all on the purpose for which the book is written.

The chief objective of this introductory text is to stimulate interest in, concern about, and understanding of, the problem of underdevelopment. It is our belief that this objective can best be achieved by focusing on *processes* of development and underdevelopment. As geographers we are particularly interested in finding out how and why in the course of time these processes have differed from place to place.

Like every other textbook, the present one constitutes a compromise. It does not contain separate chapters on population growth, ecological deterioration, international trade relations, and various other important issues. Instead, we thought it more appropriate to deal with these subjects in a number of different places, including the four regional case studies. Throughout the book we have been guided by our firm conviction that insight into the complexity of the development problematique is fostered more by analyzing thoroughly a limited number of key topics than by dealing rather superficially with 'all' aspects of development and underdevelopment.

Since our main concern is to *explain* processes of development and underdevelopment in different places, *theories* are given a prominent place in this book. Students who question the relevance of theoretical discussions should remember that no explanation is possible without theory. Facts cannot explain; they remain mere facts, isolated and meaningless, unless they are 'tied together' by some conceptual framework. Theory is needed to discover how apparently unrelated facts and events interact with each other in numerous and often unsuspected ways.

A small amount of theory is presented in chapters 1 and 2. The major theoretical chapters (14 through 16) have been purposely placed where they appear; not at the beginning or the end of the book, but following the rather factual and descriptive chapters in Parts Two and Three, and preceding the case studies in Part Five. This arrangement has several advantages: (1) it avoids 'turning off' at an early stage students who are not particularly theory-minded; (2) it offers the reader an opportunity to reflect in a meaningful way on the material presented in Parts Two and Three; and (3) it permits students to test the various theories when reading the case studies at the end of the book, thus enabling them to find out for themselves which theories are most useful for explaining spatial patterns of development and underdevelopment.

Some of the most difficult questions with which we have struggled concern the case studies. How many should be included and, more importantly, which countries should be selected? Our choice of countries was influenced by two important considerations: (1) each country should be discussed in considerable detail so as to enable us to trace its particular process of developmental change through history, and (2) each country should differ in a number of important respects from the others, so that together they would introduce the reader to a wide variety of past and present circumstances that have contributed to underdevelopment. This variety is necessary in order to be able to adequately test the theories presented in Part Four. On the basis of these criteria, only four countries were selected: Ethiopia, India, Cuba and Taiwan.

Whereas the number of tables has been deliberately kept to a minimum, we have not refrained from repeating ourselves in various places. A certain amount of repetition has been included on purpose, based on the argument that most humans are unable to absorb and digest everything they read when they are exposed to it only once.

We are indebted to Professor Stanley D. Brunn, Chairman of the Department of Geography at the University of Kentucky and Editor of *The Professional Geographer,* for spending many hours of his precious time correcting an earlier version of the manuscript and for making numerous useful suggestions. We are also grateful to Professor Alan C. Best, Department of Geography, Boston University, who encouraged us to rewrite the Epilogue.

Autumn 1984   H.A. Reitsma
                                                          J.M.G. Kleinpenning

Contents

PART ONE   THE THIRD WORLD'S UNDERDEVELOPMENT IN PERSPECTIVE

The period 1945-1955: reconstruction and disinterest / The period 1955-1965: decolonization and optimism / The period of growing skepticism: 1965-1975 / 1975-1985: Global crisis and global interdependence

Underdevelopment and underdevelopedness / Awareness and underdevelopedness / Development as a culturally relative concept / Garrett Hardin's lifeboat ethics (box) / Underdevelopment defined / Measuring underdevelopment: a dilemma / Diversity and underdevelopment

PART TWO   THE RURAL-AGRICULTURAL SCENE

Rural and urban areas / The agricultural sector / Third World crises (box) / Drugs production in the Third World (box)

Large landholdings, labor relations and tenancy / Land settlement in North America (box) / Problems in areas with excessive fragmentation of landownership / Other aspects of the legal framework / Land reforms: accomplished results – possible alternatives / Colonization as an alternate approach

Crop rotation, fallow and fertilization / The use of seed, seedlings and breeding stock / Inadequate protection of crops, livestock and farmland / Irrigation / Machines versus human labor / Low productivity / A world of paradoxes

Poorly developed livestock raising; poorly fed animals / Marginal livestock production: an explanation / Possibilities for expanding and improving livestock raising

Subsistence agriculture / Harvesting rice in Indonesia (box) / Market-oriented agriculture: plantations and agribusiness / Market-oriented agriculture: fazendas and haciendas / Reflection

Groups of agricultural producers / The role of the agricultural sector in the development process / The changing nature of the agricultural sector / Agriculture: problem child of the future

PART THREE THE URBAN-INDUSTRIAL SCENE; CORE-PERIPHERY RELATIONS

Manufacturing: still in its infancy / The structure of manufacturing / Industrial productivity / Reasons for the low degree of industrialization / Recent attempts at industrialization / Some models of industrialization / Problems of recent industrialization / Export-oriented industrialization / The spatial distribution of manufacturing / Brazil's greatest inferno (box) / Christaller's central-place theory (box) / Conclusion

A sector characterized by growth and diversity / The informal tertiary sector as an urban refuge sector / The tertiary sector: an overcrowded sector

/ The tertiary sector: also an attractive and functional sector / The tertiary sector: a dominating sector

PART FOUR   THEORIES OF DEVELOPMENT AND UNDERDEVELOPMENT

PART FIVE   FOUR CASE STUDIES

List of Tables

List of Figures

List of Photographs

Table of measures; approximate conversion values

1 mile	1.6 kilometers	1600 meters
1 kilometer (km)	0.62 mile	3274 feet
1 yard	0.9 meter	90 centimeters
1 meter	1.1 yards	40 inches
1 foot	0.3 meter	30 centimeters
1 meter	3.3 feet	39 inches
1 inch	2.5 centimeters	25 millimeters
1 centimeter	0.4 inch	10 millimeters
1 square mile	2.6 square kilometers	260 hectares
1 square kilometer	0.4 square mile	100 hectares
1 acre	0.4 hectare	4000 square meters
1 hectare (ha)	2.5 acres	10000 square meters
1 kilometer	1000 meters	3274 feet
1 meter (m)	100 centimeters	1000 millimeters

0^0 centigrade (C)	32^0 Fahrenheit (F)
10^0 centigrade	50^0 Fahrenheit
20^0 centigrade	68^0 Fahrenheit
30^0 centigrade	86^0 Fahrenheit
40^0 centigrade	104^0 Fahrenheit
50^0 centigrade	122^0 Fahrenheit

PART ONE

THE THIRD WORLD'S UNDERDEVELOPMENT IN PERSPECTIVE

Chapter 1   This changing world

During the 19th century and the first half of the 20th century, most scholars in the developed countries believed that only the temperate mid-latitude areas were suited for industrial development. Tropical countries, they argued, would make a serious mistake if they tried to develop manufacturing. Since they were unfit for industrial production, low-latitude areas would progress more rapidly if they continued to exchange their agricultural products for the manufactured goods from the temperate zone.

According to *environmental determinism*,[1] the temperate zone and the 'torrid' zone each had its specific natural potential, and it would be in the interest of all countries if patterns of international trade reflected these *comparative advantages*. Thus, an *international division of labor,* based largely on climatic differences, was proposed. It was not until about World War II that this 'Eurocentric' picture of the world became undermined, although not completely abandoned.

Since 1945, views concerning the problems of development and underdevelopment have undergone numerous and sometimes drastic changes. Such changes have occurred both in developed and underdeveloped countries. The primary purpose of this chapter is to describe and explain these changes, especially those that have taken place in the economically advanced societies. This we do at the risk of being accused of making some unacceptable generalizations. The problem is that at particular points in time views on development and underdevelopment have not always been the same in all industrialized countries. For example, since about the time the United States became militarily involved in Vietnam (1965), the plight of the Third World has received far more attention in Western Europe than in America, not only in the news media and government circles, but also in academia and high schools.

Partly because Europeans are exposed to more information on the low quality of life in the Third World and partly because they live in a more socialistically minded environment, they tend to be more inclined than Americans to sympathize with, and provide economic support to, the poor and hungry in Africa, Asia and Latin America (see Table 1). Generally speaking, Europeans are more aware of the great disparities in today's troubled world and appear better informed about the causes of underdevelopment. Notwithstanding these differences in exposure and percep-

---

[1] Environmental determinism is the belief that human activities are strongly influenced, if not determined, by physical or natural conditions, primarily climate.

Various other terms and concepts used in this chapter may be new to the reader. They are not explained here, but may be looked up in subsequent chapters (consult index).

tion, we will endeavor to present a broad outline of the ways in which attitudes toward the Third World's problems have changed on both sides of the North Atlantic.

Table 1. Net flow of official development assistance from selected countries as a percentage of gross national product, 1960-1980.

	1960	1965	1970	1975	1980
Western Europe					
Austria	N.A.	0.11	0.07	0.13	0.23
Belgium	0.88	0.60	0.46	0.62	0.50
Denmark	0.09	0.13	0.38	0.50	0.73
France	1.38	0.76	0.66	0.51	0.64
Netherlands	0.31	0.36	0.61	0.65	1.03
Norway	0.11	0.16	0.32	0.65	0.85
Sweden	0.05	0.19	0.38	0.70	0.79
Switzerland	0.04	0.09	0.15	0.15	0.24
United Kingdom	0.56	0.47	0.37	0.32	0.35
West Germany	0.31	0.40	0.32	0.28	0.43
North America					
Canada	0.19	0.19	0.42	0.51	0.43
United States	0.53	0.49	0.31	0.20	0.27
Oceania & Japan					
Australia	0.38	0.53	0.59	0.54	0.48
Japan	0.24	0.27	0.23	0.24	0.32
New Zealand	N.A.	N.A.	0.23	0.47	0.33

Sources: Todaro (1977), p. 334; World Bank, World Development Report 1982, p. 140.

For the sake of organization, the period 1945-1985 is divided into four ten-year periods. It goes without saying that this periodization is an arbitrary one and that there are no well-defined 'boundaries' separating one period from another. Different periods could have been chosen, but they would probably be not more satisfactory. The years 1955 (Bandung Conference of non-aligned African and Asian states)[2]; 1965 (escalation of the Vietnam conflict and the year before UNCTAD had been established)[3]; and 1975 (Karachi Conference of the Third World Forum)[4] happen to mark

[2] This conference, held at Bandung, Indonesia, was attended by delegates from 29 countries, representing more than half of the world's population. It was intended to build closer relations between African and Asian states, to forge an African-Asian declaration of neutrality in the Cold War, and to speed the end of colonialism. Several trade, aid and cultural agreements came out of the conference. For years, the Bandung-conference spirit of African-Asian non-alignment and cooperation was hailed as its most important result.

[3] In the early 1960s, Third World countries complained about the terms of international trade: the prices of the manufactured products they had to import were high, whereas the prices of the primary goods they produced for export were low, thus frustrating their efforts to obtain rapid economic growth. Although they were parties to the General Agreement on Tariffs and ▶

4

important moments in the history of the Third World's relations with (most of) the rest of the world and Western attitudes toward the development problematique. The following brief characterizations may serve as a useful frame of reference:

1945-1955 – period of Western disconcern
1955-1965 – period of optimism and high expectations
1965-1975 – period of growing skepticism
1975-1985 – period of pessimism and reevaluation

During the first ten years after World War II, the developed countries displayed very little interest in the (not yet discovered) problem of underdevelopment, preoccupied as they were with their own economic reconstruction and the growing East-West (Cold War) conflict.

Between 1955 and 1965, by contrast, the Third World received considerable attention. Both in the developed and underdeveloped countries it was widely believed that the poor countries were merely lagging behind and that with outside help they could catch up with the rich countries.

The period 1965-1975 was dominated by widespread disillusion emanating from the realization that development was a much more complex process than had previously been realized. Earlier theories of development were challenged and were partly replaced by more radical (neo-Marxist) theories which emphasized the negative effects for the Third World of its relations with the developed capitalist countries.

Since 1975, there has been a growing sense of frustration brought on by the worldwide economic crisis and the rapidly increasing indebtedness of most underdeveloped states. At the same time, Third World demands for the creation of a New International Economic Order (NIEO), together with expanding exports of manufactured goods by such Newly Industrializing Countries (NICs) as Brazil, South Korea and Taiwan, have led to a mild North-South confrontation.

On the following pages, each of the four periods is discussed in some detail. In an attempt to explain the prevailing mood in each period, the

Trade (GATT), they were critical of it and demanded a conference to consider means for establishing 'equal exchange.' A United Nations Conference on Trade and Development (UNCTAD) met in 1964, chiefly to consider the trade needs of underdeveloped countries and create a permanent UNCTAD, especially with a view to accelerate economic development.
[4] A group of social scientists from the Third World met in Santiago, Chile in 1973 and decided to organize a Forum, open to all social scientists from the Third World with a predominant interest in the development of their societies. The chief purpose of the Forum is to act as spokesman for the Third World. An inaugural meeting was held in Karachi, Pakistan in 1975 to discuss external and internal elements of the crisis confronting the Third World. The participants agreed on the need for an intellectual revolution to overcome the dependence of the Third World and for profound changes in the national and international economic order that the underdeveloped countries face today. For a detailed account of the functions of the Third World Forum, its views regarding development strategies and the need for a New International Economic Order (NIEO), see Todaro (1977), pp. 413-416.

dates of many important events are presented. What follows is essentially an historical account of changing attitudes, perceptions and theories about development and underdevelopment, culminating in the growing aware- ness that we live in an increasingly *interdependent* world in which the reasons for the present (1984) economic recession in the North (= developed countries) are related to those which have thus far inhibited development in most of the South (= underdeveloped countries). Accord- ing to this interdependency perspective, the interests of poor countries and rich countries are complementary and compatible, rather than conflicting and irreconcilable.

The period 1945-1955: reconstruction and disinterest

Prior to 1945, only a few scholars showed interest in problems of develop- ment, much less in problems of underdevelopment. In fact, the term 'underdevelopment' had not yet been coined, nor had the term 'Third World'. In the years following World War II, the developed countries were in no mood to worry about the low level of development in the rest of the world. Most faced serious problems at home, especially the need to recover from widespread war damage, reestablish international trade relations and adjust their economies to peace-time conditions. At the same time, Western countries were confronted with the threat of spreading commu- nism – first in Europe (which had become divided along the so-called 'Iron Curtain') and later in Asia, where the Chinese revolution of 1949 was followed by the Korean War (1950-1952). In an effort to speed up the recovery of Western Europe and at the same time block the spread of communism, the United States in 1947 adopted General Marshall's plan to provide massive reconstruction aid to its European allies.

Virtually the only countries which showed some interest in what is now generally referred to as the Third World, were the colonial powers: Belgium, France, the Netherlands, Portugal and the United Kingdom. This interest was highly selfish and had little or nothing to do with concern for the low and often declining standards of living among the indigenous populations. Faced with demands for independence by some of their over- seas dependencies, they tried to protect their interests as best they could. From 1946 until their defeat at Dien Bien Phu in 1954, the French were bogged down in a costly war in Vietnam (the first Indochinese War), followed immediately by an eight-year armed conflict in Algeria (1954-1962). The Netherlands fought an intermittent war (1946-1949) in Southeast Asia in an attempt to prevent the independence of Indonesia. Whereas the British barely resisted the drive toward independence in South Asia – India, Pakistan (including Bangladesh), Burma and Ceylon (now Sri Lanka) – they encountered problems in Kenya (Mau Mau revolt, 1952-1954), Iran (nationalization of the Anglo-Iranian Oil Company in 1951) and elsewhere.

Quite naturally, France, the Netherlands and the United Kingdom were

6

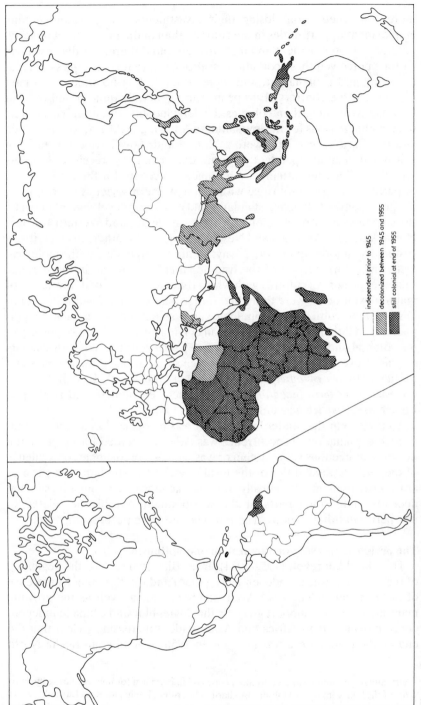

Fig. 1. Geography of decolonization, 1945-1955.

independent prior to 1945

decolonized between 1945 and 1955

still colonial at end of 1955

more concerned about losing their investments, cheap resources and employment opportunities in the colonies than in the problems of poverty, illiteracy, unemployment and malnutrition found there. Hardly anyone in Europe perceived these conditions as *problems,* that is, as topics demanding study and explanation, and there certainly was no widespread guilt feeling. On the contrary, Europeans were generally quite proud of what they had wrought in their colonies. Understandably, questions concerning the possible reasons for the low standards of living in Africa, southern Asia and the Caribbean region were seldom asked. South America, most of which had been independent for more than a century, received even less attention. Thus, few attempts were made to account for the large income disparities and social injustice within non-Western societies or to explain the great contrasts in living standards and economic development between the colonies and former colonies, on the one hand, and Western Europe, North America, Australia and New Zealand, on the other. Instead, it was customary to look upon 'tribal' ways of life as interesting anthropological facts which formed part of the traditional cultures found in those areas. Like the 'primitive' cultures with which they were associated, low levels of material well-being were described rather than explained – not by economists but by cultural anthropologists and sometimes by human geographers. And if there was little interest in delving into the causes of poverty in the colonial and ex-colonial areas of one's *own* country, Western scholars displayed even less interest in the problems that afflicted the colonies and former colonies of *other* countries. Just as the Dutch East Indies (Indonesia) were *terra incognita* for the French, Portuguese and British, so French West Africa was unknown outside France.

To the extent that underdevelopment was recognized as a problem that needed explanation, its occurrence was either accounted for in terms of a deficient indigenous value system or was seen as a predictable consequence of the limited possibilities of the local physical (mostly humid tropical or arid) environment. Practically no one advanced the hypothesis that deprivation in some parts of the world might possibly be related to prosperity in other regions. The few who did were purposely ignored.[5]

The period 1955-1965: decolonization and optimism

The Mau Mau revolt (1952-1954), Dien Bien Phu (1954), the beginning of the Algerian war of independence (1954) and the Bandung Conference of newly independent Afro-Asian states (1955), as well as the growing material and moral support given by the Soviet bloc and China to independence movements in Africa and Asia, made it increasingly clear that the end of the colonial era was in sight. In 1956, several countries in North

---

[5] Virtually no attention was paid to the theories on imperialism formulated during the early years of the 20th century by Hobson, Bukharin, Hilferding, Lenin and Rosa Luxemburg (see chapter 16).

8

Africa (Morocco, Tunisia and Sudan) achieved independence, followed in 1957 by Ghana (formerly Gold Coast). Similar developments took place in Southeast Asia. The French ended their rule in Indochina (Kampuchea, Laos and Vietnam) in 1956, while the British granted independence to Malaya in 1957. The process of decolonization greatly accelerated in 1960, when thirteen French colonies in Africa obtained independence and Belgium decided to terminate its control over the Congo (now Zaire). By 1965, there were only a few colonies left, the largest being the Portuguese territories of Angola and Mozambique and the British colony of Southern Rhodesia (later Rhodesia, now Zimbabwe),[6] all located in southern Africa (see Figures 1 and 2). Meanwhile, Egypt had nationalized the Suez Canal (1956), China had started its Great Leap Forward (1958) and Cuba had launched its (socialist) revolution (1959).

The above developments were accompanied by a large increase in the number of international (mostly UN) organizations, many of which collected and disseminated a wealth of information (e.g., population and economic census data) on Third World countries. For the first time in history, agencies, businessmen, scholars and students everywhere could obtain reasonably reliable and comparable statistical information on parts of the world which had hitherto only been available to relatively few government officials in a limited number of 'mother countries.' In the meantime, the number of independent states grew, resulting in a vast expansion of the world's network of diplomatic relations and a concomitant increase in the number of traveling diplomats, trade missions, economic advisors, etc. Upon achieving independence, Third World countries became members of the United Nations, enabling them to bring their development problems and need for aid to the attention of *all* developed countries. At the same time, the newly independent states became represented in the many UN organizations. Due to the increased contacts and information there emerged – *both in the poor and the rich countries* – an awareness that there were immense differences in economic development and living conditions in the world. Clearly, a new era was appearing on the horizon, underscored by the fact that for the first time development and underdevelopment were becoming accepted as legitimate research topics to be studied by social scientists.

By 1955, Japan and Europe had fully recovered from the war devastation and were beginning to experience greater prosperity than ever before. The unchallenged leader in the world was the United States, whose Marshall Plan aid program had been incredibly successful. The Korean War had ended (1952) and the threat of communism had abated somewhat, especially in Western Europe. International trade was

---

[6] In November 1965, the white minority rebelled against colonial status and declared Southern Rhodesia independent, changing its name to Rhodesia. Fifteen years later (Southern) Rhodesia became the independent country of Zimbabwe with a black majority government.

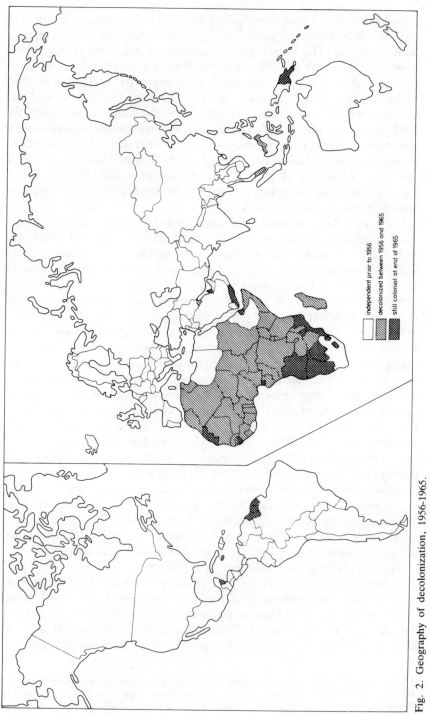

independent prior to 1956
decolonized between 1956 and 1965
still colonial at end of 1965

Fig. 2. Geography of decolonization, 1956-1965.

back to normal and the world economy was expanding at an unprecedented rate. New technological inventions followed each other in rapid succession, allowing productivity in manufacturing to jump by leaps and bounds. Meantime, high-yielding crop varieties (e.g., hybrid corn), improved farming methods and increased application of artificial fertilizers and pest controls resulted in equally impressive increases in agricultural productivity.

In brief, the trials and tribulations of the Great Depression (1930s), the Second World War and the Korean conflict belonged to the past and the future looked bright and inviting. Most importantly, the reconstruction of Japan and Europe had shown that radical changes could be brought about quickly and that foreign aid was capable of setting in motion and sustaining a long-term process of economic expansion.

The conclusion drawn from these experiences was that the Third World countries, too, could be developed in a reasonably short period of time. After all, it was believed that the 'less-developed'[7] regions merely lagged behind in their development and could catch up if they traveled the same road the advanced countries had traveled, that is, modernize and industrialize. Most possessed a large surplus rural population which could and should be absorbed into manufacturing, thus reducing overpopulation and underemployment in the rural areas while broadening their economic base by building up their secondary sector. The rich countries were prepared to provide financial aid and send technicians to get the development process underway, and it was believed that Western technology and value systems could be transmitted ready-made. Where necessary, land reforms could be carried out, so as to bring about a fair distribution of agricultural landownership. Such reforms would not only reduce income inequality, but also provide a basis for democracy and expand the market for industrial goods.

Development was seen as a 'trickling down' process, whereby economic *growth* and resulting gains in per capita GNP would create new jobs and other favorable conditions necessary for the wider distribution of the economic and social benefits of growth. Once the process of growth had been set in motion, it would reinforce itself and even accelerate. If necessary, the rich countries could provide the technical assistance needed to overcome certain bottlenecks or raise the rate of growth by increasing the amounts of foreign aid and/or investment.

An important reason for the willingness among the industrialized countries of the West to offer support to the Third World countries was the conviction that by enabling them to raise their standards of material well-being and create greater equality, they would help reduce the chance that leftist revolutions might occur.

---

[7] The terms 'less-developed,' 'underdeveloped' and 'developing' are used interchangeably.

11

It was this well-intentioned faith and almost boundless optimism, as well as the East-West rivalry and the fear of another Cuban revolution, which inspired President Kennedy to launch the Peace Corps, call for the founding of the Alliance for Progress for aiding Latin America, and declare the 1960s the First Development Decade. At the same time, the development of the poor countries was seen as economically beneficial to the developed countries. Apart from the possibility that investments might be profitable and that development would make scarce resources available to the industrialized states, the old doctrine of comparative advantages was by no means dead, so that an international division of labor or an international 'harmony of interests' would be beneficial to all countries, both in the North and the South.

The euphoria and high expectations of the 1955-1965 period were in part a direct consequence of the decolonization process. Now that the former colonies had become independent sovereign states which could plan their *own* future and promote their *own* interests, progress was virtually guaranteed. Nothing could stop them from becoming developed, so it seemed. Not only Western observers were convinced of this, but also the leaders of the newly independent states. Optimism was also fueled by the rapidly improving possibilities to plan and program growth through the use of econometric models. Finally, the hopeful and elated mood was boosted by the realization that governments, much more so than in the past, could play a major role as creators of favorable conditions for development by providing loans to entrepreneurs, carrying out agricultural reforms, making infrastructural improvements, and offering incentives for the sake of attracting foreign investors.

It should be clear from the above that around 1960 it was common to think of economic development as a fairly simple and straightforward, evolutionary process, and that the only thing the less-advanced countries had to do was to follow in the footsteps of the industrialized countries. Western economic systems, it was believed, could be diffused lock, stock and barrel from one area (the core) to another (the periphery).

While such high expectations were a source of inspiration for Rostow's *The Stages of Economic Growth* (1960) and help explain why it became a bestseller, it, in turn, convinced many Western and Third World politicians and economists that the process of development required little more than removing a number of obstacles and supplying various missing components, such as capital, technological know-how, and management.

Looking back at the 1955-1965 period, one can only express amazement at the fact that apparently few people noticed, or chose to notice, that most South American countries had failed to become developed *despite the fact that they had been independent for a hundred years or more*. No less surprising is that little attention was paid to the widely differing resource endowments and social, cultural and demographic characteristics of the many newly independent states. Finally, it is rather incomprehensible that development experts focused attention almost exclusively on industrial development, so that many countries neglected their agricultural sector. This agricultural neglect is difficult to understand in view of the fact that Rostow had made it abundantly clear that a substantial increase in agricultural output was an absolute necessity for sustaining a long-term drive towards balanced economic development.

The period of growing skepticism: 1965-1975
The optimistic mood of the late 1950s and early 1960s begun to dissipate around 1963 and had disappeared altogether by 1965. In rapid succession, the world had been shaken by the Cuban missile crisis (1962), a border war between India and China (1962), serious racial problems in South Africa (1963), rebellions in Portugal's African colonies (1963-1965), and anti-American riots in the Panama Canal Zone (1964). While the United States was becoming deeply involved in Vietnam, the Peace Corps idealism was losing much of its earlier elan. China's Prime Minister Chou En-lai, during a visit to Africa in 1964, had declared that the entire continent was ripe for revolution. Furthermore, at the newly created UN Conference on Trade and Development (UNCTAD) in Geneva, also in 1964, the Third World countries had complained about the nature of aid programs and had expressed dissatisfaction about unfavorable trade conditions, calling for stable prices for raw materials and stable terms of trade. Finally, 1965 saw an armed conflict between India and Pakistan over Kashmir, mass murders and economic chaos in Indonesia following an attempted communist coup, and the unilateral declaration of independence by Rhodesia's white minority.

These developments set the stage for a period of growing skepticism and uncertainty regarding the process of development. A 1965 UN publication, *The United Nations Development Decade at Midpoint,* left no doubt about the fact that most Third World countries were making very little progress. Indeed, the results of the growth-and-modernization approach – also known as the diffusionist approach – were downright disappointing. The harder individual countries in Latin America, Asia and Africa tried to stimulate *autonomous* (independent) development – mostly through import-substitution industrialization – the more they seemed to become dominated by foreign economic interests, especially by American and European-based multinational corporations.

Instead of the anticipated 'trickling down' process, which was supposed to bring about a more even distribution of income, many societies became characterized by ever greater income disparities. So-called 'backwash effects' were often stronger than the hoped for 'multiplier effects' or 'spread effects' with their forward and backward economic linkages. As a consequence, spatial inequality became rather more than less pronounced. Because subsidized industrial growth was concentrated in a limited number of large cities – frequently looked upon as 'growth poles' from which development was expected to diffuse to smaller settlements and surrounding rural areas – the rural areas of many countries experienced an alarming decline in employment opportunities. The result was that large numbers of rural families migrated to the cities even though only a few found jobs or adequate housing there.

Partly as a consequence of the often massive rural-to-urban migration and the abandoning of farmland that sometimes accompanied it, and partly because governments and foreign advisors neglected to stimulate agricultural production, one country after another was confronted with growing food shortages. Countries which had traditionally been self-sufficient or had been net exporters of foodstuffs, suddenly found themselves being dependent on food imports. Aside from the negative effect this had on their balance of trade, the food imports – usually purchased in the developed countries in the temperate zone – made a mockery of the doctrine of comparative (natural) advantages. At the same time, the world was experiencing an exceedingly rapid rate of population growth, causing many scientists to predict widespread malnutrition and future famines. The Sahel drought of the late 1960s and early 1970s as well as crop failures in 1972-1973 in much of Asia served as a rude warning that these dire predictions might well prove to be correct.

Every year, so it seemed, prospects for development and better opportunities for all members of Third World societies were becoming smaller. One thing became clear: growth was not the same as development for often it resulted in more underdevelopment and greater inequality. Little by little, development experts began to realize also that development was more than just economic development, that the much vaunted Green Revolution could have serious adverse social and environmental effects and cause political unrest, that foreign economic aid could do more harm than good, and that there were many more vicious circles, bottlenecks, institutional and structural barriers inhibiting development than had been thought possible at the beginning of the First Development Decade.

Whereas in 1960 there had been general agreement on the meaning of 'development,' by 1970 there was widespread uncertainty and even disagreement, with various authors feeling an urgent need to redefine the concept (see Chapter II). The euphoria and naiveté of the preceding period gave way to disenchantment and cynicism. In numerous industrialized countries, particularly the United States, the Third World became looked upon as a bottomless pit, and the issue of providing development aid was becoming increasingly controversial. This new perception, together with the declining Cold War polarization in Europe and growing opposition in the United States and abroad to providing economic assistance, caused the United States and several other donor countries to cut back their aid programs (see Table 1).

Another development was taking place which compelled Western politicians and economists to do some serious rethinking about the conventional

14

(modernization-diffusion) approach to solving problems of underdevelopment. Starting around 1965, there was a virtual explosion of publications (in the English language) that were highly critical of the evolutionary 'stages' approach to development. Especially the writings of A.G. Frank (1964 and later) became influential. Older Marxist – and particularly Leninist – theories of imperialism were revived and adapted to formulate the 'dependency perspective.' According to its proponents, underdevelopment is a relatively recent phenomenon caused by a net transfer of funds from the poor and dependent countries to the rich and dominant countries. Development and prosperity in the captalist core, so these largely neo-Marxist authors maintained, was directly related to underdevelopment and squalor in the periphery. Through foreign investment, unequal trade and profit extraction, Third World countries were becoming increasingly impoverished – a *process* sometimes referred to as 'the development of underdevelopment' (Frank 1966).

As a consequence of the avalanche of critical writings, many new terms and concepts came to dominate the development literature, including core and periphery, dominance-dependence relations, neo-colonialism, internal colonialism, growth-without-development, dependent (subservient or subordinated) development, profit extraction, surplus appropriation, deteriorating terms of trade, unequal exchange, imperialist exploitation, enclave economy, and polarization. The more radical authors called for socialist revolution in the periphery and advocated that the Third World countries should 'delink,' that is, break off relations with the capitalist West. This latter position was taken by Rodney, among others, who in 1972 published a book on the history of the relations between Africa and Europe. Both the title, *How Europe Underdeveloped Africa,* and the contents shocked many people into the realization that it was high time to reinterpret and rewrite the colonial and neo-colonial history of Africa, Asia and Latin America.

While Western views about the nature and causes of underdevelopment were being modified by neo-Marxist writings on dependence and imperialism, it became increasingly fashionable – particularly after the thaw in US-Chinese relations in 1971-72, China's admission to the UN in 1972, and last but not least, the construction of the Tanzam railroad by China (1970-75) – to point out that China had made a great deal of progress and had managed to do so largely on its own, that is, without foreign investment and with very little aid (from the USSR until about 1958). The Chinese development model, as it was called, had considerable impact on many development theorists and became a source of inspiration for a number of Third World countries.

Tanzania, as early as 1967, had decided to adopt a modified version of China's *self-reliance* approach to development. According to its advocates, self-reliance (or autonomous and equitable) development is necessary to prevent a developing country from losing control over its resources and become dependent on, and exploited by, foreign economic interests. Resources, in this context, refers not only to raw materials, but also to capital, labor and human creativity.

Although self-reliance has received (and continues to receive) enthusiastic support from many quarters, it remains questionable whether it is an appropriate approach for a small and relatively resource-poor country like Tanzania. In recent years, even China – which is more than a giant Tanzania – has found it expedient to offer incentives to foreign investors in the hope of getting them interested in setting up joint industrial ventures on Chinese soil.

It is clear that between 1962 and 1972 there was a dramatic turnabout in the way many European and North American development experts perceived the problem of development in the Third World. In summary, a few of the many important lessons learned during this period include:
(1) The process of development is exceedingly complex, e.g., a necessary change of one element in the production system usually requires complementary changes of a number of other elements.
(2) Given the diversity in size, location, physical resources, population density, human resources (literacy, skills) and value systems among the Third World countries, no single development model can be applied everywhere.
(3) The road to development followed by most developed states cannot be followed by the underdeveloped world because today's possibilities differ in many important ways from those of a hundred or two hundred years ago.
(4) Entrepreneurial ability cannot be 'exported' successfully from developed to underdeveloped countries.
(5) During the early stages of industrial development, sophisticated methods of production tend to be inappropriate; they are too expensive, create few jobs, and often require more skill than is available.
(6) Powerful interest groups within Third World countries – e.g., the new urban elite, large landowners and moneylenders – are inclined to do everything they can to prevent or subvert all radical changes which are likely to affect adversely their wealth and power.

Of course, other lessons were learned, although often too late and after irreparable damage had been done; they will be discussed in their proper context in later chapters.

1975-1985: Global crisis and global interdependence

The Second Development Decade (1970-1979) never did have much of a chance. From the very beginning, informed people everywhere knew that the gap between rich and poor countries was not getting smaller (although there were a few exceptions), and that living conditions in the poorest countries – the so-called 'basket cases' – were actually deteriorating. Notwithstanding the fact that countries like Cuba and Taiwan were making considerable progress, it was evident that the majority of them were not

16

catching up, that they were no closer to Rostow's 'take-off' stage than they had been at the time of decolonization, and that the process of under-development had by no means been arrested. If the First Development Decade had been a disappointment, the Second Development Decade was turning out to be a disaster.

In view of these developments, it is not surprising that the Third World countries in 1974 demanded the creation of a New International Economic Order (NIEO), based on the principles of equity, equality of all sovereign states, interdependence, common interests and worldwide cooperation. It was not so much a redistribution of wealth they wanted, but a redistribution of future growth opportunities.

Apart from the fact that the rich countries rejected or evaded the proposal for the simple reason that they were unwilling to give up their privileged position, a reordering of the world economic system was becoming less attainable due to the deepening economic crisis. Since 1973, the world has been plagued by a host of problems: greatly increased energy costs, high rates of inflation, massive unemployment, economic stagnation, high interest rates, and rapidly growing indebtedness, especially in the Third World. In 1982, interest payments on loans amounted to nearly 50% of the total value of exports of the Third World countries. Debts were accumulating faster than they were being paid off.

One immediate consequence of the economic recession has been the increasing reluctance of some rich countries to provide development aid. More serious has been the decline in demand for raw materials from Third World countries, thereby causing prices to fall. Predictably, reduced sales at lower prices, together with greatly increased prices for imported oil, fertilizer and other petrochemical products, have resulted in large trade deficits for many underdeveloped states. Another consequence of the recession has been the rising tide of protectionism in the industrialized countries. On both sides of the North Atlantic, demands have been heard to restrict imports of consumer goods from such low-wage countries as South Korea, Taiwan, Hong Kong and Singapore.

Clearly, then, the global crisis has greatly reduced the prospects for development, which explains why the skepticism of the 1965-1975 period has been replaced by outright pessimism. The debt problem is particularly disconcerting. If the banks in the developed countries fail to recover the billions of dollars that Third World countries have borrowed, the international financial system, and thus the world economic system, may well become paralyzed. In other words, not only are the underdeveloped countries dependent on the developed countries, but in some respects the developed countries are dependent on the underdeveloped countries. And ironically, the greater the debt becomes, the more dependent the creditor countries become. This realization that we live in a mutually dependent or *interdependent* world is very unsettling for the advanced countries because it means that they are not as much in control of their own destiny as

17

they have been accustomed to believe. Whereas prior to the oil and debt crises most relations between developed and underdeveloped countries were seen as one-way (asymmetric) relations, many of them today are looked upon as two-way interdependent (or symmetric) relations, making the developed countries almost as vulnerable as the underdeveloped countries.

Since about 1975, a sense of frustration, helplessness and impatience has made itself felt in the South, the East and the West. Frank (1982) talks in this respect about a global confidence crises. While the Soviet Union is haunted by unrest in Poland, armed conflict in Afghanistan, and disappointing agricultural productivity at home, China is faced with growing income inequality, inefficiency, underemployment and economic stagnation. The end of the Vietnam war has not brought peace and economic progress to Indochina, on the contrary, conditions have greatly deteriorated as indicated by the exodus of many thousands of Vietnamese refugees ('boat people') and the occupation of Kampuchea by Vietnam. The Middle East remains as divided and unstable as ever. The independence of Angola (1975), Mozambique (1975) and Zimbabwe (1980) has not resulted in any improvement in their living conditions. Since the Soweto uprising (1976), South Africa's racial timebomb has been ticking louder and louder. Today, Uganda is in worse shape than it was prior to the ouster of President Idi Amin (1979); the once promising East African Community (Kenya, Tanzania and Uganda) has collapsed. For years, the Horn of Africa (mainly Somalia and Ethiopia) has been the victim of internal struggles as well as great-power rivalry, with far more money and effort being allocated to the forces of destruction than to the development of human and physical resources. After several armed conflicts (especially 1977-1978), the region has a massive refugee problem and is confronted with recurrent famines. Countries like Ivory Coast, Ghana, Nigeria and Gabon, which for a number of years seemed to be making considerable progress, are no closer to providing their people an acceptable level of material and mental well-being than at the time they achieved independence (around 1960). If anything, Africa teaches us that development, however defined, remains as elusive as it was at the beginning of the First Development Decade, only now we are more aware of it (Hyden 1983).

Unfortunately, prospects for true development – as opposed to mere economic growth – are hardly better in Latin America. Uruguay, which was once known as 'the Switzerland of South America,' has steadily moved downhill. Brazil, frequently referred to as a NIC with almost unlimited possibilities, is precariously balancing on the edge of bankruptcy and knows at least as much squalor, inequality and social injustice as it did prior to its 'miraculous' industrial surge that started around 1964. In spite of the fact that Mexico ranks as the world's fourth largest oil exporter, its foreign debt nearly equals that of Brazil ($94 and $100 billion, respectively, in 1984), while poverty, malnutrition and unemployment continue to drive many citizens out of their native country. As the news media remind us almost daily, highly unstable Central America is sinking ever deeper into the underdevelopment morass, victimized as it is by oppressive governments and competing external forces. Even Cuba, which has successfully eliminated many aspects of underdevelopment, continues to struggle with serious problems (see Chapter 19).

In Asia, meanwhile, Indonesia, the Philippines, Bangladesh, India, Pakistan and Sri Lanka appear to be fighting a losing battle against poverty, hunger, unemployment, low productivity, inequality and corruption. Like Iran and Iraq, most of them spend more money on the production or purchase of arms than on efforts aimed at improving the quality of life.

Many Third World countries struggle with a variety of urban problems. Particularly alarming are the rapidly expanding shantytowns (slums) and widespread underemployment in the 'informal' tertiary sector. Another common problem is the unfavorable hierarchical structure of urban places, characterized by a shortage of medium-sized cities and regional market centers – many of which are stagnating or even declining – and the much too fast expansion of one or two excessively large cities.

A different type of problem for the Third World is its increasing diversity, causing ever greater divisiveness. While oil-exporting countries like Nigeria, Indonesia, Venezuela and Mexico favor high oil prices, the economies of oil-importing countries have been crippled by a twentyfold increase in oil prices between 1973 and 1982. Since most Third World countries are exporters of (unprocessed) raw materials and importers of manufactured goods, they naturally support efforts to raise the prices of the former and reduce those of the latter. This trading picture, however, works to the disadvantage of those NICs whose foreign trade is dominated by imports of raw materials and exports of manufactured products. Similarly, capital exporting countries like Kuwait, Saudi Arabia and the Gulf States are in favor of high interest rates, whereas other states – most of which are already heavily indebted – prefer low interest rates. In view of these and other conflicting interests, it should surprise no one that the Third World finds it increasingly difficult to speak with one voice.

Having discovered that earlier growth-oriented development strategies failed to raise the quality of life for the masses in most Third World countries, development experts have desperately searched for alternative strategies. Around 1976, the 'basic needs' approach became fashionable. As the term suggests, it aims to assure every human being of having access to the necessities of life: food, clothing and footwear, clean water, decent shelter, fuel, health care and elementary education. This strategy, proponents argue, can best be realized through equitable redistribution, small-scale operations, labor-intensive production, local participation in decision making, self-sufficiency and simple (adapted, appropriate or intermediate) technology. Attention is focused on the rural areas (where most of the population lives) and on the production of food crops. Through the introduction of appropriate technology, attempts are made to stimulate the processing of agricultural products and other natural resources in villages and small urban centers.

At first, many developed countries were not particularly enthusiastic about the basic needs approach. They were afraid that it might cost them too much in the form of development assistance. Although this view was often heard, they probably were more concerned about the fact that the new strategy might work to their disadvantage as it would reduce industrial investment opportunities, lessen the Third World's dependence by limiting its need for capital and food imports, and result in a shortage of certain agricultural raw materials – and thus in higher prices – due to a shift from the production of industrial crops for export to the production of food crops. For essentially the same reasons, most Third World countries supported the basic needs approach. More recently positions have become more or less reversed. With the onset of economic stagnation, growing unemployment, reduced sales, and falling profits, the developed countries have begun to welcome the basic needs approach as an opportunity to restrict Third World production of manufactured goods. Reduced competition from Third World manufacturers, of course, fits well into the emerging protectionist policies of the developed countries. Many Third World countries, on the other hand, appear to have become less enchanted with the basic needs strategy, worried as they are that it will result in less industrial growth than is needed to 'catch up' with the developed countries and that it will relegate them for good to second-rate status in the international economic system. In part, this fear is nurtured by the fact that it is uncertain how the goals of the basic needs approach can be materialized. Tanzania's *ujamaa* villages, for example, are considered a failure by many authors. It is also widely believed that countries which lack a tradition of cooperative endeavor are ill-suited to the self-reliance/basic needs model of development.

A variant of the approach just discussed is that of *collective self-reliance*, which some observers consider the most appropriate strategy for overcoming certain development constraints experienced by individual Third World countries. This strategy entails a form of loosely integrated economic development by a number of neighboring countries. An example is CARICOM, or the Caribbean Community, comprising Antigua, Barbados, Belize, Dominica, Grenada, Guyana, Jamaica, Montserrat, St. Kitts-Nevis-Anguilla, St. Lucia, St. Vincent, and Trinidad and Tobago. Each participating country is allowed a measure of specialization depending on its specific comparative advantages. One favorable aspect of collective self-reliance is the larger common market, allowing for scale economies. Others include less external dependence due to increased trade between member states and enhanced bargaining power *vis-à-vis* third parties, a greater diversity of resources, a larger pool of expertise, and stronger representation in international organizations.[8]

Although in theory collective self-reliance has much to offer, it is likely to encounter a variety of problems when put into practice. Sooner or later the participating countries will face such difficult questions as: How much must each member contribute to a particular collective project (e.g., a factory or power plant) and in which country should it be located? Another potential problem is that the largest, most favorably located, most richly endowed, or most highly developed country is likely to become the dominant member of the group, forcing its will upon the other members. The result may be a typical core-periphery situation which is far more beneficial to the dominant country than to the rest of the collectivity.

Closely associated with the self-reliance and basic needs approaches is the idea – supported by many European development experts – that foreign aid should above all benefit the poorest of the poor, e.g., landless laborers and individuals employed in the urban informal sector. This approach has been suggested in response to the frequently heard criticism that in earlier years a substantial proportion of all foreign aid had ended up in the pockets of the small wealthy elite, thereby exacerbating the already excessive income inequalities found in most Third World countries. Although this 'target' approach may be defensible on humanitarian grounds, it is debatable whether it is sound from a purely economic or efficiency point of view. This so-called efficiency-vs-equity debate has much in common with the question often raised by development geographers: Should a developing country try to maximize total national production (GNP) or should it give priority to the promotion of spatial equality?

Over the years, the objectives of economic aid programs have undergone drastic changes. Whereas 25 years ago much emphasis was given to large, expensive industrial projects in urban areas or near ports, today attention is more evenly divided between large and small projects as well as between urban-industrial and rural-agricultural schemes. No doubt, objectives will continue to be modified, depending on past experiences, prevailing contemporary theories and definitions of development, the nature of the requests for aid by the recipient countries, and last but not least, the donor countries' motivations for providing assistance. As far as the latter aspect is concerned, it is unfortunate that much economic aid is given for the wrong reasons, e.g., for selfish political, strategic or economic reasons. All too often, development assistance has been offered in order to aid or protect private investments in the recipient country, to help polluting industries relocate in underdeveloped countries, to make available needed non-

---

[8] Since 1980, nine states in southern Africa – Angola, Botswana, Lesotho, Malawi, Mozambique, Swaziland, Tanzania, Zambia and Zimbabwe – have formed an economic alliance, the Southern Africa Development Coordination Council (SADCC). The chief purpose of this collectivity is to reduce southern Africa's dependence on South Africa.

renewable resources, or to promote the sale of capital-intensive durable goods (e.g., tractors) to the aid-receiving country. For example, there have been allegations that the Green Revolution in underdeveloped countries has been encouraged by the rich countries, not so much for helping the fight against starvation as for creating overseas markets for the (multinational) producers of fertilizers, insecticides, herbicides, water pumps and agricultural machinery. But even when aid is given for the right reasons and with the best of intentions, it often does more harm than good. Sometimes, failure is caused by corruptive practices, while at other times it results from inadequate feasibility studies, lack of skill, hastily drawn-up projects, unfamiliarity with the ecology of humid tropical or arid environments, ignorance of local cultural values, etc. Ideally, each individual aid project, no matter how small, should be carefully studied beforehand and, what is more, thoroughly evaluated afterwards.

Since development is an extraordinarily complex process, it is no easy task to come up with an appropriate development strategy or aid program. Geographers have a task to remind others that there can be no such thing as a standard formula to be applied everywhere. Physical, social, cultural, demographic, economic and political conditions as well as historical experiences vary from country to country, from region to region, and from one locale to another. Countries also differ from each other in terms of size, relative location, distribution and hierarchy of urban places, and the quality and density of transportation and communication networks. Whereas some countries have a relatively homogeneous population, others are characterized by ethnic heterogeneity; some have a long tradition of cooperative or collective activities, whereas others do not. There are countries which cannot get along with neighboring states (e.g., Somalia and Ethiopia, or Iraq and Iran), which rules out collective self-reliance. Others (e.g., Zambia and Tanzania) may well be able to use this same strategy to their mutual advantage. In other words, development is not something that should be left up to engineers and economists. Agronomists, soil scientists, sociologists, political scientists as well as physical and human geographers should be consulted in order to tailor both broad development strategies and individual projects to the unique interplay of endogenous conditions and exogenous processes affecting the area under consideration. Just as a particular theory cannot explain underdevelopment everywhere, so geographic differentiation precludes that one single model of socioeconomic development can solve underdevelopment everywhere.

22

Chapter 2   The concept of underdevelopment

In the preceding chapter we have seen that since World War II people everywhere have become aware that there are immense disparities in social and economic development separating the 'have' from the 'have-not' countries. We have also seen that views concerning possibilities to alleviate poverty and underdevelopment have varied over the years. An initial mood of naive optimism was later replaced by growing skepticism – even pessimism – when it was discovered that the road to development was a long and tortuous one.

Underdevelopment and underdevelopedness

As a consequence of the interest in problems of underdevelopment, terms like *developing countries, less-* and *least-developed countries, underdeveloped countries* and *Third World* have become household words. Since the late 1950s, the usage of these terms has been so common that it hardly seems necessary to explain what they refer to. Nevertheless, in this chapter we will dwell on the meaning of these concepts. Our main purpose is to find out more precisely what is meant by 'development' and 'underdevelopment.'

It is our opinion that a country or people considers itself developed when material and immaterial needs are reasonably satisfied. Before pursuing this notion further, it is important that we distinguish between *development,* by which we mean a process, and *developedness,* which refers to a state of being (as opposed to becoming) developed. Likewise, we can make a distinction between *underdevelopment* as a process and *underdevelopedness* as a condition. The processes of development and underdevelopment move in opposite directions, resulting respectively in developedness and underdevelopedness. Development is a progressive process consisting of a series of parallel and successive changes which enable an underdeveloped country to become developed. Conversely, underdevelopment is a retrogressive process which eventually leads to a state of underdevelopedness.

Taken literally, developedness and underdevelopedness are relative terms, i.e., every country or society may be said to be underdeveloped in the sense that it is less developed than it might be. This point was made in 1960 by the American geographer Richard Hartshorne, who explained that even in the richest and most advanced countries all material and spiritual needs are not satisfied for everyone or in all parts of the country. To this point we can add that it is impossible to reach some envisioned, utopian situation of complete developedness, because new needs will surely emerge.

Several important conclusions can be drawn from the above discussion. (1) Development is a never-ending process of change which has progressed further in some parts of the world than in others. The result is a continuum ranging from comparatively advanced countries, often referred to as 'core' countries, via a wide variety of moderately developed countries, which may be labeled 'semi-peripheral' countries, to comparatively backward or 'peripheral' countries. (2) The developmental stage (high, moderate or low) in which a country finds itself, represents a multidimensional situation in which important needs (food, shelter, clothing, health, education, recreation, social security, personal freedom, religion, culture, etc.) are satisfied to a larger or smaller degree. (3) Since development is a continuing process, the meaning of developed varies with place and time. (4) Fully developed societies do not exist. All we can say is that a particular society may be moving toward a higher level of developedness or a higher degree of needs satisfaction for more people.

When comparing developmental changes in various countries, it is significant to realize that such changes may take place more rapidly in some countries than in others. If two countries, A and B, both experience *absolute* progress, but A advances faster than B, the latter country obviously falls behind the former. Country B, then, becomes underdeveloped *relative to* country A. This observation has particular relevance in the event the people in B are aware of their country's relative stagnation and become increasingly frustrated by the fact that the satisfaction of new needs lags behind their expectations. In that case, underdevelopment may be viewed as a growing discrepancy between raised expectations and the existing level of needs satisfaction, irrespective of how high this level of needs satisfaction may be. By the same token, if the income gap between two classes in the same society widens, resulting in greater inequality, the disadvantaged class can be expected to become dissatisfied and restless even though its standard of living may be experiencing uninterrupted absolute improvement.

The relative meaning of developed and underdeveloped is so essential that it cannot be stressed enough. Hartshorne was correct when he wrote that "peoples all over the world are aware and envious of the highly developed economies of the more advanced countries," adding that by common usage the term underdeveloped "is taken to refer to countries whose level of production is notably below that of a group of countries generally recognized as relatively advanced" (Hartshorne 1960, p. 17). Indeed, the high level of needs satisfaction obtained in the rich countries has come to be looked upon as the universal measure of developedness. In the First World as well as in the Third World, people have accepted First World standards of material and immaterial well-being as the norm. And what is more, that is the norm which the Third World countries feel they should aspire to reach. To put it in different words, Western development has become synonymous with development, while progress has become synonymous with change in the direction of Western levels of productivity and prosperity. The countries which are furthest removed from reaching these goals are generally identified as *least*-developed.

We can summarize the above discussion in one short sentence. Since developedness and underdevelopedness are relative concepts, the Third World is considered underdeveloped simply because the First World is considered developed. This statement does not mean that the Third World's underdevelopedness has been caused by the First World. Although it is unquestionably true that past and present processes of development in the First World were/are causally related to past and present processes of underdevelopment in the Third World, it would be incorrect to state as Rodney has done in his book *How Europe Underdeveloped Africa,* that the poverty in the Third World is entirely and exclusively the result of colonial and neo-colonial activities of the capitalist First World.

Awareness and underdevelopedness

On the basis of what has been said above, we conclude that it is possible to recognize two types of underdevelopedness: one involving awareness and another which does not. One of the clearest examples of the first type may be encountered in the slums of the larger cities. Many slum dwellers in the Third World live in self-built hovels without indoor plumbing, electricity or heating. The unpaved streets either are dusty or muddy. The people are poorly dressed and most children walk around on their bare feet. Apart from the fact that educational facilities and medical services tend to be of inferior quality when compared to those in better neighborhoods, many people cannot afford to make much use of them. A few blocks away there usually is considerable wealth: beautiful homes, luxurious hotels, well-stocked supermarkets, paved avenues, and elegantly dressed ladies and gentlemen dining in expensive restaurants. Day in day out, the poor are painfully reminded that they are pariahs – victims of an unjust and highly unequal society which condemns them to a wretched life in filth and poverty.

A small band of Indians living somewhere in the Amazon region serves as an example of the second type. Despite their extremely simple way of life, their primitive huts (without running water, electricity or heating), periodic famine, high death rate, etc., it is unlikely that they consider themselves poverty-stricken. Living in isolation – far away from centers of modern development and high levels of material well-being – they are totally unaware that they are underdeveloped. In no way do they feel disadvantaged. As a matter of fact, chances are that they perceive their limited needs as quite well satisfied. However, a visitor from Rio de Janeiro can be expected to regard them as underdeveloped and look down on their 'primitive' way of life. Even an inhabitant of one of Rio's *favelas* (shantytowns) is likely to think of these Indians as being deprived.

Until about a century ago, much of humankind lived in isolation – often

1. Crowded living conditions in India. Note the absence of furniture. Most homes have no running water, no kitchen, no bathroom, no bedrooms and inadequate storage. (VDO)

in highly inaccessible and therefore 'remote' areas. Few people ever traveled more than one or two hundred kilometers from their place of birth.[1] Mass media, libraries, telephones, photographs, world atlases and encyclopedias were unknown in large parts of the world. Besides, most people were unable to read. Even as late as 1940, the indigenous population of Africa, Asia and Latin America knew practically nothing about life styles and living standards outside their immediate surroundings. Since then all that has changed. Quite suddenly virtually the entire Third World has come into contact with the economically more developed areas and has discovered, so to speak, its relative backwardness.

Meanwhile, the rapidly accelerating process of rural-to-urban migration in most Third World countries has resulted in large numbers finding out that within their own countries there are those who enjoy all kinds of comforts and luxuries they had never even dreamed of. Not only have the rural migrants become aware of their poverty, but quite naturally they have acquired new tastes.

The post-World War II information explosion has caused a similar process of growing awareness in the developed countries. One of the great discoveries of the late 1940s and 1950s was that there was a 'world' of

[1] 100 km equals 62 miles. See also the list of measures on page XXII.

26

2. Outdoor health lesson in rural Togo, Africa. Officials travel (by bike) from village to village to teach people the basics of health care and hygiene. (WHO/VDO)

incredible poverty – often accompanied by widespread undernourishment and starvation – which eventually became known as the Third World. Before long, governments, churches and many individuals found the immense disparities in prosperity unacceptable. Moral indignation demanded that efforts be made to help the Third World countries combat economic stagnation, poverty and hunger. Western politicians often saw the misery and suffering as a potential source of unrest, revolution and armed conflict, and therefore as a threat to world peace. Economic assistance and humanitarian relief aid, they hoped, would reduce the risk of upheavals and so safeguard Western investments in the Third World. Western business leaders and industrialists, too, supported the idea of stimulating economic growth because it afforded them a chance to expand their operations and thus their earnings. Last but not least, the East-West rivalry or Cold War played a role: both sides tried to win over allies by providing foreign aid.

Development as a culturally relative concept

Over the years, critics have frequently pointed out that Western scientists tend to look at the problems of underdevelopment[2] from a Western or Eurocentric point of view. Although we agree that this is a correct observation, we disagree that it is a valid criticism. It is only logical that Westerners view and perceive Third World conditions in terms of the circumstances they are most familiar with. To expect them to do otherwise, thereby distancing themselves from the cultural values which have molded them, would hardly be reasonable. At the same time, it strikes us as just as logical that people in the Third World, who wish to see their countries achieve a higher level of economic development, take the First World's (or for that matter, the Second World's) economic accomplishments and level of prosperity as examples. Given the fact that the most prosperous countries generally also are the most highly industrialized, it is perfectly understandable that Third World countries equate industrialization with development. Thus, factories have come to symbolize progress, and wage labor, production for the market, and commercialization of agriculture have become regarded as solutions to the problems of underdevelopment. In other words, development must be seen as "a culturally relative term which necessarily reflects Western attitudes and standards and may not take into sufficient account the differing values of given cultures in countries described as being inferior in terms of those standards" (Ginsburg 1960, p. xiv).

Scientifically speaking, there is no objection whatsoever to using circumstances in one place as a model for guiding development in another place. The consequence, perhaps unfortunately, is that Western prosperity has become the universally accepted standard. This is the way it is, and it is unlikely to change in the near future. This standard means that a process of Westernization is reshaping, and will continue to reshape, life in much of the Third World, especially in countries which travel the capitalist road to development. But pretty much the same changes are apparent in such socialist countries as Cuba and China. Only time will tell whether a country like Iran – currently in the midst of a fundamentalist Moslem revolution – will succeed in keeping Western influence at bay. However, even if the Iranians succumb to the forceful diffusion of Western values and norms, their present resistance raises an all-important question: Just how wise is it for Third World countries to emulate the West and try to catch up with it?

Western-type development, i.e., modern development, not only squanders nonrenewable resources, but causes excessive environmental pollution and ecological damage. As Rifkin (1981, p. 139) has pointed out, a simple peasant farmer can produce ten calories of energy for each calorie

---

[2] We should use the term underdevelopedness, but here and elsewhere in this book we prefer to be guided by common parlance and use underdevelopment instead. Likewise, development is used in lieu of developedness.

28

expended, whereas the modern American farmer uses up ten calories of energy to produce one calorie. It is highly unlikely that this planet can support Western standards of living for all humanity. For that reason, less ambitious development goals would seem much more realistic. Many scientists now believe – in this age of pessimism and global crisis – that the most that can be done for the Third World is to eliminate the worst forms of deprivation. Solving these problems would be quite an impressive accomplishment, so they maintain.

However reasonable this 'lifeboat solution' (see box) might appear to some people in the developed countries of the West and East, it is anything but reasonable to assume that the peoples of the Third World will go along with it. Chances are that they will feel shortchanged and will demand a much more even distribution of wealth on a global scale. Justifiably, they will argue that they, too, are entitled to have the opportunity to satisfy more than only the most elementary needs. There is little reason, then, to expect that the development problematic will ever be resolved equitably for all humankind.

Garrett Hardin's lifeboat ethics

In 1974, Garrett Hardin wrote an article entitled "Living on a Lifeboat," which was published in the journal *Bioscience*. In it, the author paints a metaphorical picture of the world in which each developed country is represented by a lifeboat partly filled with comparatively rich people. The poor also are in lifeboats, but theirs are overcrowded and about to sink. Due to rough weather, the poor continuously fall out of their boats. While trying desperately to keep their heads above water, they hope to be admitted to a lifeboat of the rich. What are the rich passengers to do? Should they pull the poor aboard and run the risk of drowning themselves by admitting too many? In Hardin's view the rich should do nothing.

Every life saved now, Hardin claims, will diminish the quality of life for subsequent generations. Much of the world is already overpopulated, causing unprecedented ecological destruction. Survival demands that humans govern their actions by the lifeboat ethics. Thus far, the wealthy countries have already done a great deal of harm to the poor countries – and to the world at large – through their well-intentioned but misguided attempts to help them. If they keep up their ill-conceived aid programs, human existence everywhere will sooner or later be threatened by global catastrophe.

The fact that the study of underdevelopment does not date back more than a few decades does not mean that underdevelopment is a recent phenomenon. Nothing could be further from the truth. Indications are that since time immemorial great contrasts in development and prosperity have been the rule rather than the exception. Until the 20th century, these differences were not generally perceived as burning issues, at least not on a global scale. There was no widespread indignation demanding that excessive disparities in well-being be ameliorated, much less eliminated. The present worldwide awareness of the rich-poor contrast makes the post-war period unique and without precedence in all human history. For the first time, underdevelopment is being experienced as a problem and, again for the first time, more or less universal, albeit ill-defined, standards of developed and underdeveloped have found acceptance. Partly because of the many rapid technological and other changes which characterize the present era, these standards are constantly in flux.

Underdevelopment defined

Since the terms developing countries, less-developed countries and underdeveloped countries have become household words, they have often been used incorrectly. The result is considerable confusion.

This confusion could have been avoided if the original meaning – dating back to the late 1940s – had been left intact. The terms then were used to refer to countries in which the majority of the people were impoverished, poorly fed and not too healthy, where the economy was marked by low productivity and stagnation, and where poverty constituted a formidable obstacle to economic progress. Notwithstanding the lack of precision in this description, we believe that it conveys the essence of the problems with which Third World countries are confronted. In conformity with the spirit of the above description, we propose to define an underdeveloped country as *a country with a weak economic structure and with extreme poverty among the masses of the generally rapidly growing population who have become increasingly aware of their poverty*. Since this definition differs somewhat from those of others, a few explanatory notes are called for.

I. The reason that we have returned to older interpretations of underdevelopment is that we believe it desirable, even necessary, to emphasize the relative nature of the concept. Underdeveloped countries are above all countries which, in terms of economic development and prosperity, find themselves at a great disadvantage or far behind when compared with the so-called rich countries. Their level of production is notably below that of the more advanced societies. In this context it is worth noting that Warren (1982, p. 169) concludes that "There is no reason to abandon the view that underdevelopment is *non*-development, measured in terms of poverty relative to the advanced capitalist countries."

II. *Poverty* is the inability to satisfy one's needs. In the voluminous literature on underdevelopment far more attention is paid to material needs than to non-material needs, such as religious and political freedom and the protection of human rights. Indicative of this bias is that basic needs are usually, although not invariably, defined in terms of such material needs as shelter, food, clothing, clean drinking water and fuel. Quite apart from the low level of material well-being, human rights are seriously violated in virtually all Third World countries, no matter whether we are dealing with

30

3. Population explosion in the Indian subcontinent. In many Third World countries children make up about half the population. Here, children in densely populated Bangladesh receive free food donated by rich countries. (VDO)

4. Logging operations in Gabon, Africa. Most Third World countries are exporters of raw materials. Exploitation of natural resources is often in hands of foreign enterprises. (UN/VDO)

the Philippines or Tanzania, India or Argentina, South Africa or El Salvador, Vietnam or Haiti. Democracy is unknown in most Third World countries and more often than not basic freedoms – e.g., freedom of speech, uncensored information, freedom of movement and the right to organize labor unions and political parties – are conspicuous by their absence. In this regard, the countries belonging to the socialist Second World may be said to be underdeveloped as well.

III. By *weak economic structure* we mean more than the disadvantages associated with the fact that Third World countries are dependent on – or subordinated by – the more advanced (capitalist and socialist) countries. Dependency is by no means unimportant, but it is only one aspect of economic weakness. Moreover, dependency often is a result, rather than a cause, of a host of other structural weaknesses. Part and parcel of the weak

5. Bangladesh. Labor-intensive production of gravel for road construction. A poor infrastructure is a common problem in the Third World. (M. Edwards/VDO)

economic structure are things like: (a) high percentage of population employed in the primary sector, (b) low agricultural productivity, (c) underutilization of physical and human resources, (d) fragmentary industrialization, (e) overabundance of very small factories or work shops, (f) shortage of employment oppportunities in the secondary sector, (g) an excessively large and for the most part unproductive, even parasitical, informal tertiary sector, (h) inadequate infrastructure, (i) insufficient technological know-how, (j) lack of managerial skill, (k) widespread indebtedness, (l) limited purchasing power, (m) overdependence on a very small number of mostly primary exports, (n) dependence on foreign investment capital, (o) dependence on imports of capital goods, such as machinery, and (p) extraction of profits by foreign investors, in particular transnational corporations. Many of these phenomena are not consequences of colonial or neo-colonial dependency relations with economically stronger and dominating core countries, but are for the most part inherent features of backward societies.

IV. Besides economic weakness and widespread poverty, *rapid population growth* is a fundamental characteristic of most underdeveloped countries (Fig. 3). The demographic 'explosion' – with annual growth rates of 2 percent or more, as compared to less than 1 percent in the developed countries – heavily taxes the natural environment and puts an enormous burden on the economy. In India, for example, every year

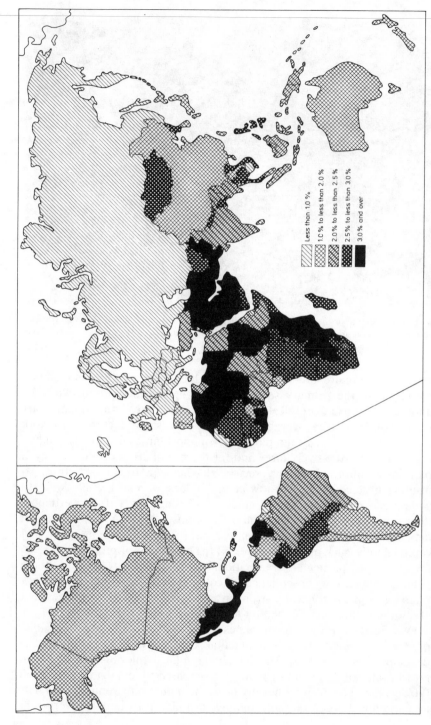

Fig. 3. Average annual rate of population growth, 1970-1981. *Source:* World Bank, *World Development Report 1983.*

Less than 1.0 %

1.0 % to less than 2.0 %

2.0 % to less than 2.5 %

2.5 % to less than 3.0 %

3.0 % and over

an extra 15 million mouths need to be fed. But man does not live by bread alone; every human being born needs air, water, space, unspoiled scenery, manufactured goods as well as schooling, medical care and work. Schooling, alone, requires such immense 'demographic investments' – absolutely necessary if the poverty cancer is to be arrested – that not enough capital resources are left to strengthen the economy, create new jobs, raise the standard of living, improve the infrastructure and, at the same time, take measures to avoid ecological disaster. In many African countries, more than one-quarter of government expenditure is on education, mostly on teachers' salaries.

V. The basic characteristics of underdevelopment just discussed are not isolated phenomena, but together form a large and complex system of cause-and-effect relationships. This internal relatedness of the underdevelopment syndrome can hardly be overemphasized because it, more than anything else, constitutes the crux of the dilemma facing the Third World countries. As we will explain in a later chapter, the Third World countries are caught, so to speak, in a maze of interacting and mutually reinforcing vicious circles from which they cannot escape easily. It would appear that they can be freed only through massive injections of foreign aid or through the discovery and exploitation of a valuable natural resource like oil. Although these may be necessary conditions for putting into motion long-term processes of development, they are not in and of themselves sufficient to guarantee that sustained economic growth will indeed materialize.

VI. In order to measure whether certain countries are underdeveloped or how underdeveloped they are, it has become almost standard procedure to look at a large number of indicators, including per capita GNP, per capita energy consumption, infant mortality rate, adult literacy rate, per capita calorie intake, the number of automobiles per 100,000 inhabitants, and percentage of population employed in manufacturing. Frequently, as many as forty such indicators are used. An interesting aspect of this approach is that it matters little which indicators or variables are used, or whether one uses just a few indicators or a great many. Regardless of how underdevelopment is measured, the results produced by one method tend to differ little from those obtained when another combination of indicators or composite index is used. Some countries (e.g., Mexico, Malaysia and South Africa) always score higher than others (e.g., Haiti, Bangladesh and Ethiopia). Because of the similar results obtained using few or many variables, various authors have recommended comparing countries on the basis of just one, two or three indicators. The reason that even one single variable, e.g., infant mortality rate, can give a fairly accurate picture of a country's relative underdevelopedness, is that it has intimate cause-and-effect relations with most other variables.

It is our opinion that all variables may be divided into three broad groups: (1) those which pertain to economic weakness, (2) those which form an aspect of poverty, and (3) those which are associated with rapid population growth. These three groups, we suggest, may be regarded as the basic elements or key characteristics of underdevelopment. The forty or so individual indicators, in other words, are merely aspects or expressions of these three key characteristics.

VII. A final point that needs attention is that despite some similarities, every underdeveloped country is unique. The mix of economic weakness, poverty, awareness and rapid population increase manifests itself differently in each country. To a large extent, these differences can be explained in terms of unlike historical processes and different natural environments, including differential resource endowments. Equally important are differences in religion, culture, leadership and location. Obviously, then, *one* theory cannot and does not account for underdevelopment everywhere.

Stated differently, underdevelopment is such a complex phenomenon that it is no sinecure to explain it, even when we make use of all the theories that have been put forward over the years. For this reason we have not included an explanation in our definition of underdevelopment, this in contrast to the definition formulated by D. Senghaas. He has defined underdevelopment as "the structural heterogeneity of peripheral social formations and the concomitant obstruction of an autonomous development of productive forces resulting from the international division of labor caused by the dominance of the capitalist mode of production" (Senghaas 1974, p. 24).

We have several objections to this sort of definition. First, the concept of underdevelopment is given a meaning which it did not originally have. According to Senghaas, its basic features are not poverty, low productivity and rapid population growth, but structural heterogeneity, peripherality and lack of autonomous development. Second, his definition implies that there is only one factor which allegedly causes underdevelopment, i.e., the constraining effect which capitalism exerts on indigenous development. Third, it cannot be assumed *a priori* that autonomous development – whatever that may be – is better, more balanced and/or more rapid than non-autonomous or dependent development. Fourth, according to Senghaas's definition with its built-in explanation, countries like China and Mongolia cannot be described as underdeveloped because they are neither integrated into the capitalist world system nor dominated by foreign capitalist interests. Fifth, Senghaas denies the possibility that there may have been underdevelopment prior to the rise of capitalism, e.g., in ancient India. Since he ascribes underdevelopment to an external factor, namely capitalist penetration, he also denies that internal factors might have played an important role. Sixth, structural heterogeneity – which may be described as the interwoven coexistence of the modern, capitalist mode of production and the traditional, pre-capitalist mode of production, whereby the former dominates and exploits the latter – is found not only in the Third World, but also in the First and Second Worlds.

Our objections should not give the reader the impression that we totally disapprove of Senghaas's explanation. Rather, we believe that his definition is one-sided, incomplete and too much a product of dogmatic Marxist thinking.

Measuring underdevelopment: a dilemma

Thus far we have talked about poverty and economic weakness as if there can be no disagreement about the meaning of these concepts. But what exactly do we mean by them and how can they be measured?

Even if we assume that poverty refers to the inadequate satisfaction of perceived needs, we are still faced with the problem of how to determine whether or not a particular need is adequately satisfied. No less troublesome is the qualification 'perceived.' Should a transistor radio or bicycle be considered a need when 30 or 60 percent of the people perceive it as such? In other words, what makes something a need? What should be the quality and size of a house or hut before it meets the local demands for shelter? Should it have windows, a fireplace or some other heating system, a bathroom with running water and a separate kitchen? And what happens to the meaning of poverty when, perhaps as a consequence of an increase in income or exposure to Western housing standards, expectations are raised? When that happens, people become more demanding, so that a dwelling which used to be acceptable may become perceived as unfit for providing adequate shelter.

The concept of *basic needs,* which has received considerable attention in the development literature, does not solve our problem. Aside from the fact that advocates of the basic needs approach to development frequently, though by no means always, ignore non-material needs, it remains debatable which needs should or should not be considered as basic. What may be regarded as a basic need in one place or at one point in time, is not necessarily viewed as such in another place or at a later moment. This dilemma underlines our earlier conclusion that *development and underdevelopment are time-relative and culture-relative concepts.*

Already many years ago economists 'solved' the problem of measuring development by using per capita GNP as an indicator. This measure makes sense because the combined value of total domestic and foreign output claimed by the residents of a given country not only is a reasonably accurate measure of that country's overall economic development, but also tells us a great deal about average earnings, purchasing power and thus about the general level of prosperity. Using per capita GNP as a yardstick, however, also has its disadvantages. It may be that one extremely lucrative sector of the economy, e.g., oil

Table 2. Classification of 125 countries (with over 1 million people) based largely on per capita GNP in 1981.

Group of countries	Number of countries	Population (millions) mid-1981	GNP/capita average 1981 (dollars)	Poorest country 1981	Richest country 1981
Low-income economies	34	2,210.5	270	Bhutan ($80)	Ghana ($400)
Lower middle-income economies	39	663.7	850	Kenya ($420)	Paraguay ($1630)
Upper middle-income economies	21	464.7	2,490	South Korea ($1700)	Trinidad and Tobago ($5670)
High-income oil exporters	4	15.0	13,460	Libya ($8450)	United Arab Emirates ($24,660)
Industrial market economies	19	719.5	11,120	Ireland ($5230)	Switzerland ($17,430)
East Europan nonmarket economies	8	380.8	–	? (a)	? (b)
	125	4,454.2	–	–	–

(a) Probably Albania.   (b) Probably East Germany.

Source: World Bank 1983, pp. 148-149.

production, is far more developed than are other sectors, thereby raising the value of total output so much that it can no longer serve as a reliable indicator of overall development. Equally problematic is that per capita GNP, like every other average value, tells us nothing about the distribution of wealth. Third World countries are known to have highly skewed distributions of wealth, with most of it concentrated in the hands or bank accounts of a very small and exceptionally rich elite. At the same time, nearly all wealth may be concentrated in one small section of the country – usually in the primate capital city – with the rural masses in the remainder of the country only knowing deprivation.

Notwithstanding these drawbacks, per capita GNP continues to be the single most commonly used variable for measuring and comparing levels of economic development. Looking at the 1981 data published by the World Bank, we notice that there are immense differences in per capita GNP, ranging from $80 in land-locked Bhutan and Laos to more than $20,000 in oil-rich Kuwait and the United Arab Emirates. Switzerland was in third place ($17,400), followed by Sweden ($14,900), Norway ($14,000) West Germany ($13,500) and Denmark ($13,100). The US was eighth ($12,800), Saudi Arabia ninth ($12,600), Canada thirteenth ($11,400) and Japan seventeenth ($10,100).

In view of these disparities, the World Bank has divided all countries with more than 1 million inhabitants into four income groups: low, lower middle, upper middle and high-income economies. By listing the high-income oil exporters (Libya, Saudi Arabia, Kuwait and the United Arab Emirates) as well as the industrial market economies and the East European nonmarket economies as separate groups, the World Bank has come up with a classification consisting of six types of countries (see Table 2).

Considering that nearly half the countries (60 out of 125) belong to the two middle-income groups, it makes little sense to divide the world up into rich and poor countries. A poor-rich dichotomy simply does not exist (see Figures 4 and 5). If we made such a crude division nonetheless, and used a per capita GNP of $2,500 as the differentiating value, we would find that well over half of all countries – together accounting for approximately 80 percent of the world population – would be designated as poor. Somewhat surprisingly perhaps, a few countries which are usually thought of as belonging to the Third World, namely, Argentina, Chile, Uruguay, Venezuela, Trinidad and Tobago, and South Africa (see Figure 4), as well as the two city-states of Hong Kong and Singapore and, of course, the four rich oil-exporting countries would then not belong to the group of poor countries. For this reason, we might want to employ a per capita GNP of $5,000 as a more appropriate cutoff value. This cutoff would result in having several countries not generally regarded as forming part of the Third World, i.e., Portugal, Yugoslavia and Greece, and probably also one or more East European nonmarket economies, joining the ranks of the poor countries.

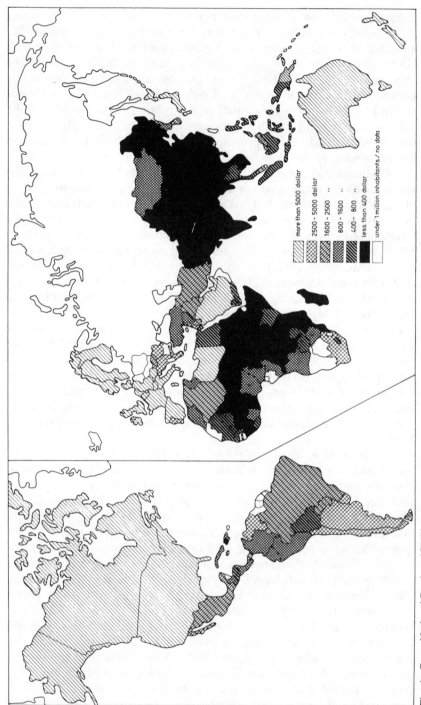

Fig. 4. Gross National Product (GNP) per capita, 1981. *Source:* World Bank, *World Development Report 1983.*

more than 5000 dollar

2500 – 5000 dollar

1600 – 2500 „

800 – 1600 „

400 – 800 „

less than 400 dollar

under 1 million inhabitants / no data

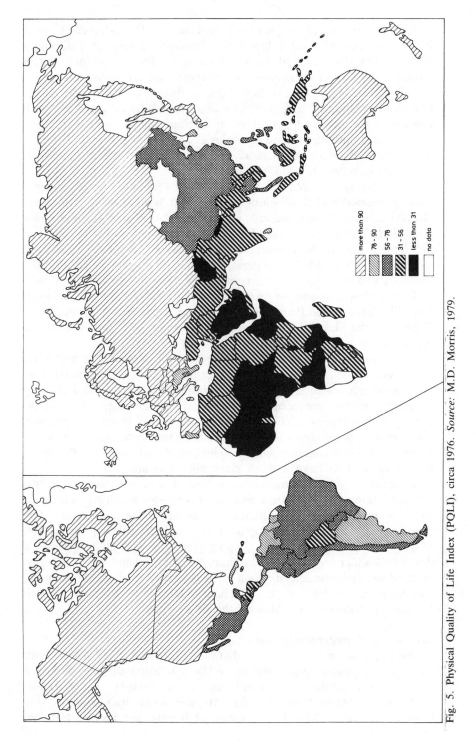

Fig. 5. Physical Quality of Life Index (PQLI), circa 1976. *Source*: M.D. Morris, 1979.

more than 90

78 – 90

56 – 78

31 – 56

less than 31

no data

41

A few years ago, M.D. Morris of the Overseas Development Council in Washington, D.C. developed the Physical Quality of Life Index (PQLI). On the basis of three indicators – life expectancy, infant mortality and adult literacy – each country can score from 0 to 100 points. Figure 5 shows the results of this method of measuring degrees of development/underdevelopment. An important asset of PQLI is that it eliminates the distorting effect of an extraordinarily large per capita GNP in such underdeveloped countries as Libya. For this reason, Figure 5 may be said to portray a more realistic picture of the geography of underdevelopment than does Figure 4.

When trying to decide which countries should be considered underdeveloped and thus belong to the Third World, we soon discover classifying most of them presents no problem. No matter which criterion is used, Ethiopia always qualifies, whereas Sweden never does. Most problematic are the high-income oil exporters and such borderline cases as Uruguay, South Africa, Portugal, Albania and Singapore. In addition, there are countries for which it is hard to obtain quantitative data, such as Cuba, Mongolia and North Korea. Finally, there are a few special cases like Taiwan and Puerto Rico which are not members of the World Bank or the United Nations because they are not considered independent sovereign states.

Using our definition of underdevelopment for determining whether a given country belongs to the Third World, it must be characterized by (1) a weak economic structure, (2) widespread poverty, (3) a growing awareness among the people that they are poverty-stricken, and (4) rapid population growth (Fig. 6). Here, too, we are faced with problem cases because some countries do not meet all four criteria. For example, Uruguay does not have a rapidly growing population, while South Africa cannot be said to have a weak economic structure.

In summary, we conclude that regardless of how underdevelopment is defined, there will always be a number of countries which straddle, so to speak, that definition. This situation is not surprising if we realize that development and underdevelopment are multidimensional in nature. Moreover, the maps in this chapter clearly reveal that there is a developed-underdeveloped continuum, rather than a dichotomy. Switzerland and Sweden are found at one extreme of this continuum, and Kampuchea, Bhutan, Laos, Chad, Bangladesh, Ethiopia, Nepal, Burma, Afghanistan and Mali at the other end.

Diversity and underdevelopment
One might be inclined to think that the ten 'basket cases' listed above must have a great deal in common. While it is true that they all have a very low per capita GNP, there also are a number of remarkable differences between them. To illustrate this point, literacy rates vary from 10 percent in Mali to 66 percent in Burma; per hectare fertilizer

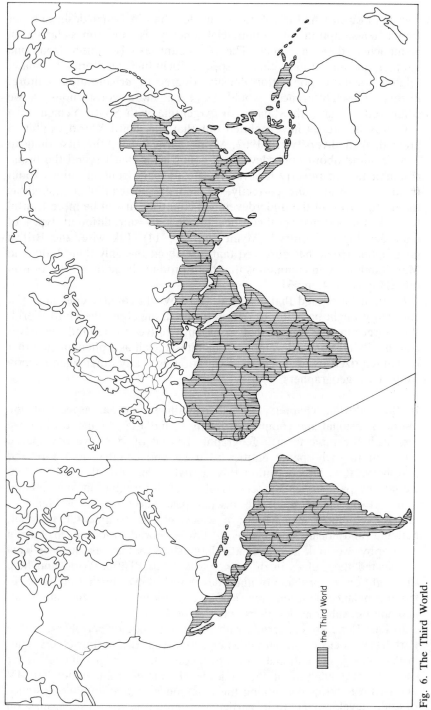

Fig. 6. The Third World.

the Third World

43

consumption in Chad is 150 times smaller than in Bangladesh; and per capita consumption of commercial energy is ten times larger in Kampuchea than in Nepal. The ten countries also differ from one another in numerous other respects, including landforms, climate, relative location, population density, degree of urbanization, culture, history, etc. Differences would be even more conspicuous if we compared China with Malawi, or Argentina with South Yemen.

Others before us have pointed out that the Third World exhibits a great deal of diversity. In 1967, Myint warned that "the first thing to bear in mind about underdeveloped countries is that beyond the broad common fact of poverty it is rarely safe to make generalizations about them . . ." And quite correctly, he added: "Instead of a monolithic theory to cover all the underdeveloped countries, it will be more fruitful to look for alternative theoretical models to suit different types of underdeveloped country" (Myint 1967, p. 14). Likewise, the British geographer Hoyle has observed that just about the only thing India and Mauritania have in common is that both produce large quantities of iron ore (Hoyle 1974, p. 3).

It might be argued that a typical Third World country does not exist and that it might be better to refrain from talking about *the* Third World. We agree in the sense that it is imperative to remind ourselves continually that underdevelopment manifests itself as a phenomenon that is characterized by as much areal variation as is any other phenomenon studied by geographers.

In the following chapters, we will examine numerous aspects of the multidimensional and complex problem of underdevelopment. Since we approach the topic from a geographical point of view, we pay special attention to such spatial entities as town and country, and core and periphery. It is largely within this spatial framework that we explore structures, patterns and processes of areal differentiation and integration. At the same time, we discuss past and present problems of underdevelopment at a variety of scales: global, continental, regional, national and local. Guided by a time-honored tradition in human geography, we look at man-land relationships as they manifest or have manifested themselves in different parts of the Third World and help shed light on the problem of underdevelopment. We further endeavor to strike a balance between empirical investigations, on the the one hand, and theoretical considerations, on the other.

In Part II we are concerned with the countryside or periphery, and in Part III we focus on urban nodes or core areas. In the four case studies in Part V, it is the national state which constitutes the spatial context for our historical analysis of the underdevelopment problematic. Part IV deals with theories concerning the emergence and continuing existence of underdevelopment. In it, particular attention is given to the question of whether underdevelopment is caused mainly by internal conditions, by external relations, or by a combination of past and present internal conditions and external relations.

PART TWO

THE RURAL-AGRICULTURAL SCENE

Chapter 3   Introduction

Rural and urban areas

Geographers like to look at the problems of the Third World from a spatial point of view. This can be done in a number of ways. One is to approach the subject on the basis of the *core-periphery dichotomy,* in which the core, also called *center,* represents the more developed urban areas, and the periphery the less developed rural areas. The core area of a country is characterized by at least some modern economic activity, a fairly good infrastructure, a rather high network accessibility, and a concentration of people. Via its harbor(s) and/or international airport, it possesses reasonably good connections with core areas in other countries. Most important, we usually find here the national capital with its powerful political elite, business leaders and top executives of industrial enterprises (often foreign-owned), most of whom maintain close relations with the developed countries of the world. In other words, the core is the country's political and economic nerve center, the site of headquarters, and the place in which national decision making is centered.

6. Education in rural Zimbabwe, Africa. As in many countries, there is a shortage of schoolhouses and teachers. (J. den Hengst/VDO)

Because of the concentration of power and influence in the core area, the remainder of the country may be characterized as peripheral, that is, dominated by the decision-making core area. Generally speaking, the periphery has little or no modern industry, is highly inaccessible, lacks health centers, schools and other services (e.g., electricity), has few off-farm employment opportunities, and is, at best, only marginally integrated into the network of international economic relations. Characteristically, the periphery occupies a weak and *dependent* position *vis-à-vis* the powerful core area. The periphery tends to be exploited by the core – a situation often referred to as *internal colonialism*. Like former colonialism and present-day neo-colonialism, internal colonialism is based on unequal relationships.

One thing should be clear from the preceding discussion: core and periphery are wedded to one another. Earlier we used the term dichotomy, but because core and periphery belong together – forming integrated parts of a single system of dominance-dependence relationships – a clear dichotomy does not exist in reality. By definition, there can be no periphery without a core, and *vice versa*. The two concepts can be separated only in theory. Functionally, core and periphery are inseparable. In the following chapters we treat them separately for practical and didactic reasons only. It is important to be well aware that the rural-agricultural periphery is closely tied to the urban-industrial-political core, just as the Third World as a whole, known as the world's *Periphery*, forms a closely integrated part of a larger worldwide system of economic relations: the so-called *World Space-Economy*. In this World Space-Economy or Capitalist World System, the Third World occupies a dependent, peripheral position *vis-à-vis* the developed countries. The latter countries, collectively referred to as the world's *Core*, play a dominant role in this neo-colonial relationship at the global scale. It is often assumed that this relationship is advantageous for the dominant Core and disadvantageous for the dominated, subservient Periphery.

The agricultural sector

The economy of the Third World's rural areas is almost everywhere dominated by agricultural activities, including nomadism. Living conditions are grim for the majority of the farming population, no matter whether they own or rent the land they cultivate. Most landless laborers are even worse-off. Invariably, rural incomes are so low that people barely manage to survive. Many needs cannot be satisfied, often not even the most basic necessities: food, clothing and shelter. In large areas, demands for clean drinking water and fuel for cooking outstrip supplies by a wide margin and shortages become more critical all the time, usually at increasingly rapid rates.

7. Water hole in the Sahel zone of West Africa. Besides using it as drinking water, women carry water to their gardens to irrigate subsistence food crops. Elsewhere, people depend on water from rivers or lakes. (VDO)

8. Fuel wood in Burkina Faso (Upper Volta). Too poor to purchase gasoline, people cut down virtually all trees and shrubs. In semiarid regions like the Sahel this practice leads to widespread ecological damage, wind erosion and desertification. (VDO)

51

Third World crises

In recent years, there has been much talk in the economically developed countries about an impending energy crisis, caused by occasional shortages of oil. This so-called crisis, however, is absolutely nothing compared to the rapidly spreading fuel crisis in many parts of the Third World. Wood – the major and sometimes only fuel people can afford – is becoming a scarce commodity. This is particularly true around cities and in semi-arid and arid regions. People have to walk ever longer distances – often an hour or more and usually on bare feet – to gather dead wood, to be carried home on their backs. Especially women do this heavy work, sometimes assisted by children. At the same time, charcoal is becoming a scarce and therefore increasingly expensive source of energy. Already, millions of people are unable to enjoy one cooked meal every day.

In many areas, also water (for cooking, drinking and washing) has to be hauled over long distances. Again, it is mainly women and children who perform this arduous task. Every day, millions of cans, pots and buckets are filled with water – often from rivers, lakes and hand-dug wells – and carried home while the sun stands high in the sky at temperatures approaching 35^0C (95^0F) or more.

In addition to growing shortages of wood and clean water, many Third World countries struggle with a housing crisis, a soil erosion crisis, an unemployment crisis, and various other crises. Compared to the Third World, people in the prosperous countries have very little to complain about. Real shortages are hardly known in the developed countries. On the contrary, if anything, people in the rich countries have too much of almost everything, including leisure, luxury and security. In sharp contrast to the underdeveloped Periphery, the Core countries may best be characterized as being 'overdeveloped.' In this highly unequal world, a small, affluent minority has far more than the large, impoverished majority. On a global scale, inequity is much more prevalent than is social justice.

In nearly every Third World country, over half the working people are engaged in agriculture and in many at least 75 percent is so-employed (see Fig. 7). This fact alone is sufficient reason for starting our analysis of the Third World's weak economic structure with a discussion of the agricultural sector. Agriculture is so dominant as a means of livelihood that our treatment of the rural areas is limited to a discussion of agriculture. And in order to discuss it in detail, several chapters are devoted to this important topic.

Another reason that we focus considerable attention on agriculture is that many problems which manifest themselves in other sectors of the economy cannot be grasped adequately unless we have an understanding of the agricultural dilemmas. For example, industrial expansion can

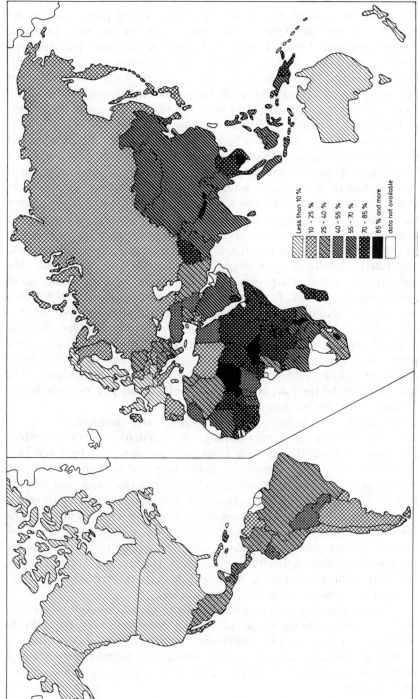

Fig. 7. Percent labor force in agriculture, 1981. *Source:* World Bank, *World Development Report 1983.*

Less than 10 %
10 - 25 %
25 - 40 %
40 - 55 %
55 - 70 %
70 - 85 %
85 % and more
data not available

often not be realized due to a lack of purchasing power among the majority of the population – the poor tillers of the soil. Domestic demand for manufactured goods is frequently so small that industrial growth can easily lead to wasteful overproduction or uneconomic underutilization of investments, especially of machines and other expensive capital goods. In both cases financial losses and eventual bankruptcy may result, which, in turn, will further aggravate the already serious unemployment problem found in most Third World cities.

Until not so long ago, it was widely believed that industrialization was the key to development, that once the process of industrial expansion had picked up momentum and reached a certain stage, modernization of other sectors of the economy would follow more or less automatically. In other words, industry was seen as the motor which could set in motion the entire, multifarious process of economic development. It has become abundantly clear in recent years that development cannot be achieved simply by building factories. A much more comprehensive, diverse and integrated development strategy is required, one in which the agricultural sector must play a leading role and must be given preferential treatment. It is now generally realized that development is more than economic development and that agriculture should function as the basis on which the process of development is to be founded. Without a sound farming system and a productive and prosperous agricultural population, prospects for industrial development and improving living conditions may be said to be so dim as to be virtually non-existent. The well-being of the rural areas or periphery of a country is inseparably tied to that of the urban-industrial core region.

Agriculture, including livestock raising and horticulture, is an extremely diverse economic activity. A systematic description which provides a picture that is both clear and complete can be given in a number of ways. For example, we could first deal with the natural and societal conditions under which agriculture is practiced and then indicate how these conditions affect agricultural production. Although geographers often use this approach – usually paying special attention to the physical environment (climate, soil, slope, drainage) – we will discuss the agricultural complexity by focusing on the manner in which, and the purpose for which, agricultural enterprises (farms) are organized. We will also attempt to indicate how agriculture is influenced by natural, economic, social, political and other factors.

Although our approach – centered on the organization of production units – enables us to shed light on many relevant aspects of Third World agriculture, it does have its limitations. For this reason, we will combine it with a second approach, one in which the farming population is divided into a number of groups, each of which has its own attributes and problems.

Looking at the organization of agricultural production, four aspects can be recognized. These are:

1. *the legal framework* or the landownership and tenure relations which form the juridical context within which agricultural production takes place. Agricultural enterprises that may be distinguished on this basis include private farms, tenant farms, collective or communal farms and state farms;
2. *the technical operation,* that is, the way in which and the degree to which the production factors nature, labor and capital are utilized;
3. *the production scheme,* which comprises all plant and animal products raised on a farm, their relative importance and the functional relations which may exist between them; and lastly,
4. *the functional aspect,* which refers to the purpose for which agricultural production takes place. Commonly, a distinction is made between (a) production for home use and (b) production for sale. The first type, known as self-sufficient agriculture or subsistence farming, tends to be characterized by small-scale production of a wide variety of food crops. The second type, the commercial farm, often is a larger and more capital-intensive enterprise that specializes in the production of an industrial crop or a food crop. Such cash crops may either be grown for the local (domestic) market or for export.

Looking at those directly involved in the production of agricultural goods, it is possible to identify several groups:

1. small private farmers (who own their land);
2. small farmers who do not own the land they work (tenants and squatters);
3. medium-size to large farmers who either own or rent their land;
4. large landowners; and
5. agricultural laborers, including many who migrate seasonally.

Although the latter typology is rather crude and incomplete, it helps us to acquire an insight into the many problems of Third World agriculture.

The four above-mentioned aspects of agricultural production will be discussed separately. This does not mean that the variegated phenomena are not related to one another. Nothing could be further from the truth. In fact, the various aspects are so thoroughly intertwined that we can distinguish between them but not really separate them. Likewise, the problems and possibilities for progress of one group of agriculturists (e.g., small tenant farmers) are often closely related to those of one or more other groups (e.g., large landowners). Because agricultural reality is such a complex constellation of interrelated phenomena and processes, we will in the following chapters frequently refer back to concepts and facts already dealt with or anticipate those which are yet to be discussed.

The legal framework is presented in the following chapter; the technical aspects in Chapter 5; the production scheme is discussed in Chapter 6; and the functional aspects are the main topic of Chapter 7.

Drugs production in the Third World

In a number of Third World countries, some of the better farmland is used for the production of marihuana, poppies and other drugs-producing crops. Because of the high prices paid for these lucrative crops, an increasing number of small farmers grow them, thereby reducing the acreage in food crops. In Northeast Africa, including Ethiopia, production of *khat* is the principal source of income for several million farmers. About 90 percent of the marihuana consumed in Europe is imported from Africa. In Bolivia, more than 13,000 farmers grow coca plants. Coca plantations in Bolivia, Peru, Colombia, Ecuador, Venezuela and Brazil together occupy thousands of square kilometers. Bolivia has been called a cocaine-imperium, as it is ruled by a small group of rich cocaine dealers. Some 100,000 farmers in Turkey grow poppies, from which opium is extracted. Opium is the raw material from which morphine and heroin are manufactured. About 70 percent of the heroin smuggled into the US comes from Turkey, where every year approximately 35,000 ha (86,000 acres) are planted in poppies. The most important opium-producing region in the world is the so-called Golden Triangle, located in Thailand, Laos and Burma. (Source: *Troef*, vol. 6, no. 1, 1982).

Chapter 4   The legal framework of agricultural production

Large landholdings, labor relations and tenancy

In quite a few underdeveloped countries, much of the agricultural land is owned by a very small number of individuals, even though a large proportion of the population – often the majority – depends on agriculture for a living. Large landholdings are particularly common in many Latin American countries. In the early 1960s, more than 50 percent of all farmland in Latin America was in the hands of no more than 1.5 percent of all landowners; a situation which has not changed much since then.

The origin of large landownership in Latin America dates back to the beginning of the colonial period. When Spain and Portugal conquered the then sparsely populated region, much of the land became Spanish and Portuguese Crown land. The Kings or their representatives gave much of the land to various dignitaries and officials without paying attention to the question of whether the way in which they distributed the land was fair. Persons with influence and favorites of the royal families managed to acquire exceedingly large tracts of land, which they often were able to expand further through illegal means. Others who had not been granted land simply appropriated a piece of Crown land, which they were subsequently allowed to keep. Much land was originally handed out for temporary use – chiefly for livestock grazing purposes – but it frequently happened that such usufructuary rights eventually became recognized as legal ownership. Thus, many large estates (*estancias* or *haciendas* in Spanish; *fazendas* in Portuguese) came into being early in Latin America's colonial history. One of the objectives of this land policy was to advance the settlement process, but as it turned out, it retarded rather than promoted the settling of the land.

Land settlement in North America

The history of settlement in Latin America contrasts sharply with that of North America. Both in the US and Canada, *homestead* legislation played a decisive role, resulting in a settlement process that was not only fair but also efficient. Thanks to this rational method of land distribution much of North America was opened up, settled and made productive by medium-to-large farmers who owned the land they cultivated. Because the homesteaders all received the same amount of land (in a certain climatic region), North America's land settlement system has contributed significantly to laying a foundation for an egalitarian society. And an egalitarian society – in which everyone's opportunities are more or less equal – serves as a foundation for democracy. By contrast, the Latin American land distribution systems virtually assured from the very beginning that egalitarian-democratic societies would not evolve.

Since the colonial era – which in most of Latin America ended around 1830 – the concentration of landownership in a limited number of hands has proceeded unabatedly, thereby exacerbating social inequity. Eventually, a small and influential *elite* was in control of nearly all the land. Sometimes they enlarged their already immense properties by purchasing additional tracts, usually at incredibly low prices. They acquired land not only for the sake of prestige, but also for investment purposes. That this egocentric and often ruthless behavior endangered the livelihood of other population groups was of no concern to them. It was mainly this elite of large land-owners who, during the early years of the 19th century, forced Spain and Portugal to give up their colonial possessions.

During the colonial period, lands belonging to the indigenous population had been protected, at least to some degree. But in the 19th century, when liberalism was seen as the key to progress and development, the oligarchy in various Latin American countries enacted laws enabling Indians to sell their land. As a consequence, landownership became even more concen-trated, while the Indians' resource base deteriorated to an alarming degree. After 1900 – when 84 percent of the land in Mexico was in the hands of one percent of the overwhelmingly agrarian population – the process of land concentration still continued in many parts of Latin America, now partly as a result of increasing commercialization and mechanization of agricultural production.

Another region in which large landholdings were common at an early date is the Middle East. During the Ottoman Era (from the early 16th century until the fall of the Ottoman Empire after World War I), the rulers handed out much 'public domain' to government officials and the military. Most considered farming below their dignity and preferred to live in urban settlements, usually leaving cultivation of their land to sharecropping tenants.

Some large landowners originally were tax collectors in the vast Turkish Empire. Since many private farmers had to pay more tax than they were able to, they became heavily indebted. The only way they could pay off their debts was by selling their land. This enabled money lenders – among them many tax collectors – to become the owners of large holdings (Tamsma 1956, pp. 8-10). Because tenants had to pay high rents or give the landlord an excessively large share of their crop, land was a most attractive investment. In fact, renting out land was so profitable in the Middle East that most large landowners lived in splendor. However, for every fabulously rich landlord there were hundreds, if not thousands, of exploited and poverty-ridden sharecroppers who desperately struggled to stay alive. Although this process of land concentration was later halted by *land reforms,* still today it sometimes happens that a hopelessly poor farmer must sell his land to pay his creditors.

One reason why an extremely uneven distribution of landownership tends to have disastrous consequences in Third World countries is that there are hardly any employment opportunities available outside agriculture. Most people must farm, whether they like it or not. The result is a great demand for farmland. And because nearly everywhere in the Third World the population is growing at a rapid rate, *land hunger* is becoming increasingly acute. In quite a few countries the pressure on the land would not be so severe if much of the land were not owned by a small minority of large landlords.

Brazil in 1980 was characterized by a highly unequal distribution of land (Table 3). Small farms (less than 20 hectares or 50 acres, which is not much considering the low levels of productivity) accounted for 65 percent of all farms but only 5.3 percent of Brazil's farmland. Farms with 1,000 hectares (2,500 acres) or more constituted only 0.9 percent of all production units, but made up 45.8 percent of all agriculturally productive land.

Fully 76 percent of the farms were classified as *minifundios,* which are too small to allow farmers to raise their standard of living above mere subsistence level. This class accounted for only 12 percent of all agricultural land. The large farms or *latifundios,* on the other hand, occupied 85 percent of all farmland. A mere 2 percent of all farms, with the remaining 3 percent of all land, were classified as *empresa rural,* that is, large enough to allow efficient organization and an acceptable living standard. Although these figures may not be completely reliable and we can question the various definitions, it is nevertheless clear that farmland in Brazil is very unevenly distributed.

Using data for 1950, A.G. Frank (1969b, p. 249) has concluded that 62 percent of Brazil's agricultural population consisted of landless laborers. If we add to this number all those families whose farms are too small to be economically viable, the *de facto* landless would account for 81 percent of Brazil's total farm population. In other words, most Brazilians who depend on agriculture for a living do not own enough or any land, partly because others own much more than they need and often more than they know what to do with.

Table 3. Distribution of farms and farmland in Brazil (1980).

| Size class | Number of farms | | Total area | |
ha	Absolute	Percentage	Absolute (ha)	Percentage
0-10	2,603,576	50.4	8,994,718	2.4
10-20	770,903	14.9	10,740,555	2.9
20-50	853,318	16.5	26,356,491	7.1
50-100	391,600	7.6	27,359,432	7.4
100-200	261,275	5.1	34,729,980	9.4
200-500	169,566	3.3	51,963,514	14.1
500-1,000	58,462	1.1	40,242,666	10.9
1,000-2,000	27,258	0.5	37,177,888	10.1
2,000-5,000	15,119	0.3	44,372,957	12.0
5,000-10,000	3,529	0.07	24,104,766	6.5
10,000-100,000	2,348	0.05	48,997,988	13.3
100,000 and over	62	0.001	14,547,048	3.9
(not specified)	10,562			
Total	5,167,758	100	369,587,872	100

Source: IX Recenseamento Geral do Brasil, 1980. Sinopse Preliminar do Censo Agropecuário. Fundação IBGE.

In Brazil, as in other Third World countries, there are many miniature-size farms, the *minifundia* and *microfundia*. Even when their land is ill-suited for intensive cultivation, farmers must try to grow as much as possible in order to avoid starvation. They must put in many hours of labor per hectare, but because they lack the knowledge and/or means to produce high yields, their output usually is very low . This problem occurs in particular in areas where the soil is not too fertile or where the better land has been bought up by enterprises – often foreign-owned – which use it for large-scale plantation production. In several Central American and Caribbean countries, the juxtaposition of marginal, low-yielding minifarms and well-organized, modern plantations is a common phenomenon. However, similar contrasts can be encountered elsewhere in Latin America, in Africa and in much of South and Southeast Asia.

Even when the land is well suited for farming, incomes from *minifundia* often are insufficient, so that the farmer must rent one or more additional plots. Or he/she can try to earn some extra money by hiring himself/herself out as a part-time or seasonal laborer on a nearby *latifundium*. Since this is not always possible, many a *minifundista* (small farmer) is forced sooner or later to borrow money – usually at a high interest rate. One crop failure or some other misfortune may raise his/her debts to the point where no other choice remains but to sell his/her few hectares, thus exacerbating the glaring contrasts between the wealthy landowners and the destitute dispossessed.

The terms 'large landowner' and 'small farm' mean different things in different places, depending on ecological conditions and levels of agro-technical development. In most humid tropical environments – where soils tend to have limited fertility due to leaching – *slash-and-burn* cultivators need at least 50 to 100 ha (125 to 250 acres) to make a meager living. The rapid depletion of the soil fertility requires them to keep most of their land in fallow at any one particular time. In this system of *shifting cultivation* – or *ladang* agriculture – fields must be rotated continuously. After a given clearing has been farmed for two or three years, it must be returned to nature (that is, left idle) for fifteen or twenty years before being cultivated again.

By contrast, a Southeast Asian farmer with 10 ha (25 acres) of properly irrigated land can grow two crops a year (without ever having to leave it idle) and may be considered a large landowner by other members of the community who have only one ha (2½ acres) of farmland.

Unlike the intensively cultivated *minifundia,* much land belonging to the large landowners is used extensively. Inputs of labor and capital per hectare are small. The owners often do not live on their property but in town or sometimes even in another country. They own a great deal of land not because they depend on it for making a living, but for investment or prestige reasons. Many of these absentee landlords know little about farming and are not interested in making the land productive. Important exceptions to this pattern are the large agricultural enterprises that produce for export, in particular the *plantations* (see Chapter 7).

Extensive utilization of the land may result from unfavorable natural conditions, such as poor soils and aridity, which make intensive cultivation

9. Shifting cultivation in the Amazon Basin of northern Brazil. Forestry experts estimate that Brazil annually loses about one million hectares (2.5 million acres) of tropical forest through burnings. Farmers have burned off the land, cultivated it for two or three years, and moved on to repeat the same destructive process elsewhere. (FAO/VDO)

uneconomical or downright impossible. In many instances, however, owners possess so much land that they earn enough money using it in a non-intensive way. Especially in Latin America, livestock grazing (or ranching) is practiced on many large landholdings, even though intensive crop production may well be possible. This is an example of *qualitative underutilization*. Sometimes only a small portion of the land is used, with the remainder lying idle: a form of *quantitative underutilization*. The larger the landholding, the greater the chance that it is used far below its capacity.

Underutilization also occurs because large landowners frequently have other, possibly more important, sources of income. They may be moneylenders, merchants, or have a business in town. Understandably, they are easily satisfied with low per hectare yields, especially when they look upon landownership as a status symbol. It is particularly these underutilized, large landholdings which are commonly referred to as *latifundia*.

Although extensive land use may make economic sense from the owner's point of view, it usually has a number of undesirable consequences when looked at from a societal perspective. It means, first of all, that the output of food is less than it could be, thus possibly contributing to malnutrition of the local population. It could even be a factor causing famine. For example, the recurring food shortages in Northeast Brazil are not caused solely by droughts. They are in no small measure directly associated with the *structural weaknesses* of the agricultural sector. In the semiarid interior, large expanses are used for extensive grazing, while in the more humid coastal zone, much land is used for the production of commercial crops, such as sugar, cocoa and tobacco. Production of staple food crops, therefore, is rather neglected. Barely adequate supplies of foodstuffs in periods of favorable weather conditions readily turn into severe shortages when adverse (dry) weather strikes.

There are also other factors which help explain the relative underutilization of large properties. The limited purchasing power of the majority of the people – both in rural and urban areas – does not particularly foster intensive cultivation. A substantial increase in output would immediately result in serious marketing problems simply because people cannot afford to buy more than what they need for their survival. In a sense, the large landowners, too, are the victims of a structurally unfavorable situation which they themselves have created by monopolizing a considerable portion of good arable farmland.

Low-intensity land use has an unfavorable effect on income levels and, thus, on savings. The resulting shortage of capital makes it difficult or impossible to make investments during periods of improved market conditions.

An entirely different combination of unfavorable social conditions is encountered when we study *labor relations* and *land tenure patterns* in areas with numerous large landholdings. In countries or regions where the majority of the people derive their livelihood from agriculture and where employment opportunities in agriculture expand more slowly than does population, large landowners obviously have a great deal of power. While the demand for land is great and growing, the supply of human resources exceeds the demand. This means that labor relations as well as tenure conditions are unfavorable for those who do not have any or enough land. By the same token, they are favorable for the few who have more land than they need or can cultivate by themselves.

In view of the above, it is not surprising that rural wages are abysmally low, working days long and social security provisions (e.g., unemployment payments) often non-existent. Most laborers can only find temporary (seasonal) work, rather than permanent employment, and being totally dependent on their employers, they can be laid off any moment and for just about any reason. Being at the landowner's mercy, the laborers' daily existence is plagued by constant insecurity. Seasonal unemployment is particularly widespread in areas where plantations are the chief providers of employment. Characterized by specialized production (monoculture), plantations have widely fluctuating demands for labor power. As a consequence, the human resources also tend to be underutilized. The term 'sub-proletariat' is sometimes used in this context. It refers to those members of society who are worse-off than the ones who can sell their labor power all year round for more or less reasonable wages: the proletarians.

In large parts of Latin America, *hacienda* laborers used to receive no wages. Instead, they were allowed the use of a small piece of the landlord's land for growing crops for home use. As this *peonage* system tied the workers to the *hacienda,* the owner was guaranteed an adequate supply of labor whenever needed. This arrangement was not entirely disadvantageous to the workers. At least they had some land which they could cultivate when there was little or no work to be done on the *hacienda.* Nevertheless, peonage meant that their position was a very weak and dependent one. Not only was 'their' piece of land limited in size and/or quality, but at certain times of the year they were obliged to work for the landlord, often ten to twelve hours a day and four or five days a week. These peak periods usually coincided precisely with the times that much work had to be done on their own plots. The obvious consequence was that the *peons* were unable to take proper care of their subsistence crops. It would seem, then, that this system of *servitude labor* offered far greater advantages to the *hacienda* owners than to the landless laboring class.

In recent decades, the peonage system has lost in importance largely as a result of the increased supply of human labor. The *hacienda* owner nowadays can easily obtain seasonal workers when he needs them. Wages being low, many landlords now prefer employing temporary wage laborers. This does not mean, however, that the feudal peonage system has disappeared altogether.

A widespread form of land tenure in the Third World is that of *sharecropping.* The tenant farmer or sharecropper does not pay the landlord a set amount of rent – either in the form of money or produce – but a certain percentage of the total yield. Thus, the more the sharecropper produces, the more he/she must surrender. In addition to providing the land, the landlord often also provides other means of production, such as fertilizer, seed, insecticides, implements, tools as well as living quarters, storage facilities and possibly credit and food. This form of tenure means that the tenant can operate an entire farm without having to invest much money in inputs. Sometimes, the sharecropper only contributes labor. In a sense, sharecropping can be seen as a joint venture with shared risks. If yields are low, both parties suffer a loss, and when crop failure strikes, the landlord loses part of his investment.

The manner in which the produced crop is divided between tenant and landlord is determined by a variety of factors. Very important, of course, is whether the landlord provides all, many or only a few production means. Also important is how high human labor is valued, which depends both on the culture and the supply-demand situation on the labor market. Unfortunately for Third World tenants, after several decades of rapid population growth, there often is an abundance or even an overabundance of available labor.

Sharecropping agreements in the Third World differ from those in more developed countries. Whereas a landlord in southern Europe receives at most half the crop, his counterpart in the Middle East tends to receive a considerably larger share. After centuries of unfavorable tenure conditions, climatic vagaries and ruthless exploitation by tax collectors and moneylenders, most Mid-Eastern farmers are so impoverished and deprived that they have nothing but their lowly valued labor power to offer. Under such circumstances, landowners will allow the sharecropper and his family no more than they need to avoid starvation – or, in Marxist parlance, just enough to guarantee the reproduction of the tenant's labor power. If natural conditions are not too unfavorable and yields reasonable, the *khammes* may receive $\frac{1}{5}$ of the crop in exchange for his labor. The landlord, who provides the other four means of production – land, irrigation water, manure and draft animals – gets the remaining $\frac{4}{5}$. This distribution is common in areas where land reforms have not been carried out.

It is obvious that the sharecropper's position is a precarious and extremely vulnerable one. Even the smallest stroke of bad luck may necessitate him to call on a moneylender for a loan. Because of a lack of creditworthiness – he possesses no collateral – the sharecropper must pay an exorbitantly high interest rate. As a result, he is likely to remain in debt for the rest of his life.

In those parts of Brazil where land has yet to be cleared, tenants are allowed to keep the entire crop, at least for a few years. The owner only furnishes the land; all other means of production must be provided by the tenants. The latter can use the land without surrendering part of the crop or paying rent, but in order to be able to grow crops they must make it fit for cultivation. After several years, the landlord terminates the contract and the tenants move to another piece of uncleared land. In this way, the owner gets his land cleared for free, which he can then use himself for the production of crops or livestock.

No matter whether the amount of rent is determined in advance (land tenure in the narrow sense of the word) or whether landlord and tenant each receive a certain percentage of the crop (sharecropping), there are additional lease conditions that are none too favorable for the tenant. For example:

1) Tenure periods are almost always short, usually for only one year or one growing season. *Continuation rights,* which are common in developed countries, are often unheard of.
2) *Amelioration rights,* the privilege to be compensated for having made lasting improvements, also are unknown in most Third World countries.

3) In developed countries, the tenant is often entitled to get part of the rent refunded in the event of crop failure or some adversity beyond his/her control. This *remittance right* exists hardly anywhere in the Third World.
4) In the case of sharecropping, the landlord frequently determines which crops are to be grown. This arrangement may work to the tenant's disadvantage,
5) Seldom is there a written document in which the conditions of the tenure contract (lease) are laid down.

In many parts of the Third World, there exists no strictly businesslike relationship between sharecropper and landlord. Instead, the relation is more or less feudal in nature. By this we mean that the landlord plays an important role in the social life of the tenant and his family. In Latin America, he often is the godfather of the tenant's children and may serve as patron and advisor (counselor) for his tenants. The tenant occupies a subservient position and is required to provide all kinds of services (menial tasks) for the landlord. This relationship – known as *patronage* – clearly resembles the serf-lord relationship that existed in medieval Europe. In recent years, however, the patronage system has lost some of its importance.

Land tenure systems such as described above are not only disadvantageous for individual tenants, but also have disastrous effects of the national economy as a whole. Most tenants are not motivated to take adequate care of the land; they farm with a minimum of effort and cost. The high rent or crop share, the short tenure period, and the absence of the rights of amelioration, continuation and remittance discourage them from fertilizing sufficiently or from improving or even maintaining the quality of the soil in some other way, e.g., through careful crop rotation or contour plowing. Since the land does not belong to them, they are unlikely to be concerned about soil erosion. Although climate, slope and soil conditions may favor tree crops and other perennials, the tenants generally prefer to grow annual crops for they cannot take the risk of planting an orchard for the next tenant.

Sharecroppers are not particularly interested in doing their utmost to maximize output. With half or more of the crop going to the landowner, it is easy to understand that the poor sharecropper is unwilling to make investments or to 'break his back.' Because landlords are afraid that tenants will not produce up to capacity, they are often reluctant to provide them with expensive, modern means of production or take proper care of maintenance. The result becomes a vicious circle which seriously interferes with efficiency, thus keeping productivity at levels that are often abysmally low. Many people are undernourished and occasionally famine strikes. Meanwhile, the tenants are unable to save, making it virtually impossible for them to raise their standard of living or become independent farmers who own their own land.

The above-described situation is not necessarily static. In recent decades there have been numerous changes – often associated with the so-called *Green Revolution*. But these changes, unfortunately, do not always constitute an improvement in the living conditions of the majority of the rural population. As a consequence of the population explosion (due to a combination of high birth rates and low or declining death rates), both the demand for land and the supply of laborers expand continuously. This situation strengthens the already powerful position of landowners. At the same time, the problems of tenants and landless laborers are exacerbated by technological developments. With the diffusion of modern innovations, such as electric water pumps, pickup trucks and agricultural machines, large landowners increasingly realize that it may well be more profitable to do the farming themselves than to rent their land to tenants. Clearly, the possibilities to rent land have declined in many areas. Increased mechanization, of course, also means a reduction in the demand for labor. Indications are that this mechanization trend will continue, thereby causing even greater social inequality (or *polarization*) and higher levels of rural unemployment. Such changes are likely to foster unrest and political instability, e.g., growing demands for radical change and for greater social justice. As we know, there already is a great deal of dissatisfaction in many Third World countries, witness Central America where pauperization and marginalization of the masses go hand in hand with growing disparities between haves and have-nots.

Problems in areas with excessive fragmentation of landownership

Large landholdings are not dominant everywhere in the Third World. In many areas they are totally absent, particularly there where the shortage of farmland has reached alarming proportions. Here we find the opposite of large holdings: excessive *fragmentation*. Not only are the fields (plots) tiny, but the farms are minuscule.

Extremely small farms have come about in a number of ways. The most common causes are high population density and a long history of splitting up farms among heirs. The clearest examples of inordinate *land hunger* and excessive fragmentation are found in South Asia, especially in the relatively flat and low-lying plains and delta areas which for many centuries have been used for intensive crop production. Most farmers have no more than one hectare, sometimes less. A five-hectare (12-acre) farm may be considered large. In spite of irrigation, tremendous labor inputs, relatively high per hectare yields and the possibility of raising at least two crops a year, outputs are barely or not quite sufficient to feed the farmer and his/her family.

Agriculture in much of Monsoon Asia is very labor intensive, partly because the farmers cannot afford to buy mechanized implements. Another reason is that the plots are too small for the use of machines; often they are even too small to allow the use of draft animals. If all plots belonging to one farmer were located next to another and were not separated by little dikes, labor-saving machines could be used, but this is rarely the case. Besides, the fields can usually only be reached on foot over narrow footpaths.

Rapid population growth further aggravates the unfavorable *man-land ratio*. Already half a century ago there was no unused cultivable land left on the island of Java (Indonesia), and since that time the rural population has more than doubled. The result has been a sharp decline in average farm size and an uninterrupted increase in the input of labor per hectare. As there are limits to further intensification, standards of living have been adversely affected. More and more people are poorly fed or go hungry much of the time. It is almost certain that the situation will become more hopeless as the years go by. In his classic study of Indonesia, *Agricultural Involution,* Geertz uses the term 'treading water' to describe the desperate situation facing the Javanese farmers. That is precisely what they are doing: laboring hard to keep their heads above water, without getting ahead. Being a strenuous activity, treading water cannot be kept up for long.

Part of the predicament is that most farmers on Java do not own their land and are unable to save any income earned. Capital-requiring improvements, therefore, cannot be made. Because the farmers have no savings or anything else to fall back on, even one poor crop can be disastrous and have lasting effects, especially when the farmer is forced to borrow money. Furthermore, periods of severe undernourishment can be detrimental to the physical and mental well-being of the farmers and their families. Since most people have no medical insurance, they are not likely to consult a physician until it is too late. Even a short stay in a hospital can mean permanent indebtedness.

In parts of Monsoon Asia, a considerable proportion of all farmland belongs to others than those who do the farming – sometimes to affluent urbanites who obtained the land as moneylenders. Because of rising land values, they increasingly look upon land as an attractive commodity for investment purposes. Land speculation has assumed enormous proportions especially in the vicinity of larger cities. Many farmers who used to own their land are now sharecroppers or have become managers for urban owners of farmland.

Not only in Java but also in other parts of Asia there are millions of rural families that depend entirely on wage labor. As the demand for land continues to grow, tenure contracts and wage labor conditions become ever more unfavorable for the landless ruralites. In fact, the wages of the rural *sub-proletariat* are often so low that it is more appropriate to talk of *wage slavery* than of wage labor.

Other aspects of the legal framework

In a number of Third World countries, part of the land is collectively owned, that is, it belongs to the entire local community. Sometimes, individual members can use part of the land for raising crops. Every now and then, all the land is redistributed with every farmer receiving a different piece than he or she had before.

67

Although this system has a number of advantages, it also has some serious drawbacks. The periodic redistributions inhibit farmers from taking proper care of the land or making lasting improvements. Back-breaking activities, such as the removal of heavy boulders or the construction of drainage channels, fences and terraces, are often left undone. Understandably, few farmers are willing to make these improvements unless they are assured that they can farm their parcel of the collectively owned land permanently.

Collective landownership occurs in a number of African countries. In the past, much of tropical Africa was characterized by a rather favorable relation between population and available land. Low population densities made shifting cultivation with its long fallow periods possible. Improvements were not needed and therefore did not take place. During the past half century or so, however, conditions have drastically changed. Population growth and expansion of commercial crop production have led to the permanent occupation of the better soils in most areas, so that farmland is becoming an increasingly scarce commodity. At the same time, there has been a substantial expansion of privately owned land and a concomitant reduction of communal landownership – a development which has been encouraged by the former colonial powers. Manshard (1970) has argued in favor of individualization of landownership in areas where communal ownership rights still prevail. In his opinion, collective ownership has decidedly negative effects both on present and future agricultural productivity. Besides, he believes that farmers should have greater security.

One major disadvantage of communal ownership is that it makes it difficult or impossible for a farmer to obtain credit because he or she possesses no collateral. And without a loan, productivity can often not be raised. Private ownership, on the other hand, means that farmers have collateral. Moreover, collective ownership discourages intensive cultivation or promotes the persistence of *ladang* agriculture. Now that population densities have increased and will continue to do so in coming years, Manshard believes that it is of the utmost importance that systems of landownership and land use be adapted to the new circumstances.

We should not conclude from the preceding that collective ownership always interferes with agricultural development. The system also has its advantages. It can stimulate collective cultivation, thereby avoiding the drawbacks of inefficient production on tiny, scattered plots. Collectivization allows for division of labor (specialization) and makes possible the purchase of expensive, modern equipment, such as tractors. It also enables farmers to take on large projects that enhance productivity, e.g., irrigation schemes or the construction of terraces. Collectively they are better able to obtain the credit needed to pay for expensive irrigation equipment, such as water mains and electric or motorized water pumps. Whether or not such improvements take place depends in no small measure on the degree to which the group is convinced that together they can accomplish more than they would if they did the farming on a purely individual basis. This conviction will stimulate motivation and enhance group solidarity, factors which are important to foster the mutual trust without which cooperation is likely to founder.

Land reforms: accomplished results – possible alternatives

In the preceding sections we have focused attention on the occurrence of a very uneven distribution of landownership in much of the Third World. Many observers believe this inequity to be a major cause of the social and economic underdevelopment of the rural areas in the Third World and that it contributes significantly to agricultural stagnation. It is hardly surprising, therefore, that *land reform* is often suggested as a necessary measure for alleviating the many serious problems which afflict the rural areas. By land reform we mean above all the redistribution of agricultural land so as to arrive at a more equitable distribution among the entire farm population. This can be accomplished by splitting up the large landholdings into smaller units to be handed over to landless laborers, tenants and small farmers.

It may seem paradoxical, but the fact is that land reforms have not yet been started in all Third World countries with a highly uneven land distribution. Where they have been instituted, results generally have been disappointing. In only a few countries have land reforms been radical.

The moderate character of many land reform programs becomes clear in a number of ways. To begin with, usually only a small proportion of the land belonging to large holdings is expropriated. Exempted from expropriation are often all fields which are well cultivated as well as all estates for which the owners have, or say they have, short-term plans to make considerable investments for the purpose of raising productivity. It is not always clear, however, what is meant by 'well cultivated' or by 'considerable investments.'

Land reforms are also moderate in the sense that they tend to be limited to those parts of the country where they can be carried out most easily. Elsewhere, the large landholdings are left more or less intact. Moderate land reforms are further characterized by the fact that landlords receive a liberal compensation for the loss of land; where land reforms are more radical, little or no compensation is given.

Expropriation regulations often are not only mild, they also tend to be put into effect at a dilatory pace. To begin with, reform proposals usually take very long to pass through various administrative bodies before they become enacted. When they finally have been codified, a multitude of exemptive clauses may make the reforms so complicated that it is difficult to carry them out without considerable delays. Enforcement is further complicated by all kinds of loopholes.

Another problem which causes delays is the absence of a cadastral registration system. This means that first an inventory must be made of all real estate properties. Once this is done, it may turn out that the amount of money available for compensations is so small that only a limited number of large holdings can be expropriated. Landowners who are faced with the loss of land often decide to go to court to appeal the expropriation decision, leaving no stone unturned to obstruct or slow down the expropriation procedures. When all legal ways to prevent the loss of land have been tried, landowners can resort to other methods, including subdividing their land and having it registered in the names of relatives or even servants. This explains that in the process of land redistribution, officials sometimes 'discover' that the landownership structure happens to be less inequitable than had been assumed!

Because of the many complications, it is not uncommon that very little is accomplished 10 or 20 years after taking the first steps toward land reform. In the meantime, the number of landless families may have reached an all-time high, while the few fortunate farmers who did benefit from the reforms often were not the neediest but those who for some reason or other were relatively influential. Moreover, where former landowners have received handsome compensations, the *power structure* is unlikely to have undergone fundamental change. With the money they have received they are often able to maintain – and perhaps even strengthen – their dominant position, for instance, by using it to make a killing in the urban real estate market, starting a profitable business, or by becoming successful rural land speculators. Real progress in the sense of creating a more equitable society by improving the living conditions and opportunities of the poor and dispossessed, has failed to come about. Apparently, development is as elusive as is happiness, especially when there are powerful forces, such as vested interests, greed and narrow-minded egotism (e.g., so-called 'lifeboat ethics'), which pull in the opposite direction.

Evidence of the limited effects of land reforms can be found in most Latin American countries. During the 1960s, detailed, comprehensive programs were worked out for many areas. These were largely the result of pressure by the U.S., which would not provide foreign (economic) aid unless land reforms were carried out. Instead of being serious efforts to ease tensions and promote social justice, they were meant to satisfy Washington's demands. So, the land reforms that were enacted often were mere formalities – a façade. Some were extremely vague and put into effect very slowly. Just about everywhere the story is the same: influential landowners doing everything they can to postpone or frustrate radical efforts to change the rural power structure.

Effects have been equally limited in India and Pakistan. Already in the 1940s the elites of these (then colonial) states advocated land reform in the hope that they would get the support of the rural masses for their struggle for political independence. After independence was achieved in 1947, they formulated land reforms and began to implement them. The reforms were not particularly drastic and thus far they have done little to improve the quality of life among the millions of impoverished downtrodden villagers. It was not so much the very poorest who benefited from the land redistribution, but the rural middle class, that is, the larger tenants and farmers who already owned their land. According to Joshi, this group at first sided with the very poorest just so the first steps toward redistribution would be taken. As soon as this was accomplished, they used their political influence to prevent the reforms from benefiting the poorest. In the end, they were quite successful in making themselves the chief beneficiaries (Joshi 1970).

Even in Mexico, where over 2 million people have been at the receiving end of land reforms introduced after the 1910-1917 revolution, rural areas are still plagued with serious problems. In 1968, there were again 3.3 million landless laborers, accounting for 54 percent of the total agricultural labor force. By 1970, concealed unemployment in the *ejidos* (native village communities) was estimated at 58 percent of the working-age population. Here, again, land reforms were not very sweeping – even though they were usually described as 'radical' – and were not implemented rapidly enough.

Meanwhile, the rural population increased faster than did the number of job opportunities outside the agricultural sector of Mexico's relatively stagnant economy. To make matters worse, large agricultural enterprises have come into existence, especially in the northern part of the country. These modern *neolatifundios* account for about two-thirds of all irrigated land, possess nearly three-quarters of all agricultural machinery and receive approximately half the total credit that the government extends to the agricultural sector. Small *ejidatarios,* most of whom have not benefited from land reforms, receive a pitiful 4 percent of all government-provided agricultural credit.

Land reforms in Third World countries frequently fail to produce the desired results because the large landowners almost always are influential enough to be able to pull the administrative strings or exert pressure on the political leaders. Thanks to direct and indirect influence on high government officials – who may be relatives or friends – they sometimes succeed in preventing reform proposals from being signed into law. By contrast, the poor and often illiterate rural masses are usually not organized and have therefore little political clout.

If reforms cannot be stopped, politicians who represent the interests of the large landowners will see to it that all kinds of exemptive clauses are written into the laws or they make sure that formulations are worded in such a way that there are ample legal possibilities to avoid expropriation. The influence of large landowners is so great not only because some of them hold high offices in government, but also because they tend to have close relations with the political elite and with the officials who are in charge of land reforms. This collusion opens the door to favoritism (or nepotism) and a host of corruptive practices against which the poorly organized tenants and laborers, who can ill-afford to hire attorneys, are unable to defend themselves. Vulnerable and powerless as they are, the landless poor are at the mercy of precisely those whose interests are diametrically opposed to theirs.

Land reforms which are not primarily intended to redress disparities and to correct social injustice can hardly be expected to help bring about a more egalitarian society. The Iranian land reform program of the 1960s, for example, was deliberately designed to eliminate political rivals of the shah and concomitantly create a class of agricultural capitalists whom the administration could count on for support and allegiance. Although the shah hoped that the land reforms would stimulate economic growth and agricultural modernization, serving the interests of the poorest in society was certainly not the prime objective. There are other countries where land reforms have been resorted to as a means to strengthen the position of the entrenched oligarchy.

At one time it was believed that redistribution of land alone was sufficient to improve conditions in the agricultural sector. Past experiences, however, have clearly demonstrated that more is required to produce satisfactory and lasting results. To increase agricultural production and make it possible for new landowners to raise their living standard, a large variety of measures must be taken. Together these are commonly referred to as *agrarian reforms*.

Besides land, the new owners need other means of production. Someone who has been a landless wage laborer all his life, possesses no tools, no implements, no farm buildings and, above all, no capital. If he only receives land, he will have to borrow money to make the necessary purchases. But as we have seen already, indebtedness may eventually force him to sell his land, thereby nullifying the effects of the land reform. It is imperative, then, that the government permit farmers to obtain cheap loans. Low-interest or interest-free credit must be available not only during the initial stages but also in subsequent years in order to enable farmers to develop their farms into efficient, profitable, viable production units. Without profits, farmers will not be able to save money, pay back the loans and become truly independent, self-reliant operators. Savings are also essential for making the investments needed to maintain, or further increase, productivity. Finally, savings are important for raising rural standards of living and levels of spending which will have a stimulating effect on the non-agricultural sectors of the economy.

Agricultural extension services also must be provided, and if illiteracy is widespread, educational facilities will need to be established. No less important is the fostering of businesslike attitudes, so that farmers can make the right financial and commercial decisions. They should also be taught the basic elements of bookkeeping. If it is considered desirable to have the farmers produce more for the market, that is, practice cash cropping, a host of other measures may have to be taken, including the building of roads and storage facilities and providing reasonably cheap transportation. It may be necessary to break the monopolistic power of the many intermediary traders who buy up crops for extremely low prices and sell them for huge profits in urban markets or to export companies. Since the middlemen often are the only persons with transportation means, they command a strong bargaining position *vis-à-vis* the farmers, who may be

10. Girls in Benin, Africa, are taught how to clear the land and raise crops. (J. van den Berg)

poorly informed and poorly organized. Finally, medical facilities need to be furnished and housing conditions improved. All the above and more are required if *agrarian reforms* are to make a lasting contribution to real rural development.

Too many attempts at reform have not gone beyond the land redistribution stage. Even when intentions were good, not much was accomplished due to lack of money, knowledge and experience. Results are often disappointing because of the immense complexity of agrarian reforms; too many different and difficult measures must be taken at the same time. If only one or two aspects are neglected, results may fall far short of the envisaged goals. Failure is not only caused by unwillingness or active opposition on the part of certain interest groups, but also by a country's inability to improve the entire 'production climate.' Mexico's experience shows that even if reforms are reasonably successful, the favorable effects may be wiped out in a relatively short period of time by rapid population growth.

Despite the fact that land reforms can relieve social problems and raise agricultural productivity in areas dominated by large landholdings, they can also have serious drawbacks. If large estates are subdivided into small production units, a new landownership structure will emerge which may not be conducive to modernizing and rationalizing agriculture. In Western Europe and North America, average farm size has increased significantly in recent decades because many farms were too small for mechanization and efficient use of labor; they could not compete effectively and incomes were

73

low. Similar problems exist in a number of Third World countries, and they may well become more urgent and widespread if drastic land redistribution measures are pushed through.

In addition to long-term disadvantages, land reforms can lead to short-term problems. If all large agricultural enterprises are subdivided, there is a danger that all well-run, efficient farms are eliminated. This explains why well-managed, modern production units often are exempted from redistribution. However, leaving them intact means that so-called 'radical' land reforms are in effect much less radical than their proponents would have us believe. In Cuba, many plantations have not been subdivided – this despite the Revolution. First they were made into cooperative enterprises and later into state-owned farms. In Indonesia, somewhat similar developments have taken place. The chief reason is that the authorities do not want to sacrifice the advantages of *scale economies* that come with large-scale production. Governments may be particularly reluctant to break up large, efficient units that are important producers of food for the domestic market (e.g., cattle ranches) or export crops (e.g., sugar plantations). Since sugar is Cuba's leading export and foremost earner of foreign exchange, the Castro regime has made sure that the sugar estates were not subdivided into small farms, but were maintained as large state enterprises. For the same reason, many former colonial plantations in other Third World countries have been left intact.

Another problem is that land reforms tend to be extremely costly, especially when landowners are eligible for compensation. Just drawing up the plans and putting them into effect requires a large number of salaried officials. Besides, there may be drawn-out law suits which greatly add to the paper work and thus to overall expenses.

Considering all these problems, it is easy to understand that land reforms are not advocated by everyone. Many experts believe that rural living conditions and agricultural productivity can be improved without land redistribution. They favor drastic changes in tenure conditions and labor conditions. These changes include establishing minimum wages, allowing tenants a larger share of the crop, and setting maximum rent price limits. At the same time, continuation rights and amelioration rights could be introduced, and short-term lease contracts outlawed. A strongly progressive tax structure could be very helpful not only in reducing social inequality but also in creating funds with which the development process can be financed or speeded up. In order to stimulate greater productivity, the government could impose a special tax on unused or underutilized land. In other words, much could be accomplished if the government were to increase its influence on, and control of, the use of land, labor and capital.

The above reforms are easier said than done. Large landowners usually do everything they can to dodge or thwart government policies which go against their vested interests. The government also may lack the political power or will to enact the required laws and/or to prosecute offenders. A

11. Newly built settler's home in the Amazon Basin, Ecuador. Although the dwelling is not yet finished, it is already inhabited. (M. de Vreede)

further complication may be that land reforms are widely believed to be the best strategy for alleviating the rural-agricultural problems and have become a hot political issue – an ideal – which must be realized at all cost. Because proponents of land reforms frequently consider all other approaches ineffective or insufficiently radical, they are not likely to be satisfied until every large landholding is eliminated. To them, land reform is the panacea – the only remedy for all rural ills – and they may fight for it until the bitter end.

Colonization as an alternate approach

In some Third World countries, the conclusion has been reached that fundamental changes in the socioeconomic structure need not necessarily be realized through land reforms. Instead, colonization of sparsely populated areas is seen as the solution. This line of thinking is particularly evident in Brazil and the Andean countries where we find densely peopled regions with *minifundism* and a sizeable landless proletariat as well as extensive 'empty' areas in the humid tropical Amazon lowlands. Colonization of the latter regions could relieve the population pressure, absorb much of the (future) population increase, create employment opportunities, reduce food imports and raise exports.

When the Spanish conquered the Andean region, most of the native people lived in the coastal areas and in the highlands; very few inhabited the lowlands east of the Andes. During the colonial period, attention remained focused on the first two regions because precious metals were available there and also because they were the only areas where the Spanish could exploit the indigenous population as providers of cheap, subservient labor power. As a consequence, the economic and demographic focal points remained centered in the coastal areas and on the *altiplano* (high plains), while the eastern lowlands remained isolated and practically uninhabited. This same situation still exists today.

The Brazilian portion of the Amazon Basin is far more extensive than those of Peru, Ecuador, Colombia and Bolivia. For centuries, Brazil has had a very sparse population. Portugal was too small to provide many immigrants, non-Portuguese citizens were generally not allowed, or did not want, to settle in the colony, and the native population grew very slowly. This emptiness made it possible for the settlers to select the best locations. While the eastern seaboard became relatively densely populated, the interior remained virgin territory. For example, the vast North, which accounts for 42 percent of Brazil's total area, had only 3.6 million inhabitants in 1970 – about 4 percent of the country's total population. Today, the North still has a population density of no more than one person per square kilometer. Opinions about the 'carrying capacity' (in terms of numbers of inhabitants) vary greatly. It has been estimated that the Amazon Basin could support an agricultural population of some 50 million. Although some observers believe this to be an overly optimistic estimate, we can safely say that the Amazon Basin remains underpopulated and underutilized.

In order to promote the colonization of the Amazon region, the five countries have launched various settlement plans. Most of these initiatives do not predate the early 1960s. The best known is undoubtedly Brazil's plan – announced in 1970 – to open up its portion of the Amazon Basin. The plan called for the construction of a number of highways and for the settling of at least 100,000 families within a 5-year period. Large homesteads of 100 ha or more would be made available.

So far, only a fraction of Brazil's ambtious plan has been realized, and the accomplishments of the Andean states are equally disappointing. In Peru and Bolivia, colonization of the eastern lowlands has absorbed no more than about 10 and 20 percent of the population increase in their respective *altiplano* regions. Most families are not interested in moving to the Amazon lowlands but prefer continuing their miserable existence in the highlands or migrate to the more developed coastal zone or to the cities where employment opportunities are believed to be better.

A reason why few opt for the Amazon region is its humid tropical climate, which differs markedly from that of the cool highlands as well as from the semiaridity in Northeast Brazil and the subtropical conditions in southern Brazil. Probably more important is that the governments initiating colonization projects have not promoted them with much vigor. Investments tend to be insufficient and enthusiasm is rather low-key. Colonists are therefore confronted with all kinds of problems – apart from being faced with tropical diseases and mostly infertile soils. Such problems include: inadequate agricultural extension services, poor educational and medical facilities, delays in the provision of consumer goods and production means, insufficient credit facilities, poor accessibility, and the often high cost of living. Not infrequently, colonization schemes are poorly organized, resulting in all kinds of land conflicts, including several settlers claiming the same piece of land. Another serious problem is the remoteness from urban markets, making commercial crop production virtually impossible. Under such conditions, the life of the settlers is anything but easy, and in many instances they can practice only a rather primitive form of subsistence agriculture.

Colonization has often meant that rural problems and poverty became more widespread – the exact opposite of what was anticipated. Indeed, few projects are truly successful in the sense that both the rural standard of living and the level of agricultural productivity can be called satisfactory (Kleinpenning 1973, 1975; Schuurman 1980). Meanwhile, no significant change has occurred in the familiar demographic pattern. The interior lowlands remain very sparsely and irregularly populated, while other rural areas become more overpopulated. And sadly, the uneven distribution of landownership has not changed much either.

Chapter 5   Technical aspects of agricultural production

In the preceding chapters we focused attention on landownership structures and discussed the negative effects of the uneven distribution and excessive fragmentation of agricultural land. We looked at land reform and colonization as means to bring about a more equitable distribution of land, raise agricultural productivity, and improve living standards of the rural poor. The emphasis was on the legal framework within which agricultural production takes place, but little has been said thus far about actual production techniques.

In this chapter we well examine how and to what degree nature, labor and capital are utilized for the realization of agricultural production. If we compare agriculture in Third World countries with that in developed countries, we soon discover that the former displays a number of technical weaknesses and that agricultural extension, which could change this, still is in its infancy. What these weaknesses are will become apparent when we examine the production process more closely.

Crop rotation, fallow and fertilization

Generally speaking, *crop rotation* is practiced less in poor than in rich countries. The soil fertility is therefore less well maintained, resulting in lower yields. In addition, insufficient crop rotation means that plant diseases are more likely to develop and spread. The use of manure or artificial fertilizer also leaves much to be desired, both in terms of quantity and quality. Farmers who do make efforts to improve the soil fertility, usually do not do so frequently enough because they are unable to purchase sufficient fertilizer. In many areas, little or no manure is available due to the lack of livestock. Even in countries where farm animals are abundant, often not much manure is applied to the land. In India, most cow dung is used as fuel – mainly for cooking purposes – and every year some 400 million tons (wet weight) go up in flames and smoke. In much of Latin America and Africa, virtually no crop farming is practiced in areas where animal husbandry is important. And in areas where manure *is* available (because the farm animals are kept inside or spend the nights in a kraal), manuring is often limited to only a few fields, usually those located closest to the settlements.

Insufficient manuring may mean that farmers must leave their fields in *fallow* for shorter or longer periods, thereby limiting the total acreage under cultivation. Besides, without applying manure or fertilizer, it is no use trying to cultivate infertile soils. Altogether, then, much land is not being used for food production. This fact, when combined with the low yields, can easily lead to food shortages, especially in periods of sustained population growth.

In large parts of the Third World, farmers do not manure at all, but simply exploit the natural soil resources. Without replenishing the fertility, the soil gradually degenerates and may eventually turn into useless wasteland. Robbing the soil of its nutrients is known as *soil mining* or *predatory cultivation* – the opposite of soil conservation. This practice is particularly common in the humid tropics, where many agriculturists simply burn down a piece of forest to create a clearing. After only a few years of cropping, the soil becomes exhausted and yields approach the danger point. The clearing is then abandoned and a fresh piece of forest is set on fire. After a rest period of perhaps 25 years, during which the soil is given a chance to recuperate, the old 'fields' may be cleared and cultivated again. This so-called *shifting cultivation* is most widespread in tropical Africa, but is also practiced in sparsely populated areas of tropical Asia and Latin America.

Since shifting cultivation requires a great deal of land, it is only practicable in areas with a very low population density. Gourou has calculated that if a particular clearing is cultivated for only one year and then left idle for the next 24 years, one square kilometer (250 acres) can support no more than 12 people (Gourou 1966, pp. 45-6). With an increase in population density, the fallow period must be shortened. If this means that the soil can no longer recuperate, its nutrient content will be reduced and yields will decline. Soil depletion, together with growing population pressure, may ultimately result in permanent damage to the soil structure, so that water can no longer be absorbed and retained. Cultivation is not possible anymore and the original wild vegetation cannot return either. Unprotected by vegetative cover, the soil is exposed to sunshine and rainfall and starts to erode. As a consequence, less land is left for more people; a situation which spells famine and tragedy.

Another disadvantage of shifting cultivation (or *ladang agriculture*) is that it offers limited possibilities for the production of tree crops. Years ago, shifting cultivators in Malaya and on the Indonesian islands of Sumatra and Borneo (Kalimantan) decided to plant rubber trees, enabling them to partly abandon their traditional ladang agriculture. Such an adaptation is the exception rather than the rule. However, since ladang farmers generally fail to replace old trees, they may eventually be worse off than before. While the trees produce, they become used to, and dependent on, cash income. When the rubber trees stop producing – after about forty years – the farmers find themselves without this income.

Although ladang agriculture does not require all that much labor, there are several peak periods. The busiest period comes towards the end of the dry season when a piece of forest is cleared and the crops are planted. After planting, not much work needs to be done until harvest time. This means that for several months a considerable amount of available labor is idle, all the more because in areas where shifting cultivation predominates, few alternative employment opportunities exist. The result is that the level of material well-being tends to be low. In areas where the man-land ratio becomes less favorable, it generally declines even further.

The use of seed, seedlings and breeding stock

The quality of seed, seedlings and breeding animals is often low in the Third World. Careful selection hardly ever occurs. Normally, seeds and seedlings are taken from the previous crop, so that existing diseases and deficiencies are rarely eliminated. The absence of good storage facilities adversely affects the quality of the seed – occasionally the seed even becomes totally useless. Selective livestock breeding, too, is not commonly practiced in Third World countries.

In the developed countries, years of research have resulted in high-yielding, well-adapted and highly resistant plant varieties and animal breeds. Nearly all these efforts were aimed at improving typically mid-latitude crops and livestock. Thus far, relatively little research has been done to help farmers in tropical regions increase their production, and agricultural science is still in its infancy in most of the Third World.

Efforts to improve tropical crops have been limited by and large to commercial crops grown for export, such as sugar, coffee, tea, rubber and sisal, mostly produced on modern foreign-owned plantations. Much of the research on these crops was done by former colonial powers whose economies sometimes depended in no small measure on the extremely lucrative trade in 'colonial wares.' In the Netherlands, for example, special schools of tropical agriculture were established, and for many years the study of tropical agriculture was no less important than the study of temperate agriculture. But while the production of tropical export crops attained a high level of sophistication, production of tropical food crops did not benefit from scientific breakthroughs. It was continued in the same old traditional ways and with antiquated methods.

Only recently has more attention been given to the Third World's agricultural problems and have efforts been made to rectify the past 'colonial neglect.' Increasingly, attempts are being made by scientists in the developed countries to develop high-yielding, hybrid food crops that are well adapted to tropical conditions, e.g., rice, corn, millet and wheat. Nevertheless, much work still needs to be done in coming years in order to make the countries of the Third World self-sufficient in food production. Extension services need to be upgraded and expanded so as to enable Third World farmers to learn about, and correctly apply, the latest innovations in the realm of crop and livestock production.

In the past, a variety of efficient farming methods, hybrid plant varieties and high-quality animal breeds – developed in the temperate zones – could have been adopted by Third World cultivators, especially those living in non-tropical areas. Usually, however, they (or their countries) lacked the financial means to do so. Even if there had been sufficient funds, few farmers would have known about these possibilities or would have been able to take advantage of the innovations due to lack of organization and inadequate infrastructural facilities. The situation has somewhat improved in the sense that today there are foreign aid programs through which high-

12. Dr. Norman E. Borlaug. Production of high-yielding wheat varieties in Mexico, 1951. (VDO)

quality methods of production are made available. On the other hand, a few technical improvements cannot by themselves raise agricultural productivity significantly. In addition to 'miracle' seeds and modern machines, farmers also need to have access to a more or less continuous flow of information and advice. Because of these limiting factors, the Green Revolution – which in the 1960s was widely praised as the solution to the Third World's food problem – has accomplished less than what had been anticipated.

By *Green Revolution* we mean above all the use of new, genetically improved varieties of food crops which are capable of producing much greater yields than the traditional varieties that are still being grown by the majority of Third World farmers. In order to obtain these higher yields, ample use must be made of other modern inputs, including artificial fertilizer, pesticides and insecticides. Another prerequisite is the availability of adequate amounts of irrigation water and, thus, of a well-organized and properly functioning irrigation system.

The first experiments to develop high-yielding varieties (HYVs) were started in the 1940s. Besides their high yields, these new varieties have other advantages; they mature earlier and suffer less from high winds or heavy downpours because of their shorter, stronger stems. New wheat varieties were first developed in Mexico – by the American agronomist Norman E. Borlaug – and have made it possible to increase per hectare yields from 0.9 tons around 1950 to 2.6 tons in 1964. From an importer of wheat, Mexico during the 1960s developed into an exporter.

New rice varieties were developed in Asia, especially in the Philippines. Yields have nearly doubled, partly as a result of the fact that the new HYVs mature sooner than the old varieties. In tropical areas with favorable irrigation conditions, the early maturing hybrids make it possible to grow two to three crops a year! Research is continuing and new varieties of grain crops – sometimes adapted to local soil and climate conditions – are being developed. Major efforts have been launched to promote the use of HYVs in many food-deficient countries, and today they are grown by millions of Third World farmers.

The much-heralded Green Revolution received a tremendous boost in 1968 because of abundant harvests in several Asian countries. These successes caused many agricultural experts to become convinced that the world's food problem could be solved. Soon thereafter, the Food and Agricultural Organization (FAO) of the UN announced that it would try to expand the area planted in HYVs sevenfold between 1970 and 1985. Mainly through this expansion, the FAO hoped to raise the output of food by about 4 percent each year. Confidence and optimism reigned, and India's Prime Minister Indira Gandhi predicted that India would soon become an exporter of grains.

Since 1968, the optimistic expectations concerning the Green Revolution have been tempered by the realization that the introduction of HYVs is not so simple. To begin with, the new seed is more expensive than the old seed – a problem particularly for the poorest farmers. A greater obstacle is that the HYVs are very demanding. They require large quantities of chemical fertilizer, well-controlled supplies of irrigation water, rather intensive cultivation and proper protection against weeds and pests. If one of these conditions is not met, yields may well be lower than if 'regular' seed had been used. In fact, some HYVs are so vulnerable that the threat of total crop failure hovers, so to speak, constantly over the fields and, of course, over the heads of the farmers.

Many small farmers lack the money to purchase the necessary inputs and when credit is made available, they often fail to make use of it, afraid as they are to take risks. Bad experiences with high interest rates, unscrupulous moneylenders and years of indebtedness have made them suspicious. Not infrequently, they see the new agricultural methods as something that will benefit the moneylenders more than themselves. Sharecroppers realize that most of the increase in output will not be for them but for the landlords, and they cannot be blamed for being afraid that the higher yields will motivate the landlords to make the tenure conditions even more unfavorable than they now are. In fact, this is precisely what has happened in many places.

The poor farmers also tend to distrust the government officials who supply them the new seed, fertilizer and pesticides and who provide them the necessary information. Again, they may be quite justified for being skeptical and overly cautious. As Utrecht (1971) has pointed out, an important reason for the disappointing results of the Green Revolution in Indonesia during the 1960s was the corruption and tactless behavior of many officials. Moreover, the farmers were often treated as objects and had no say in the local planning of agricultural programs (Pearse 1980).

A common problem is that landowners decide to rent out less land than previously. Instead, they prefer to do more of the farming themselves – with the help of machines – and reap all the benefits of increased productivity themselves. In the Punjab region of India, for example, large farms (40 ha and over) expanded by about 40 percent between 1956 and 1968. Agricultural commissioners were particularly interested in the larger farmers since they often were the only ones who were financially able to purchase the high-yielding seeds, fertilizers, insecticides, water pumps and gasoline for the pumps and machinery. Besides, large farmers could obtain credit more easily and often had land that was more fertile and/or better irrigated. They are more likely therefore to be successful than are the small farmers and tenants. And because large farmers are less of a risk, it is understandable that the government of a poor country is more inclined to invest its scarce financial resources in their farms – e.g., by offering them 'soft loans' – than in those of small farmers. At the same time, ambitious agricultural advisors realize that it is to their personal advantage if agricultural production in their area is increased dramatically in a short period of time, which explains why they may spend more time helping the large farmers than the small ones.

The result of the above preferences and priorities is that rich farmers tend to become richer and many poor farmers end up being worse-off than before. Increasing mechanization often causes more rural unemployment and lower agricultural wages, while tenure conditions become more unfavorable for the landless. Apart from the fact that it is technically very difficult to successfully effectuate the Green Revolution on tiny, fragmented farms, poor farmers usually cannot afford *all* necessary inputs, so that they may suffer partial crop failure. Crop failure, in turn, may be the cause of serious indebtedness and loss of land. Thus, the Green Revolution can be a boon for large farmers and landowners, but it frequently is a mixed blessing for small farmers and landless laborers. In many rural areas the Green Revolution has contributed to greater inequality. It is hardly surprising that most rich farmers and large landowners favor Green Revolution programs, if only because they tend to reduce the need for radical land reforms.

Various seemingly unimportant aspects have occasionally turned out to be formidable obstacles to the introduction of HYVs. For example, the larger size of the wheat or rice kernel has made it impossible to use the traditional grist mills, and sometimes the flour is poorly suited for baking bread. It is also possible that the people do not like the taste of the new grain or that the straw cannot be used as animal feed. Some HYVs have such short stems that they do not produce enough straw or that they are difficult to harvest by hand.

Mention must also be made of the fact that the Green Revolution can lead to greater *regional* disparities. Since poor countries are interested in using their scarce capital resources as effectively as possible, they are inclined to promote the production of HYVs in those parts of the country that offer the best possibilities for making the Green Revolution a success. They will select the regions with existing irrigation systems, fertile soils, fairly large farms, a reasonably good infrastructure and, preferably, with relatively prosperous and well-educated farmers. The areas selected obviously are the most developed, most productive and most affluent parts of the country, that is, those which suffer least from population pressure, unemployment and recurring food shortages. By funneling investments into these comparatively prosperous and well-endowed areas and thus raising productivity there, other parts of the country will fall further behind, at least in a relative sense. They may also suffer an absolute loss, for example, when increased output in the favored areas causes grain prices to decline and farmers elsewhere receive less for their crops. In other words, the Green Revolution can give the competitively strongest areas an extra boost to the detriment of the less-advantaged areas. And the widening disparities may well become a source of widespread discontent and political unrest (Frankel 1972).

The Green Revolution is a product of modern agricultural science. It has been a great success in the sense that the world production of food has experienced a dramatic expansion since the early 1960s. Several Third World countries which used to be victims of regular food shortages, now are self-sufficient or produce surpluses. This represents a tremendous accomplishment considering that today many more mouths must be fed than 20-25 years ago. In 1981, Bangladesh – the international 'basket case' with nearly 100 million people in an area no bigger than Florida – produced so much food that it ran out of storage space. As a result, large quantities of grain spoiled or were consumed by an exploding rodent population. Meantime, the price of rice took a nose dive, thereby threatening rural incomes. To protect the small farmers, the government decided to support the price at an artificially high level. Not only did this measure contribute significantly to Bangladesh's indebtedness, but shipments of free food were halted by rich countries.

We may conclude that the Green Revolution can be called successful when looked at from a purely technical point of view. It has helped to alleviate hunger in many Third World countries and hopefully will continue to do so in coming decades. At the same time, it tends to have some undesirable social and political side-effects – including growing disparities between small and large farmers as well as between richly and poorly endowed areas, causing tension and dissatisfaction – which cast a dark shadow over the Green Revolution. Another problematic aspect of the Green Revolution is that it makes Third World countries *dependent* on the developed countries (or their multinational corporations) with regard to the various required modern inputs, such as the high-yielding seeds, pesticides, chemical fertilizers, irrigation equipment, agricultural machinery and know-how. Many Third World farmers who used to practice self-sufficient agriculture in 'splendid isolation,' now are *dependent* on world market prices of oil products, including fertilizers. In view of the steep rise in oil prices – from about $3 a barrel in 1973 to $40 in 1981 – it is not difficult to understand that this dependence can have disastrous repercussions, not only for individual Third World farmers, but also for their governments' treasuries. Increasing national indebtedness could possibly force the Green Revolution to a grinding halt.

Inadequate protection of crops, livestock and farmland

Third World farmers usually lack the knowledge and information to protect their crops and farm animals adequately against diseases. Relatively cheap insecticides and herbicides are seldom produced locally and retail outlets which sell these goods are often not available in much of the country. Overseas imports usually are quite limited due to insufficient foreign exchange or are beyond the means of most farmers.

An additional problem is that the crops of many Third World farmers are threatened by wild animals. This is particularly true when agriculture – e.g., shifting cultivation – is practiced in more or less unspoiled natural environments. To protect their fields against damage by animals, farmers often put up fences, but they may still have to guard their crops against wild pigs, deer, rodents, birds and other animals. According to De Schlippe (1954), the Zande of southern Sudan build special huts amidst their fields in which armed men spend the nights for a number of weeks prior to harvest time. And Grossman (1981) informs us that farmers in Papua New Guinea have a

13. Traditional granaries in the savanna region of Mali, Africa. (G.J. Wijchers)

hard time keeping their domesticated animals, especially hungry pigs, out of the fields.

Protection against small parasites, such as insects, is virtually impossible in most Third World countries because of the absence of chemical insecticides. Even if they were available, little can be done against certain plagues, such as locusts. In Southwest Asia and Northeast Africa, enormous swarms of locusts occasionally wreak havoc by wiping out *all* crops as well as part of the natural vegetation. Other problems result from poor storage facilities. Not only rats, mice and all kinds of insects cause huge losses, but molds and fungi can destroy large amounts of stored food, especially in the humid tropics.

Weed control is very time consuming if it has to be done by hand and without the help of chemical weed killers. On the irrigated rice paddies and the fields of the ladang cultivators, protection of the planted crops from competition by weeds requires a major and almost constant effort on the part of the farmers.

Mention should also be made of the fact that because of their lack of financial means, knowledge and equipment, Third World farmers are unable to protect their fields or crops against various natural disasters, such as floods, occasional night frosts and soil erosion.

In summary, Third World farmers are relatively easy victims of crop failure. Major exceptions to this general rule are the farmers – chiefly in

14. Tunisia. Thousands of olive trees have been planted, partly in an effort to arrest the process of desertification. (VDO)

South, East and Southeast Asia – who practice agriculture on irrigated fields, often on terraced slopes. Dependable water supplies and well-functioning irrigation systems assure them of outputs that are highly stable over the years.

If crop failure strikes in the Third World, the consequences can be detrimental. Without savings and insurance policies, and without governments that can come to the rescue, it often means almost immediate famine. Or it can mean the beginning of permanent indebtedness for the farmers. In recent decades, disasters appear to have occurred more and more frequently, partly as a result of growing population pressure and increasing livestock densities. Especially in the Sahel region of Africa (the semiarid zone stretching from Senegal to Ethiopia), *overgrazing* has led to massive destruction of the natural vegetation and so has contributed to the process of *desertification*. The carrying capacity of the land has become overtaxed, resulting in repeated crop failure, widespread starvation and a frightening increase in the number of refugees.

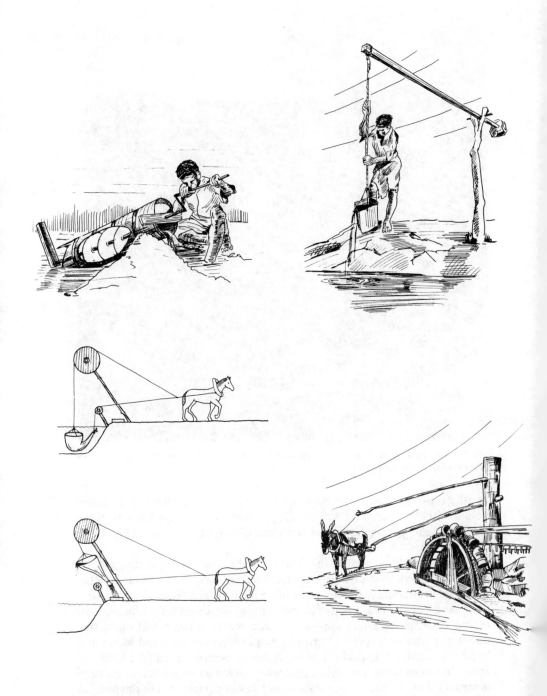

Fig. 8. Traditional devices for lifting water. *Sources:* After H.E. Hurst, 1957 and J. Weulersse, 1946.

Irrigation

Irrigation is a very important agricultural technique. In many areas it is practiced much less than it could be, which is unfortunate because the advantages of irrigation are many, including:
- greater crop variety;
- reduced dependence on often unpredictable precipitation and thus less chance of crop failure;
- longer growing periods in areas with dry seasons;
- possibility of multiple harvests in a single year;
- land can be farmed year in year out (no fallow needed);
- soil fertility is maintained more easily (by silt);
- less seasonal unemployment;
- higher yields per hectare and per farmer; and
- crop production is possible in arid regions.

Insufficient knowledge and technological capability explain why until recently little use was made of groundwater. The methods used for drawing water to the surface (see Figure 8) were quite simple and required a great deal of muscle power. The result was that only very limited areas could be irrigated. With the introduction of electric and motorized pumps, irrigation has become possible almost anywhere, including many arid regions. It goes without saying that not all deserts can be transformed into gardens, if only because the often excessively high costs constitute a limiting factor which should not be underestimated.

Within the Third World, irrigation agriculture is most advanced and widespread in Monsoon Asia. Much of it is concentrated in delta regions and other flat, usually low-lying, areas. In some areas entire mountainsides have been terraced and irrigated. Most irrigated land in used for intensive rice cultivation, allowing rural population densities to reach extremely high levels.

Irrigation systems require constant attention as well as the close cooperation of all farmers involved. Even short periods of social or political turmoil can render them ineffectual. At the end of the 1960s – following several years of political instability – at least 60 percent of the irrigation systems on the island of Java were in a state of partial disrepair.

By far the most common form of irrigation is *surface irrigation*, that is, the flooding of the fields. This method has a number of disadvantages: it is labor-intensive and requires large quantities of water. A network of canals and ditches must be constructed and dikes must be built. The land has to be flat and almost perfectly horizontal. In hilly areas this means that enormous amounts of soil must be moved. These terracing activities must be carried out in such a way that the fertile topsoil ends up on top. Another disadvantage is that in areas with an arid climate (and a low relative humidity), too much salt ends up in the soil due to evaporation of the irrigation water. In the long run, the accumulation of salt may make the land unfit for agricul-

15. Labor-intensive production of rice on irrigated terraces on the island of Bali, Indonesia. Mechanization is virtually impossible in much of Monsoon Asia. (R. Burgler)

ture. Finally, irrigation on terraced slopes can be dangerous in the sense that if something goes wrong – for example, if a dike breaks, perhaps as a result of the burrowing activities of certain animals – water will cascade down the slope, possibly destroying crops and washing away the rich topsoil and dikes on lower-lying terraces.

Modern methods of irrigation, using overhead sprinklers or perforated tubes, do not have these disadvantages. On the other hand, they are generally unsuitable for irrigated rice production, while requiring substantial capital investments and a fair amount of technical know-how. Moreover, expensive fuel is needed to operate the pumps.

Outside Monsoon Asia, very little irrigation is practiced in the Third World. Both in Latin America and Africa (except Egypt), farmers have traditionally avoided the low-lying alluvial plains and deltas. Besides occasional floods and rather unpleasant (hot, steamy) weather conditions, there is the incidence of diseases, such as malaria, making the lowlands rather unfit for human habitation. The most fertile soils and most easily irrigated areas are therefore not being used for agricultural production. With the help of modern technology, insect sprays and of course large investments, many of these lowlands could be transformed into habitable and highly productive areas. It is far from easy, however, for ladang cultivators to become irrigation farmers. For them it means much more than learning new farming methods; they must adopt an entirely different way of life. If rice is introduced as the major staple, not only their diets but also the ways

16. Preparing land for crop production in the savanna region of Nigeria. (World Bank/VDO)

they prepare their meals must undergo drastic changes. Because few things are more difficult than changing one's way of life, it is not surprising that many recently developed irrigation schemes in Africa have not been very successful. It is tragic that these problems, together with the lack of funds, preclude numerous potentially productive areas in the Third World from soon making significant contributions to solving local problems of malnutrition, hunger and occasional famine.

Machines versus human labor

Agriculture in the Third World is hardly mechanized. The overwhelming majority of the farmers rely on human and animal labor. Their tools and implements are simple and sometimes poorly adapted to environmental conditions. Handtools, such as the hoe and digging stick, are still used in many areas. Ladang cultivators never use plows. Where plows are used, they usually are pulled by bullocks, donkeys or other animals, and can do little more than loosen a thin layer of topsoil. Although the use of tractors has increased – especially on the large *haciendas* and *fazendas* in Latin America – they still play a minor role in Third World agriculture. And as long as oil prices remain high, there is little likelihood that this situation will change much. In fact, in many areas the sharp rise in the price of oil since 1973 has caused a decline in the use of tractors and other machines.

The non-use of adequate tools means that yields often are considerably lower than they could be. Meanwhile, the input of human labor in sowing,

17. Harvesting rice on newly reclaimed and irrigated land along the Niger River in Mali, West Africa. (FAO/VDO)

cultivating, weed control, harvesting and threshing is enormous. Although output per hectare may be reasonably high – particularly on the small, intensively cultivated and irrigated farms in Southeast Asia – output per farmer is very small. Even when the majority of the people are employed in agriculture, food surpluses are so small that large quantities must be imported so as to be able to feed the rapidly growing urban population.

Other agriculture-related activities, e.g., transportation of crops and processing, are often not mechanized. As in the past, the 'agricultural civilizations' of the Third World remain characterized by a production process in which the use of simple muscle power plays an all-important role.

As indicated above, per hectare input of human labor is greatest in the irrigated rice producing areas of Monsoon Asia. Gourou has calculated that in those parts of the Tonkin delta (northern Vietnam) where two rice crops a year are grown, it amounts to 625 man-days per year (Gourou 1966, p. 120). A moment's reflection reveals that this is an extraordinarily large, almost incomprehensible, amount of labor. It means that one farmer cannot work more than half a hectare (1 acre). According to Andreae (1964, p. 221), many Southeast Asian farmers put in 800 to 1200 man-days per hectare per year.

This exceedingly intensive use of the land is necessitated by the unbelievably high rural population densities. Since most farmers have less than 1 hectare, they must, in order to avoid starvation, utilize every square inch of land. Because many have been doing this for decades, the soil fertility has gone down and the land has become overexploited. In order to prevent declining yields, the farmers must invest more and more time, e.g., regularly checking every plant and replacing weak plants with healthy ones.

In the meantime, population grows relentlessly, causing pressure on land to mount and farms to become ever smaller. Clear examples of this process of related changes can be encountered in Java, where agriculture has evolved into horticulture. Geertz has referred to the increasingly labor-intensive production of rice and other food crops on miniscule farms as *involution* – a process that in Java started around 1830 with the introduction by the Dutch of the so-called 'culture system,' forcing Javanese farmers to plant part of their land in sugar cane or some other export crop that was highly profitable for the Dutch.

A concrete expression of this desperate situation of 'involuted' agriculture is the Javanese *bawon* system in which landless villagers (e.g., old widows) are allowed to help gather the harvest of those who do farm some land. In exchange for their services, they are given a small proportion of what they have harvested, usually no more than one-tenth. In recent years, however, more and more farmers try to shirk their obligations toward the village community and no longer allow anyone to help taking in the harvest. Declining farm size and continuing pauperization make it increasingly difficult for them to share their harvest with others. Furthermore, farmers who have successfully adopted the Green Revolution, often have developed a commercially minded attitude. Using small agricultural machines – which they may have purchased on credit – they are able to take care of the harvest by themselves and pay off their loans. Thus, there is less demand for labor, causing the *bawon* system of 'shared poverty' to lose importance, which is unfortunate because it serves as a useful buffer mechanism, or community-based insurance policy, against starvation of the landless poor (Palte & Tempelman 1975).

Not only Southeast Asia, but also other Third World regions experience a growing overabundance of labor in the rural areas. As a consequence, wages decline, poverty spreads and sooner or later many villagers – especially young men – head for the cities, hoping to find employment there.

It seems obvious that the introduction of labor-saving agricultural methods and machines does not solve the problems of densely populated rural areas. On the contrary, it might well aggravate the situation, as is often the case. More promising, it would seem, is the introduction of techniques which allow higher yields per unit of land. It is indeed unfortunate that many Third World countries as well as aid-providing countries have put too much emphasis on labor-saving devices and 'efficiency.'

In areas with an abundance of unused land suitable for agricultural production, the introduction of labor-saving techniques may be called for, especially if the demand for labor exceeds the supply. In other parts of the Third World, such techniques can only be expected to cause massive unemployment and widen the gulf between the rich and the poor. Eventually, the majority of the rural population may become *marginalized*, that is, deprived of possibilities to provide for themselves because they have no land, no work, and worst of all, no hope for the future. Living below the poverty level, the rural destitute – dressed in rags, living in hovels which do not protect them against cold and rain, and permanently undernourished – may either become apathetic or decide sooner or later to rebel against the established system of social injustice which victimizes them.

Low productivity

As already noted, per hectare yields tend to be low in the Third World. A few years ago, average corn yields were 1200 kilograms per hectare in Latin America and 800 kg in Africa, compared with 3000 kg in the US. Per hectare wheat yields of 700 kg in India compared with yields of more than 3000 kg in Europe, and rice yields were approximately $3\frac{1}{2}$ times lower than in Europe. Some differences are even greater, for example, the yearly production of milk is about 160 liters per cow in the Far East, 410 liters in Latin America, but more than 2000 liters in Europe. Most conspicuous is the contrast in output per farmer, not only because Western farmers make extensive use of modern machines and have larger farms, but also because they enjoy far more favorable tenure conditions. Besides, they tend to be in better health, are better educated and better informed, have a more adequate infrastructure at their disposal (including extension services, price supports and various subsidies), and are therefore more highly motivated than are most Third World farmers.

The low level of productivity has important repercussions. It means, among other things, that a very considerable proportion of the total working population must be employed in agriculture (Figure 9). Whereas the average US farmer produces enough food for more than 50 persons and a European farmer can feed at least 20 persons, in underdeveloped countries most farmers raise barely enough to feed their own family. Consequently, agriculture makes a much smaller contribution to a Third World country's GDP than might be expected on the basis of the large size of its agricultural labor force (see Figure 9).

A world of paradoxes

Various authors have observed that the Third World is full of paradoxes. Concerning the agricultural sector, the following contradictions can be listed:
1. Although per hectare yields are low and many people are malnourished, vast areas in the Third World remain underutilized.
2. Despite the fact that more than half the working-age population is engaged in agriculture, many inhabitants do not have enough to eat.
3. Even though the majority of the people are farmers, the Third World as a whole is becoming increasingly dependent on food imports.

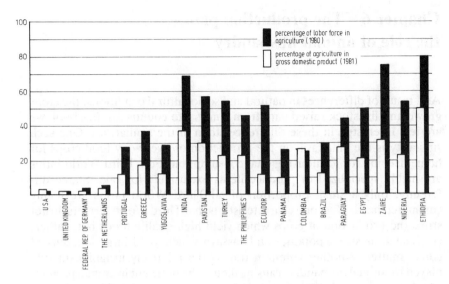

Fig. 9. Percent labor force in agriculture (1980) and agriculture's share in GDP (1981); selected developed and less-developed countries.
Source: World Bank, *World Development Report 1983.*

4. Agriculture employs far more people than does any other sector of the economy, yet its contribution to most countries' GDP is very modest.
5. The people who work hardest and make the greatest contribution to a country's total agricultural output, frequently are the lowest-paid and most impoverished members of society.
6. Even though agricultural productivity is low, much valuable farmland is lost due to inadequate measures to prevent soil erosion.

Several of these paradoxes have already been explained. Others, which have not yet received sufficient attention, will be discussed more fully in the next chapter.

Chapter 6   The production plan –
the role of animal husbandry

As a result of differences in natural and sociocultural conditions, the crops grown and livestock raised vary from country to country. In this book we are less interested in these differences than in the similarities. One such similarity is the emphasis on the production of every-day food crops for home use and for local or regional consumption. Few Third World farms are highly specialized or produce items exclusively for sale. Stated differently, only a small proportion of all Third World farms are highly commercialized. A second characteristic is that Third World farmers do not stress the production of crops which yield high-quality foods but, rather, crops such as sweet potatoes and cassava which yield large amounts of edible matter. Another common trait is the relatively insignificant role played by animal husbandry, causing diets to be deficient in animal protein. This last-mentioned characteristic is discussed in some detail in the following paragraphs.

Poorly developed livestock raising; poorly fed animals

Although farm animals, such as poultry, pigs, sheep, goats and cattle, are fairly common in much of the Third World, they generally play a minor economic role. If crops and livestock are raised on the same farm, the mutually advantageous (or symbiotic) relations between crops and livestock usually are of limited importance. In places where crop farming and livestock raising are practiced by different ethnic groups – e.g., in East Africa – there usually exist no functional relations between the two economies. The tillers of the land do not grow feed crops which they could trade for manure with the cattle raisers. Neither the herdsmen themselves nor the crop cultivators use the livestock as draft animals. Thus, neither group benefits from the possibilities offered by the other group. Of course, a similar lack of symbiotic relationships can be found in the developed countries. However, there is an important difference: whereas mixed farming is fairly common outside the Third World, it is extremely rare within the Third World.

Much livestock farming in the underdeveloped countries is marginal at best, occupying an inferior position as far as the production of food is concerned. Feed crops are usually not grown and improved pastures or special hay fields often do not exist. Most farmers do not purchase manufactured animal feed, so that the livestock must find something to eat for themselves, usually on land that is unsuitable for crop production, fallow land, stubble fields, wooded areas or along roadsides. Goats, sheep, pigs and poultry often roam around freely, scavenging for their food.

Apart from the low-quality feed, there generally is no selective breeding and little protection against diseases and parasites (ticks). Veterinary facilities are inadequate or missing altogether. Quantity and quality of animal products, e.g., meat, milk and eggs, tend to be rather low. Cattle and other large livestock sometimes are too weak or in too poor health to be used as draft animals.

Although India has an enormously large cattle population – more than 200 million – cattle have very little economic value. The cow is sacred in Hinduism and most people do not eat beef; cow slaughter is banned in many areas. Cows, however, do produce some milk, while bullocks (steers) are used for draft purposes, especially plowing. Even though cattle and water buffaloes are considered sacred, they are poorly fed and often half-starving. Feed crops are barely grown in most of India.

In Third World areas where livestock do play an important role in the rural economy, e.g., parts of Brazil, Burkina Faso (Upper Volta) and Botswana, they are often not fed well either. Because fodder crops are rarely grown and there usually is no money to purchase feed, the animals are dependent on natural vegetation. Fenced meadows and improved (e.g., irrigated) pastures are virtually unknown in much of the Third World.

People who live in semiarid (steppe) or arid (desert) environments and who depend for their living on livestock raising, usually have adapted to the unfavorable natural conditions by constantly migrating with their herds. Such *pastoral nomadism* is practiced in a number of areas, including the African Sahel region – a transition zone between the Saharan desert and the wooded savanna to the South. The Fulani of northern Nigeria, for example, migrate southward during the long dry season (October-May) and return home at the beginning of the wet season after having sold part of their herds in south-central Nigeria. If they did not practice this 'horizontal transhumance,' their herds would have to be much smaller and fewer people would be able to subsist on livestock raising*. Despite these regular migrations, few people can be supported by this way of life; natural pastures simply cannot produce large quantities of high-quality feed.

Looked at from a purely economic point of view, livestock raising is quite important in South America, where many *haciendas* and *fazendas* specialize in commercial beef production. In some regions, such as the Andean countries, it developed during the colonial era, whereas elsewhere, e.g., Argentina, it did not acquire prominence until the end of the 19th century. Production is partly for the domestic market and partly for export. A characteristic feature of these enterprises is their extensive use of land. The cattle graze on wide expanses of poor quality pasture and are not well taken care of. Although selective breeding is practiced here more than in Africa, it could be improved considerably. As is the case in other parts of the Third World, mixed farming is poorly developed.

* Transhumance is the seasonal movement of livestock between mountain pastures (summer) and lowland areas (winter) under the care of herders or in company with the owners.

18. Cattle disease control on the Argentine pampa. Gauchos herd cattle into paddocks to sort out cows and calves. (UN/VDO)

The Latin American livestock economy can be explained in terms of (1) the predominance of large landholdings which do not foster intensive land use, (2) the relatively small and often distant domestic market, (3) high transportation costs, inhibiting large-scale crop production in many areas, (4) availability of cheap labor, (5) the high cost of most inputs, such as fertilizer, and (6) a shortage of extension services and agricultural experts.

Marginal livestock production: an explanation

Although it is far from easy to provide a satisfactory explanation for the relative unimportance of livestock farming in the Third World, we can identify a number of underlying reasons.

To begin with, much of the Third World was very sparsely populated until recently; large parts still are. Intensive use of the land was not necessary, so that there was no demand for animal manure. The fertility of the soil could be maintained or restored simply by leaving the farmland idle for long or short periods of time. This practice was far easier than keeping livestock and applying manure to the land. Slash-and-burn cultivation, furthermore, prohibited the use of plows because of the presence of tree stumps, roots and heavy tree logs in and on the cleared land. Having no plows, the cultivators had no reason to keep draft animals.

Secondly, the humid tropics are not particularly conducive to livestock

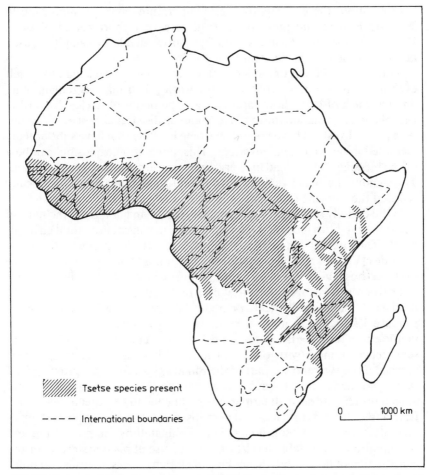

Fig. 10. Tsetse fly infested areas. *Source:* J.I. Clarke (ed.), *An Advanced Geography of Africa*, 1975, p. 342.

raising. Most natural pastures are of inferior quality – the grasses have a low nutritional value and often grow so tall that grazing becomes difficult. In many areas, leguminous plants like clover and alfalfa – which are excellent as forage – are virtually absent. Good hay is difficult to come by and does not keep well in warm humid climates.

A serious obstacle is the occurrence of a multitude of animal diseases which make it difficult to keep the livestock healthy and productive. Special mention should be made of sleeping sickness, caused by parasitic insects (*trypanosomes*) and transmitted by the tsetse fly. The disease is marked by fever, protracted lethargy, tremors and loss of weight. Tsetse flies fortunately do not occur in Asia and Latin America, but in tropical Africa they afflict an area of at least 10 million km², several countries having hardly any areas that are free of this scourge (Fig. 10).

99

In addition, the consistently high temperatures make it impossible to keep fresh meat and milk for more than a very short period of time. Refrigerated storage facilities are often not available or cannot be used because of the lack of electricity.

Although the effects of modern veterinary science have begun to be felt even in the most remote corners of the world, their impacts remain quite limited. Lack of know-how and funds are the major obstacles. Nevertheless, cheap innoculations have reduced animal diseases almost everywhere. As a result, livestock have not only become healthier but have substantially increased in numbers in many areas. This 'population explosion' can be a mixed blessing as it can lead to overgrazing, soil erosion and desertification. Throughout the Sahel region, serious ecological damage has drastically reduced the carrying capacity of the land in recent years.

In the densely settled areas of tropical Asia, man has altered the natural environment into a more amenable and more manageable cultural environment. The present landscape is almost entirely the product of human activities. Various animal diseases have become all but wiped out, but here livestock husbandry is a luxury that farmers cannot afford. This becomes clear when it is realized that it takes 5 to 10 kilograms of feed grains to produce 1 kilogram of meat, or many kilograms of grass, hay, etc. to produce 1 kilogram of milk. In other words, livestock production is very inefficient in terms of the output of calories per unit of farmland. Clearly, subsistence farmers with only 1 hectare of land would endanger their survival if they were to use part of their land as pasture or for growing feed crops. No matter how desirable it is that the human diet contains some animal protein, most small farmers are compelled to be vegetarians. Apart from a few chickens or ducks and perhaps one or two pigs or goats, human existence in much of Monsoon Asia is dominated by the production and consumption of vegetable foodstuffs and the use of plant materials for the construction of homes and the making of clothing, tools, utensils and other material possessions. In much of South and Southeast Asia, people live what may be called a 'vegetarian way of life.'

Some religions have a limiting impact on livestock raising. Just as Hindus do not consume beef, Moslems (and also Jews) do not eat pork. Pig raising, therefore, is practically absent from the Moslem world, which stretches from Mauritania and Morocco in Northwest Africa to Pakistan and Bangladesh in South Asia and parts of Indonesia in Southeast Asia. Sheep and goats usually are the chief suppliers of meat. The absence of pigs may be perceived as a loss as they are excellent scavengers which can subsist on household refuse. Besides, goats have the disadvantage of being quite destructive, especially certain tree-climbing breeds. It is believed that over the centuries, goats have caused considerable damage to the environment in the Middle East and the Mediterranean countries of Europe, including destruction of vegetation, soil erosion, choked river channels and concomitant malaria problems. In some cultures, the consumption of milk is prohibited or severely restricted (Simoons 1961).

Possibilities for expanding and improving livestock raising

It would appear from the preceding discussion that there is ample reason to take steps to promote livestock production in the Third World and to integrate it with crop production. In order to make this possible, the French agronomist René Dumont and other experts believe that drastic changes are needed in the ways farm animals are fed; the quality of the feed must be improved and the production of forage expanded. Dumont speaks of a *révolution fourragère* or 'forage revolution.' In Monsoon Asia, where agricultural production is heavily concentrated in delta regions and other low-lying plains, there is a great deal of unused or underutilized land available at higher elevations and on slopes. Pastures could be developed here. There are various types of plants, both in southern Asia and in other parts of the world, which could be used to convert relatively infertile and unproductive slopes into reasonably productive meadows. Likewise, the introduction of certain 'exotic' plants could substantially raise the carrying capacity of natural pastures in areas that suffer from periodic droughts. And the long fallow periods in areas where shifting cultivation is practiced could be used for growing fodder crops. Such changes would permit the raising of livestock. Besides producing meat and milk, they could be used as draft animals. At the same time, manure would become available for fertilizing the cropland.

Professor Dumont is of the opinion that nearly everywhere livestock production can be expanded and improved by integrating it with crop production, thus making agriculture as a whole more intensive and more diversified. The result, of course, would be improved and better-balanced diets. But as Hodder (1971, p. 114) has pointed out, all possibilities and limitations have not yet been adequately investigated. There still is a great need for more research, especially with regard to the production of animal feed. Also, rural sociologists and other social scientists should study the problems that arise when wet-land rice farmers or ladang cultivators adopt a system of mixed farming. Changing over to a new type of farming and thus to a different food package can be very difficult and may even be a traumatic experience. Apart from the fact that farmers have to learn new agricultural techniques, work with new tools, get used to taking care of livestock and perhaps revise their 'agricultural calendar,' the entire rural community may have to make important adjustments in its way of life.

Chapter 7 Functional aspects of agricultural production

A fourth aspect of the way in which agricultural enterprises are organized is the functional aspect. By this we mean the purpose for which production takes place. Most common in the Third World is the production of food crops for home consumption, usually on small farms. Besides subsistence agriculture, there are large agricultural enterprises which produce for the market.

Subsistence agriculture

Subsistence farming does not mean that everything produced is consumed by the farmer and his or her family. Although production of food for home-use is the farmer's first and foremost objective, a small surplus is usually produced for commercial purposes. By selling this, the farmer acquires money for a few necessary purchases, to pay taxes and rent (in case he or she is a tenant), and to pay off the moneylender or the bank.

The surpluses produced by subsistence farmers usually are so small that, even in countries where the majority of the people are engaged in self-sufficient agriculture, not enough food is produced to feed the entire population. Some of the reasons for the very low degree of agricultural commercialization in the Third World have already been mentioned. Together with some additional factors they include:

1. Traditional production techniques result in low levels of output per farmer, per hectare and per head of livestock.

2. Much land is either not used or underutilized, especially in areas of shifting cultivation.

3. Where farming is intensive, small or miniscule average farm size inhibits production of saleable surpluses.

4. Unfavorable tenure conditions virtually preclude high levels of productivity, particularly for sharecroppers.

5. Collective or communal landownership tends to discourage intensive farming.

6. Traditional kinship relations involving equal sharing of output hamper individual motivation to maximize production because most people are reluctant to work hard for the benefit of others. Surplus production that could be sold or traded is therefore limited.

7. Domestic and local markets are small. Levels of individual purchasing power are low, the urban population tends to be limited, urban centers are often far away or inaccessible, marketing facilities may be inadequate and the cost of transport may be prohibitive.

8. Possibilities of selling produce to food-processing industries frequently are restricted due to low degrees of industrialization. Production for export usually offers few opportunities because of competition from large,

19. Intensive rice production on tiny irrigated plots in Sierra Leone, West Africa. Children carry the harvested rice to the village where it is threshed with simple tools. (A.W. Haas)

Harvesting rice in Indonesia

Age-old customs, values and beliefs generally form stubborn obstacles to far-reaching sociocultural changes. Taboos tend to be extremely persistent, no matter how irrational they may seem to outsiders. In Indonesia, religious belief has it that farmers must use a special little knife for harvesting their rice crop and that they should be careful not to cut more than one rice plant at a time. This practice is necessary to appease the ghosts. It is obvious that this custom stands in the way of mechanization or, for that matter, the use of such handtools as sickles and scythes. Nevertheless, harvesting with sickles has gained in importance in recent years, although every farmer makes sure that at least a small part of his or her crop is harvested with the traditional *ani-ani* knife. Replacement of the knife by the sickle or scythe may be seen (by Westerners) as a step forward on the road to development. But the introduction of more efficient, labor-saving tools has greatly aggravated the unemployment problem among the women of rural Java, many of whom are now without any income. This example illustrates how arduous and full of potholes the road to progress can be.

modern, well-managed, specialized enterprises – often foreign-owned plantations – which produce products of high and uniform quality. Production for foreign markets may be adversely affected by poor connections with ports, lack of organization, inadequate packing facilities, fluctuating prices, tariff barriers and import restrictions in overseas countries.

To the above list we can add that small farmers who produce for the market, usually depend on a long chain of intermediary traders. Because these traders often are the only people able and willing to transport the produce, they enjoy a monopoly position and pay the farmers exceedingly low prices. In the absence of marketing cooperatives, small producers are totally dependent on these middlemen, not only for shipping their products but also for the delivery of all kinds of industrial goods, artificial fertilizer and other agricultural inputs. If at the same time these traders happen to be landowners, storekeepers and/or moneylenders – combinations which are not uncommon – their power is all the greater. In other words, the middlemen are in an excellent position to exploit the small farmers and appropriate nearly all the surplus value produced. This situation represents a form of *internal colonialism,* based on unequal dependence-dominance relations.

The farmers, unorganized as they usually are, have no alternative but to accept the low prices offered by the trader-moneylender. If they refuse to sell, the produce will spoil and the farmers will be without the income they need for paying taxes and rent and for paying off their debts. Another important reason for the low prices is that the small impoverished farmer must sell his or her crop immediately after it has been harvested, that is, precisely when the supply is greatest and the price is lowest. The farmer lacks the facilities to store crops, especially not the more perishable ones, and wait for prices to go up. Furthermore, if the farmer is in debt, he or she is often required to pay back in kind, rather than in the form of money. This means, in effect, that the crop has been sold before it has been harvested, making it impossible to postpone selling it until prices have become more attractive.

A particularly traumatic dilemma arises when a farmer is so strapped for money that he or she has to sell the entire crop without being able to keep some of it as seed for the next season. The potential seed is sold when the price is low, but a few months later the farmer must buy seed for a much higher price – often from the same trader-moneylender to whom he/she has sold his/her last harvest. And because the farmer may not have the money to pay for this expensive seed, it must be borrowed, usually from the same trader. Breaking out of this vicious circle of persistent indebtedness is often not possible, so that children may inherit their parents' financial obligations. They, too, may have to pass their debts on to their offspring, often resulting in *debt bondage* or *debt peonage.*

In the former British colonies, *Marketing Boards* have been established (by the British) for the purpose of guaranteeing reasonably stable and presumably fair prices to the producers. Although the Marketing Boards in some countries have had beneficial effects on prices, at least for a number of years, they generally pay prices that are too low and are in effect government-controlled instruments for siphoning surplus value from the rural areas to the urban centers or to the provincial or national coffers. Many Marketing Boards are rife with excessive red tape and rampant corruption. Farmers sometimes do not receive their payments until months later, a problem which did not exist prior to the introduction of the Boards, that is, when farmers were still dependent on local trader-moneylenders.

Frustrated by rock bottom prices, corruption and bureaucratic delays, many farmers in Nigeria, Tanzania and other Third World countries have decided in recent years to stop producing for the market. They either have reverted to pure subsistence agriculture or have quit farming altogether and left the countryside in the hope of finding better opportunities in the city.

Another reason that farmers receive little for their products is that in countries with few paved roads it is anything but simple for a trader to collect small quantities of perishable produce from a large number of farms and deliver it to an urban market. Even a short delay, caused by impassable roads or engine trouble, may mean that much of the cargo is spoiled by the time it reaches its destination. And by driving over bumpy roads, tomatoes and other soft fruits easily become damaged, especially when they are not packaged properly.

In view of the problems discussed above, it is not surprising that many farmers who live close to a marketplace or a well-traveled highway, deliver their produce themselves. They either ride a donkey, travel by bus or walk (often an hour or more), and sell their green peppers, bananas, beans, corn and perhaps a few chickens directly to the consumers.

In Kenya, many farmers, nearly all of whom are women, travel by privately operated *matatu* – a small, usually Japanese-made, covered pickup truck, that can perhaps best be described as a minibus or a rural taxi, although it is used also in town. Frequently, these *matatus* carry a dozen or more people, each with at least two baskets, boxes or sacks full of home-grown vegetables, potatoes and fruits and possibly some live poultry. Such circumstances clearly do not encourage production for sale. In the Third World, a subsistence farmer must make a tremendous effort and put up with a great deal of inconvenience if he or she wants to earn just a few dollars. But these few dollars they desperately need for the purchase of basic goods, including new or secondhand clothing, shoes, kitchen utensils and fuel, or to pay for the education of their children.

Market-oriented agriculture: plantations and agribusiness

Despite food shortages, many Third World countries export agricultural products; often their export trade is even dominated by agricultural goods. Obviously a paradoxical situation exists, especially when it is realized that in recent years a growing number of Third World countries have become highly dependent on food imports.

A considerable proportion of these agricultural export commodities are

20. Rural marketplace in the Gambian portion of Senegambia, West Africa. (J. Zwart)

grown on large, commercial farms which produce chiefly or exclusively for
foreign markets. In some countries, these specialized enterprises account
for virtually the entire production of agricultural exports and are the major
earners of foreign exchange. If that is the case, we refer to these countries as
plantation economies, the purest examples of which can be found in the
Caribbean region. It is these same commercial enterprises or plantations
which have contributed significantly to the increase in agricultural exports
from the Third World since World War II.

   Plantations are difficult to define, but in general they have many of the
following characteristics:
(1) They are large in size, sometimes thousands of hectares. In some
     regions (e.g., in several Central American republics), they occupy a
     large proportion of all cropland and are typically found in the more
     productive and more accessible areas.
(2) They are located in tropical and subtropical regions.
(3) Plantations usually produce crops that can only be grown under
     tropical or subtropical conditions. Perennial tree crops (e.g., coffee,
     tea, rubber, banana, cocoa, coconut and oil palm) are common, but

106

also various annuals (e.g., cotton, pineapple and sugar) play an important role.

(4) Production is specialized. Usually only one crop is grown (*monoculture*), although sometimes a second or third crop is raised. This specialization contrasts sharply with the *polyculture* of the subsistence farmer.

(5) Production on Third World plantations tends to be for export to the prosperous, industrialized countries of Western Europe and North America (which for the most part have no tropical and subtropical climates).

(6) On many plantations, the crops are processed, at least partially. Examples are pineapple canneries, sugar refineries and tea factories.

(7) Most plantations represent huge capital investments, making them into modern, technologically advanced enterprises capable of raising uniform, high-quality products.

(8) The capital investments usually come from the affluent countries; many Third World plantations are foreign-owned, often by multinational corporations.

(9) Management, too, often is in foreign hands. By contrast, the unskilled and poorly paid labor is supplied either by the local population or by migrants from other Third World countries.

(10) In contrast to the small subsistence farms, plantations are highly mechanized and use the most modern farming methods. Many have their own maintenance and repair shops as well as a private water supply system and generator station.

(11) Sometimes the workers live on the plantation and have their own garden plots. In that case the plantation owners may provide medical, educational and recreational facilities for the laborers and their families. Larger plantations sometimes provide separate (segregated) recreational facilities for the foreign executives, including a 'club,' a tennis court and a pool.

(12) Owing to the use of machines, high-quality seeds, pesticides, chemical fertilizers and irrigation, output per laborer is considerably higher than on nearby subsistence farms.

Summarizing the above, we can describe a plantation as a large-scale, modern, specialized enterprise, located in the tropics or subtropics, often partially industrial in character, on which foreign capital, know-how and management combine with indigenous human resources for the purpose of producing high-quality agricultural commodities for export.

In more than one sense, the plantation constitutes a 'foreign' element in the economy and landscape of the tropics and subtropics. In addition to foreign management, foreign capital and foreign agricultural methods, the crops which are produced for foreign markets often are not indigenous: e.g., rubber trees in Malaysia and Liberia have been introduced from the

Amazon Basin. This explains why Gourou and others have characterized the plantation as 'exotic.'

The exotic character implies that agriculture in many Third World countries has a *dualistic* nature – consisting of two entirely different sectors, one 'modern' and the other more or less 'traditional.' In some respects, the two sectors are antagonistic. With regard to production for export, the large commercial estates compete with the small farmers. More importantly, they also compete for land. By occupying large expanses of the more fertile land, the plantations limit the expansion possibilities of self-sufficient agriculture. This fact explains why in Jamaica and other plantation economies, much subsistence farming occurs in areas that are rather unproductive, hilly and relatively inaccessible. Where rapid population growth has led to considerable pressure on the land – or an unfavorable man/land ratio – an increasing number of small farmers must try to eke out a living on land of marginal quality. Thus, plantation agriculture contributes to the *marginalization* of part of the rural population in a number of Third World countries.

Plantations offer employment opportunities, are earners of foreign exchange and, by paying taxes to the government of the country in which they operate, form a source of income for their 'host' country. These may be seen as advantages. Unfortunately, however, the disadvantages usually more than outweigh the advantages (see Beckford 1972).

By occupying a great deal of land, plantations restrict the possibilities to produce foodstuffs for the domestic market. A paradoxical situation results: part of the agricultural output disappears to overseas markets while the Third World people themselves often do not have enough to eat and suffer from low-calorie and protein-deficient diets. A second disadvantage is that most of the profits are transferred to the countries from which the initial investments originated. The foreign management, moreover, spends much of its earnings abroad, usually in the developed countries.

If plantations are a country's chief foreign-currency earners, it is highly dependent on the world-market prices of its exports; prices over which it has no control and which may fluctuate markedly. This situation makes a country whose exports are dominated by one single commodity, say, sugar or cocoa, dangerously vulnerable. At the same time, plantations often remain 'enclaves' or economic islands without local *forward* and *backward economic linkages*. Because they import their means of production (e.g., machines and fertilizer) and export their products, they generally fail to stimulate related economic activities such as services and processing activities. In short, since their forward and backward linkages are with the outside world – especially with the capital providing and know-how generating 'metropole' – they have very limited *multiplier effects* for the country in which they are located. Apart from hiring some unskilled workers, they create hardly any employment for the local population. A final disadvantage is that the capital-intensive imports needed for the operation of the plantations consume a substantial portion of the foreign exchange their exports earn.

In several countries, the number of plantations has decreased in recent decades as a result of expropriations. Some have been divided up into a large number of small farms, while others have been nationalized and turned into state-operated farms. Some owners themselves decided to quit. In Central America, the United Fruit Company has sold much of its acreage because other investment opportunities, e.g., hotels, supermarkets and television stations, became more attractive. Yet, it is difficult to discern a general trend since in some countries large foreign-owned agricultural enterprises have been expanding. For example, in recent years immense expanses of land in the Amazon region have been acquired by multinational concerns.

Today, it is not uncommon for foreign enterprises to expand their activities to the marketing of export commodities which they themselves have not produced, supplying indigenous farmers with all kinds of modern production means, and even providing agricultural extension services. As a result of these developments, farmers who have entered into a contract to produce for the company – a fairly common practice in sugar cane production – are able to increase their output. In this way, foreign enterprises extend their influence on, and domination over, the agricultural sector.

The most pronounced form of agribusiness exists when multinational concerns like Lever Brothers (Unilever) control the industrial processing (in their own factories) as well as the distribution of the final products in the importing countries. This linkage is called *vertical integration,* whereby the same enterprise takes care of the entire chain of activities: the production of inputs (such as artificial fertilizers and pesticides, irrigation equipment and implements); raising the crops; canning, packing, etc.; shipping the finished products to market (possibly on company-built roads and railroads or in company-owned vessels); and finally wholesaling and retailing the goods (sometimes in company-owned chain stores). At the same time, the multinational is likely to be active in the field of research, especially as regards agricultural production and processing, and may have its own agricultural experiment stations as well as an agronomic training center.

Market-oriented agriculture: fazendas and haciendas

The agricultural picture of Latin America differs from that of the rest of the Third World. Here, *fazendas* and *haciendas* occupy a position somewhat between the small subsistence farms and the plantations.

Most *fazendas* and *haciendas* resemble the plantations in some respects; they are large in size and geared to commercial production. But there are also important differences. Apart from the fact that many date back to the colonial era and therefore are older than most plantations, they are neither foreign-owned nor the property of large transnationals. Many produce not for export but exclusively for the domestic market*.

Among the reasons that most *fazendas* do not produce for export are lack of interest on the part of the owners; unfavorable location with regard to ports, resulting in high transport costs; and insufficient quality of the products. The domestic orientation has both its advantages (e.g., less foreign competition) and disadvantages (limited markets).

A third difference is the lower level of productivity. Plantations are modern, efficient and well organized. High profits enable their owners to make the investments necessary to maintain or improve the competitive position of the plantations. Or else, they can obtain the needed capital in the 'metropolitan countries.' Besides, they can easily import know-how. For the *fazendas* there is less need to be modern and efficient. Lack of domestically available capital and know-how, furthermore, makes it difficult for the owners to adopt advanced, rational production methods.

In some respects, then, the *fazendas* and *haciendas* resemble the self-sufficient farms with their 'antiquated' methods of production. Nonetheless, they can compete successfully with subsistence farmers who produce small surpluses for sale, owing to the fact that they are large and cheap producers and are more specialized. The *hacendados* and *fazendeiros* are better educated and better informed, making it easier for them to adjust to changing market conditions. They are also better able to obtain credit than are the small subsistence farmers, enabling them to employ somewhat more modern methods.

Fazenda-like commercial enterprises that produce chiefly for the domestic market can also be found in Asia and Africa, but there they are much less common than in Latin America. The explanation for this contrast must be sought in the difference in colonial history, the strong impact of Iberian culture – including the widespread occurrence of large landholdings – and the generally higher standard of living of the Latin American population.

Reflection

In the preceding sections we have, while discussing the purposes for which agricultural production takes place, distinguished three types of enterprises: (1) the small, largely self-sufficient farm, (2) the large, modern, often foreign-owned plantation with its specialized production for export, and (3) the large but less rationalized *fazenda* or *hacienda* which produces mainly for the national market.

Despite their differences, all three confront us with the problem of underdevelopment. This is particularly true of the first type, which at best allows a modest level of material well-being. More often than not it breeds

---

* Confusion in terminology results because in Latin America the terms *fazenda* and *hacienda* are used to refer to all large agricultural enterprises, no matter whether they produce for the world market (e.g., coffee *fazendas*) or for the domestic market (e.g., many cattle ranches).

poverty and destitution. On the traditional *haciendas* and *fazendas,* underdevelopment manifests itself in the form of inefficiency, underutilization and low productivity, which, in turn, result from limited demand (i.e., low purchasing power), shortage of capital and know-how, and lack of entrepreneurial capability. Although the plantation is a very successful business undertaking, it is a product of economic penetration and domination by foreigners. It is exotic, that is, not a product of endogenous development. As a means of exploitation by external business interests which skim off surpluses, it contributes in a most fundamental and significant way to the complex of features known together as *dependent development* or underdevelopment.

The three agricultural enterprise types we have dealt with are not the only ones that occur in the Third World; they are simply the most common types. In addition, there are small farmers who are highly commercialized, such as the smallholder rubber producers in Malaysia and the small cocoa growers in Ghana. Their production of subsistence crops is often insufficient, so that they must purchase much of their food supply. In times of low prices for rubber or cocoa, they can experience considerable hardship and serious undernourishment.

Another type consists of bio-industries or agricultural factories which specialize in the production of livestock products, e.g., meat, milk or eggs, and which usually buy all their feed supplies. In the Third World, this new type of agricultural enterprise is emerging especially in the vicinity of the larger cities. Mention must also be made of the fact that rather modern, commercial farms of intermediate size can be found in the Third World, e.g., in a number of irrigated areas in northern Mexico. Owing to the availability of irrigation, they can be worked intensively and make an important contribution to supplying the Mexican market with a great variety of products.

The latter types of enterprises are far from common and play a relatively minor role in Third World agriculture. Only at the local scale do they have importance, which is not sufficient reason for us to discuss them further in this broad survey of Third World farm types.

Chapter 8 Conclusions

Groups of agricultural producers

The largest single group of Third World agriculturists consists of *small landowners,* most of whom have little or no education, are poor, grow subsistence food crops, use relatively unsophisticated production methods and find it hard to obtain credit. For them, farming often is a way of life, rather than a business. Their children usually help with the farm work. Although they do sell some of their produce, making a profit generally is only of secondary importance. To make ends meet, one or more members of the family may have to sell their, usually unskilled, labor power. In spite of the fact that small landowners outnumber most, if not all, other socioeconomic groups in society, they usually have little or no political power.

Small tenants are even worse off because they have to pay rent – either in money or in kind – and are virtually unable to obtain credit. It is not uncommon that they spend much of their time working for the landlord. Because of their problems to eke out a living, many tenant families live on the edge of starvation. Death rates among the children of these bonded laborers tend to be well above the national average.

A separate category are the rural *squatters,* usually to be found in sparsely populated, inaccessible areas. They are farmers who have simply settled on a small piece of land, cleared it, and now use it for growing food crops. In the interior of North Brazil these *posseiros* are a common phenomenon, but there are also squatters in the eastern lowlands of the Andean countries. Their existence is very uncertain. The land they occupy often belongs to a large landowner who could have them evicted. Private armies of thugs are sometimes deployed for this purpose. If the land belongs to the state, the chances that the squatters will be pushed off usually are less. Squatting is probably more widespread in Brazil than elsewhere. Using false documents, large landowners in Brazil often claim huge areas, and since this practice started many years ago, a given piece of land may be claimed by several individuals. In recent years, *posseiros* have begun to organize themselves into small armed bands in a desperate effort to defend their small plots of land against greedy large landowners.

Then there is the rural *middle class* – farmers who own or rent a reasonably large tract of land, and who may be fairly well educated. In most Third World countries, their number is very small. These are the farmers who know how to take advantage of credit facilities, subsidized high-yielding seed varieties, pesticides, artificial fertilizers and other agricultural inputs made available by the government to help the poor

112

masses. They are also likely to be the ones who benefit the most from irrigation schemes and other governmental efforts to increase the country's agricultural output. The Green Revolution, in particular, has been a bonanza for many of them. As a group, they are more business-minded than are the small peasants for whom agriculture tends to be a way of life. The middle class produces chiefly cash crops. Part of the profit they make is invested in farm machinery and other productivity-enhancing inputs. They frequently employ farm hands, at least seasonally. This is a particularly common practice on white-owned farms in countries like Zambia and Zimbabwe.

Most *large landholders* use their land extensively; per hectare investments of capital and labor are rather limited. In effect, their land is underutilized, producing only a fraction of what it could produce. Often they do not reside on their property but instead live in the city (*absenteeism*), where they may have a business and/or are active in politics. Their farms, if we can call them that, are run by managers and most of the work is done by seasonal laborers. The owners can easily obtain credit and take advantage of all kinds of government measures to stimulate agricultural production. Their farms in recent years have become increasingly mechanized and there is a tendency to utilize the land somewhat more intensively than in past years, no matter whether they specialize in crop or livestock production.

Landless wage laborers form the last category. Traditionally their number was very limited, but the past half century or so has witnessed a dramatic increase in the use of farm hands. They are typically a 20th-century phenomenon and their number is still rising. To some degree, they are the victims of rapid population growth and mechanization. But as we have already seen, they are also the innocent victims of other circumstances, such as the ruthless practices of intermediary traders, moneylenders and the landholding elite. To these adverse conditions we may add a host of additional factors, including urban expansion, corruption (by government officials), natural or ecological disasters (e.g., erosion, desertification, soil exhaustion), wars and other political upheavals (refugees), discriminatory legislation (e.g., against Blacks in South Africa), cultural traditions (e.g., the caste system in India which, although now outlawed, makes it almost impossible for 'untouchables' to own land), colonial land policies which have enabled European settlers and large concerns to appropriate large expanses of arable land, thereby causing unfavorable man/land ratios among the indigenous population (e.g., in Kenya, Zimbabwe and much of Latin America), and low prices for commercial crops (almost everywhere in the Third World) resulting in indebtedness and desperation sales of land by small farmers.

Wages tend to be extremely low and work is usually only seasonal. This rural sub-proletariat belongs to the most impoverished of the Third World's inhabitants. Yet, they are better-off than the millions of landless individuals who are unable to find work. Every year, many of the wretchedly destitute starve to death*. At the time of the North-South 'Survival Summit' at Cancún, Mexico (in October 1981), the number of human beings living in absolute poverty was estimated at nearly 1 billion. At that same time, there were approximately 10 million refugees in the Third World.

The role of the agricultural sector in the development process

Developments which have occurred in the rich countries during the past few centuries clearly demonstrate the tremendous importance of a productive agricultural sector and a reasonably prosperous rural population. Almost invariably, these formed the basis on which economic progress was founded. This is not surprising when it is realized that at the moment when a country reaches its take-off stage and enters a period of sustained economic growth, the majority – sometimes, the overwhelming majority – of the people are farmers. According to Rostow (1960), who coined the term 'take-off stage,' Britain reached this crucial point in its economic history around 1802, France and the United States around 1860, Japan around 1900, Canada around 1920 and Mexico around 1955.

By forcing the farmers to pay taxes, a productive and prosperous agricultural sector can play an all-important role as provider of the capital needed for industrialization and infrastructural improvements which, in turn, are likely to have beneficial effects on agricultural output. By exporting part of its surplus production to foreign markets, the agricultural sector can also earn substantial amounts of foreign currency, to be used to pay for imports of expensive capital goods, such as agricultural and industrial machinery. Furthermore, a productive agricultural sector can feed the growing urban population and/or supply upcoming industries with raw materials, thus saving foreign exchange. Lastly, a prosperous farming population can play a critically important role as a market for domestic producers of industrial goods. In brief, the agricultural sector is capable of serving as a springboard for the development of other sectors of the economy. This situation is only possible when the farmers are productive and relatively affluent. If their surpluses are small and their standard of living low, they cannot be the driving force which sets in motion and sustains a period of economic growth.

One of the great tragedies of the Third World is that the agricultural sector is weak and, to make matters worse, is getting weaker. Instead of generating capital, it often consumes capital originating from other capital-starved sectors of the economy or made available by foreign aid donors – usually in the form of loans. In many countries, the agricultural sector does earn foreign exchange, but usually the amounts are insufficient to pay for

---

* At present, there are some 500,000,000 seriously undernourished people in the Third World. Starvation claims approximately 50,000,000 lives annually (FAO, Agriculture Toward 2000).

114

21. Fleeing from famine in the Sahel, 1979. Many rural families migrate to cities, usually ending up in a shantytown or squatter settlement. (WHO/VDO)

the imports needed to push a country past the take-off stage of economic growth. To add to the misfortune, in recent years spreading agricultural stagnation in the Third World – combined with unprecedented rates of population increase – has necessitated massive imports of food which drain the importing countries of their sorely needed foreign currency. Notwithstanding these imports, a growing number of countries experience widespread starvation or occasional famine. Many farmers are not able to produce enough to feed their own families, let alone sell part of their pitiful harvest. And impoverished as they are, most Third World farmers are unimportant as buyers of manufactured goods, thus hampering the development of the secondary sector of the economy. Specifically, the low purchasing power of the rural majority does not allow industrial enterprises to enjoy the advantages of scale economies which come with mass production. Without these advantages, Third World manufacturers easily fall victim to foreign competitors who are able to produce more economically.

Finally, because the rural population is too poor to contribute much to the national treasury (in the form of taxes), the government is often unwilling and/or unable to develop an adequate rural infrastructure and provide the many services needed to make agriculture more productive. In nearly all Third World countries, rural areas are characterized by poor roads, a shortage of schools and health centers, a near-absence of electricity

115

and other energy supplies, no telephones, few physicians and virtually no agricultural extension facilities.

According to Lipton (1977), this situation is partly the result of an *urban bias* – the tendency among national and lower-level governments, political leaders and civil servants, to favor the urban centers at the expense of the countryside. However this may be, the consequence is that the rural population cannot break out of the vicious circle of low productivity → poverty → low productivity. Often, the only thing they can do, driven by utter despair and hunger, is to escape the rural misery and flee to the cities.

The changing nature of the agricultural sector

Because Third World agriculture tends to be characterized by low levels of technology and an emphasis on the production of crops rather than livestock, it is frequently described as traditional. This term is not altogether incorrect, since it does display a number of antiquated features. On the other hand, Third World agriculture, including subsistence farming, has undergone drastic changes as a result of contacts with the affluent industrial countries, or, if you wish, because the Third World has become integrated into the world economic system. In some areas, particularly in parts of Latin America, indigenous agriculture has even been completely wiped out.

Important (structural) changes were set in motion in many areas by the colonial powers when they forced the indigenous population to pay taxes and started to market industrial goods in the colonies, thereby creating new wants and needs among the people. In order to be able to pay the taxes and purchase the imported manufactures, people needed to have money. Often this meant that they decided to devote part of their land to the production of cash crops, a development which was encouraged by a growing demand in Western countries for all kinds of exotic (especially tropical) products, such as pepper, cloves and other spices as well as sugar, indigo, cotton, tea and coffee. The new contacts led to the growth of urban centers and thus to the emergence of domestic markets. As a consequence, agriculture became less purely self-sufficient. Meanwhile, large-scale commercial enterprises, mainly plantations and mining operations, came into existence, requiring fairly large numbers of laborers.

The commercialization of agriculture implies that it has become susceptible to ups and downs in demand on the world market and accompanying price fluctuations. Stated differently: Third World farmers have become dependent on circumstances over which they have no control. In later chapters we will see that this *dependence* can have undesirable, and according to some observers even disastrous, consequences for Third World countries.

Another change which occurred as a result of the Western contacts was the introduction of a wide variety of 'new' crops into the indigenous agricultural ecology. A host of crops that have found a niche in African and

116

Asian agriculture since 1500, were brought over from the Western hemisphere, e.g., tomatoes, corn and various kinds of beans. A Brazilian rubber tree species (*hevea brasiliensis*) was introduced in Malaysia, Indonesia, Sri Lanka and West Africa. Other crops were diffused in the opposite direction from the 'Old' World to the 'New' World, e.g., citrus, rice and soybeans.

Farming techniques have undergone some dramatic modifications as well. New tools and methods – including irrigation – were introduced, especially on European-managed plantations, and subsequently spread to nearby subsistence farmers. More recently, a whole battery of new agricultural methods have been adopted in areas where the Green Revolution has made inroads.

Although these various changes can have certain favorable effects, e.g., greater productivity and increased variety of diet, they often lead to sharper internal disparities between the haves and have-nots. In particular, changes and innovations have a tendency to further aggravate the already hopeless situation in which millions of small landowners, tenants and landless laborers find themselves. For these groups, mere survival has become increasingly uncertain. Clearly, this process of rural-agricultural deterioration – frequently accompanied by sociopolitical disintegration – cannot be labeled 'traditional' either.

Agriculture: problem child of the future

Owing to its many problems and the fact that the majority of the Third World's inhabitants depend on it for a living, the agricultural sector has begun to receive more attention lately. More and more people, both in the Third World and in the West, are becoming alarmed by the realization that, due to explosive population increase, the demand for food is expanding more rapidly than is food production. Because of political upheavals, ecological disasters and other unforeseen setbacks (e.g., delayed land reforms), output of food often is considerably smaller than had been anticipated. Hunger and starvation spread as stockpiles of food continue to dwindle, and massive emergency shipments of foodstuffs are needed at ever shorter intervals in order to avoid mass famine. In the fall of 1981, for example, there was practically no food left in Tanzania, and president Nyerere sent out urgent pleas to the rich countries to donate food in order to avoid catastrophe. Late 1984, virtually all rich countries pitched in to help avert mass starvation in Ethiopia.

Belatedly, it is being realized that indigenous agriculture has been sorely neglected; that for several decades people had been misled by the erring belief that industrialization could and would solve the Third World's grinding poverty. Except in a few Newly Industrializing Countries (NICs), industrial expansion has failed to create sufficient new employment opportunities. In other words, industrialization has not been able to raise income levels in most of the Third World. Neither has it contributed much to improving levels of agricultural productivity. Without doubt, one of the great challenges facing humankind is the problem of how to produce substantially more food while keeping down the prices of foodstuffs. Solving this problem is a task – a moral obligation – which should rank high on our list of priorities, where 'our' refers primarily to that segment of humanity that is so fortunate as to have never gone to bed with an empty stomach.

Theoretically, agricultural production can be expanded. Large areas are still not being utilized or are underutilized. Productivity can be increased almost everywhere through improved tenure conditions, a more equitable land distribution, expanded infrastructural facilities, more irrigation, seed selection, selective breeding, increased fertilization, price controls, credit facilities, etc. Many experts remain convinced that the world can feed a population several times larger than the present one.

On the other hand, efforts to raise agricultural output have not always been successful; sometimes they have been downright disappointing. Thus far, a relatively small proportion of the Third World's farmers has benefited from such efforts, mostly those whose existence was not too problematical to start with. The result is that the poor-rich gap has widened. To make matters worse, exploitation of the poor by the rich has become rampant in much of the Third World, and so has corruption. Famines have plagued humankind from time immemorial but, as far as we know, most of them occurred locally and were separated by fairly long intervals of relative food abundance. Today, emergency shipments of food supplies to famine-stricken areas around the globe are a frightfully common phenomenon. The question is whether we will still be able to do the same in twenty or twenty-five years from now when there will be one billion more mouths to feed.

Paralyzed by economic stagnation, much of the Third World is presently barely able to keep its head above water or, to paraphrase Geertz (1963), it is caught in a situation of 'treading water.' Eventually the people may drown of exhaustion. Will the prosperous countries of the world allow this tragedy to take place?

PART THREE

THE URBAN-INDUSTRIAL SCENE;
CORE-PERIPHERY RELATIONS

Chapter 9   The Secondary Sector

Although some manufacturing is found in the countryside, e.g., tea factories and sugar refineries, most of it is concentrated in and around urban settlements. Manufacturing activities in the Third World are largely concentrated in port cities and capital cities. Often, a country's largest city is its national capital as well as its most important port city, making it the dominant center of political and economic power. Here we find the most influential members of society (the elite), the headquarters of all major industrial concerns, the major banks, the most important educational institutions, and representatives of foreign governments and businesses. If the country has an international airport, it is usually located near this *primate city*. Not infrequently, a major share of all secondary economic activity is found in this one urban center: 30 percent in Accra (Ghana); 35 percent in Lagos (Nigeria); 50 percent in Conakry (Guinea); 62 percent in Dar es Salaam (Tanzania); 75 percent in Freetown (Sierra Leone); 81 percent in Dakar (Senegal); and 100 percent in Banjul (Gambia), Monrovia (Liberia) and Libreville (Gabon).*

Manufacturing: still in its infancy

Far fewer people are employed in the secondary sector of the economy than in primary activities (agriculture, fishing, forestry, etc.). This is true even when construction and mining are included in the secondary sector. In 1978, only eleven Third World countries had more than 30 percent of their adult population employed in secondary activities. Among these were such special cases as the tiny city-states of Singapore and Hong Kong. As for the remainder of the Third World's countries, in about one-third the value was between 20 and 30 percent; in one-third between 10 and 20 percent; and in one-third less than 10 percent. Since these figures pertain to the entire secondary sector – including mining, construction and public utilities – it is clear that the proportion employed in manufacturing is even smaller.

We should realize that many of those belonging to the 'secondary labor force' do not work in large factories but in small workshops or what are called cottage industries. Small enterprises with no more than a dozen employees and a low consumption of energy (few machines) tend to be predominant. Although large factories are few in number, they neverthe-

---

* Source: Mabogunje 1980, p. 167.

less contribute significantly to the secondary sector's share of a country's Gross Domestic Product (GDP).*

Various *indicators* can be used to measure a country's degree of industrialization. For example, we could use manufacturing's contribution to the GDP. Or, we could take the proportion of the working population employed in manufacturing. Because every single indicator has its disadvantage, a number of them can be used in combination, e.g., by means of a so-called *composite index*. In addition to the two indicators already mentioned, energy consumption per capita, steel consumption per capita, and industrial output per capita are often used in order to arrive at an index of industrialization (Table 4).

Table 4. Various indicators used for measuring the degree of industrialization; selected countries.

Indicator	USA	Indonesia	India	Malawi	Brazil	Ecuador
Manufacturing's percentage share of GDP (c. 1981)	23	12	18	13	27	11
Gross industrial output per cap. (c. 1981) in US$	4,281	593	53	46	594	593
Energy consumption per cap. (1980)*	11,626	266	210	59	1,102	629
Industrial exports as % of total exports (c. 1980)	68	2	59	10	39	3

* kilograms of coal equivalent
Source: World Bank, *World Development Report 1983.*

None of these indicators tells us anything about the degree to which the manufactured goods are being purchased (and consumed) by the inhabitants of individual Third World countries. After all, a considerable portion of the total industrial output may be exported, while, at the same time, other manufactured products may be imported. Furthermore, the per capita consumption figures represent averages. Because most Third World countries are characterized by extreme socioeconomic disparities between the impoverished masses and the wealthy few, averages are rather meaningless. The small, affluent minority often consumes a far greater share of total industrial output than does the remainder of the population. Most people, both in the urban areas and in the countryside, lack the means to purchase such basic commodities as footwear and clothes, let alone bicycles, furniture and all kinds of appliances.

* GDP equals GNP plus income earned in the country but sent abroad, minus income earned abroad but sent into the country. GDP tends to exceed GNP in debtor countries, while the reverse tends to be true for creditor countries.

122

No matter how we measure the degree of industrialization, it is clear that Third World countries have very little industry when compared with developed countries. In fact, a low level of industrialization is so characteristic that many observers believe that underdevelopment can be equated with the near-absence of manufacturing. In their opinion, to be developed is the same as being industrialized; development in this light can only be achieved through industrialization.

The above views have been criticized ever since it became clear that there were countries which experienced considerable industrial growth without losing many of the essential characteristics of underdevelopment, such as widespread poverty, illiteracy, starvation, low productivity and glaring inequity. In other words, growth is not the same as development and does not necessarily result in development, which explains the expression 'growth without development.' It has become increasingly apparent during the past two decades that underdevelopment is not the same as low industrial output and, perhaps more important, that underdeveloped is not the same as not-yet-developed.

The view that underdeveloped countries are countries that have not yet been developed was widely held during the 1950s and early 1960s. The so-called 'pre-industrial countries' were simply thought to lag behind; they were believed to be at about the same stage of development that the European countries were just prior to the Industrial Revolution. If only they would follow the example set by the European countries, that is, industrialize (and urbanize), development would come automatically.

A most important point is that the situation underdeveloped countries find themselves in today differs very markedly from the situation the now-developed countries were in about a hundred years ago. The world has not stood still during those hundred years, but has witnessed a great many drastic changes. These developments mean that the not-yet-developed countries of today do not have the same possibilities that the now-developed and industrialized countries had at the dawn of their period of industrialization and urbanization.

When Europe started to develop, most of it was rather sparsely populated (in contrast to countries like India, Bangladesh and Egypt today); population growth was moderate (whereas the Third World now experiences explosive rates of population increase); there still were 'empty spaces' – especially in the Western Hemisphere – where many Europeans could migrate; development and modernization came from within, rather than from without; changes occurred at a slow pace, so that proper adjustments to them could be made; the various developments – political, social, economic, technological, scientific, etc. – all took place more or less simultaneously as progress in one field influenced progress in all other fields. Furthermore, Europe had the advantage of not having to compete with industrially highly developed areas elsewhere in the world.

The process of development in Europa was not only gradual, but also

123

rather harmonious. This is a far cry from the haphazard, fragmentary process of change that has come over the Third World in recent decades. Another contrast is that the Third World countries have become accustomed to a wide variety of sophisticated industrial products, e.g., modern machines, prior to attaining their own industrial infrastructure. Most of these products must be imported and, because they are expensive, have an unfavorable effect on a country's balance of trade.

Despite fairly rapid rates of industrial expansion in the Third World, its share of the world's total output remains lilliputian. With well over half the world's population, it contributes only about 10 percent of the total production of manufactured goods. Considering that many Third World areas are richly endowed with all kinds of natural resources, including energy resources like petroleum and water power potential, this may come as a surprise. By contrast, several developed countries are highly industrialized, even though they have hardly any industrial raw materials. Among these are Denmark and Japan. Also Finland and Switzerland are not well endowed with mineral resources, yet they are highly developed and prosperous.

The structure of manufacturing

Some Third World countries are more industrialized than others. At the upper end of the scale we find countries like Brazil, which supplies 90 percent of its demand for consumer goods and 75 percent of its demand for capital goods. At the lower end of the scale are countries like Niger and Burkina Faso – both landlocked – which have hardly any manufacturing at all.

In general, we can say that most Third World countries do have:
(1) industries which process agricultural and mineral raw materials destined largely for export (often referred to as 'export valorization industries'); and
(2) industries which produce basic consumer goods for the home market.

(1) The processing of agricultural produce tends to be particularly important. These industries have been developed for the purpose of reducing the perishability of agricultural goods and/or the cost of shipping them to overseas markets. Examples are sugar mills, seed crushing mills, canneries, slaughter houses and tanneries. Countries which export minerals, such as copper and bauxite, usually have ore smelters and refineries, again for the purpose of lowering transport costs. Many of these industries are not located in urban centers, but are found near the farms and mines that provide the raw materials.

Since most of these processing industries produce for export, they are not adversely affected by a limited domestic market. And because many of them are foreign-owned, they normally do not suffer from lack of capital. As a result, they tend to be more modern and better equipped than are most enterprises that produce for the domestic market.

124

22. Jute mill in Bangladesh. Jute is the country's major industrial crop, and jute products its leading export. (M. Edwards/VDO)

(2) The second category includes factories producing utensils, tools, textile, clothing, footwear and foodstuffs. Because they cater to the basic needs of the people, their market usually is fairly large, even though the purchasing power of the majority of the population is extremely low. Not infrequently, these industries are protected against foreign competition by tariff barriers. Protection, however, often results in inefficiency or high-cost production as well as in poor quality goods. Sometimes, they produce more than the domestic market can absorb. If this leads to exports, the overcapacity constitutes an advantage, providing the country with badly needed foreign exchange. Overcapacity, on the other hand, can also result in greater inefficiency, expensive subsidy programs and bankruptcies.

In most instances, overcapacity results not so much from insufficient demand as from the fact that a large part of the domestic demand for manufactured goods is supplied by foreign producers. Since the 1950s, many Third World countries have tried to become less dependent on foreign imports by launching so-called *import-substitution* industrialization programs (see pp. 134-135). Apart from the fact that this development policy has failed to make the countries less dependent on the industrialized countries, it has, by offering subsidies and protection, made it profitable for foreign enterprises – especially multinational concerns – to move in and start producing the basic consumer goods previously imported from the developed countries. Competition from these better managed and more

23. Textile mill in Mexico. Most industrial enterprises in the Third World are much smaller, employing only a few workers. (M. Pellanders)

efficient foreign-owned industries means that often only a small portion of the total domestic demand is supplied by factories owned by nationals.

In most underdeveloped countries we find few if any:

(a) Industries producing sophisticated luxury goods, such as washing machines and television sets. The local market is usually still too limited. Due to widespread poverty, there is not much demand for these products, making mass production (with its scale economies) impossible. This means that local producers are unable to compete against large-scale foreign producers. Especially countries with a small total population are faced with this problem, and it so happens that many Third World countries have only a few million inhabitants.

(b) Industries requiring a large number of highly trained workers. For example, because of the lack of sophisticated skills, it is very unlikely to find factories that make computers (although India is an exception in this respect).

(c) Industries which depend on a large number of other industries for supplies of parts and/or materials, that is, industries with many *backward linkages*. An example is the automobile industry. Most of these backward linkages are absent in Third World countries, so that parts and materials must be imported, in which case we are dealing with little more than an assembly industry.

126

(d) Industries which are very capital-intensive, such as the petrochemical industry.

All these industries – (a) through (d) – occur to some extent in the Third World, but usually only in the more populous countries, such as India, Brazil and Mexico, all with rather large domestic markets. Like Taiwan, South Korea and Singapore, they have many highly qualified workers as well as people with advanced technological and managerial skills.

The industrial picture of the Third World clearly is an incomplete one; some branches are missing, while others are not fully developed. The number of inter-industrial linkages, therefore, is limited, not only within a given country but also among the many countries which together make up the Third World. International trade patterns reflect this situation: as a group, the Third World countries trade more with the industrialized countries than they do among themselves, a fact which, according to many observers, means that the Third World countries occupy a dependent position *vis-à-vis* the developed countries.

Industrial productivity
In addition to the weakness or absence of a large number of branches, Third World countries are generally characterized by relatively low levels of industrial productivity. As a consequence, production often is rather expensive, making it difficult to compete successfully with more efficient producers in developed countries. Moreover, the quality of their products and of the services they provide their customers sometimes leaves much to be desired.

In an effort to strengthen the competitive position of their industries, Third World countries frequently resort to protectionist measures, such as import duties on foreign-made goods. Or, they subsidize domestic manufacturers in an attempt to keep down prices. Aside from the fact that such economic policies can be a heavy drain on the national treasury, they have the tendency to encourage even greater inefficiency, poor management, and the production of low-quality goods. Both protectionism and government subsidies carry the danger in them of stifling any incentive and motivation among executives with the result that they no longer do everything they can to produce top quality goods as efficiently as possible.

The low level of productivity is in no small measure a consequence of a shortage of skilled and experienced workers and managers – a situation which reflects the inadequacy of existing educational facilities. To some degree it may also result from *brain drain*, that is, the loss of highly qualified people who have left for greener pastures in countries where wages and salaries are well above those back home. A particularly serious victim of this type of selective out-migration is Sudan, many of whose ablest and best-trained citizens have found employment in the rich oil-producing countries around the Arabian (or Persian) Gulf.

24. Transportation problem in Kenya, East Africa. During the rainy season, many roads in Africa become impassable. (H. de Bruyn/VDO)

Additional factors which adversely affect productivity are: widespread malnourishment among the workers, inadequate infrastructure, poor services, and the absence of an 'industrial heritage' among the overwhelmingly rural population. A limited domestic market may be another reason for the low productivity. Faced with the problem of insufficient demand for their products, factories occasionally operate below capacity.

Manufacturers in most Third World countries repeatedly struggle with such problems as delayed arrivals of spare parts, brown-outs and black-outs, serious transportation and communication problems (e.g., break-downs, impassable roads and port congestion), temporary shortages of supplies, and inadequate maintenance facilities. The machinery is often outdated, either because there is no money to replace it with new and more efficient equipment, or because it was bought secondhand in a developed country.

Sometimes, Western development aid consists of old, written-off, but still functioning, machines. Although it may be argued that secondhand equipment is better than no equipment at all, it does mean that the Third World countries are faced with the problem of not being able to compete effectively with the more developed countries, thus making it extra difficult for them to catch up with the developed countries. Besides, secondhand machines naturally require more maintenance and repairs: precisely one of the most critical bottlenecks in Third World countries where technological know-how, industrial tools, and spare parts are in short supply. It is hardly surprising, then, that lengthy industrial breakdowns are far more common in poor countries than they are in rich countries.

Finally, mention must be made of the fact that factory workers often have to do their jobs under highly unfavorable conditions; in buildings which are poorly ventilated and in which the temperature is either too high or too low. Air pollution, noise, exposed belts and other moving parts, poorly insulated electrical wires, dangerous chemicals, inadequate waste disposal and other hazards claim high accident rates. Proper insurance against injuries or benefit payments are usually not provided by the employer, and most individual workers cannot afford to take out private insurance policies. All in all, working conditions in many factories and workshops are such that they preclude high levels of productivity.

Reasons for the low degree of industrialization

The relative absence of industrial development in the Third World cannot be ascribed to a shortage of available natural resources. Although some countries are indeed poorly endowed, others are not. The largest proven oil reserves are found in the Third World and many countries have enormous hydroelectric potential or are rich in minerals. Agricultural possibilities, too, are quite favorable in a large number of industrially undeveloped countries. Clearly, if all the locally produced raw materials – both agricultural and mineral – were processed in the Third World countries themselves, many of them would have considerable importance as industrial producers.

If we want to understand the low degree of industrialization, we must return to about 1750. At that moment in history, the very first signs of the Industrial Revolution became apparent, which eventually led to the emergence of a modern industrial sector. This development did not take place in what is now known as the Third World, where conditions were far from amenable to large-scale industrial development.

One important drawback to industrial development in the Third World is the relative lack of coal. China is the only Third World country today which possesses large, favorably located, and easily exploitable supplies of coal. But coal is no longer the important source of inanimate energy which it was during the second half of the 18th century and the entire 19th century. The existence of most mineral resources in the Third World, moreover, was not discovered until the 20th century.

The Third World countries also lacked a good infrastructure and suffered a shortage of capital. Technical knowledge was limited and, generally speaking, at a much lower level than in Europe, while population densities often were extremely low. Thus, both the labor force and the market potential were very small and certainly much more restricted than today.

Apart from the fact that the majority of the currently prosperous countries had fewer of these drawbacks, they had the advantage of being the first ones to experience the Industrial Revolution, enabling them to pursue their industrial development without being adversely affected by competition from other parts of the world.

In a sense, Europe's head start was the principal reason for the Third World's late start. While industrialization progressed in Western Europe – and later also in North America – the Third World became increasingly drawn into this process, but in a way which further reduced its chance of becoming industrially developed. Africa, South and Southeast Asia, and Latin America became the suppliers of industrial raw materials and food-stuffs for the rapidly industrializing and urbanizing countries. They also began to play a role, albeit a minor one, as markets for manufactured goods from Europe initially and later also from North America and Japan. In the meantime, many Western countries, especially the United Kingdom, prof-ited greatly from this international trade. Thus, the Third World countries became integrated into a worldwide network of economic relations; their role in this international system being forced upon them by the then-developing countries.

Once this *international division of labor* had come into existence, it was difficult to change it. Instead, it tended to perpetuate itself and so became ever more entrenched, pulling the developed and underdeveloped parts of the world further and further apart, both in terms of average living stan-dards and opportunities to achieve further progress. In most of the Third World, conditions for industrialization became increasingly unfavorable, so that industrial development became virtually impossible.

Attempts by Third World countries to change this course of events were consistently frustrated by the industrialized countries and therefore failed or, at best, resulted in uneconomical production which could not compete against more efficient production in the economically advanced countries. To this fact we must add that nearly all Third World countries were colonies until after World War II. The 'mother countries' usually made sure that no potentially competitive industries would develop in their colonial 'posses-sions.' While exploiting them, the colonial powers took advantage of their dominant position and assigned to their colonies the subservient role of producers of cheap minerals and agricultural commodities. Thus, a world space-economy embracing a dominant 'center' and a dependent 'periphery' came into existence, which has been maintained ever since. Notwithstand-ing the fact that today the old colonial order no longer exists, the world remains characterized by the sharp contrast between a prosperous, in-dustrially developed North and an impoverished, industrially backward South.

Recent attempts at industrialization

The late 20th century has brought about a growing awareness in many Third World countries that they should try to promote industrial develop-ment. During World War I, the interruption of international trade made it clear that they had become highly dependent on the industrialized countries. Between the two World Wars, this awareness of dependence and vulnerability only grew, especially in Latin America, when, as a result of the economic crisis of the 1930s, foreign demand for their raw materials and foodstuffs declined drastically. In a number of Latin American countries, economists and governments became increasingly concerned and began to formulate ideas as to how they could make their countries less dependent on the rich world. Brazil, Argentina and Mexico were particularly active in this respect, and all three arrived at the conclusion that they should stimulate industrialization. They decided they should process their own raw materials and, perhaps more important, reduce their imports of industrial products from Europe and North America.

The Second World War again underlined the Third World's vulnerable position. No less significant were some developments on the political front: serious cracks began to emerge in the until then largely unchallenged colonial structure. In 1947, India and Pakistan achieved political independence, followed by Indonesia two years later. These developments served as eye-openers in the sense that a growing number of people – both in the underdeveloped and developed countries – began to realize how great the differences in development and wealth were. For the first time, people everywhere became aware that there was a so-called 'Third World'; that there were many poverty-stricken, less-developed or underdeveloped countries. And for the first time, underdevelopment was seen *as a problem,* not in the last place because it became increasingly realized that most Third World countries were faced with a virtual population explosion, the likes of which the world had never before experienced. Partly as a result of this unprecedented growth in numbers of people, many countries struggled with a deepening crisis concerning the satisfaction of such *basic needs* as food, firewood, water, shelter, and clothing.

At that same time, industrialization was widely viewed as *the* measure of economic independence and respectability, so that it was advocated and promoted as an important, if not the most important, way to eliminate underdevelopment. Understandably, the post-war years witnessed the emergence of innumerable industrial enterprises, not only in the newly independent countries of Africa and Asia, but particularly in the Latin American countries. This drive toward industrialization was also a response to the rapid increase in population, the massive migration from rural to urban areas, and the rise in unemployment levels in the cities.

The idea that industrialization is necessary to eliminate, or at least alleviate, underdevelopment seems logical when we realize that industrial expansion does offer some important advantages:

(1) It creates employment, not only for the urban population, but also for rural-to-urban migrants who leave the countryside because they cannot find work in the often neglected agricultural sector.

(2) It raises the level of material well-being because the secondary sector

tends to be more productive than agriculture, allowing it to pay higher wages.

(3) Industrial goods have greater marketing possibilities. Hence, industrialization is more likely to stimulate economic growth than does increased agricultural production.

(4) Industrialization usually has favorable effects on other sectors of the economy because it can provide them with productivity-enhancing and labor-saving capital goods.

(5) It can raise the demand for agricultural raw materials (industrial crops, especially) and for all sorts of services, e.g., in the realms of trade, transport, storage, repairs, information, data processing, communication, and insurance.

(6) It makes a country less dependent on imports, which means a saving of foreign exchange. Reduced dependence on foreign products can also be an important advantage in times of an economic crisis or a war.

(7) Industrialization broadens the economic base, thereby making a country less vulnerable. Over the years, demand for agricultural goods has grown more slowly than demand for industrial goods, causing an unfavorable development in the *terms of trade* for countries whose foreign trade is dominated by agricultural exports and industrial imports. For example, today many more tons of rubber must be exported than 25 years ago for the purchase of one tractor. Or, a farmer in Ghana must now produce considerably more cocoa beans than in 1960 in order to earn enough money to buy a bar of Swiss-made chocolate. As long as these trends continue, producers of agricultural commodities will end up in an increasingly perilous situation – they are caught in a special sort of cost-price squeeze. At the same time, by making the economy more diversified, industrialization can contribute to lessening a country's dependence on the export of just one or two commodities.

(8) Industrial development can have a long-lasting influence on the entire society, making it easier for the people to accept, adjust to, or cope with, a host of changes, including the omnifarious and pervasive process of *modernization*, which may be said to consist of "the growth and diffusion of a set of institutions rooted in the transformation of the economy by means of technology" (Berger *et al.* 1974, p. 15).

As pointed out above, too many Third World leaders and Western advisors have come to look upon industrialization as the only way that countries can become developed. This view has resulted in attention being focused almost exclusively on the secondary sector. The consequence has been that agriculture, the rural areas, and thus the majority of the people, became neglected. Many economists and development specialists were convinced that once industry had reached an advanced stage of development, the agricultural sector would follow more or less automatically. This view still exercises considerable influence in a number of countries, which is surprising in view of the fact that many scholars have been warning over and over again that 'genuine' development is unlikely, or even impossible, so

132

long as agriculture is neglected. W.W. Rostow stressed this point in his 1960 bestseller *The Stages of Economic Growth,* pointing out that a productive agricultural sector and prosperous farming population are preconditions for industrial development. "Agriculture must supply expanded food, expanded markets, and an expanded supply of loanable funds to the [industrial] sector" (Rostow 1960, p. 24).

The thought that industrial expansion would irrevocably lead to agricultural development was (and is) a serious miscalculation. Many countries which could feed themselves twenty years ago, today need to import large amounts of food. Rural living conditions have greatly deteriorated while unemployment rates have reached alarmingly high levels, forcing a swelling stream of ruralites to move to the cities. A significant proportion of the rural migrants, however, fails to find employment in the secondary sector and either 'escapes' into the *informal sector* (see chapter 10) or remains unemployed – living in miserable hovels in the rapidly expanding shantytowns.

Some models of industrialization

If a Third World country wishes to industrialize, it must decide which path to follow, i.e., it must choose a particular strategy. In theory, various models are possible, for example, it can start its industrialization process by first building up *basic industries,* such as power plants, blast furnaces, and cement factories. Or, it can begin with the development of industries which produce *capital goods,* such as machines, trucks, and cranes. Another possibility is to give priority to the production of *consumer goods* (e.g., household appliances, clothing, and office furniture) during the early stages of industrialization.

Basic industries produce raw materials, semifinished products, and energy. They are called basic because once they exist, they can function as a basis for the development of a host of other industries. They have many *forward linkages,* meaning that they provide the materials and goods needed as inputs by factories which make finished products. Basic industries have additional advantages. They usually do not require large numbers of skilled workers but only a few highly trained technicians (engineers) who can, if necessary, be attracted from abroad. Further, they are relatively simple in the sense that they have few *backward linkages,* that is, they require a limited number of supplies. Blast furnaces, for example, need little more than iron ore and coal (or some other source of energy); this in sharp contrast to an automobile factory, which requires a great many backward linkages.

Countries which are rich in mineral resources and sources of energy have good opportunities for developing basic industries as a foundation for further industrialization. An important advantage of basic industries is that they make the country less dependent on imports of industrial raw materials and semifinished products, so that in times of war or serious shortages of foreign exchange – the latter possibly resulting from high prices and/or devaluation of the national currency – other branches of the second-ary sector are less likely to be adversely affected.

On the other hand, basic industries also have their disadvantages. They demand enormous capital investments and provide relatively little employment. Besides, they cannot function effectively unless there are other industries which buy their products. If there are not enough customers – that is, forward linkages – in the country itself, part of the output must be sold abroad, or else the basic industries must produce below capacity. Export may be difficult because Third World countries often produce less efficiently or turn out products of lower quality than do the older in-dustrialized countries.

Considering these drawbacks, Third World countries frequently decide to build only certain basic industries, e.g., cement factories and power plants. Generally speaking, only the larger and more populous countries which already have a substantial number of industries producing consumer goods, e.g., Argentina, Brazil, China, and India, have elected to develop a broad array of basic industries.

In the Third World, industries producing *capital goods* have received even less priority than have the basic industries. This is understandable on account of the fact that they require large numbers of highly qualified and experienced workers. No less important is that they – being producers of machines and industrial equipment – cannot prosper unless there are other industrial branches which purchase their products. If there are few such customers, it usually is more economical to import the needed capital goods. Third World countries theoretically could export their surplus of capital goods, but competition from the more highly industrialized coun-tries, in terms of price, quality, and service, is such that penetrating foreign markets is extremely difficult for them.

Considering the disadvantages associated with strategies calling for the development of basic industries or the production of capital goods, we should not be surprised that most Third World countries have emphasized the production of *consumer goods,* not in the last place because there exists a large, and growing demand for them.

Since most consumer goods were imported previously, many countries have adopted an industrialization policy commonly known as *import substitution.* In this model, special emphasis is placed on the production of relatively simple goods that do not require immense investments, compli-cated production techniques and a large pool of highly skilled labor.

According to its advocates, the import-substitution approach would accomplish the following:
(1) Reduce dependence on foreign producers.
(2) Save foreign exchange.
(3) Raise employment opportunities.
(4) By processing domestically produced raw materials, rather than ex-porting them unprocessed, dependence on foreign markets will decrease.

(5) The new industries could possibly export part of their output, thus earning foreign currency.

(6) Industrial wages would raise the purchasing power of the (urban) population and so expand domestic demand for manufactured goods.

(7) Greater demand, in turn, will stimulate increased production, thus allowing manufacturers to benefit from scale-economies.

(8) Greater demand for domestically produced raw materials will increase earnings in the primary sector, especially in mining and agriculture.

(9) Through its favorable effects on technological know-how and industrial skills, import substitution might open up possibilities for subsequent economic development.

(10) By lowering exports of raw materials and imports of manufactured goods, the disadvantages of unequal exchange and agriculture's deteriorating terms of trade will be reduced.

In brief, import-substitution industrialization was believed to be *the* remedy for the problems of underdevelopment; it was expected to contribute significantly to alleviating poverty, unemployment, economic stagnation and, last but not least, reduce dependence on the economically advanced countries.

Problems of recent industrialization

Import substitution, aimed primarily at the production of consumer goods, was easier said than done. If lack of capital was a bottleneck prior to World War II, it was an even greater problem in the post-war period because the industrial production processes which Third World countries wanted to adopt from the more developed countries had become more capital-intensive over the years.

Savings in the Third World usually are insufficient for financing comprehensive industrialization programs. The majority of the population – in the rural areas as well as in the cities – is caught in a vicious circle of poverty: low incomes → no investments → low productivity → small profits → limited savings. Besides, most households are unlikely to invest their savings in industrial projects. The same applies to people who have commercial capital at their disposal; they usually prefer to invest their savings in trade transactions rather than buy long-term industrial stock. And because most Third World countries had so little industry to begin with, there was not enough industrial capital available to sustain a rapid rate of continued industrialization, making it extra difficult to catch up with countries which already possess a high degree of industrialization.

Problems are further aggravated by the fact that the wealthy people generally prefer to invest in land or spend their money on luxury consumption, e.g., sumptuous mansions. If they do invest in industrial enterprises, they frequently do so in the more developed countries, either because they find this safer or because they expect higher returns. If there were a progressive tax structure, the wealthy elite could play an important role in ameliorating the problem of scarce capital, but more often than not the rich use their political power and influence to make sure that they do not have to pay a great deal of tax, or else they know ways – usually through 'connections' – to evade the system.

Another serious problem is the lack of knowledge and experience. In Europe and North America, the gradual process of industrialization in the course of the past 200 years has created a favorable climate for industrial development, a 'human infrastructure' of attitudes and entrepreneurship which serves as the basis on which modern industrial society is founded. Most Third World countries have had no more than a few decades of industrial-technological and industrial-organizational experience, which is hardly enough for building up well-functioning production and distribution systems. The experience, moreover, is often quite limited because management was, and sometimes still is, largely in the hands of foreigners. Many workers are inadequately trained, while highly skilled technicians are in short supply, partly as a result of the brain drain to high-salary countries. Adoption of production processes and organization methods that have been developed in the technologically advanced countries is therefore far from easy. Furthermore, the possibilities for industrial research are totally insufficient, so that Third World countries are unable to keep up with, and adjust to, the latest developments, making it difficult for them to compete successfully with foreign producers.

To solve the problem of not having enough capital, Third World countries have borrowed extensively from the governments of rich countries, from private sources, and from international organizations, such as the World Bank and the International Monetary Fund (IMF). Large sums have also been granted by the rich countries as development aid.

Much of the industrialization, however, has been accomplished in another way, viz., by attracting foreign enterprises. This strategy has an important advantage in that several essential inputs are provided by the foreign entrepreneurs, e.g., capital investments, technical know-how, managerial expertise, and organizational talent. Thus, the Third World country itself need not contribute more than a small part of the total human infrastructure (or social overhead, as it sometimes is called); often only unskilled and semiskilled workers. Partly as a result of this model of industrialization, many Western enterprises have developed into giant multinational or transnational concerns which no longer restrict their activities to one single country.

Another conspicuous aspect of the post-war industrialization process is that in many countries the state (that is, the government) has become an active entrepreneur, either by setting up enterprises with state capital or by participating in semi-state enterprises. The latter often are joint ventures with foreign concerns.

Import-substitution industrialization has been successful in reducing the need to import consumer goods. It has also had a favorable effect on the employment situation and has enabled governments to collect additional revenues through industrial taxation. But at the same time, it has brought forward new problems, and the over-all effects of import substitution have been rather disappointing. Or, perhaps, expectations were too high.

The many loans, patents, and licenses proved to be exceedingly costly and have had disastrous repercussions for the balance of payments of many countries. Trade balances were also adversely affected by imports of raw materials, semifinished products and, particularly, expensive capital goods. As a consequence, foreign exchange reserves often failed to expand, and in some instances declined. Meanwhile, the growing influence of foreign concerns meant that dependence on foreign technology became greater than it had ever been.

Over the years, industrial researchers in the technologically advanced countries have developed capital-intensive, labor-saving production processes, while assuming that cheap raw materials could easily be obtained on the world market. In many Third World countries, these raw materials are not available, and frequently the only input they have to offer is a large supply of unskilled labor. In other words, what they need is *not* highly sophisticated, capital-intensive methods of production, but labor-intensive processes. By importing modern technology, relatively few new jobs are being created.

Although industrial output has increased markedly and manufacturing's contribution to many a country's GDP has experienced a remarkable rise, the proportion of the population employed in the secondary sector has grown less than had been anticipated by proponents of the import-substitution strategy. In fact, few fundamental changes have taken place in the employment structure of most societies, although we should not neglect to mention that industrialization has resulted in the emergence of a small elite (or bourgeoisie) of industrial workers who earn wages well above those in other sectors of the economy, and certainly much higher than the agricultural wages.

Industrialization has for the most part failed to have a stimulating effect on the economy as a whole. Few backward linkages have had a chance to develop within the Third World as many of the needed inputs are still being imported. Much of the profit made by foreign-owned enterprises ends up in the developed countries – or metropoles – instead of being invested in the Third World. Even many domestically owned enterprises do not plow enough of their profits back into the business. As long as investing abroad is (or is thought to be) more profitable, reinvestments can be expected to remain too small to ensure vigorous industrial expansion and future economic viability. In addition, transnational corporations withdraw large sums of money in exchange for the technological and managerial expertise they make available.

All in all, import-substitution industrialization has rarely resulted in balanced economic development. Foreign businesses have operated in a highly selective manner. While investing heavily in profitable branches – in which they often acquired a dominant position – they carefully avoided putting money into less promising branches.

Another undesirable repercussion of the massive 'penetration' by foreign companies is that many a Third World country has lost part of its political independence. In order to protect the interests of these companies, Western countries sometimes interfere either directly or indirectly in the internal political affairs of Third World countries. Not many under-developed countries have been successful at avoiding this outside inter-ference. A notable exception is China, which since about 1960 – when it began to fear Soviet domination – has followed the road of self-reliant development. Prior to that time, China had accepted a great deal of aid from the Soviet Union, but then, sensing that it was becoming too depen-dent, broke off relations and withdrew, so to speak, behind its 'bamboo curtain,' imposing upon itself a high degree of isolation. There are other countries, among them Tanzania, which have made valiant efforts to keep foreign interests and influences at bay, but sooner or later circumstances compelled them to relax their self-reliance approach and call upon foreign businesses or governments to help out with the difficult processes of in-dustrialization and economic-technological modernization.

In recent years, import-substitution industrialization has come to a vir-tual standstill in some countries. The reason is that the most promising industrial branches have been developed, whereas less profitable branches have not. This problem of unbalanced or fragmentary industrial develop-ment is particularly common in countries with only a few million inhabi-tants – of which there are all too many, especially in Africa. But even in more populous countries, the purchasing power of the average citizen usually is so small that the size of the domestic market is too limited to make it economically worthwhile to develop certain industries. People who cannot afford to buy shoes, certainly have no money for tennis rackets, alarm clocks or electric space heaters.

There are other reasons why the domestic market tends to be small. In the absence of a network of all-weather roads, transport costs often are prohibitive, so that a large number of manufactured goods become too expensive for most people. Inasmuch as many industrial enterprises oper-ate below capacity, or for some reason or other do not function very economically, their products frequently are unnecessarily expensive.

Notwithstanding the demographic explosion, demand for manufactured goods has grown less than might have been expected. This is particularly true of countries where the rapid rate of population growth has been accompanied by a decline in the standard of living.

138

Another obstacle to sustained industrialization is the often inadequate infrastructure. Upgrading it is of course extremely costly, especially for large countries with a relatively small or highly dispersed population. If large sums of money are spent on roads, bridges, electrification, communication networks, etc., insufficient means may be left to realize what the development plans call for in the first place, namely, industrialization. Basic industries are often absent or incapable of providing the products and materials which manufacturing enterprises need in order to function properly. And in many instances, a considerable proportion of a country's foreign exchange must be spent on imports of food and agricultural raw materials because the agricultural sector is not productive enough to satisfy the country's demand for agricultural goods.

The import-substitution model of development frequently exacerbates the already wretched conditions in the rural areas by discriminating against the agricultural sector. By protecting the new industries – via high tariff walls and/or subsidies – manufactured goods tend to be priced too high when compared with agricultural commodities. At the same time, rural wages are considerably lower than urban-industrial wages, partly because of deliberate government efforts to keep food prices as low as possible. Thus, farmers pay high prices for industrial goods while receiving low prices for their crops. Quite correctly, Mabogunje (1980, pp. 162-3) speaks of a "situation of [internal] *unequal exchange*," pointing out that this "progressively aggravates the disparity in real income between the rural and urban areas of the country, and in turn, stimulates the growing [rural to-urban] exodus . . ." Also, because the *terms of trade* between the rural and urban areas generally are biased against the former, import-substitution industrialization has accelerated the rate of capital transfer from the rural to the urban areas, thereby intensifying the pauperization of the rural-agricultural population (Mabogunje 1980, p. 90).

In short, by penalizing the rural-agricultural sector, the import-substitution strategy discourages agricultural expansion and robs the countryside of many of its young and more ambitious people. It also contributes to a much too rapid rate of urbanization, resulting in masses of unemployed and uprooted people living in squalid shantytowns.

Despite the fact that already in the early 1960s many observers – especially Latin American economists – began to question, or even denounce, the import-substitution model of development, it still is the dominant strategy in much of the Third World. This being so, it is hardly realistic to expect that many underdeveloped countries will make much progress in the foreseeable future and join the small group of NICs (Taiwan, South Korea, etc.) which have successfully moved beyond import substitution to export-oriented industrialization.

Export-oriented industrialization

The problem of a small domestic market can be partly overcome by producing for export. To do this successfully, it is essential that the export products can compete on the international market. For reasons already discussed, most Third World countries are unable to produce high-quality goods. And when they *are* capable of producing low-priced goods of reasonable quality, they often find it difficult to capture a corner of the world market. The more highly industrialized countries, interested as they are in protecting their own industries and employment opportunities, frequently erect tariff barriers or employ import restrictions (quotas, duties) to keep out cheap foreign products. These measures help explain why the number of Third World countries which have been successful at promoting *export substitution* – the so-called NICs – is still very small.

In various parts of the Third World, groups of neighboring countries have organized *common markets* for the purpose of enlarging the limited national markets and enhancing economic cooperation, e.g., by pooling natural and human resources. Examples are the Caribbean Free Trade Association (CARIFTA), which later became the Caribbean Community (CARICOM), the Andean Common Market, and the now defunct East African Economic Community (Kenya, Tanzania, Uganda). Thus far, the results have been disappointing. Most Third World countries have approximately the same economic possibilities and the same problems, making meaningful economic integration and a functional division of labor very problematic. Besides, the smaller, weaker members of such regional economic communities are understandably concerned about becoming dominated, and perhaps disadvantaged, by their larger and economically stronger partners. The consequence may be a 'sub-imperialistic' dependency relationship – e.g., between landlocked Burkina Faso and Ivory Coast – which is to the detriment of one country and to the advantage of another.

The above problems notwithstanding, there has been an appreciable increase in export-oriented industries. Most are partly or wholly owned by foreigners who have been attracted by the very low wages that Third World countries have to offer. Also important are the tax exemptions and other financial benefits allowed by certain countries in an attempt to promote industrial growth. Some countries even have established special free-trade zones – usually in port cities, such as Dakar, Senegal – for the purpose of attracting foreign industrial investment.

A factor which has acquired importance in recent years is the general absence of pollution-control legislation and stringent safety regulations in Third World countries. In the developed countries, polluting industries (e.g., aluminum refineries, pulp and paper mills, and chemical industries) are required to make increasingly expensive investments in order to comply with a host of environmental protection and worker-safety regulations. As a result, production costs have become so prohibitive in some branches of

140

industry that factories either have to close down or move to Third World locations. Although the governments of most underindustrialized countries seem to be aware of the dangers of industrial pollution, they are so keen on raising industrial activity and creating new jobs that they are willing, even anxious, to grant polluting industries permission to locate within their borders. This is particularly true of labor-intensive industries, including textile mills and factories producing artificial fibers, both of which cause considerable water and air pollution.

For the purposes of advancing the New International Economic Order (NIEO), various rich countries have taken steps to encourage labor-intensive industries to move to low-wage Third World countries. International development organizations, such as the World Bank, also have made their contributions in this respect. Several Third World countries, especially Hong Kong, Singapore, Taiwan, South Korea, Malaysia, Mexico and Tunisia, have taken advantage of this policy by offering the necessary infrastructural facilities, but, unfortunately, also by restricting the power of labor unions. As a result, these states have experienced an impressive increase in the number of labor-intensive, export-oriented industries, with a total of well over 1 million employees. Particularly important are leather goods industries, textile mills, and factories producing electronic equipment. Although there are exceptions, the majority of these industries do not require large numbers of highly skilled workers.

Foreign enterprises either construct the required buildings themselves or rent already existing facilities. Sometimes, they also build water supply systems, power stations, and service roads. As a rule, they import all the machinery and other capital goods needed. This means that production takes place in a modern, efficient way, thus combining the advantages of mechanization with that of low wages. Sometimes raw materials and other inputs are produced locally, but in many instances they too are imported. In the latter case, the host country only provides very few inputs – often only the unskilled labor force.

For the sake of protecting already existing, domestically owned industries, the foreign 'guest industries' are often not allowed to produce for the home market – only for export. Thus, the entire output is shipped out of the country, usually with the same ships or planes that bring in the raw materials and semifinished goods. Under those circumstances, the foreign enterprises are little more than economic *enclaves* – not unlike the foreign-owned and foreign-managed plantations – with few forward and backward linkages with other sectors of the local or regional economy. Because of their enclave nature, these industries are referred to as being 'footloose.' Looking at them from the industrialized countries' point of view, they may be called 'runaway industries,' that is, industries which have fled the high wages, social security premiums, labor unions and stringent environmental-protection controls in their countries of origin.

A large number of examples of *runaway industries* can be found in northern Mexico. Since 1961, the Mexican government has put into effect a National Boundary Development Program, whose principal objective it is to expand industrial employment opportunities for the rapidly growing population in the border area. In order to stimulate industrial growth, the Government has improved the physical infrastructure and developed completely serviced industrial sites. Special measures have been taken to facilitate imports and exports across the U.S. border. Foreign enterprises wanting to locate in northern Mexico are required to pay wages that are well above the minimum wage and can only employ people who are jobless. All products must be exported to countries other than those that belong to the Latin American Free Trade Association (LAFTA), of which Mexico is a member.

U.S. enterprises have found it very attractive to locate branch plants in the Mexican border zone. Although the wages they have to pay are higher than in Asia and Puerto Rico, they are some 25 percent lower than those in the U.S. Nearness to the U.S. means that the costs of transporting raw materials to the factories and manufactured products to U.S. markets are relatively low. Top executives also can visit plants in northern Mexico more easily than those in distant countries like Taiwan and Malaysia. Many U.S. firms with operations in northern Mexico have their headquarters in a city just north of the boundary. Frequently, the more capital-intensive manufacturing processes are also situated there. An added advantage is Mexico's political stability, making it a relatively safe place for long-term investments.

For Mexico, the principal advantages are: jobs, industrial experience and revenues in the form of value added taxes. In 1978 alone, more than 400 new factories started operations, together employing some 75,000 workers. Particularly important are various assembly activities and the production of textiles, apparel, leather goods, and plastic products.

Other countries with many foreign industrial enterprises are Hong Kong, Taiwan, South Korea, Singapore, and Malaysia. Most of these industries are owned by U.S. and Japanese concerns, but also European companies have made large investments. Although foreign-owned industries are most common in the dozen or so NICs – virtually all located in Southeast Asia and Latin America – they can be found in every Third World country except for a few communist countries, such as Cuba and Mongolia.

It should be clear that foreign-owned, export-oriented industries have some disadvantages for the countries in which they are located. Apart from making them highly dependent on the more developed countries, there looms the danger that they close down or move out when other Third World countries offer greater economic advantages, such as lower wages, thereby allowing for better returns on investments. Because of cut-throat competition within the capitalist system, *footloose* capitalist enterprises are quick to adjust to changing economic circumstances and new opportunities, i.e., moving from low-profit, high-risk areas to high-profit, low-risk places.

142

Another disadvantage, as we have already seen, is that foreign-owned export industries do not produce many *multiplier effects*. Being economic enclaves, they normally fail to stimulate the regional or national economy. Most inputs come from abroad, including many services. If only part of the total manufacturing process takes place in the Third World country, which often happens, the skills learned tend to be quite limited. Virtually all key activitities, including research, management, and production planning, remain in the hands of foreign decision makers or are centered in the headquarters in the rich, industrialized countries. It is especially these latter activities which Third World countries need so desperately for their development.

There are other disadvantages. Wages must be rather low in order to guarantee that export-oriented industries can compete on the international market. A greater handicap is that much of the profit leaves the country and that most of the better-paid employees spend their income abroad. This constant outflow of capital (or *surplus extraction*) means not only that domestic purchasing power does not expand much, but also that insufficient capital is available for subsequent industrial investment. In other words, for its economic expansion and modernization the country remains dependent on foreign sources of capital.

Despite these drawbacks, export-oriented industrialization appears to be a successful approach for a limited number of small states, e.g., Singapore and Hong Kong. For most other Third World countries, however, it cannot possibly solve the problem of economic underdevelopment.

The spatial distribution of manufacturing

The industrial geography of many Third World countries is characterized by a high degree of concentration in a very small number of locations, normally the capital city and one or two other urban centers. In Uruguay, almost all manufacturing is found in and around Montevideo, and in Peru over two-thirds occurs in or near Lima. Greater São Paulo dominates the spatial pattern of manufacturing in Brazil, having more industry than the Netherlands. Similar patterns of spatial concentration exist in Tunisia, Tanzania, Ghana and many other Third World countries. The reason for this high degree of *localization* is that in most underdeveloped countries only a limited number of areas possess the infrastructural requirements needed to make industrial production possible.

The large cities and their immediate surroundings usually constitute the largest and most accessible markets. Not only do they have many inhabitants, but income levels are higher than elsewhere in the country. The primate capital cities, in particular, have more than their fair share of high-salaried foreign and government officials, industrialists, senior executives, physicians, educators, and other professionals.

Another advantage of the larger cities is that they are the only places in which semiskilled and skilled laborers are available. Due to the massive

143

rural-to-urban migration, there also is a large supply of unskilled workers that far exceeds the demand. While industrial enterprises take advantage of this pool of cheap labor, governments often are interested in promoting industrialization in an attempt to hold down unemployment and social unrest in the large cities.

Most big cities compare favorably with smaller urban centers in terms of the quality and quantity of services and infrastructural provisions. Connections with other major cities as well as with overseas suppliers and markets tend to be reasonably good. In addition to trade facilities, the larger cities offer industrial entrepreneurs a wide variety of other important advantages, including banking facilities, a nearby airport, availability of electricity, a water supply system, sewerage, and telephone service. In the event one or more of these basic services are inadequate, they can be expanded or improved more easily and cheaply there than in most other, more remote, parts of the country.

Large cities offer *agglomeration advantages*. Once a few industries are present, they help to make an urban place more attractive for other industrial enterprises by supplying the latter with inputs or by buying their products. Such local industrial linkages are crucially important in the Third World, more so than in the industrialized countries. In view of the rather poorly developed transportation and communication systems in most Third World countries, proximity to industrial suppliers and customers can mean the difference between whether or not a certain enterprise can produce economically, withstand foreign competition, and make enough profit to enable it to make the reinvestments necessary to keep up its efficiency and competitive position or to expand its operations and enjoy scale-economies.

Finally, we wish to draw attention to the fact that capital cities offer specific advantages not to be found in other places. We are referring to the presence of a host of governmental institutions and related agencies, making 'bureaucratic circuits' there shorter than elsewhere in the country. As a result, long delays (in obtaining permits, financial support, etc.) are less likely to interfere with the proper functioning of the economy. Besides, proximity to government officials and decision makers allows for high-level personal contacts that can be extremely advantageous for ambitious manufacturers who are determined to stay ahead of competitors by continuously making adjustments to new developments and by adopting the latest industrial innovations.

Summarizing the above, we conclude that circumstances are such that industrialization in Third World countries is highly concentrated in one or two locales. The result is a pattern of extreme spatial polarization, in which a small number of economically dynamic urban centers contrast with many smaller towns and vast rural areas which experience economic stagnation or even decline. Often neglected by the government or disadvantaged by development policies, agriculture deteriorates, unemployment rises, stan-

144

dards of living decline and many farmers become marginalized. With rural poverty becoming more intense, many people decide to leave the countryside and head for the larger cities, thus reinforcing the processes of uneven spatial concentration and polarization.

Many observers see the emergence of this center-periphery pattern as a highly undesirable development which should be reversed as soon as possible. They regard the too rapidly growing urban core areas, and especially the primate cities, as parasites which systematically and relentlessly drain the rural areas of their livelihood in much the same way that former colonial powers exploited their colonial possessions. In both cases we are confronted with a dominance-dependence relationship in which enrichment of the dominant core is dialectically associated with impoverishment of the subservient periphery. The result is extreme disparity, not only socioeconomic disparity characterized by a small wealthy elite and large masses of pariahs for whom the future holds little in store, but also spatial disparity whereby the development of one region is causally related to the underdevelopment of another region.

Brazil's greatest inferno

A vivid description of an example of *unequal development* appeared in *Newsweek Magazine*, May 17, 1982. Under the headline "The Brazilian Powerhouse," the following portrayal was given of São Paulo:

From the air, it is a tangle of broad expressways, glossy skyscrapers and shimmering lights; on the ground, it is a hopeless maze of congestion and smog. São Paulo, Brazil's largest city, seems at once to enchant and offend. Two modern subway lines define the city's limits – and limitations. One line runs north beneath the miles of factories and south past the polished mansions of the rich. The other is pushing west toward the one-family homes of the middle class, and east to the squalid slums of the migrant poor . . . "I can think of no other place in the Western world," says Brazilian Sen. André Franco Montoro, "where the gap between rich and poor is greater than it is here."

. . . Once a tiny coffee-processing village straddling the Tropic of Capricorn, the city now houses South America's biggest industrial park and one of the Third World's largest concentrations of multinationals. São Paulo – the city and its surrounding state – contributes half of Brazil's tax revenues, produces two-thirds of the nation's manufactured exports and shelters the majority of Brazil's Fortune 500-size companies. In fact, São Paulo generates so much economic activity that its projected output for 1982 is a stunning $110 billion – a figure that would give it the seventeenth largest gross national product in the world. "Let's face it," says one businessman, "São Paulo is very, very First World."

Like any First World city, São Paulo suffers the tensions of a population whose rich get richer and whose poor barely get by. "Vigorous growth has translated into a widening gap between the opulence of a few and the difficulties of many," says Cardinal Paulo Evaristo Arns . . . Only 30 percent of Greater São Paulo's population have access to sewage systems; the infant mortality rate is high, and tens of thousands of hungry urchins roam the streets. Almost 12 percent of São Paulo's work force are jobless, and frustration is mounting visibly in the mosquito- and rat-infested squatters' slums. Yet what began in the 1920s as a trickle of migrants from the northeast region of Brazil has become a tidal wave in the last two decades. Today, the city population is 9 million, with another 8 million jamming the suburbs – and new migrants arrive at a rate of 1,000 per day. As a result, São Paulo faces the prospect of becoming the world's second largest city . . .

. . . Paulistas are also the wealthiest people in Latin America, with an annual per capita income of $4,000 – more than twice that of the average Brazilian. They buy half of all consumer goods purchased in Brazil, consume 40 percent of the electricity, drive more than 40 percent of the cars, and talk on one-quarter of the nation's telephones . . .

For the urban poor, however, São Paulo can be Brazil's greatest inferno. The biggest problem is overcrowding. Brazilian officials have tried to dam the wave of urban migrants by offering tax incentives and bonuses to companies willing to set up shop in the Amazon and Northeast. But these efforts to halt the amoeba-like multiplication of urban ghettos have proven largely futile . . .

The darkest side of São Paulo can be found in the *favelas* – the squatters' slums on the city's periphery. Many of the residents are jobless migrants. They have little hope of finding steady work, and their children usually suffer from malnutrition. According to church estimates, one-third of the São Paulo population lives at or below the $75 per month minimum subsistence level. Home in these squalid slums usually means either a makeshift wooden shack with no electricity or plumbing, or a patch of mud under a bridge. Unable to afford the average $150 monthly rent for a standard one-family dwelling, São Paulo's poor live in constant fear of harassment and eviction by the notoriously intolerant Paulista police.

Life in the *favelas* invariably means life on the run – and the offspring of these fetid ghettos develop shrewd street instincts early on . . . Many are from fatherless homes, taking to the streets for sheer survival between bouts in juvenile facilities. They run in small packs, committing petty crimes to obtain food. One of São Paulo's greatest blights is a three-block area near the downtown Hilton Hotel called "Boca de Lixo" – literally, "garbage mouth." There, pimps sell young boys between the ages of 9 and 13 for an hour of pleasure. Many of the boys take hormone treatment to become more feminine. Some dream of becoming trans-sexuals; most dream of escape.

The broad gulf between São Paulo's very rich and very poor breeds a social tension that often finds release in violence . . . Although police statistics are admittedly incomplete, Paulistas say that crime is on the rise. Middle- and upper-class homes are frequently burglarized, and street crimes are as commonplace as the sidewalk vendors who sell fried corn-bread stuffed with peppered shrimp. Tired of the slow response by the police, Paulistas frequently take the law into their own hands. Spontaneous lynchings occur regularly along the area's darker streets. Urchins carry guns and knives – and most mansions have at least one weapon locked for safe-keeping in the household vault . . .

Newsweek, May 17, 1982, pp. 50-53.

Cities would not have such a dominant position in the space-economy if the governments of Third World countries had pursued a policy of decentralization and had promoted industrialization in smaller urban centers scattered throughout the country. Spatial economists and geographers have suggested that Third World countries should make efforts to bring about a Christaller-type pattern of 'central places,' so as to make possible a more even distribution of economic development (see box).

Thus far, such suggestions have received little attention or have not yet led to the formulation, and much less the implementation, of concrete policies. This is not so surprising because decentralization has serious disadvantages. Providers of capital (e.g., local or foreign banks) as well as entrepreneurs are generally interested in profit maximization; they are in business to make money, rather than to develop countries or foster spatially balanced economic growth. This means that they are interested in establishing factories in the most economically favorable locations, that is, in cities with good transportation links and other infrastructural facilities. Invariably, these are large cities or port cities.

Christaller's central-place theory

In 1933, the German geographer Walter Christaller published *Central Places in Southern Germany,* in which he presented a theory about the number, distribution and size of towns. He first simplified the complexity of reality by formulating some assumptions: (1) there are no environmental differences (e.g., there are no rivers and the land is perfectly flat), (2) rural population is evenly distributed, (3) everyone has the same income, (4) each person can travel in every direction, and (5) travel costs per kilometer are the same everywhere. Christaller further assumed that towns act as *central places* for the surrounding countryside (6), and that each person desiring a service or good in a town seeks to minimize traveling expenses, that is, goes to the nearest town (7).

On the basis of these assumptions he concluded that each central place is surrounded by a *hexagonal service area* (also called hinterland, umland or trade area), that all service areas have the same size, and that all central places are of equal size and located at equal distances from one another (Fig. 11a). In reality, however, urban places vary in size from small hamlets to large cities, and *central-place functions* vary in that some are used more frequently than others. For example, a grocery store is visited more often than a jewelry store. Every hamlet has a grocery store, but only larger places have one or more jewelry stores. Thus, hamlets have few central-place functions, the so-called *lower-order functions,* while cities have a great variety of activities; in addition to lower-order functions they have *higher-order functions.*

To draw enough customers, higher-order functions must be spaced far apart, or, serve large hinterlands. Since they are found only in larger

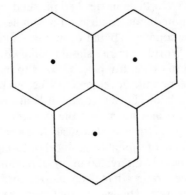

Fig. 11a. Three hypothetical central places with hexagonal service areas.

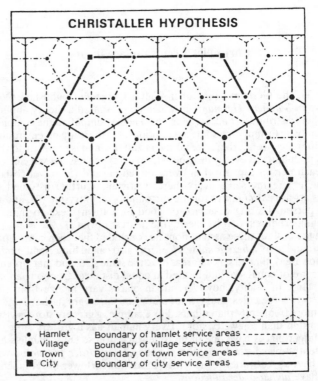

Fig. 11b. Hierarchy of hypothetical central places with their service areas.
Source: J.H. Johnson, *Urban Geography; An Introductory Analysis*, 1972, p. 102.

urban places, the number of such *higher-order central places* is much smaller than the number of *lower-order central places*. Obviously, then, higher-order places are spaced further apart than lower-order places. But because of Christaller's assumptions, they, too, are evenly distributed and have (equally large) hexagonal service areas. As Fig. 11b shows, *higher-order service areas* contain a number of small central places, each with its own *lower-order service area.*

Summarizing the above, we conclude that we are dealing with a *hierarchical* spatial structure of central places and service areas, based on a hierarchy of urban functions. At the top of the *urban hierarchy* we find the highest-order city with many specialized functions (e.g., international airport, university and government) which may serve an entire country, while at the bottom there are a great many tiny central places with few (unspecialized) functions serving small rural hinterlands.

Whereas the hypothetical picture sketched here is characterized by perfect spatial regularity, in real-world situations the pattern, of course, is much less regular. Nevertheless, the general validity of Christaller's theory is borne out on the landscape, especially in the more developed countries. Since the Christaller pattern can be said to be a rational organization of economic space in which no person or enterprise is too far removed from any low-, medium- or high-order urban function, under-developed countries might be well advised to try to steer urban development in such a way that the distribution of small, medium-size and large central places approximates the Christaller pattern.

As we will see in a later section, many underdeveloped countries have an overabundance of villages and hamlets, not enough medium-size towns (or regional market centers), and one exceedingly large primate city. In other words, they have a highly irregular urban hierarchy, and what is more, a very irregular spatial pattern of service areas. Often, there are too many very small service areas and too few of medium-size. Such an unbalanced spatial structure is a detriment to economic development because large parts of the country lack easy access to the medium- and higher-order urban services needed to maintain high levels of productivity. Generally speaking, regions which do not have the right mix of central-place services are characterized by underutilization of human and natural resources.

For many enterprises in the Third World it is absolutely essential that they can enjoy the advantages of being located in a big city, otherwise they would not be able to compete successfully with foreign producers. A vigorous decentralization policy could easily scare off foreign investors and/or result in fatal diseconomies, bankruptcies, and a concomitant loss of jobs. We should also keep in mind that decentralization is easier said than done – even in developed countries – if only because it is very costly. The building of roads and railroads as well as the provision and maintenance of other infrastructural facilities – just for the sake of dispersing industrial activity – cost more than the majority of underdeveloped countries can afford. For the time being, it seems wiser that they attract industrial activity and create jobs than worry about future disadvantages of uneven industrial development.

In other words, efficiency now should weigh heavier than spatial inequity later. This is the conclusion many capitalist observers have arrived at, hoping that a more equitable distribution will come about at a later stage. Radicals tend to disagree with this view. They point out that the decline in spatial inequality that has occurred in many industrialized countries (Williamson 1965), and which some people expect will eventually take place more or less automatically in the Third World countries, is highly unlikely to occur unless strongly promoted by the government. Since they see spatial inequality as one of the foremost problems of underdevelopment, they are inclined to give more weight to equity, decentralization, and redistribution than to capitalist efficiency and profit maximization.

In this context, radical geographers and political economists have often cited the Chinese model of development with its emphasis on rural industrialization and self-sufficient agricultural communes as the example that Third World countries should follow. However, radicals have not explained how smaller and less densely populated countries, with less diversity in their resource endowment, should go about adopting communist China's approach to decentralized development – which, by the way, has turned out to be less successful than was once believed. Clearly, countries like Angola and Sudan cannot be compared with China. In virtually every respect, no matter whether we consider their history, culture, agricultural know-how, trade relations, ethnic composition, or geographical situation, they differ so fundamentally from China that efforts to imitate the Chinese model might well do more harm than good. In a similar vein, the Soviet model of development (with its early emphasis on basic industries) is also unlikely to be a useful model for Third World countries. We do not mean that they would do well to follow the examples set by the United Kingdom, Denmark, Japan, or even Taiwan. Not only are all countries different, having unique possibilities and limitations, but, as we have already seen, the situation in which the underdeveloped countries find themselves today differs significantly from the situation in which the now-developed countries found themselves during the early days of the Industrial Revolution.

In recent years, some of the more industrialized countries in the Third World, e.g., Argentina, Brazil and Mexico, have come to realize that it is high time to stimulate industrial decentralization. Increasingly, dispersion is being advocated in order to halt the rapid expansion of the largest cities. Many of them already are so huge that living conditions have become almost intolerable, plagued as they are by daily traffic congestion and intense air pollution. Public utilities and services are totally inadequate to cater to the needs of the millions of inhabitants and the ever growing number of industries. A growing proportion of the population, moreover, must commute over exceedingly long distances to get to their jobs.

At the same time, other parts of the country remain virtually inaccessible, empty and unproductive. Owing to the pull of the big cities, the sparsely populated rural areas sometimes become even more stagnant than they already are.

Official, government-formulated decentralization policy is often considered the only method that could possibly stem this tide of increasing regional imbalance. Various efforts have been made to accomplish this, but so far most of them have met with little success. The problem is that once a given region has acquired economic dominance, it has so many advantages over other regions that it is likely to stay ahead and further strengthen its dominant position. And paradoxically, its dominance may become greater *because of* measures aimed at decentralization. For example, if economic growth in secondary centers takes place in the form of subsidiaries belonging to corporations which have their headquarters in the primate city, is financed by banks located in the major industrial region, or in any other way is dependent on inputs coming from the dominant core region, much of the profit produced in these smaller *growth poles* can be expected to flow to the decision-making primate city or leading industrial region. If that is the case, we are dealing with a form of *internal colonialism* whereby the dominant 'metropole' siphons off surplus value from the dependent 'satellites.' Although such an exploitative core-periphery relationship can never be the objective of decentralization policies, it may well result from them, with the consequence that spatial inequality within a country does not diminish, but, instead, becomes more intensified. An additional disadvantage of *dependent* development in the smaller urban centers – especially when it consists of subsidiary establishments – is that it can lead to grave unemployment problems in times of economic recession. The reason being that when parent companies are forced to cut back production, they are likely to first close down their branch plants.

Conclusion

Prior to World II, there was very little manufacturing in the Third World. Only a few Latin American countries, India, South Africa, and one or two other states could boast limited industrial development. It was not until after 1960 – when most countries in Africa and southern Asia had gained their independence – that industrial growth made its first halting appearance in most other underdeveloped countries. Much of this initial import-substitution industrialization was concentrated in a relatively small number of cities. As a consequence, these cities have experienced a phenomenal increase in population.

Since industrial development has been decidedly one-sided, often dominated by production of luxury goods for the wealthy few, it seems desirable that in the coming years many Third World countries make determined efforts to promote a more balanced pattern of industrialization. Some sectors, especially labor-intensive industries producing goods for which there is a great demand among the large majority of the still overwhelmingly rural population, should receive far more attention than they thus far have. Because industrialization and modernization have caused extreme regional differences in employment opportunities and living standards, it would seem imperative that governments formulate policies aimed at reducing these spatial inequalities. For many countries this will mean that agricultural production, rather than manufacturing, is given priority treatment. As Rostow (1960) has pointed out: without a relatively prosperous and productive agricultural sector – capable of feeding the entire population, of providing industrial crops to be processed locally and perhaps even of producing a surplus for export (thereby earning much-needed foreign exchange) – it would seem impossible to sustain a long-term process of balanced development.

Meanwhile, efforts must be made to develop and take better advantage of locally available natural resources, such as soils, minerals, and water power. Attention must also be paid to developing an adequate infrastructure: roads, railroads, schools, hospitals, family planning facilities, public utilities, and a host of other services. The experiences of Japan (since 1869), Taiwan, Cuba and China could well serve as examples from which Third World countries can learn a great deal – probably more than they can learn from Western Europe which, because of its earlier development, was able to progress in a way which is not open to the Third World. Better yet, instead of adopting some foreign development model, each under-developed country would do well to develop its own individual model, based on intensive utilization of locally available human and natural resources. Important objectives should be: reduction of unemployment; increasing income levels; expansion of domestic demand for locally manufactured goods; improvement of the trade balance by exporting *processed* raw materials; and promotion of over-all productivity. At the same time, foreign investment should be kept within bounds and external dependence avoided or reduced as much as is feasible. In the event Third World countries have no alternative but to attract foreign capital, they should do everything they can to limit the disadvantages thereof, e.g., by establishing joint ventures, so that decision making is controlled less by foreigners.

Lastly, if corruptive practices are widespread, it is absolutely essential that every effort be made to wipe out this malignancy in the shortest possible time. No matter how richly endowed a country may be with natural resources, even the best development strategies are doomed to failure as long as the scourge of corruption is not eliminated (see chapter 15).

Chapter 10   The tertiary sector

A sector characterized by growth and diversity

Not only the primary and secondary sectors of the economy display the typical features of underdevelopment, but so does the tertiary sector.

Prior to the Age of Discoveries (note the evidence of Eurocentrism!) the division of labor was limited in most non-Western societies. Except for countries like China, tertiary activities did not gain significance until after Europeans had established more or less permanent contacts with these societies. Several factors played a role. One was that the colonial powers promoted in their overseas territories the production of primary goods for export. Together with the import of manufactured goods from Europe, this export of agricultural products and raw materials meant an increase in trade and transport activities. A second factor was that the Europeans exacted taxes from the indigenous population, thus forcing many people to work for them – mainly on plantations or in mines – or to grow cash crops which they could sell to European traders. These developments, together with the establishment of colonial administrative systems, led to an increase in tertiary activities.

The tertiary sector has continued to increase its share of the total labor force. During the past few decades, there even has been a notable accelera-tion, especially in the urban areas. With the employment opportunities in the secondary sector being insufficient to meet the demand for jobs, many urbanites – including countless migrants from surrounding rural areas – must of necessity try to find work in the tertiary sector.

In Third World cities, usually a distinction is made between *formal* and *informal* tertiary activities. Formal activities include modern services per-formed by banks, insurance companies, rental services, wholesaling and retailing outlets, hospitals, educational institutions, and all kinds of govern-ment agencies. These 'firm-centered' services are common in the developed countries with their relatively high standards of living. In the Third World they are much less important and employ only a small propor-tion of the urban population.

Far more important in terms of total employment is what Geertz (1963) calls the 'bazaar economy': a wide variety of small-scale, marginal activities and services, more commonly referred to as the *informal sector* (Hart 1973). The term 'informal' originally indicated that the people who find work in this sector are not licensed and their 'businesses' are not officially registered. Many are self-employed, practice their 'trade' illegally and pay no income tax. In fact, we might say that most of them do not officially have a job but simply keep themselves busy, at least part of the time, performing all sorts of small tasks for little money. Theirs are by and large labor-

25. Rickshaw driver and sidewalk vendors in Calcutta, India. The informal sector is an overcrowded sector. (VDO)

intensive operations requiring very little if any investment. Productivity tends to be low and working hours irregular. Included are peddlers, street vendors, hawkers, market women, retailers, rickshaw drivers, wood carvers, taxi drivers, servants, car washers, porters, night watchmen, shoeshine boys, sidewalk tailors, errand boys, cleaning ladies, (illegal) beer brewers, laundry women, and all kinds of repairmen. Some make a living as beggars, petty criminals (e.g., pickpockets and shoplifters), smugglers, drug dealers, prostitutes, fortune tellers, or witch doctors (quacks).

McGee (1971) has used the term *proto-proletariat* to refer to all the people who 'get by' in the informal sector. Also 'refuge sector,' 'unorganized reserve army' and 'lumpen proletariat' have been used in this context. The latter term is of German origin and refers to the dispossessed and uprooted who have no regular work and are dressed in rags (= lumpen). In their excellent article on hawking in Soweto, South Africa, Rogerson & Beavon (1982) talk about the 'survival strategies' of those who try to make a living in the informal sector.

Because the informal sector is so very heterogeneous, it is difficult to draw a sharp line separating it from the formal sector. Instead, there is a continuum ranging from small-scale to large-scale, from illegal to legal, from relatively unproductive to highly productive. Since the informal sector

154

26. Beer brewing in Burkina Faso (Upper Volta), West Africa. Small beer brewers are common throughout sub-Saharan Africa. (VDO)

is much less important in the rural areas, we will limit our discussion to informal activities in urban areas.

The informal tertiary sector as an urban refuge sector

Recent growth of the urban tertiary sector is largely the result of a tremendous expansion of the informal sector. In many Third World cities, no fewer than 40 out of every 100 economically active people are engaged in informal activities. This number would be even greater if children under the age of fifteen were included, many of whom earn a few quarters a week by collecting discarded tin cans, scrapwood, plastic containers, and glass bottles or by helping people find a parking place and keep an eye on their car while they are doing errands around town. Also housewives are not included in the above figure.

A substantial proportion of those who are 'employed' in the informal sector are retailers. Some own a tiny shop, others have a semipermanent stand by the side of the road. Many walk the streets of the downtown sections as peddlers, often trying to sell small articles that they themselves or relatives have made. Such 'businesses' require hardly any investment because stocks usually are very small and the quality of the goods leaves much to be desired.

155

27. Sidewalk trade in secondhand bottles, India. Also repairmen practice their trade on sidewalks. (VDO)

Street vendors often only have a few old newspapers or a piece of cloth, plastic or canvas which they spread out on the sidewalk to display their wares. If their activities are illegal, they make sure that they can quickly

156

28. Street vendors in Bangladesh. This family sells medicinal herbs and extracts. The informal sector is a refuge sector with much hidden unemployment. (IKON/VDO)

pick up their merchandise and take off. Some people practice a trade on a busy sidewalk or in the marketplace. They may be sewing clothes, repairing household goods or shoes, carving wood or decorating pottery. Again, their equipment consists of little more than an old, hand-operated sewing machine and some thread or a few simple tools and a box full of pieces of leather, metal, wood and plastic.

In many African countries, market women do not have more than two baskets of fruit and vegetables for sale, produce which they may have grown themselves. Others try to sell a few live chickens or some fish. It is not at all uncommon that they walk for an hour or more to get to the market, often on their bare feet, while carrying their merchandise by hand or on their head. On rainy days, they may be sitting in the rain all day long, without even an umbrella for protection. (Although Africa is generally known to have tropical climates, in many places – especially at higher elevations – the temperature on rainy days may not rise above 15°C (60°F), so that people shiver the entire day in their soaked clothes. At night, when the temperature may drop to less than 10°C (50°F), they are numbed by the cold in their unheated and leaky huts or slum dwellings.) If they travel to the market by bus, it sometimes happens that transportation fees equal or even exceed their earnings for that day. And when they fail to sell their produce, they usually consume much of it themselves – carrying back home again whatever is left over (Van Heur *et al.* 1982).

157

29. Drying laundry in Karachi, Pakistan. Hundreds of small launderers do the wash for hotels, restaurants, hospitals and private customers. (R. Giling)

Clearly, most of these retailers are unable to accumulate enough capital to expand or modernize their business. Thus, their activities remain small-scale and rather unproductive, barely enabling them to earn enough to feed themselves and their family. In fact, most Africans know all too well what it is like to go to bed with an empty stomach.

An important reason that incomes are extremely small in the urban informal sector is that there is considerable competition with too many people selling the same commodities or providing the same services. The combination of a dearth of paid jobs and an overabundance of people who lack the means to set up a profitable business explains why far too many of the urban poor end up doing the same kind of work.

A characteristic feature of the informal trade sector is its high degree of specialization. In some instances, this can be traced back to the division of labor that existed in pre-colonial days. But usually it is a consequence of strong competition, lack of financial means and insufficient training – including illiteracy. Many people trade in only one or two products or limit their manufacturing activities to a very small part of the entire production process. This way, experience and know-how remain so restricted that it is next to impossible for an individual to branch out and build up a large, profitable enterprise.

158

An advantage of the high level of specialization (or labor division) is that an exceptionally large number of persons can find their little niche in the urban economy, enabling them to make a meager living. In other words, the informal sector has a tremendous capacity to absorb – not unlike the intensive rice-growing economies in the densely populated countries of Monsoon Asia. In both cases the majority of the people live in a state of 'shared poverty' and the *agricultural involution* in rural Southeast Asia resembles the *urban involution* that is so characteristic of many of the Third World's cities.

The informal trade sector tends to experience both long-term and short-term fluctuations. Marketing of fruit and vegetables, naturally enough, expands or contracts with the seasons. But there are other circumstances which are responsible for (sudden) changes in activity. For example, a virtual explosion of trade activities accompanies particular celebrations or takes place on days when wages are paid to factory workers or other groups of employees. Only two or three days later the number of hawkers and other small traders may have shrunk so much that the streets almost seem deserted. These strong fluctuations are an indication that informal trade serves as an additional (secondary) source of income for people like night watchmen and car washers who cannot make ends meet without it.

It is obvious that small informal retailers, shoemakers and sidewalk tailors have little in common with factories and trade companies that belong to the modern, formal sectors of the economy. In contradistinction to what we encounter in developed countries, both the secondary and tertiary sectors in underdeveloped countries are characterized by *fragmentary modernization*. Side by side we find in Third World cities immense contrasts in organization, efficiency, and productivity – large-scale, ultra-modern enterprises as well as hawkers and rickshaw drivers; air-conditioned hotels as well as hovels made of cardboard and rags; modern, well-lit supermarkets as well as dark, dirty, little shops; expensive restaurants as well as filthy beer halls where people get their drinks served in discarded tin cans.

These contrasts do not necessarily mean that the small-scale informal activities are totally unrelated to the large-scale formal enterprises. There sometimes exist functional ties between the two, with one catering to the other. And without these mutually beneficial relations, there probably would be more unemployment and poverty than there is now. Paper mills and glass factories can produce cheaply thanks to the poor people – often children – who collect old paper and empty bottles. Various other industries make good use of discarded materials, such as tin cans, rags, and plastic containers. Without the army of self-employed trash collectors, many of these industries would not be able to survive.

Small informal enterprises often play an important role as distributors of manufactured goods or as providers of all kinds of services. Modern cigarette factories, for example, need not worry about the distribution of their product. A large number of peddlers will see to it that the cigarettes get to the customers, making formal commercial outlets – tobacco shops, etc. – largely unnecessary. The same is true of a host of other small

30. Searching through a garbage dump in Honduras. (H. Spruyt)

consumer goods, such as matches, kitchen utensils, leather goods, ballpoint pens and candy. Similarly, most factories and formal retail stores need not provide warrantees and free repair services. Almost anything can be repaired quickly and cheaply in the tiny informal repairshops, operated by individuals who have learned their trade by watching others. Not only bicycles and vacuum cleaners but also sewing machines and radios can be repaired by them.

Large manufacturers sometimes put the 'hidden' skills of these small repairmen, tinkers and handymen to good use, for instance, by having them make certain parts, such as gaskets. When supplies of parts do not arrive in time – due to congested ports, railroad breakdowns or impassable roads – factories often resort to placing orders with small repairshops. Without such subcontracts, many a large-scale manufacturer in Jakarta or Bombay would be hard pressed to stay in business. This, then, is another reason why it can be misleading to discuss the small-scale informal sector as if it were a totally separate part of the economy.

The rapid growth of the tertiary sector in recent decades leads us to conclude that it is more elastic than is manufacturing; the foregoing discussion makes it easy to explain why this is so. Since most informal activities require little or no schooling or investment, they can absorb almost unlimited numbers of people, including children. In spite of the fact that in

160

many places attempts are made to prevent the informal sector from becoming excessively large, e.g., by issuing a limited number of licenses or having traders pay a fee upon entering the marketplace, it has proved virtually impossible to control its growth.

A large and expanding informal sector is a sure sign that there is a serious shortage of permanent wage-labor jobs. This explains the term 'refuge sector' – a rather appropriate description, especially when the employment situation has deteriorated due to the combined effects of economic stagnation and rapid population growth or massive rural-to-urban migration.

Not only the least-educated and poorest segments of the urban population are forced to take inferior jobs, but the same is true of many better-trained individuals. They, too, can be victims of the weak economy with its shortage of job opportunities. Even persons with academic degrees – engineers, dentists, lawyers – may have to earn a living as taxi drivers, clerks or waiters. In some countries, e.g., India, there are far more highly trained people than the relatively undeveloped economy can use. If they do succeed in finding the type of work they are qualified for, they may well become frustrated knowing that their salary is a mere pittance compared to what they could earn in a developed country or in the rich oil-exporting countries in the Middle East. Understandably, many decide to try their luck outside their native country. Every year, some 3,000 young physicians leave India in search of better-paid work. This Third World *brain drain* explains why hospitals in Western Europe and North America often have a medical staff which includes a large number of foreigners. At the same time, most rural communities in the Third World suffer from a near-absence of medical workers!

Escape into the informal sector is also caused by relentless competition from modern industries. Many traditional crafts and small-scale manufacturing establishments – e.g., weaving, beer brewing, wagon making – have been 'destroyed' either by cheap, mass-produced imports or by efficient, large-scale production in domestic factories. One modern shoe factory employing a hundred workers can produce more, and often better, shoes than can 1,000 small individual shoemakers. In the same way that agricultural mechanization causes widespread unemployment in the rural areas, so industrial mechanization and rationalization force many urbanites to escape into the informal sector or flee their native country altogether. Just as millions of Mexicans have fled to the US, millions of 'guest-workers' from southern Europe, Africa, the Middle East, and southern Asia have migrated to Northwest Europe.

The tertiary sector: an overcrowded sector
Too many people try to make a living in the tertiary sector. Competition is fierce and earnings are for the most part barely above starvation level. Even so, rapid growth of the urban population, coupled with insufficient industrial employment, means that the tertiary sector continues to ex-

pand. Evidence of overcrowding can also be found in the *formal* tertiary sector, that is, in modern commercial businesses and service industries. A familiar sight is the excessively large number of clerks, waiters, porters, cleaning ladies, etc. in department stores, hotels, restaurants, banks, rental services and office buildings. This allows for excellent service and may be necessary to compete against the well-developed informal sector which can provide many services more cheaply. Small family enterprises also tend to employ many people, owing to the customary obligation to help as many needy relatives as possible.

Government institutions, too, are characterized by overemployment. To some degree this may be encouraged by official or unofficial government policy aimed at providing a maximum of employment. Besides, many high officials like to surround themselves with a large staff, not only so they can delegate much of their work, but also because of the prestige it affords them. Another reason is that the persons who are given a job often express their gratitude in the form of a small payment to their new boss. This is not so surprising when it is realized that government jobs usually are highly coveted; they provide a measure of status as well as security. Although salaries tend to be rather low, most government officials somehow manage to earn some additional income. The more highly educated, in particular, are anxious to find employment in the government sector – sometimes asking relatives and acquaintances for work or using bribes and other corruptive practices to further their chances. Lower officials who try to talk their superiors into hiring more people, frequently are under considerable pressure from friends and relatives. It would seem that in many Third World countries *nepotism* (favoritism shown to a relative, as by giving an appointive job) is a widespread phenomenon that is fairly taken for granted.

The abundance of people seeking employment also helps to explain why various Third World countries have armies and police forces which appear to be too large considering the low level of economic development. Although lack of internal security or social tension – either actual or potential – are often cited as reasons, it is perfectly clear that in many cases the large numbers of military personnel and police officers are a direct consequence of government efforts to create employment.

One of the greatest dilemmas facing Third World countries is the question of how to rationalize, modernize and raise the productivity of large-scale, formal enterprises without causing a decline of small-scale, informal activities. Since the number of people living in cities is likely to surge ahead in coming years, there looms the danger that urban unemployment will reach unacceptably high levels, possibly resulting in widespread unrest and social chaos.

The tertiary sector: also an attractive and functional sector
The phenomenal expansion of the urban tertiary sector is, as we have seen, a direct consequence of agricultural stagnation and insufficient

31. Urban scene in Morocco. (Message on the billboard: 'The sexiest man in the world.') (J. Poley)

employment in the still poorly developed secondary sector. There are additional reasons for its rapid growth. Most important, perhaps, is that it has some advantage over the other sectors, causing it to attract many job seekers. Apart from the prestige that is attached to having an office job, work in the tertiary sector usually is much less strenuous and less dangerous than is work in agriculture, mining or industry. Not only are hours generally shorter, but jobs in the informal sector allow more personal freedom and independence. Whereas many jobs in agriculture have the disadvantage of being seasonal – with long periods of little or no income – people who have an office job normally are assured of a regular income throughout the entire year. Moreover, it is not uncommon for officials to find ways to make a little extra money on the side, e.g., by accepting an occasional bribe.

It is incorrect to think of the tertiary sector as being exclusively a refuge sector, or to describe its expansion as unhealthy. Much of its growth was necessary due to the increase in population as well as the attainment of political independence, which required a larger governmental/administrative apparatus than had existed previously. What *is* unhealthy is that the tertiary sector has grown too much, too fast, i.e., totally out of proportion with the low productivity of the primary and secondary sectors of the economy. To put it differently, the tertiary sector is too large considering the low standard of living of the majority of the population. Since many workers in the tertiary sector contribute little to the overall economic productivity, its large size tends to hold back economic development and frustrates efforts to raise standards of living and well-being. In other words, Third World cities are caught in a vicious circle of persistent poverty.

In view of the above, we might be misled to look upon the informal sector as being parasitic in nature. But this conclusion, too, is not entirely correct because it serves a useful function as a provider of low-cost foodstuffs and cheap manufactured goods and services. If there were no informal sector, prices would be higher and many of the urban poor might not be able to survive. Or, if there were no informal moneylenders, the poor might not be able to obtain the small loans which are occasionally needed as a result of illness or an accident. Finally, it is only the informal sector which can satisfy certain traditional needs or supply craftsmen with particular materials.

In recent years, there has been a growing realization that important functions are performed by the small-scale tertiary activities. As a consequence, economists, sociologists, urban anthropologists, and geographers have done a great deal of research on the informal sector and collected a wealth of information. Probably the most important question is: Should the informal sector be stimulated or discouraged?

The consensus is that, because of its immense significance as a provider of employment, it should be stimulated. Only certain illegal and morally unacceptable activities ought to be discouraged. For the rest, attention should be paid especially to those informal activities that offer the best opportunities to raise overall productivity. Assistance should be provided and funds made available to help people help themselves, e.g., by giving them some schooling so as to become more skilled in their trade or by making it possible for them to take out loans needed to obtain better equipment and tools. At the same time, people who are interested should be given a chance to master the basics of bookkeeping and business law.

Unfortunately, the realization that the informal sector should be upgraded because it has an important role to play lives more among foreign researchers than among Third World leaders, so that small-scale shopkeepers, marketwomen and repairmen are unlikely to receive much government assistance in the foreseeable future.

The tertiary sector: a dominating sector

In most developed countries, the tertiary sector employs approximately the same number of people as does the secondary sector. By contrast, in many Third World countries the ratio is two to one or even three to one. To use Indonesia as an example, in 1980, no less than 30 percent of the economically active population was classified as being employed in the tertiary sector, while only 12 percent worked in the secondary sector. In addition to this lack of balance, tertiary activities are concentrated almost entirely in the larger cities, with the rural areas being practically devoid of them because the largely self-sufficient peasants receive so little cash that they can afford few services.

The dominant position of the tertiary sector in the cities is one of the contradictions which characterize the problem of underdevelopment. While the majority of the producers are small subsistence farmers, and industrialization – which was the motor for the development of the tertiary sector in the now-developed countries – still is in its infancy, many Third World countries already have a comparatively large tertiary sector. This is an unhealthy situation inasmuch as an overly large tertiary sector tends to keep per capita productivity at a low level. As long as average productivity is low, levels of material well-being are bound to remain low as well.

Considering the above, it seems appropriate to refer to Third World cities as service economies. Trade, transportation, banking, administration and other service industries together are the number one employer, with manufacturing trailing far behind. Whereas the growth of the tertiary sector was an indication of increased industrial and agricultural productivity and rising standards of living in developed countries, in the Third World its growth is rather an indication of a rampant shortage of jobs and widespread poverty due to stagnation in the productive sectors of the economy.

Chapter 11 Urban settlements and the process of urbanization

Urbanization in the Third World

Although the majority of the Third World population lives in small rural villages, the proportion living in urban places has grown rapidly in recent decades. In fact, urban expansion in the Third World currently outpaces that in the industrialized countries.

In 1920, only 15 million Third World people lived in cities of 100,000-plus inhabitants; by 1960, their number had reached 139 million. During that 40-year period, the total urban population of the Third World grew nearly 400 percent – from 68 million to 319 million – an urbanization rate which far exceeds anything the industrialized countries ever have experienced. Today, most Third World countries continue to experience rapid urban expansion. Average annual *urbanization growth rates* in the US and most of Europe between 1967 and 1982 were about 1 percent, but many Third World countries, especially in Africa, had annual growth rates of 4 percent or more (see Fig. 12).

In sharp contrast to the developed countries, where urbanization has been a very gradual process, the Third World is faced with a virtual urban explosion. This explosion is largely dominated by the mushrooming of large cities. In 1920, there were only 13 cities with over 500,000 inhabitants, but four decades later there already were 105. Perhaps most astonishing is that in 1980 the Third World counted more such cities than did the industrialized countries: 259 versus 230.

As a result of these above developments, more than half the world's total urban population now lives in the Third World. This is so despite the fact that the *degree of urbanization* (percent of total population living in urban places) is much higher in the developed than in the underdeveloped countries (see Table 5 and Fig. 13).

Several urban agglomerations, e.g., São Paulo, Mexico City, and Calcutta, already have more than 10 million inhabitants. By the year 2000, there are likely to be many more such giant urban concentrations. Bombay is then expected to have 19 million inhabitants and Mexico City some 30 million, making the latter the largest megalopolis in the world. It is possible that by the turn of the century, 12 of the 15 largest cities will be located in the Third World, with Tokyo, New York and Los Angeles being the only exceptions.

The process of urbanization in the Third World: an historical sketch

Many parts of the Third World have known urban settlements for a very long time. The earliest cities are thought to have emerged in Mesopotamia (present-day Iraq), but also other parts of the Middle East, China, Central

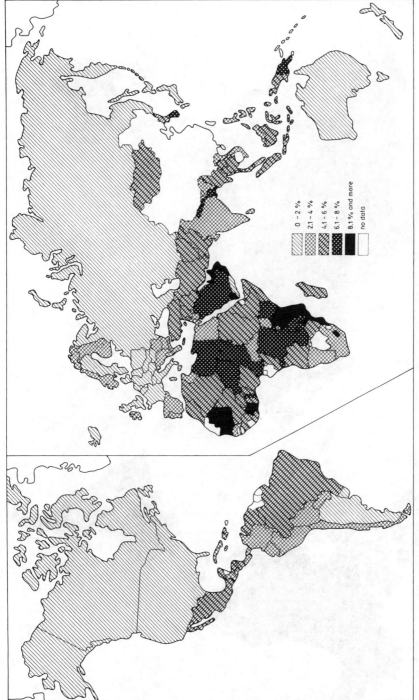

Fig. 12. Average annual urban population growth rate, 1970-1982. *Source:* World Bank, *World Development Report 1984.*

0 – 2 %
2,1 – 4 %
4,1 – 6 %
6,1 – 8 %
8,1 % and more
no data

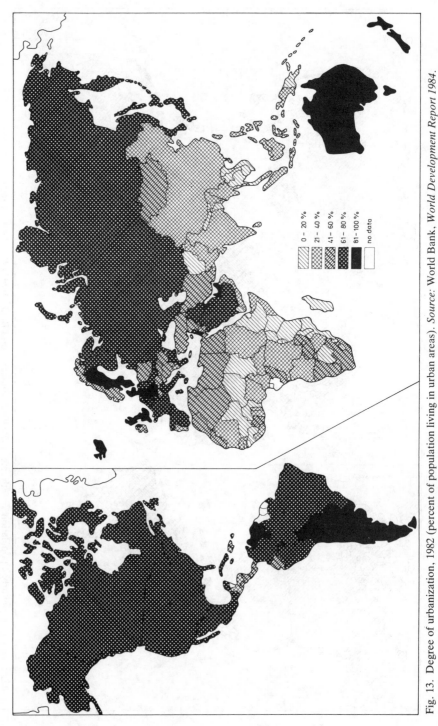

Fig. 13. Degree of urbanization, 1982 (percent of population living in urban areas). *Source*: World Bank, *World Development Report 1984*.

Table 5. Degrees of urbanization in 1920, 1950, 1960, 1970, and 1980 (based on national definitions).

| Region | Percent of total population living in urban centers | | | | |
	1920	1950	1960	1970	1980
World	19	29	34	38	40
Developed countries	39	53	59	65	71
Third World	8	17	22	26	29
Europe	46	54	58	64	72
USSR	15	39	49	57	62
North America	52	64	67	70	77
Oceania	47	61	66	71	78
South Asia	9	16	18	20	25
East Asia	9	17	25	29	29
Africa	7	15	18	23	27
Latin America	22	41	49	57	66

Sources: United Nations, various publications; World Bank, World Development Report 1982.

Asia, East Africa, and West Africa possessed cities long before the Greeks and Romans built Athens and Rome. And when the Spanish arrived in Central and South America, they 'discovered' a number of pre-Columbian cities.

Ancient urban settlements often were trade centers, located on caravan routes or on the coast; others were religious centers or had important administrative functions. Most of them did not have many inhabitants, usually not more than 50,000. It was not until the 16th century or later that cities began to become considerably larger, while at the same time many new cities appeared. The expansion of colonialism and trade with Europe contributed significantly to these developments. A hundred years after Columbus had sailed across the Atlantic Ocean, no fewer than 200 new cities had been founded in Latin America. In much of Africa, on the other hand, it was not until the second half of the 19th century – after slave trade had been abolished – and the early years of the 20th century – following the colonial partition of Africa by European powers – that many new cities came into existence.

The location of many newly founded centers was strongly influenced by the desire on the part of European traders to collect and ship 'colonial wares' as efficiently as possible. This meant that the Europeans selected locations with easy access to the hinterlands where agricultural commodities and later mineral raw materials originated. Most were situated on, or close to, the coast, making them at the same time convenient places for the distribution of manufactured goods imported from Europe. The few commercial centers which were founded further inland either were easily accessible overland or were situated along a navigable river.

With the majority of the new trade centers being located on the coast, the process of urbanization was highly peripheral in terms of its spatial pattern.

169

Port cities such as Recife (Brazil), Salvador (Brazil), Lima (Peru), Dakar (Senegal), Abidjan (Ivory Coast), Accra (Gold Coast; now Ghana), Lagos (Nigeria), Luanda (Angola), Calcutta (India), Singapore (Singapore), and Jakarta (Indonesia) all had, and still have, the advantage of offering excellent opportunities for the collection and distribution of goods. These economic advantages explain why many port cities have developed into huge agglomerations with considerable industrial and administrative significance.

This being the case, the peripheral bias has over the years become more pronounced with the result that the existing urbanization patterns of Africa and Latin America differ markedly from that of Europe. Just as the countries of Africa and Latin America have not evolved 'organically' from traditional societies, but instead are artificial creations forced upon the indigenous people by outside (colonial) forces, so also the distributional pattern of major cities is not a product of internal forces, but one imposed from without to serve the business interests of the outsiders.

Not every large city in the Third World is located on or near the coast. Many cities in South and Central America received a strong impetus from mining activities. Already in the 16th century, production of silver and other precious metals was important in Mexico and the Andean region. Some early mining settlements rapidly developed into urban places. For example, around 1600 the city of Potosí (silver mining) had more than 100,000 inhabitants. As places like Potosí grew, they developed into important markets for agricultural goods and manufactured products, thus stimulating economic activities and the emergence of various smaller trade centers in surrounding areas.

The most important urban developments in the Third World do not date back to the 16th century, but have occurred since the beginning of the 19th century. From about 1800 until World War II, the dominant factor stimulating urbanization in the Third World was the industrial development taking place in Europe and North America. This economic upsurge meant that there was a rapidly growing demand for a host of raw materials from non-Western regions. Not only mining but also export-oriented agriculture experienced a dramatic expansion. While plantations multiplied in many tropical areas, output of cash crops by small farmers increased almost as rapidly. As a result of the greatly enlarged production for export and the simultaneously increasing demand for industrial goods, economic activity as well as population became increasingly concentrated in a relatively small number of urban places. To give an example, the large-scale production of coffee led to the emergence of numerous towns in southeastern Brazil. Likewise, the phenomenal growth of Buenos Aires (Argentina), Montevideo (Uruguay), and many smaller settlements in the humid pampa region was closely associated with the production of beef and grain for overseas markets. In Southeast Asia, plantation agriculture contributed to

170

the growth of cities like Jakarta (Indonesia), Surabaya (Indonesia), and Singapore.

Although especially port cities benefited from the surge in overseas trade, the construction of railroads made possible the rise of urban centers in the interior. Both in southern Brazil (São Paulo state) and the pampa region of central Argentina, railroads have played a decisive role in opening up large hinterlands and integrating them into the expanding world economy. The same development has occurred in Africa. Northern Nigeria, for example, was made accessible by means of rail connections to the coast. Thanks to these links, the region could be transformed into an important producer of peanuts for export, and this, in turn, led to the growth of Kano and other cities in the savanna region of northern Nigeria.

Other inland cities emerged as administrative centers. With the expansion of colonialism, a growing need arose to divide large areas into smaller units so as to better be able to establish and maintain effective control. The immense French area in West Africa, for example, eventually became divided into eight 'territories': Senegal, Mauritania, Mali, Niger, Dahomey (Benin), Upper Volta (Burkina Faso), Ivory Coast, and Guinea. Even though Dakar (Senegal) remained the major administrative center for all of French West Africa, each territory soon had its own local capital.

Colonialism, trade, and integration into the world economic system fostered urban growth, but there was one factor which did exactly the opposite, viz., the lack of industrial development. While Europe and North America witnessed a truly revolutionary expansion of secondary economic activities between 1800 and 1940, hardly any manufacturing growth occurred in many countries of Asia, Africa, and Latin America. The process of industrialization in the Third World was greatly retarded by the general absence of technical knowledge, limited accumulation of capital, low purchasing power among the majority of the population, and, above all, by economic policies pursued by Western countries. The latter, in an effort to protect their industries and relative prosperity, purposely stymied the development of potentially competitive industrial production in non-Western societies. This policy was easier to foist on the colonial areas in Africa, Asia, and the Caribbean than on South America, but even in the latter region efforts aimed at discouraging industrial development were quite successful. The few industries which did come into existence were for the most part either relatively simple industries that satisfied basic needs, or processing industries whose main purpose it was to lower the transport costs of mineral and agricultural raw materials that had to be shipped to industrialized countries. Thus, the process of industrialization in the Third World was highly fragmentary and unbalanced, with many branches lacking altogether. And this, of course, slowed down the urbanization process.

At the same time, the colonial powers neglected to develop agriculture, so that the rural population remained relatively unproductive and poor.

Only the production of export crops – largely on plantations – received considerable attention, but this benefited at best a very small proportion of the rural population. As a consequence, the rural areas were incapable of making a significant contribution to the process of urbanization. Most rural areas remained highly isolated and backward, geared toward self-sufficient food production. Agricultural surpluses which could have stimulated trade were hardly produced, while the demand for goods not locally produced was equally limited due to the absence of purchasing power. Prior to the Second World War, a very large share of the total population stayed almost completely outside a money economy.

Since World War II, some far-reaching changes have taken place in the Third World, causing the rate of urbanization to accelerate. One such change was the attainment of political independence by former colonies in Africa and Asia. Whereas in 1945 nearly all of Africa still was colonial, twenty years later it counted some forty independent states. Apart from Djibouti, Spanish Sahara, and Guinea-Bissau, only Rhodesia (Zimbabwe), Angola, Mozambique, and Namibia had not yet been 'liberated.' The latter territory – formerly called South West Africa – continues to be a colony to the present day, ruled not by a European power but by neighboring South Africa.

Attainment of political independence was associated with considerable political fragmentation, especially in Africa, and thus caused a multiplication of administrative functions. Whereas Dakar (Senegal) had served as the colonial capital for all of French West Africa, after 1960 – the year in which most French territories in Africa achieved independence – each of the new states (Mali, Niger, etc.) developed its own full-fledged national capital. Likewise, the former administrative units that prior to 1960 were known collectively as French Equatorial Africa (Congo, Gabon, Central African Republic, and Chad), became separate sovereign entities. The emergence of many new capital cities contributed significantly to the process of urbanization. Part of their early inhabitants belonged to the upper and middle classes which possessed considerable purchasing power, making the cities relatively attractive locations for various industries producing consumer goods. The tertiary sector, too, had better opportunities to develop here than elsewhere.

After having obtained independence, many countries decided to stimulate industrialization as a strategy to achieve overall economic development and raise standards of material well-being. As we have seen in chapter 9, the drive toward industrialization often took the form of import substitution, with much of the expansion of manufacturing taking place in urban centers. In some instances, entirely new industrial cities were created, sometimes in the vicinity of mining activities, e.g., Ciudad Guayana in eastern Venezuela, and sometimes on the coast, e.g., the new port city of Tema in Ghana.

172

The large excess of births over deaths also plays an important role in the process of urbanization. Aside from the natural growth of the urban population, increasing population pressure in the rural areas – frequently burdened with low levels of agricultural output, soil erosion, exceedingly low wages, a serious shortage of industrial jobs, and a totally inadequate social and physical infrastructure – has set in motion a massive rural-to-urban migration stream swelling the cities and causing an explosion of the urban, informal sector.

There are no indications that the rural areas of most underdeveloped countries will experience much economic progress. On the contrary, they are likely to suffer long-term stagnation. The density of population will increase, resulting in a growing shortage of jobs. Agricultural mechanization may further aggravate the problems of unemployment and underemployment. But with or without increased mechanization, rural living conditions are expected to deteriorate rather than improve, so that rural-to-urban migration will proceed at rates comparable to those that the Third World has witnessed during the past few decades. Rural retrogression is all the more likely if countries go on stimulating industrialization.

Some experts have suggested that further urbanization should be avoided. Specifically, they favor halting, even prohibiting, the migration from rural to urban areas. It is questionable whether these are realistic proposals. First of all, most Third World countries are not yet highly urbanized in an absolute sense; they only are highly urbanized considering the early stage of economic development they are in. Moreover, cities can play an invaluable role in promoting economic growth, both at the regional and the national level. Without urban growth poles, not much economic progress can be anticipated – at least, that appears to be the lesson which can be learned from the economically advanced countries.

Another important consideration is that efforts to discourage people from moving to the cities are unlikely to be successful. Only highly authoritarian measures might prevent rural people from moving to the cities, but such measures could in the long run do more harm than good. A radical anti-urbanization campaign could hardly be expected to solve the problems facing the underdeveloped countries. This does not mean that a *laissez-faire* approach should be adopted. In our opinion it seems imperative that Third World countries take immediate steps to:

(1) lower the birth rate, both in the cities and in the rural areas;
(2) improve living conditions in the rural areas; and
(3) create jobs in the cities.

As far as point (2) is concerned, the more attractive life in the countryside can be made, the less will be the desire among rural people to migrate to the cities. Particularly important in this respect is that governments work out thoughtful plans aimed at raising the productivity of small farmers. As Hyden emphasized in *Beyond Ujamaa in Tanzania* (1980), as long as the agricultural sector produces little more than is needed for subsistence, there can be no hope that Third World countries will overcome their persistent-poverty dilemma. Although Hyden's observation pertains to sub-Saharan Africa – see also his more recently published book *No Shortcuts to Progress* (1983) – there is ample evidence that the same conclusion applies to numerous countries in Asia and Latin America.

Contrasts in urbanization: the Third World versus the industrially advanced countries

Urban growth in the developed countries first started *after* the rural areas had reached a certain degree of economic development and prosperity. Agricultural surpluses made it possible for some people to specialize in non-agricultural activities, including commerce, administration, and crafts. These latter activities became progressively concentrated in small urban centers, whose main function it was to provide services for the rural-farm population in exchange for foodstuffs.

At an early date, many European cities became important as manufacturing centers, with different cities specializing in the production of different consumer goods. This industrial specialization encouraged inter-city trade relations; cloth made in one city was traded for metal tools, wooden barrels or pottery made in other places. Such trade led to the accumulation of small amounts of capital which could be used to expand industrial enterprises or develop new ones. Gradually, more and more urban jobs were created, not only in manufacturing but also in trade, transportation, banking, insurance, etc. Thus, cities grew and became increasingly important markets for foodstuffs and other agricultural goods, including industrial crops (e.g., flax) and livestock products (e.g., wool). Farmers were able to satisfy the growing needs of the cities by adopting improved methods of production. From the cities they were able to obtain better tools and implements, allowing them to work their land more intensively and increase their productivity. There clearly existed a mutually beneficial relationship between town and country. Growth in one sector stimulated growth in other sectors, enabling the urban as well as the rural people to further increase per capita output and enjoy a measure of previously unknown prosperity.

Urbanization in medieval Europe was essentially the result of *internal* economic development. Also after 1492 and during the Industrial Revolution, technological advancement, industrial expansion, and urbanization were first and foremost endogenous processes, based more on the often ruthless exploitation of the not yet unionized labor force than on the exploitation of overseas lands and peoples. Surely, slave trade and colonial exploits have played a role, but these activities, too, were the results of developments occurring in Europe and controlled by Europeans.

In most Third World countries, the process of urbanization has taken an entirely different course. For one thing, manufacturing was not important as a factor stimulating early urban growth. In most cities there was little or no industry until recently. Many started out as administrative centers and/or as foci where colonial wares and primary goods were shipped to Europe, and from which imported industrial goods were distributed to their hinterlands. Overseas trade lay at their foundation, making them into important transshipment points. Since this inter-continental trade was in the hands of foreigners, capital was extracted rather than accumulated. Thus, in contrast to what had happened in Europe, development of an endogenous secondary sector was inhibited. The little manufacturing that does occur in Third World cities, as we have seen, is for the most part of recent origin and is often owned and managed by foreign entrepreneurs. Industrialization is the result not of internal forces but of external, that is, foreign initiatives.

These external influences remain readily visible in the morphology of many an African or Asian city. Certain residential quarters have an unmistakably Western appearance, characterized as they are by fashionable European-style dwellings on large lots, modern supermarkets, and clubs. In contrast to the sections inhabited by the indigenous population, many 'expatriate' quarters have been planned with parks and other recreational facilities, wide streets and tree-lined avenues. Even where these sections of town have become inhabited by Africans or Asians, they retain their Western appearance. For example, open-air markets, industrial enterprises, and informal tertiary activities generally are lacking. Another conspicuous feature is the low population density, and thus the absence of large crowds of pedestrians or heavy traffic. More often than not they constitute 'islands' of peace and quiet as well as prosperity. Although one is unlikely to encounter many street peddlers, shoe-shine boys, or sidewalk tailors, the wealthy residents provide considerable employment for gardeners, night watchmen, cleaning ladies, cooks, private chauffeurs, and the like.

As we have pointed out in an earlier section, the external orientation of many Third World cities has influenced their location. Many can be found on the coast, along navigable rivers or along railroad lines. Their often peripheral location – a consequence of their function as collection and distribution points – has had a great impact on patterns of road and rail connections. To a large degree, these patterns are dominated by transportation lines which run more or less perpendicular to the coastline, linking the peripheral transshipment points to those parts of the interior that have (or had) significance as producers of agricultural goods or mineral raw materials destined for export.

Just as no roads or railways were built from the coast to inland areas lacking important resources, few efforts were made to construct links between the various cities or to connect the 'perpendicular' lines with one another. Instead of one comprehensive, integrated network with many connections, a large number of separate transportation lines, running more or less parallel to one another, were established. The interstitial areas have long remained highly inaccessible; some still are, making it very difficult to develop them and integrate them into the national economy. By the same token, few connections exist between neighboring countries, thereby inhibiting regional economic cooperation. For years, Uganda and Tanzania were members of the now defunct East African Common Market – to which also Kenya belonged – but the movement of goods across their common border was virtually impossible due to the absence of good crossboundary transport routes. To this very day, large parts of the Third World suffer the economic disadvantages of colonial-type transportation geographies which differ markedly from those of the developed countries (see Fig. 14, in which the pattern on the right allows for a high degree of economic

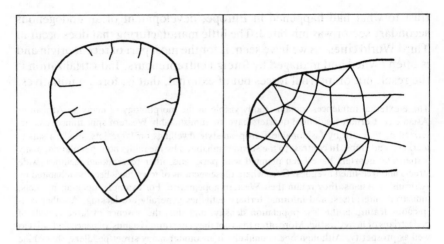

Fig. 14. Two hypothetical transportation networks (representing Africa and Western Europe).

cooperation and integration, whereas the pattern on the left makes this extremely difficult).

Primate cities

Suppose we divided all urban centers of a given country into five size-classes, e.g., very large, large, medium, small, and very small, and then counted the number of places in each category, we would obtain what is called a frequency distribution. For country X the frequency distribution might be 1, 4, 16, 64, 256, with 1024 villages. Country Y, on the other hand, might have a different *urban hierarchy*, e.g.: 3, 15, 75, 375, 1875, with 9375 rural settlements. Both these frequency distributions are too regular to be realistic, but they are more or less typical of economically advanced countries.

Most Third World countries have frequency distributions that differ markedly from the examples given above, displaying little or no regularity. The following hypothetical, and admittedly extreme, distribution may serve to illustrate the difference: 1, 0, 2, 40, 900, with 14,000 villages. It is clear that we are dealing here with a totally different hierarchy; there are, relatively speaking, too many villages and small towns, while medium-size and large cities are underrepresented. Another important difference is that the largest city is too large when compared with the two urban centers that belong to the category of medium-size cities. When the number one city is much larger than the number two city, we say that the country in question has a *primate city*.

176

Primacy measured

The term 'primate city' was introduced by Mark Jefferson in 1939. According to him, a country was characterized by *primacy* when the largest city had more than twice as many inhabitants as the second largest city. In later years, various authors have proposed different definitions. Sometimes the number of inhabitants of the largest city is expressed as a percentage of the total number of inhabitants of the four largest cities, the so-called *index of primacy* (Ginsburg 1961). In other words:

$$\frac{P_1 + P_2 + P_3 + P_4}{P_1} \times 100\%.$$

A disadvantage of these and various other primacy indexes is that they are based exclusively on numbers of inhabitants, totally disregarding the significance of urban functions. There are countries with two, or even three, leading cities of approximately the same size. These countries are not characterized by urban primacy. Examples are Nigeria, where Lagos and Ibadan have approximately the same number of inhabitants, and Ecuador, where Guayaquil and Quito are about the same size. If we focus attention on the distribution of modern secondary and tertiary activities, we find that these are concentrated to a large degree in the port cities of Lagos and Guayaquil. Each of these two cities, then, may be said to possess a high measure of (economic) primacy.

Primate cities are not limited to the Third World; we also find them in various European countries, including France, Denmark, and Austria. Primacy, however, is more common in underdeveloped than in developed countries. Furthermore, primacy tends to be far more extreme in the Third World, with the largest city being the undisputed leader in virtually every respect. In addition to being the most populous urban center, it dominates the country economically as well as politically. Invariably, it is the national nerve center (or core) where the national elite and other major decision makers are concentrated.

Primacy often has its roots in the colonial past. The colonial powers (or metropoles) usually centered all important activities in one favorably located place. Both exports and imports were funneled through this center, thus attracting commerce and other tertiary activities. Usually it had better connections with hinterland areas than other urban settlements, most of which were by-passed and remained rather isolated, so that they could not develop into central places with important service functions for surrounding rural areas. Already at an early date, such a 'bridgehead' began to attract people – both expatriates and natives – thus experiencing a considerable growth in population, sometimes at the expense of other urban centers.

At the same time, the primate city often became the administrative 'capital' of the colony, where especially the better-educated people were concentrated, in part because it had more and better educational facilities than other places. It goes without saying that it was this relatively developed and influential city which nearly always was chosen as the seat of government when a colony became an independent, sovereign state. This being the case, its growth and dominance were further enhanced, frequently at an accelerated pace. Not only did the new capital become a symbol of national pride and dignity as well as of a new and promising future, so that it received preferential treatment, but it also became the place of residence for a growing number of foreign representatives and diplomats. It is in this capital/primate city that we find stadiums, cultural centers, conference halls and other prestige symbols. And naturally enough, if the country has an international airport, it is almost certainly located in or near the capital city.

Being the major political-administrative and economic center in the country, income levels tend to be substantially higher than in other urban centers. This means that the capital constitutes the most attractive market for all kinds of services and luxury consumer goods. In effect, many Third World countries have a very large and often increasing percentage of all economic growth occurring in the primate city, which, in turn, attracts large numbers of migrants.

This trend toward economic primacy has been greatly strengthened by the post-colonial drive toward industrialization. Because of its many economic advantages – availability of labor, skill, market, and capital, as well as favorable location, agglomeration advantages, better-than-average infrastructure, and superior connections with the rest of the country – it was targeted as the most logical site for industrial expansion. In addition to attracting small-scale indigenous entrepreneurs, the primate city was favored by large, often multinational, enterprises. Since the governments of most Third World countries did not encourage industrial decentralization, and sometimes even discouraged it, industrial growth has taken place for the most part in and near the capital city. Thus, the political capital usually also is the economic-industrial capital, making it the unrivaled leader which dominates virtually all aspects of modern life in the entire country.

Although a high degree of primacy has been fostered by colonialism, or more precisely, by development from without based on exploitative overseas relationships and externally controlled decisions, primacy also occurs in countries which never were colonized by European powers. An example is Iran. There, a weak agricultural sector with a highly unfavorable land-ownership structure failed to promote the development of a hierarchical network of smaller and larger market places. Severely exploited by power-

178

ful large landowners, the overwhelming majority of crop-sharing tenants had little or no purchasing power, so that secondary economic activities were unable to flourish. The ruling indigenous elite, moreover, did not stimulate the growth of medium-sized regional centers. Instead, they favored the seat of imperial power. For centuries, surplus value was systematically siphoned away from the countryside and used consumptively by the fabulously rich nobility who lived in splendor. As was the case in colonial territories, life in Iran was dominated by parasitic rather than symbiotic relationships; by social injustice, unequal opportunity and unbalanced growth. By the time manufacturing began to acquire some importance – not until after World War II – most of it was concentrated in the relatively large capital city. Thus, Tehran's primacy (since about 1800) was enhanced to the detriment of smaller urban settlements. During the past few decades, the constant flow of oil revenues to Tehran has only served to further strengthen its dominant economic position.

Primacy is often most pronounced in small countries. Here, only one large city suffices to provide the entire country with all urban services needed. The result is that other places do not get a chance to develop into regional centers. In several small African countries, some 90 to 100 percent of the secondary and tertiary sectors are concentrated in one and the same primate city.

Finally, extreme primacy may have resulted from political fragmentation. In a sense, the city of Dakar is much too large for relatively small Senegal. Likewise, Brazzaville overshadows all other urban centers in the People's Republic of Congo. The reason is that both Dakar and Brazzaville used to be the colonial-administrative centers for areas that were much larger than are the countries in which they are now located. Prior to 1960, Dakar served all of French West Africa, while Brazzaville functioned as the colonial capital of French Equatorial Africa.

The spectacular growth of one city is a phenomenon that does not belong exclusively to the past. In many Third World countries, the same process of highly concentrated urbanization goes on unabated. What is more is that it is likely to continue for some time. Apart from the fact that few governments are convinced that they should promote a more evenly dispersed pattern of urban growth, it is far from easy – and very expensive – to reverse the trend toward increased primacy. Countries which have taken steps to create a more balanced spatial structure of urban nodes, hoping to reduce the degree of primacy, generally have not been very successful. An important reason why results thus far have been disappointing is that few of the planned growth poles have been able to attract much industry, let alone lure industries away from the primate cities. It does not seem to make much difference whether a country has a free-market economy or a centrally planned economy; failure to lessen the degree of primacy is common to both.

A high degree of primacy has a number of consequences. First of all, it means that a large share of the total urban population is concentrated in one small part of the country. Approximately one-fourth of Brazil's urbanites live in just two cities: São Paulo and Rio de Janeiro. Even more extreme is the situation in Uruguay, where nearly half of all citizens and over half the urban population live in Greater Montevideo.

Even more extreme than the uneven distribution of people is the often highly unbalanced distribution of economic activity and gross national earnings. In Latin America, an unbelievable 70 percent of all non-agricultural economic activity is centered in ten urban agglomerations, i.e., Buenos Aires, São Paulo, Mexico City, Rio de Janeiro, Santiago, Havana, Caracas, Lima, Rosario, and Montevideo. This is all the more surprising because altogether there are over 200 cities with more than 50,000 inhabitants each. In other words, Latin America as a whole is characterized by a pattern of *spatial polarization*: a limited number of urban-industrial cores surrounded by extensive peripheral areas with few non-agricultural activities (Odell 1970, p. 542). And while the primate city may suffer from excessive congestion and concomitant diseconomies of agglomeration, or if you wish, from 'overdevelopment,' much of the rest of the country may be characterized by underutilization due to too little development.

Continued economic growth in the major conurbations slows down economic growth in the smaller urban centers. The large and dynamic cities act like powerful magnets, exerting a strong pull on investments and skilled labor, thereby draining the smaller towns and rural areas of part of their lifeblood. The result is lasting economic stagnation in large parts of each country, a situation aggravated by the constant flow of tax revenues from the countryside to the urban core areas. This *urban bias* favors especially the bigger cities, that is, the centers in which the most influential decision makers already are concentrated.

The 'suction power' of the big urban centers explains why many of them are surrounded by large areas – sometimes tens of thousands of square kilometers in size – in which hardly any urban development takes place. Although such peri-urban *umlands* may contain a number of settlements large enough to be called urban, they are so completely dominated by the large metropolis that they cannot function properly as central places. Having no *raison d'être,* they are unable to prosper and grow. Not only economically, but also culturally, socially and politically they are virtual voids that have little to offer to their own inhabitants or to people in surrounding hinterlands. In fact, they barely have hinterlands or spheres of influence.

An example of the suffocating and stultifying impact that a big city has on its surroundings can be found in Peru. Within a 500-kilometer (300-mile) radius of Lima-Callao, there is not one single urban settlement that is able to function as a regional center. This entire 'under-urbanized' zone depends for its services on Lima; an urban hierarchy with nested spheres of influence à la Christaller's model, so common in the developed countries (see Fig.

11b), does not exist. Because similar voids can be found around many other primate cities in the Third World, it should not surprise us that primate cities as well as other big cities are considered by many scholars to be parasites, and that extreme primacy is frequently thought of as a formidable obstacle to genuine development.

The relative under-urbanization of large areas has its undesirable repercussions as far as spatial patterns of accessibility are concerned. The networks of roads and railroads are strongly influenced by the location of the national capital-*cum*-primate city. Whereas transportation lines radiate from the big metropolis, giving it excellent access to a large *tributary area,* smaller urban centers lack such radial systems of diverging transport routes, thus making it difficult for them to draw surrounding rural areas into their spheres of influence. Few are important as market towns or as centers of secondary and tertiary activity. A mutually beneficial relationship between them and the farming population barely exists. With many rural areas being highly inaccessible – located as they are in the interstices between major roads radiating from the capital city – modern agricultural development is next to impossible. Agricultural innovations cannot penetrate, or, if they do reach the small rural communities, farmers are hard pressed to take advantage of them due to the inability of local towns to provide them with the necessary services, credit and information. Progress, thus, passes them by, turning the rural-farm areas into stagnant, poverty-stricken backwaters.

In brief, the absence of a hierarchical system of central places and, more specifically, the lack of medium-size towns, discourages over-all economic development. Economic backwardness, in its turn, virtually prohibits the development of a spatially balanced structure of smaller and larger regional centers needed to raise agricultural productivity. In this sense, extreme primacy may be looked upon as being dysfunctional. Itself an expression of spatial inequality, it fosters ever greater regional disparities, polarization and internal colonialism.

Although above-mentioned observations generally apply to the large majority of Third World countries, we must not forget that each country represents a unique case. Realizing this, we must exercise extreme caution when formulating policies aimed at improving the urban settlement structure of a given country. For example, a high degree of primacy tends to be less dysfunctional in small states than in large ones. Or, urbanization strategies which may well be sound for relatively highly urbanized and economically advanced countries, such as Argentina and Brazil, could have detrimental consequences for countries like Ethiopia and Tanzania, both of which have less than 20 percent of their population living in urban centers and possess very little industry. Whereas the first two countries may be well-advised to stimulate a limited number of industrial centers with approximately 200,000 inhabitants each, for the latter two countries it would seem more appropriate to try to create a large number of small market towns that can provide essential services for the farming population in their immediate surroundings.

Primacy and regional disparities can also have undesirable *political* consequences. The people in the more backward and isolated parts of the country may become dissatisfied and restless, particularly if they have become influenced by rising expectations. Sooner or later they are likely to demand better services, higher prices for their products, higher wages, lower taxes, and perhaps more political influence. Incensed by the fact that they are victimized by social injustice and unequal opportunity, they may even start an insurgent or separatist movement. Desires to secede are particularly likely in ethnically heterogeneous countries where various ethnic groups (or 'tribes') each inhabit 'their own' territory. In such *multinational states,* the disadvantaged group or groups often resent that one or more other ethnic groups – located in the dominant core area – have all the political power and enjoy a higher standard of living than they in the dependent periphery. They feel, and frequently are, discriminated against and exploited, as well as looked down upon, by inhabitants of the core. Since ethnically heterogeneous countries are particularly common in Africa – almost every African state has a number of ethnic territories within its boundaries – it is not surprising that this continent has been plagued with numerous instances of internal strife, aggressive ethnic nationalism, liberation movements, and civil war (e.g., in Angola, Nigeria, Sudan, Ethiopia). As a result, there are large numbers, even millions, of refugees.

Multinational states and plural societies

A multinational state may be defined as a country in which culturally distinct groups of people (or *nations*) are concentrated in different parts of the country. Canada could serve as an example. In a plural society, by contrast, various cultural or ethnic groups live side by side throughout most or all of the country, so that they cannot claim to have their own territory. An example of a plural society is the U.S. Both the multinational state and the plural society have a heterogeneous population, but they differ in terms of the manner in which the various groups of people are spatially distributed (see Fig. 15).

It should be apparant from the figure that secessionist movements and claims of regional self-determination are more likely in a multinational state than in a plural society. Although plural societies are hardly ever plagued with separatist demands, they may be faced with continuous intergroup antagonism and discrimination. Relations can be quite tense when one group enjoys a much higher standard of living than other groups, a situation which fosters jealousy and perhaps even overt hostility. Indonesia, for example, has a substantial number of Chinese inhabitants, many of whom are employed in commercial activities, especially in retailing. Partly because they tend to be comparatively affluent, they are not well liked by much of the rest of society. Like the Jews in pre-war Germany and elsewhere in Europe, they are often made into scapegoats and discriminated against (Drake 1981).

Similar problems are encountered in several East African countries, where people of Asian origin – mainly from the Indian subcontinent – occupy an economic position not unlike that of the Chinese in Indonesia. They, too, are rather successful as retailers and enjoy a higher level of material well-being than the average Kenyan or Ugandan citizen. Like the Chinese in Indonesia or the Jews in Europe, they are highly urbanized and relatively well educated. Their different culture and physical appearance,

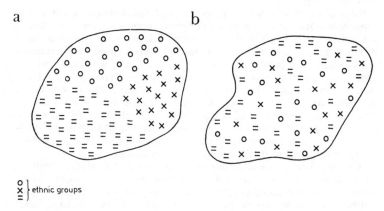

Fig. 15. Hypothetical multinational state (a) and plural society (b).

together with their relative prosperity, have bred *xenophobia* and jealousy among the African majority – the age-old problems of out-group enmity, as opposed to in-group amity. In 1973, some 30,000 Asians were expelled from Uganda, causing a detrimental brain drain from which Uganda has not yet recuperated. More recently, many Asians in Kenya became victims of hostile xenophobic feelings. In the summer of 1982, in the wake of an attempt by Africans to overthrow the Kenyan government, Asian neighborhoods in Nairobi were plundered by angry mobs of poverty-stricken Africans who looted Asian stores, demolished Asian homes, and raped Asian girls and women. Following these atrocities, many of Kenya's 100,000 Asians seriously considered leaving Kenya – their native country – afraid lest they might once again become the victims of violent out-group antagonism.

In several respects, the situations just described form a sharp contrast with the kinds of problems discussed by Michael Hechter. In his seminal work on Britain's "Celtic fringe" (1975), Hechter postulated his theory of *internal colonialism,* according to which ethnic nationalism is awakened by discrimination against a particular ethnic minority. Commerce and trade in a peripherally located ethnic region are monopolized by the

183

ethnic majority in the core. The peripheral economy is forced to be dependent on, and subservient to, that of the core, and thus becomes underdeveloped. Economic dependence is reinforced through judicial and political measures. Hechter's central theme is that there is a causal relationship between cultural differences and economic exploitation.

Discrimination and exploitation by the politically and economically dominant majority is likely to result sooner or later in dissatisfaction among members of the deprived ethnic minority. No longer willing to put up with their lower standard of living, poor public services, lack of political power, and their being treated as second-class citizens, they may demand regional autonomy or even total separation, making their region into a sovereign state.

Regardless of whether there is a causal link between cultural and economic differences, or whether peripheral minorities always do have a lower standard of living than the majority in the core, the type of political problem described by Hechter and his followers only occurs in multinational states; not in plural societies. In that sense, we could call it a *geopolitical* problem. And since so-called 'tribal societies' – especially common in Africa – are essentially multinational states in which one particular tribe often has more political and economic power than the other tribes, they are all faced with the dilemma of potential, geopolitically rooted instability. A current example of such instability is provided by Zimbabwe, in which the Ndebele people in Matabeleland are discriminated against by the Shona people in Mashonaland.

It is, therefore, all the more important that the leaders of such countries try to avoid, or reduce, regional inequalities. By the same token, efforts should be made to avoid or alleviate extreme primacy. Too much polarization in a tribal society or multinational state is almost certain to foster political unrest and possibly political fragmentation, neither of which is likely to help the urgently needed fight against poverty, hunger, and suffering in the Third World.

Components of urban growth: natural population growth and net-migration

Birth rates in Third World cities are considerably higher than in Western cities. Rates of 3 percent or more are not at all unusual, meaning that there are 30 or more life births per 1,000 inhabitants per year. Although urban birth rates usually are lower than rural birth rates, urban death rates, especially infant mortality rates, tend to be lower as well due to better drinking water, sewerage, medical services and a relatively youthful population. The result is that rates of natural increase in the cities are about as high as they are in the rural areas, on average about 2.5 percent. This alone would cause Third World cities to grow quite rapidly.

Many cities, especially the bigger ones, experience an annual increase of between 4 and 8 percent. This growth is a clear indication that migration plays an important role. We can distinguish five types of internal migration:

intra-urban, inter-urban, rural-to-urban, urban-to-rural, and rural-to-rural migration. Of these, only the second and third types contribute to the rapid expansion of the larger cities. Inter-urban migration often consists of the movement from small cities to bigger ones. The most common type of migration in the Third World is the movement from rural to urban areas. This is, of course, the only type of internal migration that can raise a country's overall degree of urbanization – no matter whether it is permanent in character or temporary, such as 'circular' labor migration. This latter term implies that the labor migrants expect to return home after having spent a year or more in the city. In Africa, most migrant laborers are males, many of whom travel over long distances and frequently across one or more international boundaries, e.g., from Burkina Faso to Ivory Coast and Ghana, or from Malawi and Mozambique to South Africa.

Rural-to-urban migration

In studies concerning the causes of the often massive migration from rural to urban areas, a distinction is usually made between *push factors* and *pull factors*. The former are unfavorable conditions in the rural areas which encourage, or even force, people to leave the countryside and settle in an urban place. Pull factors represent favorable circumstances in the cities which attract people from the rural areas.

Most push factors are economic in nature, e.g., unemployment, low wages, and insufficient opportunity to make a decent living. In an earlier chapter we already discussed the reasons for the widespread economic malaise in the rural areas. One of these is the demographic factor, that is, the rapid rate of population growth. To this factor we can add the problems of rising expectations – which often have not materialized, at least not fast enough – and the fact that owing to better information (e.g., transistor radios!) rural people have become increasingly aware that they are poor and disadvantaged. They may even feel discriminated against.

In addition to economic reasons there may be other factors which motivate rural people to migrate to a city. Among these is the low quality or absence of health care and education. Sometimes rural-to-urban migration represents an escape from social obligations or social controls. Nowadays, many young people feel tied down by the traditional values and folkways which dominate life in the small rural villages. In the anonimity of the big, bustling city they can enjoy a measure of personal freedom. Here, again, heightened awareness plays an important role, breeding a sense of frustration and boredom among young people living in the countryside.

We have just seen that cities attract rural migrants because they can offer them a number of amenities, e.g., schools and recreational facilities, that they have to do without in the villages. To these pull factors we can add the fact that most rural migrants can find one or more relatives or acquaintances in the city. Surveys have shown that many migrants consider this fact to be very important because they can rely on relatives, fellow tribesmen,

32. Moving in West Africa. Villagers migrate to the big city in search of work and better living conditions. (WHO/VDO)

etc. for providing temporary shelter and helping them to find work. But the most important pull factors are the relatively high urban wages and the diversity of job opportunities.

The fact that a large percentage of the rural migrants do not succeed in the big city, cannot find work and end up living in makeshift huts in a squalid shantytown, is clear evidence that push factors are more powerful than pull factors. Or, to put it differently, conditions are worse in the rural than in the urban areas, a conclusion which is underlined by the fact that the tidal wave of rural-to-urban migrants does not subside. On the contrary, the stream keeps swelling. With rural living conditions deteriorating, millions of people are driven by desperation to exchange their rural environment for an urban habitat.

Clearly, the urbanization process in the Third World differs fundamentally from that which the developed countries experienced. There, rural-to-urban migration was largely a response to growing employment opportunities in the cities. Besides, the push factor was less powerful. Instead of stagnation and declining productivity, growing output per farmer – made possible by mechanization and better cultivation practices – enabled many young people to leave the farms and look for work in the cities.

In spite of the massive out-migration, few rural areas in the Third World have become depopulated or now have a population with a drastically

186

altered (i.e., older) age structure. Exceedingly rapid rates of natural population growth make an absolute decline in the number of rural people virtually impossible, while at the same time maintaining a relatively young population. In most rural areas, 40 to 50 percent of the population consists of children, so that age pyramids have a very broad base. As a result, these areas are faced with unfavorable *dependency ratios,* that is, with many economically unproductive persons per 100 economically active adults. Generally speaking, the dependency ratio may be calculated with the following formula:

$$\frac{\text{children} + \text{aged}}{\text{adults}} \times 100\%$$

Most people who migrate to the cities move rather short distances, usually not more than a few hundred kilometers. This fact is not surprising considering that one tends to have more information about nearby than faraway places – an example of *distance bias.* One is also more likely to know some people in a nearby town than in a distant city. If villagers are encouraged by earlier migrants to 'make the same move,' and they do decide to go to that same city, we are dealing with *chain migration.* As suggested earlier, this type of migration plays an important part in the Third World urbanization process. Finally, short-distance migration has two additional advantages: it is relatively cheap and it makes it possible for the migrants to maintain contacts with relatives and friends who have not (yet) decided to leave the countryside.

Migration is often selective as certain age groups (or cohorts) are more likely to move than are others. People between the ages of 15 and 30 tend to be overrepresented among the migrants. And usually, more males than females move to the cities, so that sex ratios there may differ markedly from those in the rural areas. This difference is particularly true during the early stages of rural-to-urban migration. In later years, the trend may reverse, with more females than males leaving the rural areas. In Latin America, where there are relatively many urban jobs suitable for women, men are outnumbered by women in quite a few cities.

As already mentioned, not every migrant settles in the city permanently. There are those who move to a city every year, only to stay for a few months. They arrive after the crops have been harvested, find a temporary job, and return to their village by the time the next growing season starts. In addition to this short-cycle (or seasonal) migration, there are types of 'circular' migration which are much less temporary. For example, the gold mines in the Witwatersrand region of South Africa employ large numbers of migrant workers who sign contracts for a year or longer. Upon completing the contracted period they return home, which for many is Lesotho, Botswana or some other country in southern Africa. Many laborers sign subsequent contracts and return to the mines, thus spending much of their productive life away from home and family.

Circular migration in Africa

Long-distance migration of laborers is particularly common in Africa, and dates back to the colonial era. In *Which Way Africa?* (1964), Basil Davidson describes how this form of circular migration came into being and what its consequences are:

". . . land was useless without labour, and so were mining concessions. The enclosure of land and the opening of mines went hand-in-hand with pressure on rural Africans to leave their homes and work for European wages, or rather, . . . for European employers. It is here that we arrive at what was probably the most destructive element in the economic system of the [European] invaders.

Directly forced labour was used in all colonies, . . . but the British and French early came to prefer *indirect* methods of forcing Africans to work for Europeans. Their approach was simple. They applied a money tax to peasants who lived without money. Either the peasants earned the money to pay the tax, which meant going to work for Europeans – or the police seized them for 'punishment', which meant, of course, the same thing . . .

It is hard to exaggerate the extent and the effects of this imposition of the need to work for Europeans on countless millions of subsistence farmers and their dependents. It went on everywhere, and it went on recklessly. Large areas were denuded of their 'fit adult males' for long periods of time. Huge populations adjusted to colonial rule by taking it increasingly for granted that their men would annually leave home and 'migrate' to the towns and mines and white plantations . . .

The gross effect . . . was serious and continuous dismantlement of the pattern and structure of social life. And this was compensated by no corresponding gain in understanding and advancement by the men who went to the mines of the Rand [i.e., the Witwatersrand near Johannesburg, South Africa] or the Rhodesian Copperbelt [now Zambia], and there they worked as unskilled labourers beneath a colour bar of white enforcement . . .

Year after year, from one end of the continent to the other, countless hundreds and thousands of men could be found trudging on foot from territory to territory – unless their prospective employers, like the South African gold mines, had got the migrant system so well organized that they could provide lorries, trains, and even aeroplanes.

Borders and frontiers, closed or open, made no difference to this ceaseless movement of men in search of wages: the sheer need to earn money (initially to pay taxes, afterwards to ensure survival of their families) drove them across every obstacle. In an average year, for example, half the total force of able-bodied men in Basutoland [now Lesotho] is away working in South Africa. The proportion for Malawi has often been almost as high . . . In West Africa the plantation economy of the Ivory Coast rests on labour from neighbouring Upper Volta; an even larger number of peasants from Upper Volta goes annually to Ghana. A map of all these annual migrations, sketched across Africa, would show a cobweb of trodden paths."
Basil Davidson, *Which Way Africa?* pp. 39-41 and 85.

Temporary migration frequently turns into permanent migration. The more time a person has spent in a city, the smaller the chance that he or she will return to the village. Even those who do not succeed usually decide to stay, if only to avoid the humiliation of being looked upon and treated as failures by fellow villagers. Besides, the chances of finding work in the village would in most instances be very slim. Apart from an occasional visit to the village and despite efforts to maintain ties with relatives back home, urban-to-rural migration hardly occurs in most Third World countries.

Inter-urban migration is fairly common, especially in large countries with numerous cities. Sometimes it takes the form of *step migration*, with rural people first moving to a nearby small town and later deciding to move on to a larger city further away. And although they may not end up in a big city, perhaps their children will – the so-called 'generation stepwise migration.'

Since rural-to-urban migration as well as inter-urban migration tend to converge on the bigger cities, these large urban centers usually grow much faster than the smaller ones. The ultimate result is an increasingly uneven distribution of the urban population, with particularly large concentrations in the primate cities. This pattern becomes even more unbalanced in the event that the smaller urban places lose some of their regional functions due to the growing influence and dominance of the bigger cities. When this happens, the smaller towns become stagnant and may decline in population. Gradually, they lose part of their urban character and even their *raison d'être* – a process which has been referred to as *ruralization*.

Ruralization can have adverse effects on the surrounding rural area. Small farming communities need a variety of services. This is particularly true in case the farmers want to increase their output, improve or modernize methods of production, and become more commercialized and specialized. To make such changes possible, farmers need information and advice as well as credit facilities and marketing outlets. In brief, what they need is a fairly dense network of small towns which can provide these services and where farmers can get the supplies, implements, spare parts and repair services necessary to become modern agricultural producers.

Unfortunately, numerous Third World countries have a shortage of such regional service centers, while the ones which do exist may be declining in importance and losing population. The consequence is that farming remains backward, unproductive and under-commercialized. Agriculture may even decline, with many farmers sliding back into a subsistence-type of existence and living almost wholly outside the modern money economy.

Under these conditions, it is not surprising that rural people continue to move away from the countryside. Sometimes, formerly productive farmland becomes abandoned and food production declines. Meanwhile, various small rural towns and market centers experience economic stagnation and loss of service functions. The big cities, by contrast, become increasingly swamped with unskilled rural migrants, most of whom compete for small jobs in the urban informal sector. As long as these processes continue, and especially as long as the farmers do not become more productive and remain incapable of feeding the urban population, Third World countries are unlikely to solve the problems of underdevelopment (cf. Hyden 1980).

Contrasting urbanization processes

We have seen that urbanization in the Third World differs markedly from that in the advanced countries. During the Industrial Revolution, growing industrialization in Western cities created jobs which attracted rural migrants. Since natural population growth was moderate – both in the cities and the rural areas – and the push factors in the rural areas were not particularly strong, cities in Europe and North America never experienced the rapid increases in population now common throughout the Third World. Industrialization often preceded and stimulated urbanization, whereas in the Third World urbanization usually precedes industrialization. As a consequence, most Third World cities struggle with massive unemployment and have a tertiary sector which is far too large when compared with the size of the secondary sector, or, for that matter, with the overall level of economic development. In the developed countries, the urban tertiary sector did not begin to show signs of rapid expansion until the cities had become important centers of industrial activity. In the Third World, this sequence of events tends to be reversed, with the tertiary sector employing far more people than does the secondary sector. This, then, explains the term 'tertiary urbanization,' first used by M. Santos (1971).

Using past developments in the advanced countries as a yardstick, we could come to the conclusion that the process of urbanization in the Third World is taking place too rapidly. More specifically, the big cities – often primate cities – are too large. Notwithstanding the fact that Bombay, Calcutta, Cairo, Seoul, and Jakarta do not possess much industry, each has more than 6 million inhabitants, which is about six times as many as Paris had in 1851. In other words, the Third World's colossal urban agglomerations are much less the products of high levels of industrial activity, economic growth and prosperity than they are the epitome of persistent poverty, economic stagnation, and exceedingly rapid rates of population growth. In a sense, they are the most visible expressions of under-development.

Intra-urban disparities

Everywhere in the world, cities are characterized by spatial inequality. Prosperous residential neighborhoods contrast with low-income neighborhoods; old dilapidated sections with overcrowded tenements have little in common with spacious suburbs dominated by single-family homes. Unquestionably, Third World cities show the most extreme disparities, not only in terms of income levels but also with regard to population density, architecture (morphology), and quality of public services. Generally speaking, the rich are extremely rich and many of the poor are extremely poor. While there are fewer rich people than in Western cities, the poor are far more numerous. Perhaps the most notable difference is that a relatively well-to-do middle class – so dominant in Western cities – is quite small in all but a few Third World cities. Thus, the contrasts are much greater and more conspicuous; extreme wealth occurs side by side with abject poverty and deprivation. In an earlier chapter we identified similar contrasts in the rural areas, especially in Latin America and parts of Asia, where relatively few wealthy landlords are outnumbered by poverty-stricken peasants, sharecroppers, and landless laborers.

Another conspicuous contrast found in many Third World cities exists between the CBD and much of the rest of the built-up environment. This is particularly true of the primate cities. Whereas the CBD has an ultra-modern appearance – with many new and architecturally impressive buildings, luxurious hotels, air-conditioned restaurants, modern stores, beautiful conference centers, sumptuous headquarters of multinational concerns, well-maintained avenues with wide, shady sidewalks, and high-quality public services – much of the rest of the city is devoid of all these ingredients of modernity. With the exception of a few wealthy residential neighborhoods, most of it is unplanned, poorly serviced (e.g., unpaved streets and open sewers), overcrowded, and poverty-ridden.

Chapter 12 Shantytowns

Introduction

A large percentage of the inhabitants of Third World cities cannot afford to buy or rent a regular house. Instead, they build their own dwelling, using cheap materials, such as old pieces of corrugated iron, flattened oil drums, tin cans, scrap wood, old bricks, plastic and rags. Particularly the unemployed rural migrants often have no alternative; the demand for housing far exceeds the supply, and low-cost public housing generally does not receive sufficient attention. Even where the government is able and willing to provide cheap housing, it is incapable of keeping up with the large and fast-growing demand. As a result, even people who can afford a decent home frequently are unable to find one.

Large residential sections of makeshift hovels can be found in virtually every Third World city. Without doubt, they are the most visible features of urban underdevelopment. In Latin America they are often called *barrios clandestinos,* while in French speaking areas the terms *bidonvilles* and *zones d'habitat spontané* are used (*bidon* = gasoline can or jerrycan). In English, the terms squatter colony, squatter settlement and shantytown are most common. By 1960, there were some 100 million people living in shantytowns (Juppenlatz 1970, p. 23). Before long, their number will reach the $\frac{1}{2}$-billion mark! Today, close to half the Third World's urbanites live in *barriadas, favelas, bidonvilles* and similar squalid residential neighborhoods in and around cities.

Origin, location and physical characteristics of squatter settlements

Some cities have known squatters for many years. The first *favelas* in Rio de Janeiro came into being shortly after the turn of the century, when people left nearby coffee-growing areas and migrated to the city. Lima's oldest *barriadas* date back to the 1920s. In most cities, however, 'spontaneous' (read: 'illegal' or 'clandestine') neighborhoods did not become a widespread phenomenon until after World War II.

Shantytowns are often found on land that is ill-suited for urban development, e.g., on steep slopes or flat and poorly drained valley bottoms. Outside Recife, Brazil, thousands of people live in primitive wooden huts built on stilts in the heavily polluted lagoons. Others are located next to garbage dumps or dirty industries. In some cities, thousands of people live in little shacks or cardboard boxes on railroad right-of-ways, only a few feet away from the tracks. Elsewhere, people live on tiny boats and primitive rafts.

Usually, squatters prefer to build their settlements on government-owned land rather than on privately owned land. This reduces the chance

33. Residential neighborhood in Belize City, Belize, Central America. This neighborhood compares favorably with the urban slums and shantytowns found throughout the Third World. (H. Spruyt)

that they will be evicted. It is not uncommon that they occupy the land collectively, in a well-organized and carefully 'planned' manner. In a very short period of time – often at night – tens or even hundreds of families invade a vacant plot of land and quickly construct their shanties. This collective action is called forth by the fact that their occupation is illegal. By confronting the authorities with a *fait accompli*, they hope to avoid eviction.

Since most inhabitants cannot afford to pay for public transportation, they must travel on foot or ride a bicycle to work. This explains why many shantytowns are located close to factories and construction sites. Others are within walking distance from the center of town with its concentration of informal jobs. And sometimes squatter settlements may be found at a stone's throw from a wealthy neighborhood, where many of the poor people find employment as cleaning ladies, cooks, chauffeurs, gardeners, and house servants.

Most shanties are not only poorly constructed, but they also are very small and lack such basic services as running water and electricity. They leak in rainy weather and are drafty as doors do not close properly and windows are without panes. In winter they are cold because of the absence of a heating system. Since the huts are small and built close together,

34. Livingroom in India. One-room and two-room dwellings are the rule rather than the exception in the Third World. (VDO)

population densities frequently are extremely high. Instead of streets there are unpaved footpaths and alleys, too narrow to be used by cars or wagons. Open sewers are commonplace, and after a few hours of rain the entire neighborhood changes into one large filthy, stinky mudhole.

It goes without saying that shantytowns tend to be unhealthy habitats. Without running water, showers, flush toilets and washing machines it is next to impossible for people to properly clean themselves and keep their clothes, bedding and homes clean as well. If we add to this that medical services are grossly insufficient and that most people eat pretty much the same food every day of the year, it is understandable that a fairly large percentage of the inhabitants suffers from chronic ailments. Infectious diseases tend to be particularly common. It is not at all surprising, then, that death rates – especially infant mortality rates – are significantly higher than in other parts of the city.

The people

Although some adults and children go through life as beggars, most people have a job and are thus integrated into the urban economy, albeit marginally. Many are employed in the informal tertiary sector, earning barely enough to subsist. Others may have construction jobs or work in a factory. Especially in Africa, it is not uncommon that the women practice a

194

35. Squatter settlement along a river in Jakarta, Indonesia. Paved streets and underground sewers are unknown in most shantytowns. (R. Giling)

little agriculture or horticulture in the urban fringe area, sometimes selling part of the produce in the urban marketplace.

Of course, not all shantytown residents are people who have migrated from rural areas. Many have come from smaller cities, while others have lived in the big city all their lives. Some residents stay in a shantytown for a number of years, after which they move on to a better neighborhood. Then there are those who used to live in a respectable section of town but who, for one reason or another, were forced to resettle in a shantytown. All in all, there is a fair amount of mobility, with younger families and rural migrants moving in and older families moving out.

Turner (1967) and others have discovered that many rural migrants first settle in an old slum area near the center of town and later move out to an illegal squatter settlement in the urban periphery. For some the reason is that they want to get away from the noise, congestion and polluted air in the downtown area, while for others it is the desire to stop paying relatively high rents. Living in a peripheral squatter settlement is not only cheap – making it possible for people to save some money – but also enables the inhabitants to work on their own house and make it into a reasonably comfortable residence without running the risk of the landlord raising the rent. Although such center-to-periphery moves appear to be fairly common in Latin America, they are relatively unknown in most cities in Asia and Africa.

The smoldering slums

For Gervacio Peñaranda, home is a muddy hovel built of scrap wood and tin, amid the stench of open drains in a teeming waterfront slum in Manila. His six ragged children scavenge amid broken glass and trash heaps, while Peñaranda, 37, peddles bananas in order to earn $2.20 a day. "It is hard to feed my family," he complains. But things may soon get even worse. The banana vendor is one of greater Manila's 1.6 million squatters, and his family faces eviction from the shack they have 'illegally' occupied for the last seven years. Peñaranda fears that moving means starving and he vows to stay. "The relocation site is too far from work," he says.

The population of Manila is swelling at the rate of 200,000 a year. Many of them are peasants fleeing destitution in the countryside. They set up leaky lean-tos in vacant lots or huddle in abandoned warehouses, becoming an embarrassing eyesore for the image-conscious Marcos regime, as well as a tindery social and political issue. Despite church relief work, the squatters' slums are breeding grounds for prostitution, crime and even political subversion by anti-Marcos guerrilla groups.

The plight of the squatters has become a prime concern for First Lady Imelda Marcos, who as human-settlements minister controls the National Housing Authority. As part of a controversial slum-clearance scheme launched last June, she has ordered thousands of shanties demolished and their inhabitants resettled. One achievement has been the razing of the shanties that fringed Manila International Airport and offered many visitors a first dismal glimpse of the Philippines.

But the relocation plans have run into opposition. Many squatters have fought eviction with rocks, bottles and barricades. And critics charge that the government has squandered millions on prestige projects like gleaming new convention centers while ignoring the urban poor. Several modern four-story housing projects have been built with great official fanfare. But a recent World Bank report indicates that many of them are going to middle-class families, not to the neediest squatters, most of whom cannot afford the rent.

Despite the risk of jail and heavy fines, vague legislation on squatters' rights has encouraged many squatters to stay put. In the past, the government has sometimes granted longtime 'illegal' inhabitants of public property titles to their scraps of land. Last June a large squatter community in Manila's Sampaloc District won ownership rights after living in the area for 30 years.

Given the squatters' tenacity, the Marcos government is unlikely to risk urban rioting with a wholesale relocation program. The National Housing Authority has earmarked $1.5 billion over the next 15 years to improve living conditions in the slums themselves. The funds will come from World Bank loans and other sources. And last week the U.S. government chipped in $50 million to improve the lot of Filipinos living near U.S. military bases, including 28,000 squatters.

But money alone is unlikely to check the malignant growth of the slums. The Philippines has one of the highest birthrates in Southeast Asia: its population of 50 million is surging at the rate of 2.4 percent a year. During his visit to the Philippines last year, Pope John Paul II warned that the

rehabilitation of the waterfront slum would never catch up with the swelling flood of new squatters. As much as 40 percent of Manila's population now earns less than $140 a year – and hunger and lack of housing might soon push the squatters from apprehension to open revolt.
Source: T. Nater & R. Vokey (1982), The Smoldering Slums. Newsweek, Sept. 13, p. 28.

Are there solutions for the shantytown problem?

We have already seen that poverty is not the only factor why shantytowns are so prevalent in Third World cities. Another important reason is the shortage of 'normal' homes. Practically everywhere, construction of new houses lags far behind the massive influx of migrants. This being the case, the shantytown problem might be reduced by building more low-rent houses.

Although this approach could help alleviate the situation, various authors have pointed out that it may well have negative consequences for the remaining shantytowns. Provision of cheap housing will result in selective migration, that is to say, only the people who can afford to pay the rent will leave the squatter settlements. These often are the people with relatively well-paid jobs or permanent work and with more education than the average squatter. Precisely these individuals tend to play a useful role in the poor neighborhoods. Apart from the fact that they may set good examples for others, they often are local leaders without whose organizational talents, initiatives and advice the neighborhoods would be worse-off than they already are.

Additional drawbacks of the housing construction approach are, first, that it might encourage even larger numbers of rural people to migrate to the cities, and second, that it does not benefit those segments of urban society which have the greatest need for support. When low-cost housing is subsidized, it tends to discriminate against the very neediest families. The result may be a heightened awareness of hopelessness and growing apathy which, in turn, could lead to unrest, agitation and an increase in criminal or illegal activities. In order to avoid such disintegration, it has been suggested that a certain percentage of the new homes should be made available to the very poorest – homes for which hardly any rent, or no rent at all, has to be paid. This solution, however, is costly, even for such relatively prosperous Third World countries as petroleum-exporting Nigeria. In the event countries do possess the financial means to provide free housing for the poor, they probably lack the political will to effectuate such schemes. Although the latter problem is particularly common in free enterprise societies, socialist countries, too, have been less than successful in this respect.

197

Hong Kong is often cited as *the* example that could possibly be followed by other Third World countries. In 1956, Hong Kong had some 300,000 squatters. To alleviate this problem, plans were developed to build very modest six-story tenement buildings in which each family received a minimum amount of living space (120 square feet). On each floor there were communal bathrooms, laundry rooms and kitchens. Rents were so low that most people could afford them. Eleven years later no fewer than 600,000 former squatters were living in such low-cost tenements. Furthermore, each neighborhood was provided with one or more stores, playgrounds, post offices, schools and various other facilities, including regular trash collection and street cleaning. The residents were also given advice as to how they could make optimum use of, and best maintain, their limited living quarters (Juppenlatz 1970, pp. 52-62).

Hong Kong's successful approach could be adopted elsewhere. However, because Hong Kong is a unique case, it is not at all certain that its particular solution to the shantytown problem is applicable to cities everywhere in the Third World. First of all, the number of squatters formed a relatively small proportion of Hong Kong's total population. Secondly, the large influx of migrants from the People's Republic of China has slowed down considerably in the course of the years. In most other Third World countries, rural-to-urban migration has not lessened; on the contrary, it has accelerated. Thirdly, in most countries, large-scale measures to improve urban housing conditions would result in a larger than ever flow of rural people to the cities. In Hong Kong this situation is not possible because it has virtually no rural areas. Finally, mention must be made of the fact that Hong Kong, a British crown colony, has received considerable financial support for its housing schemes from the U.K. government.

Since shantytowns are such complex phenomena, caused as they are by rural stagnation, rapid population growth, low wages, widespread unemployment and underemployment, low levels of productivity, and social injustice, it is extremely difficult to find a single solution. It would seem that the only answer is a well-planned and carefully managed comprehensive socioeconomic development strategy aimed both at the rural *and* the urban environment.

Obviously, such wide-ranging and ambitious plans require immense investments and, thus, massive development aid from the rich, industrialized countries. Besides, alleviation or elimination of shantytowns cannot be accomplished in just a few years. In other words, only long-term policies have a reasonable chance of producing the desired results. Efforts geared to short-term solutions are not only likely to be ineffectual, but may well do more harm than good. An uncoordinated, piecemeal approach must be avoided at all cost, which implies that the national government must work out concrete programs and control the entire development process.

Most governments, unfortunately, do not do nearly enough. Sometimes there is a lack of concern on the part of the well-to-do politicians. Sometimes other concerns, e.g., industrialization, receive practically all the attention. Almost everywhere there is a shortage of funds and expertise for developing and carrying out integrated long-term plans. Instead of helping the squatter population, governments frequently try to simply get rid of the squatters. Few efforts are made to make the shantytowns more liveable, if only because government officials fear that this will result in making them more permanent and encourage their expansion. Instead of putting in sewage systems and water mains and providing electricity to the squatter settlements, bulldozers are sometimes used to 'solve' the shantytown problem.

Meanwhile, squatting remains illegal in a number of Third World countries, so that the squatters live in a state of continuous uncertainty. Knowing that they may be evicted any moment and that their homes may be bulldozed away, the squatters obviously are not particularly motivated to upgrade the quality of their neighborhoods. If, on the other hand, they were given legal title to the land they occupy, they might be more than willing to do whatever they can to make lasting improvements to their homes and upgrade the entire neighborhood. If the government were to encourage them and offer advice and support (e.g., free use of tools and equipment), squatters could install water mains and sewers themselves. In several places where this self-help approach has been tried, the results have been very encouraging, with many squatters interested in spending all the money and time required to make the desired improvements.

Governments could also try to avoid the creation of new (illegal) squatter settlements. This could be accomplished by designating specific tracts of land for urban expansion, subdividing them into lots and providing aid for putting in all basic utilities – the so-called 'site-and-service' projects. Although the people must build their own homes, the government can help them by supplying cheap materials, taking care of delivering the building materials, giving the people advice and allowing them to take out small loans. This site-and-service approach has several advantages: urban expansion is no longer illegal and haphazard; construction costs are considerably lower than in the case of large-scale, ready-made housing projects (as in Hong Kong); and it instills a fair amount of pride among the new residents in their 'own' neighborhood. The last-mentioned aspect is important in that it is a virtual guarantee that the inhabitants will be motivated to properly maintain their habitat.

It is encouraging that these ideas are gaining acceptance in a growing number of countries. Governments are gradually adopting more tolerant attitudes toward squatting, realizing that it makes more sense to help squatters make the shantytowns as liveable as possible than to try to bulldoze the squatter settlements out of existence.

Chapter 13 Core and periphery
in Third World countries

Sharp regional contrasts

In addition to the urban-rural dichotomy, the core-periphery dichotomy is often employed as a framework for describing the spatial differences and contrasts so typical of Third World countries.

In the core or center we find a concentration of modern industrial, commercial, and service activities. Frequently, it also constitutes the country's agricultural heartland. Agriculture there tends to be more advanced, more commercialized, and above all more productive than in the rest of the country. The higher yields are in part due to the relatively well-developed physical and social infrastructure, for example, there are more and better roads as well as more and better schools. The nearness of a large urban market – usually including the primate city – explains why many farmers grow crops for sale. The core region is further characterized by a standard of living which is above the national average, by rapid population growth and by an expansion of non-rural employment opportunities. Finally, since the national capital tends to be located in the core region, the latter almost invariably dominates the rest of the country politically, economically, demographically and also culturally.

By contrast, the periphery is overwhelmingly rural, relatively stagnant and backward, quite inaccessible, and characterized by a shortage of modern services (schools, health facilities, etc.) as well as by out-migration, subsistence agriculture, and low levels of material well-being. The periphery also has little or no political power, this despite the fact that a substantial proportion of the total population lives there.

Core-periphery differences, of course, also exist in developed countries, but there the contrasts tend to be much smaller, if only because of government efforts aimed at opening up and economically stimulating the more backward and rural parts of the country. In the industrially and technologically advanced countries – no matter whether they have an essentially free-market economy or a government-controlled planned economy – forces are constantly at work which foster geographical redistribution of wealth. These forces put pressure on the government to funnel funds from the more economically dynamic regions to the less advantaged regions. In the United Kingdom, for example, major efforts have been made to aid the 'depressed areas' – old industrial regions with high levels of unemployment. Serious efforts to accomplish redistribution are uncommon in Third World countries. In fact, as we have seen already, often the exact reverse situation exists, with the relatively prosperous core enriching itself at the expense of the periphery. Typically, the gulf separat-

200

ing dominant core and dominated periphery becomes ever wider in most underdeveloped countries. In only a handful of countries, e.g., Cuba and Taiwan, has spatial inequality been reduced in recent years.

In some instances, conspicuous spatial disparity dates back many centuries, as for example in Mexico. More commonly, core-periphery contrasts did not emerge until after capitalism had obtained a foothold during the colonial period. Certain advantaged areas became more developed than the rest of the colony and acquired a measure of dominance over the remainder of the territory's space-economy. Owing to such inherent advantages as favorable location, early head start and increasingly important political-administrative functions, this core region has continued to grow faster than the rest of the country, often attracting foreign (multinational) industrial investments. With the increasing concentration of modern economic activities in the core, other parts of the country have become progressively 'peripheralized' and subjugated. A network of unequal (or asymmetric) relations now ties the periphery to the core, often resulting in the relative, if not absolute, decline of the former and continuing growth in the latter. In other words, the periphery is being colonized, causing extreme polarization in the country at large.

Manifestations of such asymmetric relations include:

(1) The periphery supplies cheap raw materials and agricultural products to the core, where many of these resources are processed, thus creating employment opportunities and a measure of wealth there.

(2) The periphery imports relatively expensive industrial goods, some of which are produced in the core area by import-substitution industries. With declining prices for raw materials and rising prices for industrial consumer goods – sometimes artificially high due to industrialization policies – the people in the periphery are the victims of a cost-price squeeze that is usually referred to as *unequal exchange*. While the farmers have to pay more for fertilizer and other agricultural inputs, they receive less for their crops.

(3) As a result of economic stagnation, widespread unemployment and low wages in the periphery, many of the better-educated and more enterprising young people leave the countryside and migrate to the core. This way, the periphery functions as a supplier of cheap labor.

(4) There usually is not enough capital in the periphery to stimulate new economic activities. Part of the reason is that capital is siphoned off by the core. Apart from the fact that much of the tax money collected in the rural areas ends up in the cities, the rural elite (e.g., large landowners) spend a large part of their money in the core – often on luxury consumer goods – and invest capital outside the periphery.

(5) If domestic 'core capital' is invested in the periphery, e.g., in canneries or sawmills, most of the profit flows back to the national core region.

For the peripheral areas, the overall effect of above-mentioned asymmetrical relations is increasing marginalization, pauperization and deprivation. They become underdeveloped backwaters characterized by growing unemployment and out-migration. Being situated at the losing end of a dominance-dependence relationship, they are caught in a vicious circle of declining productivity, growing indebtedness, deteriorating man/land ratios, and environmental degradation (soil erosion). In utter despair, not a few people withdraw from the money economy and revert back to a food-producing, subsistence type of existence.

The crisis in the peripheral areas derives in part from the absence of a strong decentralization policy. Not only are entrepreneurs free to invest where profit margins are greatest, that is, in the relatively highly urbanized and comparatively dynamic core region, but government investments, too, are likely to be concentrated in this same, advantaged part of the country. This is particularly true in the event the government promotes import-substitution industrialization. Stimulation of manufacturing activities invariably means that the bulk of government subsidies go to urban-based enterprises. In other words, government-provided incentives are usually core-directed, giving the core region an even greater advantage (and dominance) over the periphery. Or, as Myrdal has pointed out, a 'spiral of cumulative causation' results in positive *spread effects* in the core, and in negative *backwash effects* in the periphery.

In view of this contrast between growth in one small part of the country – especially in and around the capital/primate city – and stagnation or decline in much of the rest of the country, it is not surprising that the discussion concerning regional development often focuses on the necessity to promote a more even distribution of urban centers. According to its advocates, a better-balanced pattern of urbanization, with small and medium-sized cities outside the economic heartland, will bring employment opportunities closer to the majority of the population. It will also make it easier for farmers to market their produce and to acquire the inputs and services needed to increase their productivity. Further, a more even distribution of urban places would help open up areas that have thus far remained highly inaccessible, thus making it possible for them to become more productive. In Africa and Latin America, in particular, there still are immense areas which are virtually uninhabited or so underutilized that their economic importance is negligible.

Proponents of even development and balanced urbanization realize that these objectives can only be realized by means of strong government action and carefully planned and effectively controlled long-term policies. Through a combination of fiscal incentives and penalties the government should encourage enterprises to settle in smaller towns and discourage them from locating in the core region. Such a decentralization policy has been put into effect in Puerto Rico, and the results have been quite favorable. Yet, the costs of the program were very reasonable (Odell 1970, p. 543). In larger countries, however, decentralization will require considerable financial sacrifices, if only because of the costs of overcoming the 'friction of space.' But it is precisely in these larger states where the need to

The equity-efficiency debate

Governments are faced with the problem of having to choose between two alternative policy goals: improved *equity* or greater *efficiency*. Efficiency may be defined as economic output or economic growth, and equity as the fair distribution of the fruits of economic growth.

In the early stages of modern economic expansion, there is a tendency for economic growth to become concentrated in one small portion of the country – the original core area. Other areas lag behind, so that the fruits of economic growth are poorly distributed. In later stages of economic expansion, the laggard regions are opened up and begin to attract economic activities. With the spread of manufacturing from the core to the periphery, the latter becomes increasingly integrated into the national space-economy, and the fruits of development become more evenly distributed.

According to this theoretical model, efficiency precedes equity. An early period of increasing spatial inequality is automatically followed by a period of declining spatial inequality. This, at least, is the conclusion Williamson (1965) has arrived at on the basis of the history of economic development in Western countries. Using Williamson's findings as a guideline, Third World countries might decide to adopt an 'efficiency-now and equity-later' policy, pointing out that an 'equity-now' approach might well retard economic growth and eventually produce an equitable distribution of poverty and backwardness. After all, if an equity-now policy results in economic inefficiency, thereby impairing the country's competitive position in the world, not much economic growth will take place.

In an earlier chapter we have seen that it is hazardous to assume that current developments in Third World countries can be compared with past developments in the advanced countries. In other words, Williamson's model may not apply to the Third World. In view of the fact that cities like São Paulo and Mexico City already are much larger than London and Paris were in 1850, it is indeed questionable whether spatial inequality in Third World countries will *automatically* diminish with continuing economic growth. In fact, indications are that it will not; that regional disparities and polarization will only intensify.

The dilemma is clear: what are Third World countries to do? An efficiency-first policy exacerbates the already immensely wide gulf between core and periphery, while an equity-now policy seems doomed to result in subsistence-level living conditions for everyone. Whereas the core can be expected to prefer an efficiency-first approach, the periphery is likely to favor a policy which fosters reduction of spatial inequality. Meanwhile, efficiency is likely to receive more attention in capitalist than in socialist countries, whereas socialist governments are inclined to make serious attempts to spread the fruits of economic development evenly across space. Regardless of whether a country is essentially capitalist or essentially socialist, it cannot ignore either the equity or the efficiency side of the issue. It must pursue some kind of compromise, that is to say, adopt an equity-with-efficiency policy. The critical question then becomes: How and with what types of incentives and disincentives can both objectives best be served? Obviously, a simple answer cannot be given. Since every country is unique, the answer will differ from one country to the next.

decentralize is greatest. The sooner the relentless growth of such giant urban agglomerations as Mexico City, São Paulo and Buenos Aires can be halted, the better it would be.

With few exceptions, policies aimed at urban decentralization and regional development have been anything but successful. The larger cities continue to attract many enterprises and migrants. Even if some economic activities locate in the periphery, the basic dominance-dependence structure is likely to remain intact. In fact, it may intensify. Integration of the peripheral regions into the national economy often results only in growth – not in development. Commonly, much of the profit earned by branch plants in the periphery ends up in the core where the parent companies and national headquarters are located. In other words, efforts to spread economic activity more evenly throughout the country do not necessarily diminish the periphery's subordinate position, and could well lead to greater spatial inequality. If the result is further accumulation of capital, power and influence in the core region, polarization becomes more pronounced. While the country's overall GNP grows, regional disparities grow as well, that is, *equity* is sacrificed for *efficiency*.

In case economic growth leads to excessive spatial inequality, there is a danger that the country will fall victim to social unrest and political instability. Widespread dissatisfaction in the periphery is particularly likely in times of economic recession. Since the decision makers are located in the core, they find it easier to shut down factories in the periphery than in the core. The result is that an economic slow-down tends to hit the periphery harder than the core. During a recession, moreover, efficiency arguments usually become stronger relative to equity arguments. These are well-known phenomena, not only in the Third World, but also in the advanced countries. They underscore the vulnerability of peripheral, *dependent development*.

In much the same way, the Third World as a whole occupies a vulnerable, dependent position *vis-à-vis* the developed countries which occupy a dominant position in the world economic system. It is no coincidence, therefore, that global economic recession tends to hit the underdeveloped countries harder than the developed countries.

The possible role of cities in regional development

Because regional inequality correlates rather closely with differences in urban development, the question rises what role cities can play in the process of regional development. More specifically, to what degree can they function as *growth centers* or *growth poles* stimulating economic development in the laggard regions?

Different authors have different opinions. For example, A.G. Frank looks upon the cities as 'metropoles' which exploit the countryside ('satellite'). The cities, in turn, are satellites of the rich countries which exploit the Third World. Within the international capitalist system, the cities in Third World countries function as relay stations in a network of metropole-satellite relations which tie the Third World's peasants to New York, Tokyo and Paris. By way of the urban relay stations, profits (or surplus values) are channeled to the world's major capitalist cores. While investments, technology and expensive industrial goods move down this world-embracing hierarchical structure of dominance-dependence relations, cheap raw materials and labor move in the oppositie direction. This situation is referred to by Frank as the 'development of underdevelopment' or as 'dependent development.' Also the expression 'growth-without-development' is used in this context. But whatever it is called, the important point to make is that according to *dependency theory* à la Frank, Third World cities play a negative role. Instead of being centers of growth and development, they are centers of foreign domination and exploitation.

Others, e.g., Hirschman and Friedmann, see the role of the cities as more positive. Both believe that the future of the underdeveloped countries lies with the cities because they – and they alone – have the capacity to pull the Third World countries up to a level of economic development that may some day approach that of the wealthy countries. Just as the growth of urban centers made possible the development of the advanced countries, so cities are needed to raise levels of productivity and material well-being in the Third World.

McGee has compared Frank's pessimistic view with that of Hirschman and Friedmann, and comes to the conclusion that both are exaggerated. In his opinion, both views pay insufficient attention to the reality of the actual urbanization process in the underdeveloped countries (McGee 1971, p. 13).

In contrast to the rather one-sided and negative view of Frank, Hoselitz (1960) makes a distinction between 'parasitic' and 'generative' cities. A city is generative in case "its formation, continued existence and growth is one of the factors accountable for the economic development of the region or country in which it is located." A parasitic city "exerts an opposite impact" (Hoselitz 1960, pp. 187-188). The problem of how one should establish whether a given city is generative or parasitic does not concern us here. More important is the more carefully balanced appraisal which Hoselitz's terminology allows.

There is considerable evidence that cities are parasitic, at least in a number of respects. They attract the brighter and more enterprising young people from the surrounding rural area. Wealthy landowners and moneylenders tend to reside in the cities, where they spend most of their rural-derived income. Agricultural traders, too, often live in the cities and spend most of the profit they make there. Thus, there is a constant flow of capital from the countryside to the urban centers. Additional capital is extracted from the rural areas as a consequence of unequal exchange; farmers receive low prices for their products but have to pay dearly for manufactured goods and urban-based services. Also, a disproportionately large percentage of the rural-derived tax revenues usually ends up in the cities, while much of the savings farmers have deposited in banks is invested not in the rural areas but in the cities.

Notwithstanding these parasitic relations, it would be incorrect to conclude that cities have exclusively negative influences on their surroundings. Besides offering employment opportunities to rural migrants, they may play a role in alleviating unfavorable man/land ratios in nearby agricultural regions. Cities often are important as markets for agricultural products, giving farmers an opportunity to grow crops for sale; both food crops and industrial crops. Furthermore, the rural population can take advantage of services provided by the city, including various agricultural inputs, without which crop yields per hectare and/or per farmer would be lower than they would otherwise be.

Summarizing the above, we conclude that cities tend to be both parasitic and generative at the same time. However, some cities clearly are more parasitic than others, and they are more parasitic in some countries than in others. Comparing Third World countries with advanced countries, most authors agree that cities in the former group of countries are less generative and more parasitic than those in the latter group (e.g., M. Santos 1971). It would seem that this difference can be explained, at least in part, in terms of a difference in the distribution of landownership. If much of the agricultural land is in the hands of a small number of large landowners, cities usually are rather highly parasitic. On the other hand, in countries where farmland is more equitably distributed among the agricultural producers and/or farmers' cooperatives are well developed, the parasitic nature of urban places tends to be considerably weaker.

Conclusion

Third World cities can play an important role in the process of regional development. In fact, they are absolutely necessary – just as roads, banks and schools are necessary. No modern development is feasible without communication, trade, credit, education and information, and these facilities and services cannot be provided adequately and economically unless there are urban nodes. Preferably, there should be an integrated network of smaller and larger nodes that can serve as the framework for a well-functioning space-economy. If and when such a Christallerian 'spatial lattice' is available, overall productivity can be raised well above presently existing levels. Increased productivity, both in rural and urban areas, is a *sine qua non* for development. Without it, levels of material well-being will remain low and hunger and poverty will continue to prevail. Through effective spatial integration of town and country, the rural areas can stimulate economic progress in the cities, while the cities can stimulate development in the rural areas. Just as economically healthy and dynamic cities require a productive and prosperous hinterland, so well-functioning rural hinterlands require generative urban centers.

Core and periphery, in other words, should not function as antagonistic entities with conflicting interests and with relations that are characterized only by dominance and dependence. Instead, emphasis should be placed on their *mutual dependence* or *interdependence*. The narrow-minded and self-defeating conflict of interests between core and periphery should not be stressed, but rather their *harmony of interests*. Core and periphery, or urban node and rural hinterland, need each other and depend on each other. It is up to regional planners, economists and geographers to de-emphasize and try to reduce the core-periphery dichotomy and work out realistic proposals aimed at their functional integration. Unequal, parasitic relations must be replaced by equal, generative relations which are mutually beneficial both to urban nodes and rural hinterlands.

This, of course, is no mean task, especially not for a poor, under-developed country. It requires a great deal of sophisticated, long-term planning and the careful selection of sites for future growth centers. It also requires a considerable amount of motivation on the part of the government as well as the dedication of uncorrupted officials. At the same time, it requires generous, unselfish development aid donations on the part of the rich countries. After all, the World's Core and Periphery are interdependent parts of one and the same international economic system. Here, too, parasitic-exploitative relations need be replaced by mutually beneficial, cooperative efforts aimed at greater equity for all humankind.

PART FOUR

THEORIES OF DEVELOPMENT AND UNDERDEVELOPMENT

Chapter 14   Causes of underdevelopment: an overview of theories

In the preceding chapters, attention was focused on the more important *characteristics* of underdevelopment, both in the rural areas and the urban environment. We now turn to a discussion of *theories* concerning the *causes* of underdevelopment. Our purpose is to arrive at a more complete understanding of the processes responsible for the development of underdevelopment.

Some older views

Prior to the early 1950s – when Third World problems received very little attention (see Chapter 1) – it was customary to associate the absence of modern economic development with the limited possibilities offered by certain physical (often tropical) environments and/or particular cultural traditions and value systems which, in the eyes of Westerners, impeded change and progress. As for Latin America, geographers and other scientists were apt to point out that it produced more revolutions and *coups d'etat* than stable governments and capable leaders. Instability and other adverse *internal* conditions were viewed by many as the major causes of underdevelopment.

In those days, colonialism was rarely seen as an obstacle to development. This was not surprising since many Third World countries were still colonial possessions; the suggestion that colonialism was responsible for poverty and economic backwardness would have been tantamount to condemning the colonial activities of the metropolitan countries. In fact, people in Western countries were generally convinced of the exact opposite view, i.e., that it was the God-given responsibility of the West to bestow civilization, Christianity and economic development on the overseas dependencies – the so-called 'white man's burden.' The inhabitants of the colonies in Africa, Asia and the Caribbean were commonly looked upon as primitives or heathens who were incapable of looking after themselves (see Marx's views below).

The fact that considerable attention was paid to Latin America's political instability is understandable for two reasons. One was that most of the region was not colonial, but consisted of sovereign states which had achieved independence more than a hundred years previously. The other reason was that revolutions and coups constitute radical changes which tend to go hand in hand with violence, material destruction, loss of lives and insecurity, thus causing many people to have little confidence in the economic future of their own country. At the same time, revolutions often

211

lead to the loss of political influence and economic power (wealth) on the part of the former elite. Although revolutionary changes may lay the foundation for a period of economic growth and a more equitable distribution of wealth for society at large, they are just as likely to set the stage for more revolution, instigated by those individuals or segments of society which suffered most from the previous revolution. The long-term result may well be a more or less permanent climate of turmoil and instability.

It goes without saying that extended periods of political turbulence are not conducive to economic development. The lack of economic expansion, in turn, is likely to foster widespread dissatisfaction that sooner or later is translated into demands for radical change, including attempts to overthrow the government. As a result of such conditions of self-perpetuating instability, the country is almost certain to become the victim of a downward spiral of progressive disintegration and increasing underdevelopment.

In a similar vein, the suggestion that low levels of economic development in Africa, Asia and Latin America may have something to do with the unfavorable conditions of their natural environments is not altogether without foundation. A very large proportion of the Third World is located in areas with humid tropical (Af, Am) climates, savanna (Aw) climates or hot dry (BSh, BWh) climates.

It was above all the French geographer Pierre Gourou who many years ago concluded that most soils in humid tropical areas are infertile and become exhausted after having been farmed for a few years. In addition, extensive areas – especially in monsoon-Asia – repeatedly receive so much precipitation that fields become inundated, resulting in widespread destruction of crops and in soil erosion. The humid tropical climates also are conducive to the spread of all kinds of diseases and parasites which afflict humans as much as farm animals. The low quality of tropical grasslands, furthermore, severely limits the possibilities of raising high-quality livestock. Animal husbandry is further discouraged by the fact that meat and milk readily spoil in the tropics. Finally, the combination of high temperatures and high levels of relative humidity, as well as the small diurnal and seasonal temperature ranges, do not favor hard physical labor. Working conditions in factories often are extremely unpleasant due to oppressive heat and muggy weather.

Insufficient rainfall, together with the unpredictability as to when the rainy season will set in and how long it will last, limits the agricultural potential of the semiarid and savanna regions. Crop failure occurs frequently, and as soon as the dry season lasts longer than usual – but what is usual? – natural pasturelands are likely to become overgrazed. When that happens, the ecosystem may be irreparably damaged. In large parts of Africa and the Middle East, many thousands of square kilometers of agricultural land have been lost for good as a result of a centuries-old process of desertification.

Of course, the truly arid areas, or deserts, are even less productive. Crops can be grown only where there is water for irrigation, as is the case in the Nile Valley and in scattered oases. In Africa and Asia, especially, very extensive forms of livestock raising are practiced by nomads who are constantly migrating from one patch of sparse vegetation to the next.

Since weather conditions in much of the Third World are characterized by a great deal of annual variability, crop failure is a fairly common phenomenon. In 1983 and 1984, for example, much of Africa suffered severe drought, while a few years earlier large parts of Asia had received insufficient amounts of rain. An immediate consequence of crop failure is that large numbers of small farmers are forced to borrow money. Thus, they become dependent on, and exploited by, moneylenders, traders, landlords and others who are able and willing to provide them credit. Due to the high interest rates that are usually being charged, it may take several consecutive 'fat years' before a farmer can pay off his/her debt. Squeezed dry by their creditors, most small farmers are and remain impoverished, unable as they are to put aside part of their meager earnings to 'insure' themselves against the damages of the next crop failure.

Vicious circles as causes

When it became increasingly apparent during the 1950s that under-development was far more widespread than had hitherto been realized, several development experts drew attention to the fact that Third World countries were caught in a complex web of interlocking vicious circles (see Figure 16). The various circles – each of which constitutes a chain of cause-and-effect relations in which a certain unfavorable circumstance leads to one or more other maladjustments that in turn perpetuate, or even magnify, the first – have a tendency to propel and reenforce one another. Many scholars believed that the poor countries were not able to free themselves from the vicious circles without outside help. Their suggestion was that the rich countries should provide massive assistance in the form of financial, technical and managerial aid.

The main objective of this Marshall-type approach was to stimulate growth in the modern sector of the economy and reduce the size of the so-called traditional sector. This way, they argued, Third World countries would get rid of the *dualism* or *fragmentary modernization* that character-izes their economies and tends to produce a highly unequal distribution of wealth. At the same time, foreign aid would allow them to increase the low levels of productivity found in all sectors of their economies. Since low productivity was generally regarded as one of the main bottlenecks holding back economic development, it is not surprising that it shows up in a strategic place in Figure 16. If productivity could be increased, so the experts reasoned, earnings would go up, purchasing power rise and domes-tic markets expand, so that agricultural and industrial producers would sell more, make more profit and be able to make investments in order to raise

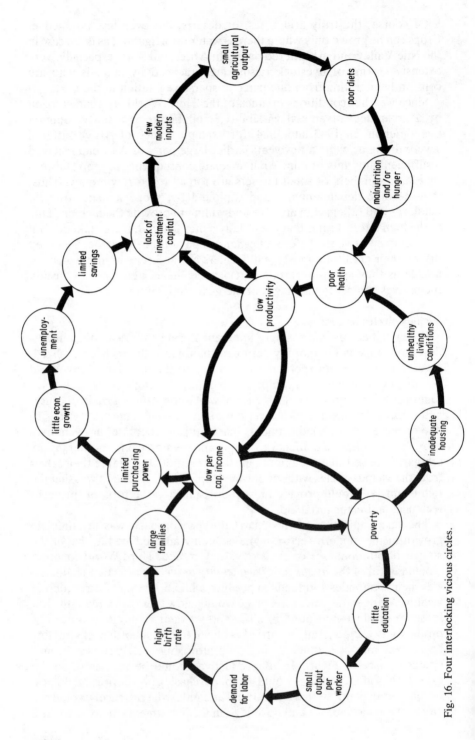

Fig. 16. Four interlocking vicious circles.

214

productivity (and output) even more. In this way, the countries would break out of the stagnation dilemma and become sufficiently dynamic to set out on the road towards sustained growth.

Colonialism as scapegoat

Before long, the vicious-circle view became the target of severe criticism. Skeptics pointed out that its proponents had not indicated how 'their magic circles' had come into existence. Some argued that no process repeats itself in time and that change follows the path of a spiral which travels either upward or downward. Others emphasized that vicious circles do not explain anything; at best they describe an already existing situation. In order to understand the problems afflicting the Third World, they claimed, it was not sufficient to note that various and often very different aspects of underdevelopment were related to one another and that this relatedness somehow caused stagnation. Instead, they called for an historical approach, that is, a thorough analysis of the sequence of events which presumably had brought about underdevelopment. They wanted to explore the historical roots of the downward-spiraling process of underdevelopment and trace it through time from its starting point to the present moment.

One of the most important consequences of this new point of view was that during the late 1950s and early 1960s colonialism became increasingly identified as *the* cause of disintegration and decline in the Third World. In rapid succession, one author after another pointed out that the metropolitan countries had had numerous disastrous effects on their colonial territories. The indigenous population had been exploited, while their traditional way of life, culture and self-sufficient mode of production had been destroyed. Forced to pay taxes, the people either had been compelled to work for wages or grow cash crops for Western markets. In some areas, the colonial rulers had employed forced-labor practices and other forms of slavery; in other areas, the native people had had to surrender part of their farmland or had been pushed off their land altogether. Through the introduction of a money economy, many farmers had fallen victim to unscrupulous loansharks and other businessmen.

In virtually all colonial areas, social differentiation had increased, frequently caused by drastic changes in landownership relations. As a result of preferential treatment *vis-à-vis* certain groups or due to deliberate divide-and-rule policies, latent hostilities between different segments of the indigenous societies, e.g., ethnic or religious groups, had sometimes developed into inter-tribal warfare or aggravated forms of discrimination.

Allegedly, colonialism had wrought equally fatal effects on the secondary and tertiary sectors. Unable to compete with imports of cheap, often mass-produced, textiles and other manufactured goods, many artisans and craftsmen were forced out of work. Meanwhile, modern industrialization in the colonies was purposely discouraged by the mother countries. The

Europeans, furthermore, controlled the often lucrative foreign trade and had developed a modern tertiary sector which they dominated.

The changes which had taken place in the colonies clearly served the interests of the metropolitan countries and their trade companies. Hence, whatever development had occurred was *dependent development,* not autonomous development. Clearly, the colonial powers and the expatriate population in the colonies had enriched themselves at the expense of the native peoples. In exchange for imported manufactures, the colonial dependencies had to supply the Western countries with raw materials. In this way, an *international division of labor* as well as a Western-dominated international trade structure had evolved which worked to the advantage of the colonial powers and to the disadvantage of their overseas territories.

The external dependence of the colonies was readily visible in their spatial organization; a modern infrastructure of roads and railroads existed only in those areas which produced primary goods needed by Western industries or which in some other way played a role in the 'rape' of the colonies by their foreign rulers. Other areas were not opened up and all too often degenerated into reservoirs of cheap, unskilled labor. Urban development, too, displayed a highly uneven spatial pattern. Only places that occupied a strategic position in the externally enforced network of economically exploitative relations, and in particular port cities, developed into important urban centers.

Colonialism also led to dramatic demographic changes. Following an initial decline in population, caused mainly by the spread of new diseases and slave trade (Africa), population numbers began to rise – usually at increasingly rapid rates – due largely to the introduction of Western health standards, insecticides (e.g., DDT) and modern medical facilities and medications. While the traditionally high birth rates remained high, death rates dropped precipitously, particularly during the last few decades of the colonial era. Combined with the slow rate of economic growth and the persistently low level of productivity, this population explosion has resulted in widespread pauperization and marginalization.

Marx on colonialism

Contrary to what is often believed, Marx considered capitalism as the most advanced socioeconomic system ever achieved and held that its expansion into the pre-capitalist (backward) areas of the world was desirable and progressive – not retrogressive. He looked upon capitalism as a superior mode of production and saw the rise of capitalism as the greatest progress in human history. Understandably, then, he welcomed its extension to non-European societies by means of direct colonialism. Since Marx regarded colonialism as the historical process of capitalist expansion, he recognized the progressive role of British colonialism in India and other overseas areas.

In 1853, Marx published an article in the *New York Daily Tribune* (June 25) which unequivocally shows that he considered colonialism as a powerful engine of positive social change. Referring to the thousands of villages in India, he wrote: "These small stereotype forms of social organism have been to the greater part dissolved, and are disappearing . . . through the working of English steam and English free trade . . . English interference . . . sweeping away both Hindoo spinner and weaver, dissolved these small semi-barbarian communities, by blowing up their economical basis, and thus produced the greatest, and, to speak the truth, the only *social* revolution ever heard of in Asia."

". . . we must not forget that these idyllic village communities, inoffensive though they may appear, had always been the solid foundation of Oriental despotism, that they restrained the human mind within the smallest possible compass, making it the unresisting tool of superstition, enslaving it beneath traditional rules, depriving it of all grandeur and historical energies . . . We must not forget that this undignified, stagnatory and vegetative life, that this passive sort of existence, evoked on the other part, in contradistinction, wild, aimless, unfounded forces of destruction, and rendered murder itself a religious rite in Hindostan. We must not forget that these little communities were contaminated by distinctions of caste and by slavery, that they subjugated man to external circumstances instead of elevating man to be the sovereign of circumstances, that they transformed a self-developing social state into never changing natural destiny, and thus brought about a brutalizing worship of nature, exhibiting its degradation in the fact that man, the sovereign of nature, fell down on his knees in adoration of Hanuman the monkey and Sabbala the cow."

A little later, Marx wrote in the same paper (August 8, 1853): "England has to fulfill a double mission in India: one destructive, the other regenerating – the annihilation of old Asiatic society, and the laying of the material foundations of Western society in Asia . . . Steam has brought India into regular and graphic communication with Europe, has connected its chief ports with those of the whole south-eastern ocean, and has revindicated it from the isolated position which was the prime law of its stagnation . . . The British having broken up this self-sufficient inertia of the villages, railways will provide the new want of communication and intercourse . . . [once] you have introduced machinery into the locomotion of a country, which possesses iron and coal, you are unable to withhold it from its fabrication. You cannot maintain a net of railways over an immense country without introducing all those industrial processes necessary to meet the immediate and current wants of railway locomotion, and out of which there must grow the application of machinery to those branches of industry not immediately connected with railways. The railway system will therefore become, in India, truly the forerunner of modern industry."

"Modern industry, resulting from the railway system, will dissolve the hereditary divisions of labor, upon which rest the Indian castes, those decisive impediments to Indian progress and Indian power."

For similar reasons, Marx favorably viewed the annexation of Mexican territories by the US, while Engels welcomed the French conquest of Algeria as an important event in the progress of civilization.

Source: Warren 1982, particularly pp. 40-44.

The views of Lacoste and Bobek

Whereas many scholars accepted the anti-colonialism point of view, others were convinced that it was no more than a partial explanation, and a one-sided one at that. First of all, they pointed out – like Marx and Engels had done a hundred years earlier (see box) – that colonial domination had some undeniably positive effects on the overseas territories. Second, they emphasized that it was incorrect, even misleading, to talk about colonialism as if it had been the same everywhere. Indeed, there had been (and still were around 1960) marked differences in the nature as well as the intensity of colonial activities. For example, Portuguese colonialism differed from British and Japanese colonialism, while Dutch colonialism in Indonesia was not the same as Dutch colonialism in Surinam. Even within Indonesia, colonial activities displayed great contrasts from one place to another, e.g., between Java and Sumatra. A third point they made was that some former colonial areas had been independent for a century or more, but remained underdeveloped. Perhaps most convincing was their argument that parts of the Third World had never been colonial dependencies or had known colonial domination for very short periods of time, sometimes only a few years (e.g., China, Thailand, Afghanistan, Iran and Ethiopia).

Few geographers have made significant contributions to the early underdevelopment debate. Two, however, merit to be mentioned: the Austrian Hans Bobek and the Frenchman Yves Lacoste, both of whom had serious reservations concerning the one-sidedness of the anti-colonialism interpretation.

According to Lacoste, underdevelopment is an extremely complex phenomenon which cannot be fully explained in terms of past colonial domination, present neo-colonial relations, certain religious values, cultural traditions, unfavorable physical conditions and/or rapid population growth. Although each of these factors may have contributed to the problem, there often are other circumstances which may well have played a more decisive role.

Lacoste has argued in favor of thorough historical analysis of factors which have caused stagnation and disintegration *prior to* the onset of modern (European) colonialism. By studying the distant past, Lacoste suggests, it may be possible to come up with an acceptable explanation for the underdevelopment of areas which have never been colonized. On the basis of various such investigations, he has arrived at the conclusion that stagnation and underdevelopment have often been caused by the selfish behavior of an indigenous elite. In other words, abject poverty among the majority of the population was brought about not by external colonialism but by *internal* colonialism, characterized by feudal-like forms of tribute appropriation. Since the peasants lacked the means and incentive to raise the level of agricultural productivity and the upper strata did not use their wealth productively, these societies did not possess the dynamism necessary for sustained economic growth. Instead, most experienced extended periods of no-growth or declining productivity.

218

By stressing that in some instances a dominant and parasitic upper class did not emerge until after the beginning of the colonial epoch, or was strengthened as a result of colonial or neo-colonial relations, Lacoste demonstrated that he was well aware that the problem of underdevelopment can have a strong external component. Nevertheless, he tended to regard underdevelopment chiefly as the product of endogenous forces which originate and grow from within societies.

Bobek's views are somewhat similar to those of Lacoste. After having studied a number of Mid-Eastern countries, among them Iran (Persia), he concluded that these societies had for centuries been characterized by what he termed *rent capitalism*. Small wealthy elites were not involved in productive activities – and thus did not contribute to their countries' GDP – but used their influence to appropriate part of the output (or surplus) produced by farmers and craftsmen. The elites did this by renting land and equipment to these agricultural and industrial producers as well as by loaning them money at high interest rates.

In contradistinction to modern capitalism in which savings and profits are used in order to expand production, a distinguishing feature of rent capitalism is the absence of such investments. The appropriated surpluses mainly serve to satisfy the extravagant desires of the wealthy elite residing in the cities.

Rent capitalism (or Oriental feudalism) already existed in the Middle East and other parts of Asia long before the birth of Christ, and may be almost as old as the earliest urban centers. Bobek believed that every ancient non-Western civilization in which cities existed was characterized by some form of rent capitalism. Since rent-capitalistic systems have undergone little change through the ages, all advanced non-Western societies have known long periods of socioeconomic stagnation and a highly uneven distribution of wealth. The harsh exploitation of the rural masses was not only responsible for widespread poverty, but was a virtually insurmountable barrier to economic progress. Quite clearly, Bobek disagreed with the thesis that modern, external colonialism is the only, or even principal, cause of underdevelopment.

Despite the fact that Bobek's ideas – most notably his rather awkward 'rent capitalism' notion – have received considerable criticism, his theory contains some useful elements. Like Lacoste, he has emphasized that internal constraints can have long-lasting repercussions for the economic development of a given society. And like Lacoste, he has made a valuable contribution to our understanding of the development of underdevelopment by encouraging us not to overlook the social, economic and political conditions that prevailed in pre-colonial, pre-capitalist days.

Imperialism theory and dependency theory

In 1917, Lenin published his *Imperialism: The Highest Stage of Capitalism*. In this essay, he turned upside down Marx's view on the progressive nature of colonial expansion, thereby erasing from Marxism the idea that capitalism can have a positive effect on the social and economic development of non-Western societies. The result has been that since 1917 most Marxists have regarded colonialism (or imperialism), and more recently also neo-colonialism, as the major obstacles to development in the Third World and, more to the point, as the chief causes of underdevelopment in the world.

Since the 1960s, these views – better known as imperialism theory and dependency theory – have enjoyed a fair amount of popularity. Notwithstanding the fact that the many advocates of these two closely related theories do not always agree on specific details, they invariably emphasize that the Third World countries occupy a dependent, or *subordinate,* place in the international economic system, or, as (neo-)Marxists say, in the 'world capitalist system.' Both imperialism theory and dependency theory are concerned with the unequal relationship which exists between the imperialist developed countries of the First World, on the one hand, and the dependent underdeveloped countries of the Third World, on the other. The main difference between the two views is that imperialism theory looks at this relationship from the point of view of the developed countries – which, according to this theory, need to establish and maintain economic control over the Third World in order to ward off the 'inevitable' demise of their capitalist mode of production – whereas dependency theory looks at this same relationship from the point of view of the underdeveloped countries. Dependency theory emphasizes the disadvantages which the exploitative activities of the imperialist countries and their multinationals have on the countries of the Third World. In reality, the two theories have borrowed so much from one another, that they have become virtually indistinguishable.

In the course of the past few centuries, and more specifically since about the 1880s, the Third World countries have become *dominated* by the prosperous and generally highly industrialized countries of Western Europe, the US and Japan. The developed countries of the capitalist First World are said to have 'penetrated' the Third World countries, thereby forcing them into a vulnerable and dependent position within the capitalist world system. An important aspect of this system is 'the' international division of labor, in which the Third World countries have been 'assigned' the inferior role of suppliers of raw materials and the First World countries maintain full control of all key industries.

Major characteristics of the Third World, so proponents of both theories claim, are its *peripheral* or *dependent capitalism* and its *incomplete capitalist transformation.* Traditional pre-capitalist modes of production (particularly subsistence farming) still survive, at least to some extent, but have become subjugated by the modern capitalist sector. The result is *dependent development.* The partial integration of the Third World into the world capitalist system makes it possible for the advanced countries to siphon off a constant flow of surplus out of the peripheral countries and into the economically dominant core countries.

Dependency theory was developed during the 1960s by Latin American scientists looking for solutions to the economic problems which their part of the world faced as well as for an explanation of those problems. Once the theory had gained some acceptance, around 1970, it became increasingly applied to other Third World areas, and before long it threatened to become a *deus ex machina* which supposedly could account for all problems of underdevelopment anywhere on earth.

What to do with theory?

In the preceding paragraphs, several theories of underdevelopment have been briefly discussed. None has escaped criticism. Just as dependency and imperialism theorists have denied that vicious circles have explanatory value, so others have rejected the theories of dependency and imperialism as too simplistic and too ideologically colored. Likewise, the views of Lacoste and Bobek have been dismissed as too limited in scope for explaining problems of underdevelopment.

All theories presented here appear to have at least one thing in common; after having obtained a measure of acceptance, they have become more or less discredited, only to be replaced by other theories. Apparently, science behaves somewhat like a fashion in that a period of diffusion and growing popularity is sooner or later followed by a period of contraction and rejection.

It is our opinion that the Third World is remarkably diverse, consisting of a heterogeneous collection of countries which are dissimilar in terms of size, climate, landforms, population density, culture, history, natural resources, economic activities, administrative efficiency, political ideology, international relations, etc. There also are important differences in location. Whereas Mexico borders on a developed country, Malawi is surrounded by underdeveloped countries. Another locational difference between these two states is that Mexico has direct access to two oceans, whereas Malawi is in the unfortunate situation of being a land-locked country without any seaports. Altogether, there are no fewer than 23 landlocked countries in the Third World, mostly in Africa, and since landlockedness constitutes a serious handicap for economic development, it is not surprising that they are strongly overrepresented among the group of hard-core, least-developed countries.

Since India is unlike Mauritania, Kuwait unlike Afghanistan, and Jamaica unlike Bolivia, it is simply impossible that one theory could explain underdevelopment everywhere. By the same token, no one single development strategy could possibly resolve the problems of poverty, malnutrition and low productivity in all Third World countries. On the contrary. If a particular development policy – export-oriented industrialization, for example – is successful in some countries, as it is in Taiwan, South Korea and Singapore, this success will make it all the more difficult for other countries to pursue that same strategy.

221

Underdevelopment, we believe, must be seen as the product of an array of complex and continuously changing interactions between past and present, between natural and human factors, and between internal conditions and external relations. The multitude of obstacles to development and the many retrogressive forces causing underdevelopment vary with place and time. In some instances – depending on place and time – exogenous forces may play a decisive role, while in other instances – again depending on place and time – endogenous factors may well be more influential. Historically oriented case studies of individual countries or regions, carried out for the express purpose of bringing to light the nature of the processes of underdevelopment, tend to support this view. At the same time, such regional analyses indicate that none of the above-mentioned theories should be discarded. All can serve as invaluable research tools that help the researcher to ask the pertinent questions. For each investigation, the researcher should make a careful evaluation regarding which theory or theories can best be employed to explain the origin and continued existence of underdevelopment in a particular region or country. Certainly, it would be a grave error to decide *beforehand*, perhaps on the basis of one's ideological convictions, which theory ought to be used. A wrong choice of theory, obviously, will lead to incorrect conclusions, and more importantly, to the formulation of an inappropriate and possibly harmful development strategy. Whereas dependency theory, for example, can contribute significantly to an understanding of the underdevelopment of Jamaica or Indonesia, it may shed little light, if any, on the underdevelopment of Uruguay or Iran.

In the next two chapters, we pay special attention to (1) Lacoste's views and (2) the views of the imperialism and dependency theorists. In contrast to the former, which emphasize the role that *internal* factors have played in the process of underdevelopment, the latter theories focus on the importance of *external* causes.

The theoretical discussions are followed in Part Five by case studies of four markedly different Third World countries, i.e., Ethiopia, India, Cuba and Taiwan. An important purpose of these case studies is to test the various theories of underdevelopment and to apply them where possible to explain past and present conditions of underdevelopment in a diversity of concrete situations.

Chapter 15 Lacoste's explanation of underdevelopment

Among geographers, it was mainly Bobek and Lacoste who prior to 1965 tried to find a satisfactory explanation for the development of under-development. Bobek has clearly stated that colonialism alone was not a sufficient explanation of the problem. His major contribution has been to point to an *internal* cause, viz., the underdeveloping effect of rent capital-ism. According to Bobek, it is incorrect to suggest that underdeveloped countries, say around 1900, were trailing the now-developed countries on the road to industrialization, because they simply were not traveling that same road (Bobek 1962, pp. 14-15). The modern industrial system could not have developed autonomously under the conditions which prevailed in countries with a tradition of rent capitalism. Firmly established cultural and political institutions as well as mental attitudes were formidable obstacles to processes of modernization and industrialization. As long as these institutional barriers are not removed and attitudes are not changed – something which requires several generations – Western-type development cannot come to fruition. In Bobek's view, massive foreign aid, including large financial injections, is an inappropriate development strategy because it will not yield short-term results in societies which remain in the grasp of an essentially feudalistic system dominated by rent capitalism.

Lacoste has dealt much more extensively than Bobek with the basic causes of underdevelopment. In this chapter we will consider in detail his views as he formulated them in the 1960s. We do so not so much because Lacoste is a geographer, but because he tried to identify the core of the problem and in doing so uncovered a number of important factors which, unfortunately, have received insufficient attention in later theories of underdevelopment, including the dependency and imperialism theories discussed in the next chapter. The fact that Lacoste published in French, rather than in English or Spanish, may be the reason that his views have remained relatively unknown, even among geographers.

Population growth as a factor of underdevelopment

In the early 1960s, Lacoste characterized the situation of underdevelop-ment as a 'permanently disrupted equilibrium' between a rapid increase in population numbers, on the one hand, and a slow rate of resource develop-ment, on the other. It is understandable, therefore, that in his analysis of the causes of underdevelopment, he has questioned whether rapid popula-tion growth forms part of the explanation of the problem.

According to Lacoste, scientists who consider a rapid rate of population growth to be the chief cause of underdevelopment, often use the following

36. Demographic investment in Cameroon, Africa. Even simple school buildings, slates and chalk cost more than many rural communities can afford. (UNICEF/VDO)

line of reasoning. Because of colonialism and other circumstances, the Third World has had for a long time less than its share of modern development. At the moment that economic progress could have begun there and the Third World could have followed the example of the Western industrialized countries, the population began to grow at an increasingly fast rate; this stifled economic progress from the very beginning. Because of the need for large *demographic investments,* it was usually impossible to make the extensive additional investments necessary to increase production per head of the population. The premature acceleration in population growth, in other words, has prevented economic growth, so that standards of living could not rise or started to decline.

Lacoste does not agree with this argument. He points out that the population explosion in the Third World began relatively late. Many of the currently less-developed regions – most of all the long since independent countries of Latin America – could have made investments to stimulate economic expansion well before becoming handicapped by rapid population increase. He also points out that the now-developed countries have had to absorb considerable population growth, particularly during the second half of the last century, although it must be admitted that this growth was not as fast as that presently encountered in most Third World countries. In the majority of the developed countries it reached no more than 1.5 or 2 percent per annum, whereas in many underdeveloped coun-

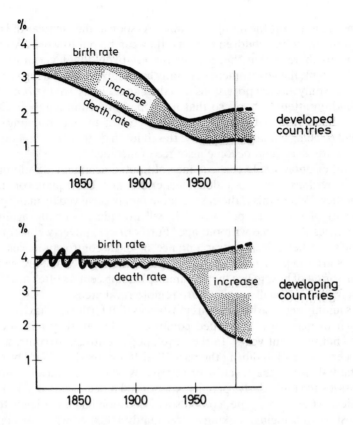

Fig. 17. Two types of demographic change. *Source:* After Y. Lacoste, 1965.

tries it has risen to approximately 3 percent since the Second World War (Fig. 17). Moreover, there were virtually unlimited emigration possibilities for Europeans during the past two centuries – an option not open to peoples of the Third World.

Nevertheless, the slow and modest economic progress must not be attributed to the unfavorable demographic situation. Other factors are primarily responsible for the problem. In Third World countries, explains Lacoste, birth rates have remained high due to the absence of economic development from which broad layers of the population could have benefitted, while the expansion of modern medical provisions has resulted in a drastic decline in death rates. The consequent acceleration in population growth, therefore, is more a *result* of economic stagnation than its cause.

Limited economic growth and the widespread poverty associated with it tend to have a number of serious repercussions. Caught in such a situation, it frequently happens that a large number of children becomes regarded as a

225

means of increasing the family's income. As soon as the physical and mental development of the children permits, they can be put to work. An important factor here is that, because of the relatively low level of economic development, the government generally has limited financial resources and can make only modest provisions for education. Nor is it able to ensure that all children attend school, so that many parents withdraw their children from education and thereby reduce the cost of their upbringing. Thus, instead of being a financial liability, the children go to work – sometimes at a very early age – and become a source of income.

Another unfavorable consequence of limited economic development is that provisions for the elderly generally are inadequate or lacking altogether. Where this is the case, a large family is viewed by many parents as a sort of insurance policy which will provide protection against the deficiencies that come with old age. Furthermore, poverty constitutes an obstacle to the widespread acceptance of birth control practices. Many parents are too poor to be able to afford contraceptives and are generally also ignorant of how to use them. Family planning centers often are few and far between, especially in the more remote rural areas.

It is mainly because of these circumstances that birth rates have remained so high in many less-developed countries, although they have declined somewhat in recent years. In the developed countries, by contrast, there has been a sharp fall during the past 50 to 100 years (Fig. 17). Owing to a substantial rise in the level of prosperity as well as drastically improved provisions for the elderly, people experienced a decreasing need for large families. At the same time, compulsory education had a tendency to raise the costs of upbringing, making a large family a 'luxury' which most people could no longer afford. In addition to the introduction of compulsory education, the ever-growing need of technologically advanced societies to better educate the children meant that they could not enter the production process until much later. Thus, the advantages of having many children diminished, while their liabilities became more apparent.

Various other social and economic developments have contributed to the decline in birth rates in the developed countries. Since there is no need to discuss these in detail, we briefly mention only the following: (1) higher earnings allowed people to save money or take out a life insurance policy so that they did not need to depend on their children to take care of them after reaching retirement age; (2) growing prosperity brought contraceptives within the financial reach of the entire population; (3) improved education, information and medical services greatly aided the widespread adoption of birth control practices; and (4) gradually, large families became increasingly less socially acceptable, exerting pressure on people to conform to the new small-family norm.

Although it is clear from the above that cirumstances having an effect on the level of births in the prosperous countries are of a different kind than those in the Third World, Lacoste does not conclude from this that rapid population growth should be regarded as *the* cause of underdevelopment. He observes rightly that the demographic changes just noted in the rich countries did not happen of their own accord. They were able to take place only because of the occurrence of a host of socioeconomic changes. As a result of the considerable increase in productivity during the past few generations, incomes rose appreciably, allowing governments to collect far more tax revenue than previously. This, in turn, made it possible to provide a wide variety of public services, including social security and high-quality advanced education. It was not just a small privileged group which benefitted from the opportunities created by these changes, but almost the entire population.

Admittedly, cause and effect cannot be easily separated in this development process because as soon as the rate of population growth began to slow down, it became possible to speed up the overall process of socioeconomic betterment. And the improved social and economic climate contributed to a further decrease in the number of births.

In the less-developed countries, on the other hand, such social and economic improvements did not occur, or occurred to a much lesser extent. Birth rates did not decline and sometimes even experienced a slight increase. What did decline, in some countries even precipitously, was the death rate. An explosive population growth was the result. If socioeconomic developments had begun before or at the same time the decline in mortality had set in, the explosive increase in numbers of people would not have taken place because birth rates would also have gone down. Now that a rapid population growth is occurring in nearly all Third World countries, it obviously impedes economic advance to no small degree due to the necessity for extensive *demographic investments,* such as the building of schools, the training of teachers, expanding infrastructural facilities, and creating new jobs.

Lacoste's views on the role of history and the impact of colonialism

As we have seen, Lacoste looks upon the recently accelerated rate of population growth primarily as a consequence of limited socioeconomic development, not as one of its causes. This means that the lack of socioeconomic development, rather than rapid population growth, requires an explanation.

In order to arrive at such an explanation, Lacoste contrasts the histories of European countries with those of non-European countries. There developed in Western Europe from the 11th century onward societies in which an independent bourgeoisie, dedicated to economic progress, freedom and equal opportunities, came to occupy an increasingly important place. In the countries outside Western Europe, such a group was either absent or failed to develop into an influential class. The level of development in most regions outside Europe was low, while the social order was characterized by a lack of dynamism, or even by ossification.

227

Such static conditions also prevailed in regions where higher civilizations had developed, as for instance in India. Since nationalistic sentiments were developed very little among the population, many of these regions suffered sharp internal, political divisiveness. Weakened as the societies were by a lack of cohesion, they made it relatively easy for the West European countries to establish colonies in large parts of the world. Lacoste attaches considerable importance to these different 'initial' situations between Western Europe and the rest of the world.

With reference to colonialism, he believes this to be a factor that has contributed significantly to the emergence of the problem of underdevelopment, but he does not agree with the view that underdevelopment is entirely a consequence of colonial exploitation. By no means does he wish to minimize the role of colonialism, but rather he tries to reduce its role to its correct proportions (Lacoste 1965, p. 213).

Lacoste posits his view on account of the following facts: (1) various parts of the Third World have never been colonies; (2) some countries which today show symptoms of underdevelopment were once important colonial powers (Spain and Portugal); and (3) a number of former colonies are now included among the developed countries, with some of them having achieved great power and prosperity (U.S. and Canada). In order to counter the proposition that colonialism is wholly responsible for underdevelopment, Lacoste puts forward two more facts: (4) nearly all of Latin America lost its colonial status at the beginning of the 19th century, but underdevelopment has increased since that time, particularly after the turn of the century; and (5) despite the fact that the majority of African and Asian colonies have become independent, this has not led to a marked reduction in underdevelopment – nor does it appear that this will happen in the foreseeable future.

Lacoste is well aware that this latter argument is open to criticism since the consequences of colonialism cannot be erased within a few years. Most African and Asian countries became independent so recently that they have not yet had sufficient opportunity to overcome the harmful effects of many years – even centuries – of colonial exploitation. This reasoning does not apply to most of Latin America, which has been independent for several generations. On the other hand, one can point out that its present underdevelopment is in no small measure attributable to the unfavorable socioeconomic and political structures – e.g., the highly uneven distribution of landownership – which Latin American countries have inherited from their Spanish and Portuguese conquerors. Particular circumstances, in other words, can have long-lasting repercussions even though the immediate causes have long since disappeared.

Following his discussion of the role of colonialism, Lacoste reaches the conclusion that, in order to find a satisfactory explanation for the problem of underdevelopment, one needs to know not only the causes of socioeconomic stagnation *during* the colonial period, but also those responsible for stagnation *since* the colonial era. In addition, one should endeavor to identify the causes of underdevelopment in countries which have never had colonial status or have been colonies for only a very short period of time.

The role of ruling elites

Lacoste believes that such an explanation for underdevelopment can be found in the existence of small minorities who hold excessive political and economic power. Powerful minorities (elites) have invariably enriched themselves at the expense of society at large; they have held back, or steered, development in such a way that the great majority of the population experienced little or no improvement in its living standards – it remained poor or became still further impoverished.

Elites may include large landowners, money lenders, traders, industrialists, mine owners, higher-level civil servants, political leaders or members of the clergy. Their role has already been discussed in another connection, but it may be well to list once again the ways in which their actions can limit the opportunities of the masses.

(a) If a small upper class has appropriated a large proportion of the land, it may be responsible for the fact that most potential cropland is used extensively, e.g., for grazing purposes; this has resulted in a large class of landless laborers or small proprietors.

(b) Since a wealthy land-owning elite tends to have considerable control over two production factors, i.e., nature and capital, it can usually exploit a third production factor, viz., labor. In an overwhelmingly agrarian society this means that wages are low while tenancy arrangements are highly unfavorable for the tenants. In consequence, there is widespread poverty as well as little social mobility – factors which help explain the relative absence of a middle class.

(c) Elites may also be responsible for the fact that available capital is not used to increase productivity, but is wasted on luxury consumption by the privileged few. Thus, physical and human resources remain largely unused. To the extent that this refers to capital obtained through the exploitation of underpaid labor power, this means that substantial 'forced savings' are produced by the subjugated peasants and other working-class people with little or no benefit to themselves.

(d) Elites may also be responsible for the flow of capital abroad, where investments may be safer or earn more profit.

(e) The ruling elite often stifles the intellectual development of the masses by not supporting the improvement and expansion of education, or worse, by deliberately opposing it. Where this is so, the reason may be that the ruling minority fears that education will make the poorer members of society more aware of their miserable living conditions and thus more restless. Besides, according to this line of reasoning, the more ignorant the masses, the less well equipped they are to organize themselves into a powerful force demanding higher wages and other social and political reforms. A largely illiterate population, of course, means that productivity stays at a low level and that economic modernization remains virtually impossible.

(f) Elites often are reluctant to make efforts to achieve a reduction in the rate of population growth, their reasoning being that a large population means lower wages and more tax payers.

(g) Because the upper class wishes to maintain or increase its political power, it uses its influence in the administrative sphere for its own benefit. It prevents the masses from organizing themselves politically, e.g., by denying them the right to form political parties. Oligarchically ruled countries rarely have such democratic institutions as free elections and strong labor unions.

229

(h) The same desire may cause those in power to be open to corruption, and to give in to attempts at bribery by foreign firms. Nepotism, too, tends to be widespread.

(i) Finally, the oligarchy may, in order to maintain its position of power, ensure that there is a large army or police force to protect its interests. A large part of the government's budget is frequently reserved for this purpose.

According to Lacoste, small powerful elites can arise in a number of ways. In many instances, they emerged during the period that the now-underdeveloped countries were European colonies. Thanks to possibilities created by the colonial system or through special relations with the colonizers, certain individuals were able to gain exceptional influence which they used to bring the production factors partly under their control.

Other elites are purely indigenous in origin, predating the moment when the areas concerned came into contact with the Western countries. Indeed, privileged aristocracies already existed in pre-colonial days and frequently facilitated the expansion of colonialism, while at the same time further consolidating their own power. Owing to special agreements with European trade companies and/or governments, elites usually managed to acquire more privileges than they had enjoyed previously.

In regions which did not fall victim to colonial domination, the upper class generally also succeeded in increasing its power. This was especially the case after 1850 when modern capitalism became more widespread, enabling elites to take advantage of new possibilities resulting from all kinds of changes associated with the emergence of a worldwide network of economic (largely commercial) relations. Especially in areas where there was no middle class, so Lacoste concludes, these developments have contributed to the underdevelopment problematic (Lacoste 1965, p. 231).

In the final analysis, it matters little whether the elite is indigenous or whether it is entirely the product of imposed colonialism. With reference to Latin America, Lacoste remarks "It is not its foreign nature which makes a privileged minority particularly harmful, but the enormity of the appropriations committed by those in power. Exploitation of the masses by an indigenous minority may be just as severe (if not more so) as that perpetrated by foreign colonialism, and frequently the indigenous elite maintains very close relations with outside [imperialist] forces" (1965, p. 235).

In order to clarify and further support his proposition that it is not only colonialism that can be held responsible for the problem of underdevelopment, but also the presence of powerful, selfish minorities, Lacoste examines a number of countries which used to have a colonial status but which are now characterized by high levels of development.

He observes that Australia, Canada and the U.S. have not come to form part of the Third World. This is because, in his view, the immigrants came mainly from West European countries with 'solid bourgeoisies.' They included many enterprising people and the majority of them believed that everyone should have the opportunity to become prosperous in the new homeland. Their attitudes have left a clear imprint on society. One of its concrete results was the Homestead Act in the U.S., under which all settlers could obtain the same number of acres of agricultural land. In these countries, 'perfectly' capitalist social structures were introduced which were totally divorced from existing pre-capitalist relationships. There was no exploitation by a ruling elite because the presence of a high degree of rural egalitarianism, powerful democratic institutions and a relatively important middle class made it impossible in Australia, Canada and the U.S. for the colonial system to promote the emergence of a privileged minority whose powers would be other than those which were purely capitalist in nature.

The American South formed an exception, at least to some degree. Cotton plantations, worked with the help of slaves, dominated economic life until the middle of last century. The related socioeconomic structure had all the characteristics that tended to foster the emergence of underdevelopment. Not surprisingly, phenomena appeared in the Deep South which were very similar to those encountered in Third World countries; today a part of the rural black population still leads a marginal, downtrodden existence by U.S. standards. That no truly underdeveloped region has emerged is due, according to Lacoste, mainly to the high level of prosperity in the remainder of the United States and the possibility of large-scale internal migration. Thus, no serious imbalance arose in the South between population growth and the development of its resource base. To this we can add that the Civil War prevented the South from sliding into a typical Third World type of situation by effectively halting the process of underdevelopment.

Generally speaking, the situation is quite different in South and Central America. The countries there, according to Lacoste, are now underdeveloped because during the colonial period an exceedingly small group of Spaniards, Portuguese and their Creole descendants gained control of the economy, in part through the acquisition of extensive areas of agricultural land and mining concessions. Highly unfavorable economic and political power structures developed in much of Latin America. The independence movements at the beginning of the 19th century were only to a small degree due to popular uprisings. They were encouraged mainly by the elites which had emerged during the colonial era, an important reason being that they felt themselves frustrated by the motherlands (Spain and Portugal) in their attempts to gain greater wealth and power. After breaking the political bonds with Spain and Portugal, the elites seized the opportunity to take possession of large parts of the crown lands that still existed, some church lands, as well as much of the land belonging to the Indians. Both during the colonial period (until circa 1825) and afterwards, a small elite within the region has regarded Latin America as a territory to be exploited for personal gain. This was possible because democracy did not get off the ground. Nearly all the countries became oligarchies, characterized by instability, corruption, inequality and social injustice.

The above observations do not only apply to Latin America, but also to many regions which were colonial possessions until after World War II. Examples include the former British and French colonies in Africa, most of which achieved independence around 1960. In many of these young sovereign states, power is now in the hands of privileged, indigenous minorities who have filled the power vacuum left behind by the former colonial rulers (see box at end of chapter).

These elites frequently form the 'bridge' enabling Western capitalists and transnational concerns to succeed in gaining influence or in maintaining and further expanding what interests they already possess. The links that the elites have with the West are often very strong, and this, by the way, also applies to those Third World countries which never had a colonial status or did so for only a short time.

Elite and capitalism in Lacoste's view

In Lacoste's opinion, the excessive power of Third World elites is related to a distortion of capitalism. It is the result of a 'veritable adulteration' of the capitalist relations of production. He elucidates this as follows. In Western Europe, where the capitalist system developed gradually, the personal dependency relationships between peasantry and landed aristocracy (so typical of the feudal system) disappeared. In theory, there exists between the capitalist and the worker only a contract, whereby the latter receives payment for supplying a certain amount of labor time. In Europe, the capitalist system liquidated archaic modes of production, while in Australia, Canada and the U.S. it spread out over practically virgin territory, so that in those areas not much elimination of pre-capitalist modes of production actually occurred.

In many regions, however, the imported capitalist system caused considerable disruption, resulting in aggravated inequality. The already powerful owners of capital further increased their influence by combining it with the power of landlord or slave owner. That is, purely capitalist power relationships were reinforced through alliance with more archaic power relationships.

This 'adulteration' of the capitalist system was in many cases a direct consequence of colonialism. At the time when the principles of free enterprise triumphed in Europe, the colonized regions were subjected to a regime of unfettered monopolies. Not content with the fact that they could profit from the technical and financial weakness of the indigenous peoples, European entrepreneurs – whose success was already assured thanks to the simple play of economic forces – demanded and obtained the support of the colonial power and its army. At the time when free trade was being hailed in Europe, the colonies remained closely subjected to tightly controlled trade relations with their mother countries. The consequence was that, through the introduction of capitalist relations of production, a small group – comprising both colonists and members of the native aristocracy – came to

232

enjoy great privileges. The changes in the traditional structures not only enabled indigenous elites to exploit the peasantry more than ever before, but also allowed them to become capitalists and make a fortune through the production of lucrative export goods or by engaging in the sale of much-wanted imported manufactures.

As far as the colonial rulers themselves were concerned, they combined the power which they exercised as capitalists with authoritarian methods of political domination – sometimes involving slavery – which were more or less feudalistic in nature. Apparently, the ideals of freedom, equality and brotherhood were meant only for Europeans; not for the indigenous populations of the colonial dependencies.

The position of the privileged minority in many overseas territories became exceptionally strong – its power exceeding not only that which the capitalist derived from the capitalist system, but also that possessed by the feudal lord in the feudal system. This monstrous capitalist system could arise only there where means of production were primitive and where the mass of the population was in a state of political subjection. Although this system applied particularly to colonial territories, brutal exploitation by ruling elites also occurred without foreign, colonialist intervention (see Bobek's view on rent capitalism in the preceding chapter).

First in Europe and later also in North America, the capitalist system grew strong by eliminating less-productive, pre-capitalist modes of production. Outside these regions it has clearly shown a tendency to incorporate these archaic modes of production. The plantation economy, for example, was until late in the 19th century a combination of capitalism (the more advanced and dominant mode of production) and a form of production based on slavery. It is necessary, therefore, to distinguish between 'adulterated capitalism' and 'normal capitalism.' In contrast to the former, the latter – also referred to as 'pure capitalism' – does not incorporate pre-capitalist modes of production or pre-capitalist (feudal) power relationships.

Lacoste attributes the fact that no adulteration of capitalism occurred in Western Europe to the considerable influence which the bourgeoisie had acquired in the course of time. As a result, relatively democratic social and political relationships emerged. At first these benefitted only the bourgeoisie, but eventually also working-class people became beneficiaries of the new, enlightened ideals of equal opportunity and political freedom.

Summary of Lacoste's view on the causes of underdevelopment

In the countries where there was a powerful middle class, where political life had developed in a relatively democratic way, and where the socioeconomic relationships were essentially capitalistic, there arose a situation which can be called developed. In areas – whether colonies or not – where there was no real middle class, where political structures were definitely not democratic and where capitalist production relationships

233

were combined with archaic ones, enabling a privileged minority to gain exorbitant political, economic and social power, circumstances have given rise to underdevelopment.

Clearly, Lacoste sees the process of underdevelopment as the complex interplay of diverse forces. Both old situations, often ones which have already disappeared, as well as more recent conditions, such as the population explosion, have played a part in the retrogressive process of under-development. Due to the selfish behavior of a small ruling minority, poverty is widespread. Limited purchasing power among the people means that there is little domestic demand for manufactured goods, and this, in turn, forms a formidable obstacle to modern economic development. Meanwhile, poverty and massive underemployment tend to favor a high birth rate which, when combined with a declining death rate, results in a rapid increase in population. Such rapid population growth often outstrips the rate of economic growth, causing ever greater imbalance between population numbers and productivity. The result is economic and social stagnation and persistent poverty.

The role of internal and external circumstances

With reference to the question whether underdevelopment is the result of internal or external circumstances, Lacoste tends to put more weight on internal factors because they are the ones which have allowed, and still allow, external factors to play an important role. The selfishness of the privileged indigenous minority formerly encouraged colonial exploitation because this afforded them a chance to enrich themselves, while present neo-colonial (or imperialistic) activities of foreign capitalists in Third World countries are possible only because they enjoy the necessary support and collaboration of the elites in those countries. In other words, we are dealing here with interactions between external and internal factors, such that the effects of certain external forces are conditioned by internal circumstances. What Lacoste precisely means becomes clear when we compare a country like Brazil – which has opened its boundaries to foreign enterprises and investors – with the Chinese People's Republic – where until recently Western investors could not get a foot in the door. Lacoste says about the less-developed countries: "Their historical evolution and basic problems are not so much caused by external factors, but are above all consequences of internal causes" (Lacoste 1965, p. 237). The only way to combat neo-colonialism, he concludes, is to get rid of the privileged minorities; without them neo-colonialism would not have much of a chance.

Evaluation of Lacoste's view

It is our opinion that in many respects Lacoste's arguments go to the heart of the matter. It is regrettable, therefore, that his view has received little attention internationally. The more recent literature on dependency relations hardly ever refers to him.

Although he points out that the problem of underdevelopment is to some extent a modern phenomenon, exacerbated *inter alia* by the current population explosion, he nevertheless makes clear that the real causes are much older. He rightly concludes that ascribing underdevelopment exclusively to forces which are at work today cannot possibly lead to a satisfactory explanation. Underdevelopment is the result of a long-term process involving a succession of political, social and economic changes. So, naturally, Lacoste attaches great significance to a thorough historical analysis.

In his own analysis of historical conditions he refers to the early lead of the West and to differing circumstances which existed in various overseas territories before the beginning of intensive contacts with the West. Unfortunately, this early geographical diversity has been taken into account insufficiently or not at all by most contemporary authors who have tried to provide an explanation for the problem of underdevelopment.

Another point in Lacoste's favor is the emphasis he places on the harmful role played by colonialism, while at the same time bringing out the relative importance of that same factor. By drawing attention to the part played by Third World elites, he makes more understandable the lack of progress during the post-colonial period as well as the limited development in Third World countries which never were colonies.

Besides providing us some valuable insights, Lacoste's view also contains a number of weaknesses. By pointing out the absence of a strong bourgeoisie in the Third World countries and by stressing that these countries were (are) dominated by powerful elites, he is in fact laying strong emphasis on the internal situation – too strong, it would seem. Notwithstanding the fact that he does pay considerable attention to the negative effects of such external forces as colonial domination and neo-colonial penetration, Lacoste has stated clearly that in the final analysis internal weaknesses have been decisive. In contrast to the dependency theorists (see next chapter), he has paid relatively little attention to colonial and neo-colonial relations between the Third World countries, on the one hand, and the developed countries, on the other.

In the latest edition of his *Géographie du sous-développement,* published in 1975, Lacoste admits to have devoted insufficient attention to the role of imperialism. He considers analysis at two levels to be necessary for a good understanding, i.e., at the international and the national level. Such an analysis should focus on interrelations and interactions of phenomena and processes at both levels. But as Lacoste has emphasized, there is the problem that imperialism and internal class relations are so closely interwoven that they cannot be separated. As a consequence, he does not arrive at a fundamentally different view concerning the 'real' causes of underdevelopment. He continues to believe in the essential role of the ruling elites because, in his opinion, it is they who make possible the imperialism of the great powers and other developed countries.

A final point of criticism is that Lacoste, in explaining the development of the prosperous industrialized countries, attributes great importance to the influence of the bourgeoisie which he considers to be responsible for the relatively democratic structures on which pure capitalism rests. Despite his often Marxist views, he fails to take into account the role of socialism, even though the latter has had an unmistakable impact on the nature of capitalism in the developed countries. The question may therefore be raised whether it is justified to speak of 'normal' capitalism. Lacoste talks about 'adulterated' or 'corrupted' capitalism in the Third World, but since socialism has modified capitalism in Western Europe, thereby removing its sharper edges, normal or pure capitalism does not occur there either.

Incidentally, Lacoste can be complemented on having recognized that there are two kinds of capitalism and that he arrived at this conclusion before others pointed to the difference between *peripheral* capitalism and *central* capitalism (see following chapter).

Africa's new privileged minorities

Because views concerning the negative role of elites are based primarily on past and presently existing power structures in the Middle East, southern Asia and Latin America, it may be of interest to see what René Dumont, one of the foremost experts on Africa, has to say about the role of the elite in an African country. We have selected Zambia for this purpose, but essentially the same observations apply to Senegal, Nigeria, Tanzania, and most other African countries.

Formerly known as Northern Rhodesia, Zambia achieved independence in 1964. Prior to that date, it was the British who constituted a small and powerful elite in the colony. Today, there still are quite a few foreigners (or expatriates), e.g., commercial farmers and people with top jobs in mining, industry, construction and education. In addition, there are numerous foreign advisers, representatives of international organizations and diplomats. Although all these foreigners may be said to form part of Zambia's privileged few, we will focus here on the African members of this select group.

In *Stranglehold on Africa*, René Dumont and Marie-France Mottin have devoted an entire chapter to Zambia's new elite. What follows is a sample of their observations, most of which are highly critical of Zambia's present leaders.

"The ruling class and the country's president were soon [after independence] building up, under cover of vague philosophical rhetoric . . . a form of neocolonialism that could never lead to true economic and political independence. But had they really set their hearts on independence, or were they merely eager to increase their privileges and prosperity?"

"So a new class-ridden society has grown up that differs from the old colonial society only in the colour of people's skins – black is now the predominant colour. But the problem is that this time the privileged minority is much bigger, and costs the country a great deal more, which means that the poor are getting even poorer . . ."

"[President] Kaunda is – rightly – afraid of urban disturbances, and has to look for support to the clique of people round him, who take advantage of the so-called 'socialist' path that gives them a chance to acquire more class privileges and don't give a damn for social justice, which should be the cornerstone of socialism. They need Kaunda to maintain a degree of political stability and to keep the balance between the tribes. In defending solely their own short-term political interests, the regime's privileged few don't even realize that they're sawing through the branch they're sitting on."

"The top government men are more colonialist than the colonials and never do more than roar through the villages [in their Mercedes] in a cloud of dust. Visits from agricultural or veterinary advisers are few and far between."

"The privileged minority refuse to see that there's a malnutrition problem, which seems pretty unimportant if you're well fed yourself . . . Even in the rural areas people are undernourished, with 82 per cent of households below the poverty line. The privileged minority, who are completely sold on Western-style food (a major status symbol because it is associated with the whites), simply don't want to know."

"The main concern of the privileged minorities is to look after their own interests, so they take advantage of the system. For instance they can obtain loans worth thousands, or rather tens of thousands, of kwachas, and many will make sure never to pay them back . . . The more you have the more you get!"

"Corruption is on the increase among the top-executives . . . a large number of influential people are jostling for advantage. The most serious aspect of corruption is that those in charge suggest more expensive solutions if they think there'll be more in it for themselves."

"The land is in the public domain, but it is the powerful few who take over the estates abandoned by the whites, and only a handful farm them efficiently. Some sell off everything . . . Others . . . manage to get hold of grants, which they have no real intention of repaying, from the same banks or official bodies that are so short of capital that they've stopped lending money to peasant farmers. But apparently Party membership counts as collateral, and as they're influential, they won't be taken to court."

". . . the privileged few, who assess the country's level of development by the yardstick, first of their own luxurious lifestyle and, second, of the number, appearance and splendour of public buildings. 'If we change our economic model and go for a more modest form of development, how shall we ever be able to build the Champs-Elysées in Lusaka?' was the ingenuous question one minister put to us. And his view is less grandiose than that of many other people who think only in terms of [a lifestyle as found in] the United States."

To the above we can add that virtually everywhere in Africa the authorities encourage the peasants to grow cash crops for export rather than subsistence crops, because this allows them (e.g., by means of export duties) to syphon off the surplus value realized on the world market. It enables them to divert resources to urban consumption or investment, that is, away from the peasants' control and mainly for the benefit of the urban-based ruling elites. The fact that this practice may result in food shortages in the rural areas, appears to be no great concern to them. According to Dumont & Mottin, a Tanzanian peasant "is required to work for 6,000 days, for very little pay, to enable a bureaucrat (who may be a mere parasite) to avoid using public transport . . . the Party prosecutes anyone who rebels against this form of forced farm labour – for which the old colonial regulations have been reinstated! Fines or even a prison sentence rain down on them. Party officials drive out in their cars to egg them on, but take good care not to dirty their hands . . ."

Source: Dumont, R. & M-F. Mottin, *Stranglehold on Africa.*

Chapter 16   Attempts at a comprehensive explanation of underdevelopment: imperialism and dependency theories

A. THEORIES OF IMPERIALISM

Classical views

According to Coppens (1979), imperialism may be defined as the existence, establishment or maintenance of international relationships of dominance and subordination between states or other collectivities. The main purpose of imperialism is to gain control over the political and/or economic life of other areas. Various explanations were given for this behavior at the beginning of this century, at a time when imperialism was still generally equated with colonialism.

Since Hobson in 1902 was the first to present his views, he may be regarded as the founder of the theory of imperialism. He pointed to the unequal distribution of income which is characteristic of capitalism and emphasized the limited purchasing power of the working population. This 'underconsumption' made it necessary for industrialized countries to seek foreign markets for surplus goods and to find external possibilities for the investment of surplus capital. The result was imperialism, characterized by considerable rivalry between the major powers. In his view, financial centers formed the dominant driving force in this process. According to Hobson, a rise in wages – leading to increased purchasing power and greater investment opportunities at home – would reduce or even eliminate the need for imperialist policies.

Schumpeter was even more optimistic than Hobson. He saw imperialism as a feudal relic within capitalism which would disappear of its own accord.

Hilferding, in 1910, also pointed to the attempts of 'capital' to gain world domination. He examined in particular the pressure which financiers put on governments to protect home markets against foreign competition and to acquire colonies for the import of raw materials as well as for the export of manufactured goods and investment capital. He predicted that inter-state rivalry would lead to imperialistic wars. Eventually, however, industrial development would spread to all corners of the globe.

In 1913, Rosa Luxemburg published her book on the accumulation of capital. Borrowing ideas from Marx, she emphasized that international accumulation of capital was necessary in order to counter underconsumption (or industrial overcapacity) in the home countries and to avoid, or ameliorate, the economic crises and social turmoil to which it could give rise. Such international accumulation of capital could be achieved by breaking open the pre-capitalist societies as markets for industrial goods and as suppliers of cheap raw materials. Without control over these non-capitalist regions, capitalism would no longer be able to expand and survive. Imperialism was, in her eyes, the expression of a worldwide armed struggle to obtain the remaining non-capitalist regions for a capitalism which, by its very nature, was bound to expand. Thus, Luxemburg stressed the military aspect of capitalism. But she did not think that imperialism could save capitalism – it could merely postpone its disintegration. Sooner or later capitalism would be destroyed by its own internal contradictions (Marx). In contrast to Hilferding, she foresaw ever greater disparities in wealth on a world scale. And as soon as there were no pre-capitalist societies left to be conquered and colonized, imperialism would come to a grinding halt and the whole capitalist system would collapse.

Bukharin (1915) and Lenin (1917) borrowed some of the ideas just mentioned and drew attention to the rise of big monopolies. According to Lenin, capitalism had entered a new stage around the turn of the century, the monopoly stage, which he regarded as the highest, that is to say, final stage of capitalism. Imperialism, which mainly served to supply opportunities for investment and larger profits outside the national boundaries, provided only a delay of execution for capitalism. Lenin was convinced that capitalism was destined to collapse eventually under the weight of its own contradictions.

All these 'classical' theoreticians were concerned with the motives underlying imperialist behavior, with the question whether or not capitalism needed imperialism for its continued existence, and with the consequences of the expansion or disappearance of imperialism for the capitalist development of Western countries. Virtually none of them paid much attention to the possible effects of imperialism on the colonial territories. Most saw the colonial dependencies merely as backward areas which were being developed and exploited for the benefit of the capitalist mother countries. The overseas territories lacked an independent historical role. Revolutionary changes, for instance, would begin in the mother countries and from there spread to the colonies, not the reverse. Most imperialism theorists were interested in the non-Western areas only to the extent that the latter had an influence on production relationships in the metropolitan countries (Coppens 1976, 1979).

Modern views

The classical views on imperialism do not play an important part today in discussions about underdevelopment, but they have influenced modern neo-Marxist views concerning imperialist behavior. Like their predecessors, neo-Marxists are interested mainly in the reasons why part of the capital produced in the prosperous countries is invested in Third World countries – a process often referred to as the international expansion of capital.

240

The proposition that the prime motive is the higher profits to be obtained outside the mother country – defended by Lenin and others – has proven to be untenable in many instances. But this argument does still apply, for example, to investments in runaway industries (e.g., American-owned factories in northern Mexico) which profit from low wages. Nor does the proposition that surplus capital can be made productive only in Third World countries provide a satisfactory explanation. The securing of cheap raw materials is now emphasized more than was done by the classical theorists (e.g., by Jalée who, incidentally, exaggerates the significance of the Third World in this respect). Reference is also made to the profitability of being able to operate behind the tariff walls erected in recent decades by underdeveloped countries which are pursuing a policy of (subsidized) industrialization through import substitution. Western multinationals, in particular, have moved in to take advantage of this Third World protectionism.

It is clear from the above that views concerning the economic motives behind imperialism are now different and less simplistic than they were at the beginning of this century. The conclusion which has been reached is that the periphery performs important functions for the core countries, although it is far from clear whether the periphery is absolutely indispensable for the capitalist heartland, making imperialism a *sine qua non* for the economic well-being of the developed countries or, for that matter, for the survival of capitalism.

However this may be, according to theories of imperialism, the export of investment capital to the Third World is more than outweighed by capital transfers in the opposite direction. An *unequal exchange* takes place by which the process of accumulation in the periphery is limited, while the rich countries providing the capital enrich themselves still further.

Capital accumulation in the developed countries is not limited to the repatriation of profits from foreign investments. Various French economists, including Palloix and Emmanuel, who have examined the question of *unequal capital accumulation,* have pointed out that the exchange of raw materials for industrial products is also unequal; Third World countries receive too low a price for their exports, while paying too much for manufactured imports. And because of *deteriorating terms of trade,* caused by the increased use of synthetic substitutes and the relatively small elasticity of demand for certain raw materials, the problem of unequal exchange tends to increase in magnitude. Furthermore, there is the difficulty of quickly reducing the output of various raw materials in times of economic slowdown as well as the problem of increased competition among Third World countries supplying primary goods. In a sense, too many poor countries export the same commodities (e.g., coffee and cocoa), keeping prices at a low level. Due to deteriorating terms of trade, Third World countries must export increasingly large quantities of primary products in exchange for the same amount of imports. Meanwhile, growing wage differentials between poor and rich countries have aggravated the problem of unequal exchange by making Third World exports continuously cheaper relative to imports.

In contrast to the older theories of imperialism, the more modern variants devote considerable attention to the consequences of imperialism for the less-developed countries. This is exemplified not only by the unequal exchange debate, but also by other neo-Marxist viewpoints. To illustrate this, we briefly present the more relevant ideas of Baran, Szentes and Mandel.

In his book *The Political Economy of Growth,* published in 1957, Baran states that surpluses in Third World countries available for expansion of productive capacity are generally greater than is often assumed. He disagrees that scarcity of capital, lack of enterprise, and rapid population growth are causes of underdevelopment. In his opinion, colonialism uprooted the traditional societies and destroyed their dynamism; after decolonization only feudal and underdeveloped capitalist structures remained. The indigenous elites indulge in overconsumption and either invest too much in other countries or in such non-productive activities as the construction of monumental office buildings. They try to protect their vested interests and privileges or expand their power by maintaining close links with Western capital which has established itself in key sectors of the underdeveloped economies.

For Szentes, the development question has an external (international) as well as an internal dimension. As a consequence of external factors, an economic and social structure has arisen in Third World countries which – more or less independently of those external factors – has become responsible for maintaining and further strengthening foreign capitalist domination. This structure inhibits true (autonomous) development. In his view, the chief characteristics and, at the same time, the major causes of underdevelopment are (a) economic dependence on foreign capitalist powers, (b) systematic creaming off of income, e.g., through profit extraction by foreign investors, (c) an open but disintegrated economy whose different branches have deformed structures, and (d) a heterogeneous society with a dualistic (traditional/modern) structure.

Mandel, starting from Marx's theory of original capital accumulation, has emphasized that Third World countries suffer a double burden. From the 16th to the 19th centuries, they were forced to make contributions to the accumulation of industrial capital in Europe. Since then they have been faced with the almost impossible task of catching up industrially. There is, of course, already an extensive industrial capacity in the Western world which floods these countries with manufactured products.

Besides the neo-Marxist theorists just discussed, mention should be made of Galtung. Although not a Marxist, he has been influenced by Marxist ideas. He believes that imperialism is a system that splits collectivities up

242

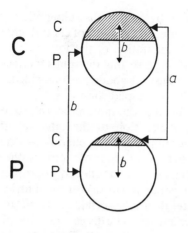

a = harmony of interests
b = conflict of interests

Fig. 18. Galtung's model of imperialist relations between core (c) and periphery (p).
Source: Galtung, 1971.

into parts which have either harmony-of-interests relations or conflict-of-interests relations, irrespective of whether they are capitalist or non-capitalist societies. In *A Structural Theory of Imperialism* (1971), he distinguishes between different kinds of imperialism – economic, political, military, communicational, informational and cultural – which influence each other and are often difficult to separate. In his model (see Figure 18), Galtung assumes two kinds of countries (developed or central vs. underdeveloped or peripheral) and four classes or interest groups (a central and a peripheral group in both types of countries). He believes that it is typical of imperialist structures that there is an intimate harmony-of-interests relationship between the central groups (elites) of the two countries. Conflicting interests exist between the central and peripheral groups *within* each country (but especially in the peripheral country) as well as *between* the two countries.

In contrast to Marx, Galtung believes that there is no 'solidarity' between the oppressed (peripheral) groups of the world. The workers in the rich countries have been corrupted, as it were, by their high living standard and would rather profit from the exploitation of the poor in the underdeveloped countries than join the 'Workers of the world, unite!' appeal in an effort to help their Third World counterparts.

In this exploitative center-periphery relationship, the privileged minorities of the poor countries occupy a key position in the sense that they form the bridgehead which enables the rich countries and their multinationals to appropriate much of the wealth squeezed out of the mass of the

Third World population by indigenous ruling elites. In other words, the harmony of interests between the elites of central and peripheral countries is based on the joint exploitation of the lower classes in the dominated countries. Galtung also suggests that the spin-off effects from the exchange of raw materials for industrial goods are one-sided, working almost exclusively in favor of the developed countries.

It is clear from all this that the more modern proponents of theories of imperialism have paid attention to the adverse effects which foreign domination has on the subjugated peripheral countries. In doing so, they have come very close to another group of theorists, the *dependencistas*. The latter have focused even more on the allegedly detrimental consequences of imperialism for the dependent Third World countries. This focus has led them to study in greater depth the social, economic and political structures in underdeveloped countries. The large majority of the *dependencistas* either originate from or live(d) in the Third World, particularly Latin America. Since their arguments show a less exclusively economic bias, *dependencia* theory nicely complements the theories of imperialism.

Because of the systematic and explicit attention given to the problems of the underdeveloped countries, the ideas of the *dependencistas* are of great importance for a more comprehensive explanation of underdevelopment. For this reason, we will discuss their arguments in considerable detail in the following section.

B. DEPENDENCY THEORY

The failure of import-substitution industrialization in Latin America

During the 1950s, a development strategy was implemented in Latin America, known as *desarrollo hacia adentro* or inward-centered development. A very important part of this strategy was industrialization for the purpose of import substitution, which was supposed to serve as the motor for numerous other economic, social and political developments. During the 1960s, the results of import-substitution industrialization proved to be disappointing and it became apparent that it contained a number of obvious disadvantages. These disadvantages have already been discussed, but will be summarized briefly here.

(1) Industrial expansion remained rather limited, mainly as a consequence of the small home market, the impossibility of being able to export on a large scale, and the limited successes in the field of international cooperation or collective self-reliance. In the smaller countries, in particular, it was not economically feasible to establish capital goods industries. Insufficient domestic purchasing power meant that many factories could not be operated at full capacity. The result was that they produced at too high a cost. Faced with widespread industrial inefficiency, governments decided to subsidize numerous enterprises. Apart from the negative effect this had on the national budget, it also tended to encourage more inefficiency.

(2) Another problem was that the adoption of modern production processes caused the expansion of much-desired employment opportunities to be quite small. Consequently, the rural exodus which had been encouraged by the establishment of industries led to an increase in unemployment in the cities.

244

(3) Imports of capital goods needed for the process of industrialization imposed a heavy burden on the balance of payments. Many countries were soon confronted with a shortage of foreign exchange and/or a growing foreign debt.

(4) Owing to inefficiency and high costs of production, industrial goods generally were unable to compete with foreign-made products, so that the hoped for increase in manufactured exports normally failed to materialize. Meantime, exports of mineral resources and agricultural commodities often suffered from deteriorating terms of trade, thus putting extra pressure on the balance of trade.

(5) In order to achieve rapid industrialization, which was supposed to reduce dependence on imports, Latin American countries became ever more dependent on foreign capital and foreign technology. The result was that foreign capitalists obtained increasing control over Latin American economies. While they established monopolies in the more profitable sectors, the less attractive sectors suffered from a serious lack of investment capital. There also began a considerable outflow of capital in the form of royalties and profits. To add insult to injury, already existing domestically owned industries were exposed to growing competition from subsidiaries of increasingly influential multinational concerns.

(6) In other fields, developments were also disappointing. For example, the traditional oligarchy retained its influence and was thus able to prevent much-needed changes in the countryside – there were virtually no large-scale redistributions of agricultural land and hardly any radical agrarian reforms. In general, the level of prosperity did not rise appreciably; poverty and other social problems persisted undiminished.

All in all, it became increasingly clear during the latter half of the 1960s that the development strategy being followed would not lead to the desired results. The economy remained weak and the Latin American countries saw their dependence on the developed countries grow stronger instead of weaker. The United States continued to play a dominant role not only in the economic field, but also politically. The U.S.-inspired Alliance for Progress, which had made the doctrine of *desarrollismo* the official development strategy for Latin America, contributed neither to progress, nor to greater political and economic independence of the Latin American countries.

Origin of the dependency theory

The situation sketched above led to a critical examination of the development approach followed thus far. This resulted in the exposure of what, in the opinion of critics, constituted *the* fundamental cause of Latin America's underdevelopment. In their view, this was the dependent position in which Latin America had come to find itself because of the rise of industrial capitalism. Saddled with socio-political and economic structures largely determined by foreign interests, the region was unable to develop autonomously. This interpretation has become known as the dependency theory.

Since dependency theory has largely arisen from contributions by Latin American scholars, it is regarded first and foremost as a manifestation of growing Third World awareness of, and dissatisfaction with, allegedly inadequate theories of development, such as Rostow's stages-of-economic-growth model.

The following individuals may be listed as belonging to the major forerunners and pioneers of dependency theory:

(1) The Argentine economist R. Prebisch, who introduced the double concept of 'center-periphery' in 1949, pointing out that the economies of peripheral countries were merely geared towards primary production and benefitted much less from international specialization and technological progress than did the central countries. Owing to deteriorating terms of trade, the peripheral countries found themselves in an increasingly vulnerable position and remained structurally subservient to the central or core countries. This situation would in all likelihood continue, if not grow worse, because the core countries could be expected to maintain, and possibly strengthen, their exploitation-oriented dominance over the periphery;

(2) Experts of the Economic Commission for Latin America (ECLA). After the failure of the inward-looking development strategy, originally propagated by ECLA, many of them took a critical look of this development-through-import-substitution-industrialization policy;

(3) The Swedish economist G. Myrdal, who noted that economic, social and political dependency relations existed between regions, not only at the national level, but also at the international level. More often than not, such relations have unfavorable *backwash effects* (e.g., outflow of surplus production, brain drain and destruction of domestic craft industries because of external competition), rather than positive *spread effects*, on the weaker, less-developed regions. Like Prebisch, he regarded underdevelopment not as an early stage of a universal development process through which all countries had to pass (as Rostow maintained), but as a phenomenon directly related to development elsewhere;

(4) The Mexican, R. Stavenhagen, who emphasized that in Third World countries the traditional sector of the economy tends to be linked to the more dynamic and aggressive modern sector in such a way that the former is subjugated and exploited by the latter. He, too, drew attention to the fact that intra-national relations often are favorable for the more developed regions and unfavorable for the less prosperous, disadvantaged regions;

(5) The Mexican, P. Gonzalez Casanova, who saw the underdevelopment of particular regions within a country as a consequence of the dominant position of the national core region or metropolis. He described this situation as 'internal colonialism.'

It is above all the American economist A.G. Frank, who is credited for having integrated the various points of view into a single theoretical framework. Although it is debatable whether he should be considered as the founder of dependency theory, fact is that his books and articles – mostly written in English – have enjoyed great popularity outside Latin America.

Finally, contributions to the dependency perspective have been made by Bagú, Bodenheimer, Cardoso, Córdova, Dos Santos, Fernandes, Faletto, Furtado, Garcia, Jaguaribe, Ianni, Marini, Paz, Pinto, Quijano, Sunkel, Torres Rivas, Vasconi, and countless others. While Frank's view has a decidedly economic emphasis, many of these Latin American *dependencistas* have focused more on the political and social aspects of the dependency problem.

The content of dependency theory

Dependency theory became widely known between 1967 and 1973 and has enjoyed considerable popularity. Many consider(ed) it applicable not only to Latin America, for which it was developed, but also to other parts of the Third World. The theory is (was) even regarded by many as the most satisfactory explanation of underdevelopment anywhere.

Despite the fact that in the past few years the dependency perspective has lost some of its popularity, we feel justified in considering its content rather exhaustively. Since the ideas of the various contributors to the theory are not wholly identical – sometimes even contradictory – and the authors mentioned above have emphasized different aspects of dependency, it would be going too far to discuss all their views in detail. Instead, we will present only the highlights.

Dependency theory holds that Latin America's underdevelopment is the result of external domination which began immediately after 1492. As a consequence, Latin America has not been able to determine its own development. The economic, social and political structures which the region now possesses were imposed from outside through asymmetrical (unequal) relationships which were, and still are, attuned to foreign interests. Spain and Portugal were the first to give shape to this development and, after political independence, it was the industrializing countries of Western Europe (particularly Britain) and later also the U.S. which assumed this role. These countries needed Latin America as a producer of cheap food and raw materials and as a market for industrial products. Today, the U.S., Britain and other core countries, through their dominant role in the world economy, make it impossible for the Latin American countries to develop.

According to dependency theory, there are two groups of capitalist countries: dominant and dominated. These have been combined by the former into a single worldwide system, that of capitalism, in which the former occupy a central position and the latter a peripheral or dependent position. Thanks to their higher place in the system, the dominant countries can determine the structure of the whole system and assign specific functions to those occupying a lower position. In the subordinated peripheral countries, their influence has led to the emergence of an inferior or dependent type of capitalism, commonly referred to as *peripheral capitalism* (Amin 1973).

Dos Santos, in a similar light, defines dependency as "a conditioning situation in which the economies of one group of countries are conditioned by the development and expansion of others." The dominant countries "can expand through self-impulsion while others, being in a dependent position, can only expand as a reflection of the expansion of the dominant countries" (Dos Santos 1973, p. 76). In other words, the dependent countries lack an autonomous capacity for development – a view which is shared by most *dependencistas*.

The subservient role which Latin American countries are forced to play in the world system has led to more or less blatant forms of exploitation. The ultimate result is underdevelopment. This means that development and underdevelopment are two sides of the same coin; they belong together as a Siamese twin. Development in one place is causally related to underdevelopment in another place since they represent two aspects of the same historical process.

This historical process is the steady expansion of capitalism from Western Europe and North America (and more recently from Japan) over the greater part of the earth, resulting in the creation of a worldwide imperialist network of colonial and neo-colonial relationships through which surpluses are funneled from periphery to center. This process of capitalist penetration into underdeveloped countries still continues. Frank puts it as follows: "underdevelopment was and still is generated by the very same historical process which also generated economic development: the development of capitalism itself" (Frank 1969a, p. 9). He foresees that Latin America will become even more underdeveloped through further intensification of its relations with the prosperous countries (e.g., in the form of additional investments, loans and imports of technological knowledge). It is no coincidence that the poorest regions of Latin America, e.g., Northeast Brazil, are precisely the areas which have had the longest and most intensive contacts with more developed countries. In Frank's view, a weakening of relationships offers the best possibilities of arriving at a higher level of development.

Whereas the classical economists (e.g., Ricardo) explained and justified differences in economic development in terms of an international division of labor based on the principle of comparative advantages, this is not the standpoint of proponents of dependency theory. On the contrary, they believe that such differences, e.g., advanced industries in core countries and plantations in the periphery, are anything but the result of mutual interests, but those of one group of countries. The consequence is a conflict rather than a harmony of interests.

In view of the above, it is understandable that *dependencistas* ascribe underdevelopment to the constraining effects of *external* obstacles, and not, or much less so, to internal deficiencies. Many Marxist authors among them fail to make a distinction between external and internal factors because they consider that irrelevant. They see underdevelopment solely as a result of capitalism; all obstacles in the path of development are inherent in the capitalist system. According to them, the ruling elites of the Third World are so closely associated with foreign capitalist forces that a revolution of the proletariat, aimed at curtailing or eliminating the feudal and capitalist bourgeoisie, would be the only way of breaking out of the present situation of dependency and underdevelopment. On the other hand, the more bourgeois and nationalistically oriented *dependencistas* do consider the distinction between internal and external forces to be relevant. In their view, the unfavorable pattern of relationships between rich and poor countries can best be modified by pursuing a development policy aimed at greater autonomy. They believe that this can be achieved by means of closer economic cooperation among Third World countries and social reforms. They do not consider development along capitalist lines impossible.

The view of the Marxist authors does not mean that they are unaware that the dominance of the developed countries usually makes itself felt in indirect ways. Dos Santos states: "external domination in a pure sense is in principle impracticable. Domination is practicable only when it finds support among those local groups which profit by it" (Dos Santos 1973, p. 78).

Capitalism creates within the dependent countries an *infrastructure of dependence,* i.e., particular institutions, social classes, etc., through which the dominating countries can exert their influence and establish a dependent or peripheral capitalism in a more subtle manner than is possible through outright colonial control. These social classes and institutions often serve the interests of the core countries more than those of their own countries. In effect, they may be little more than extensions of the *international bourgeoisie* (Wöhlcke 1977). Bodenheimer characterizes them as *client classes* and has defined them as "those which have a vested interest in the existing international system. These classes carry out certain functions on behalf of foreign interests; in return they enjoy a privileged and increasingly dominant and hegemonic position within their own societies, based largely on economic, political or military support from abroad" (Bodenheimer 1971, p. 163).

Among the client classes in Latin America are such groups as the large landowners – who have an interest in the export of agricultural goods – and the new elite consisting of persons with influential positions in the secondary and modern (formal) tertiary sectors. They form a cultural, political and social extension of the so-called *associated sector* of the economy, i.e., that part of the economy which has arisen from direct relations (imports, exports, foreign investments and loans) between the core countries and the periphery. Frank regards this international bourgeoisie as an enemy of the underdeveloped countries and the poor masses living there.

Although the emphasis has thus far been on economic aspects, dependency theory certainly does not regard dependency as something that manifests itself only in the economic field. It considers the interrelatedness of economic, social and political features to be a very close and obvious one. Economic dependence permeates social, political and cultural life in the dependent countries; the reverse is equally true. Long-standing social differences in Latin America are seen as expressions of economic dependence and weakness. This also applies to the more recent process of marginalization, that is, the growing impoverishment of millions of people who hardly take part in modern economic, social, cultural and political life.

As far as the internal situation is concerned, the dependency school has also criticized the assumption that Latin American societies are composed of two totally separate sectors: a modern and a traditional one. In other words, they reject the view of a dualistic society. This does not mean that they deny the existence of modern vs. traditional contrasts, but only that they contest that there is little or no contact between the two sectors. Characteristic of dependent capitalism is not dualism, but *structural heterogeneity,* that is, the interwoven coexistence of advanced capitalist and underdeveloped (seemingly non-capitalist) modes of production and distribution. The whole system, however, is not symbiotic in nature. Rather, it is parasitic, conditioned as it is by the comparatively vigorous, aggressive and continuously expanding capitalist sector which, at the same time, supports the associated sector. Structural heterogeneity is a consequence of the *asymmetrical integration* of the periphery into the world economy.

Various authors have pointed out that the associated sector is responsible for preempting too much qualified labor. By paying relatively high wages, it has a tendency to starve other sectors of much needed skill, yet is unable to create much employment due to its use of modern, labor-extensive methods of production. At the same time, this sector monopolizes the bulk of modern technology, the domestic capital market, government-provided infrastructural facilities, the most economically attractive locations as well as the most productive agricultural lands. For instance, in poverty-ridden Northeast Brazil, much of the fertile and well-watered coastal lowland is in the hands of large producers – including multinational corporations – who raise exclusively commercial crops on extensive and sometimes highly mechanized plantations. Meanwhile, according to estimates, over 3 million people in Northeast Brazil have starved to death in recent years due to persistent drought.

The associated sector also makes decisions about the use of other important resources, displaces competing sectors or makes them dependent upon itself through its role as a supplier of a wide variety of inputs (e.g., fertilizer). Because of the relatively high income it generates and the social services it provides for its employees, it also forces up prices. To sum up, it may be said that the modern sector can ensure economic growth, but not real development – the *growth-without-development* dilemma. This inability appears from numerous symptoms of marginality, such as open and concealed unemployment, malnutrition, illiteracy, poor housing, poor health conditions, etc.

The Egyptian economist Samir Amin, who is usually associated with the dependency school, also records these phenomena. He does not refer to structural heterogeneity, but uses the expression 'social formation,' by which he means specific structures characterized by a combination of different modes of production, one of which is dominant and conditions the development of the various dependent modes grouped around it. The latter may be either pre-capitalist modes of production which existed prior to the penetration of capitalism, or non-capitalist modes which arose later. In all instances, however, form and function of the dependent modes have been greatly influenced by the role they have come to perform with reference to the dominant, capitalist mode of production, such as supplying cheap food and services to the industrial workers in the modern sector.

Besides sectoral dominance, the *dependencistas* also point to the existence of dominating and dominated regions within the countries of Latin America. The dominant regions are much more developed because modern economic activities are largely concentrated there. Partly because they are developed, the other regions are slowed down in their development or are underdeveloped. Both in the past and in more recent times, the core

250

regions have been able to exert their dominance over the more backward regions, resulting in typical core-periphery relations which are advantageous to the former and disadvantageous to the latter. Or, to use Myrdal's terminology, *spread* effects are predominant in the region where the elite is concentrated, whereas *backwash* effects tend to prevail in the peripheral regions. Since it is mainly the core regions which maintain intensive relations with the international capitalist system, their dominance at the national level may be seen as an expression of the influence of the world system.

Geographically speaking, the most interesting aspect of dependency theory is that it relates patterns of development and underdevelopment at the national level to those existing at the global level. It also places regional and local patterns in the broader national framework of which they form integrated parts. Frank's views can be used to illustrate this. In his discussions of the spatial dimensions of dependency relations, he uses the terms satellite and metropolis. *Satellites* are entities which perform a dependent or subordinate role in the worldwide system of capitalist relationships, such that surpluses are extracted from them. The *metropolis,* on the other hand, occupies a dominant position in that same system, enabling it to appropriate economic surpluses at the expense of the satellites.

Frank uses this pair of concepts at all spatial levels. At the *local* level he draws attention to the metropolis-satellite relationship, for example, where the large landowner leases land to a tenant on unfavorable terms for the latter. At the *regional* level he refers to towns which appropriate surpluses from the surrounding countryside through the collection of rent or the unequal exchange of manufactured goods and services for agricultural products. There is a metropolis-satellite relationship at the *national* level when the economy of the more developed part(s) of a country dominates that of the other regions. In many instances, this means that the latter serve mainly as suppliers of cheap raw materials, food and labor. Lastly, at the *international* level a metropolis-satellite relationship exists where an entire country is dominated and exploited by one or more metropolitan countries. Frank regards current underdevelopment mainly as "the historical product of past and continuing economic and other relations between the satellite underdeveloped countries and the now developed metropolitan countries" (Frank 1969a, p. 4).

By using the two concepts at various levels, a particular entity can have the status of a metropolis in one situation and that of a satellite in another. For example, a small or medium-sized regional capital is a metropolis in relation to the surrounding countryside, but is at the same time a satellite of the national core region and its primate city. The latter, in turn, may be a satellite of Washington-New York, London, Paris and/or Tokyo – the world metropolises where all relationships ultimately converge and where, accordingly, the greatest concentration of surpluses, or, if you wish, the greatest accumulation of capital, occurs. Frank formulates it as follows:

"these metropolis-satellite relations are not limited to the imperial or international level, but penetrate and structure the very economic, political, and social life of the Latin American colonies and countries. Just as the colonial and national capital and its export sector became the satellite of the Iberian (and later of other) metropoles of the world economic system, this satellite immediately becomes a colonial and then a national metropolis with respect to the productive sectors and population of the interior. Furthermore, the provincial capitals, which thus are themselves satellites of the national metropolis – and through the latter of the world metropolis – are in turn provincial centers around which their own local satellites orbit. Thus a whole chain of constellations of metropoles and satellites relates all parts of the whole system from its metropolitan center in Europe or the United States to the farthest outpost in the Latin American countryside" (Frank 1969a, p. 6).

The success of dependency theory

Dependency theory has appealed strongly not only to academics but also to others, both inside and outside Latin America. Since the early 1970s, countless publications on dependency have appeared and new titles are still being added, although the emphasis has shifted somewhat in the direction of the so-called *world-system approach*. Non-Latin Americans have also made their contributions, in particular the Egyptian economist Samir Amin. He has pointed out that the origin and continued existence of the modern export economy, which is so important for Third World countries, is based to a large extent on low wages which greatly limit domestic purchasing power. In order to stimulate development, the now dominant export sector should be replaced by activities aimed at increasing the prosperity of the underdeveloped countries' own population.

Dependency theory owes much of its success to the relative absence of alternative theories. Latin American academic circles were dominated for a long time by the conventional approach to the development problem, which meant catching up with the developed countries through the attraction of capital and know-how. This approach – known as the *modern-ization model* – was based on an inadequate understanding of the fundamental causes of underdevelopment. Few development experts – mainly economists – were aware of the more profound analyses, such as the one by Lacoste, which had examined not merely the immediate causes, but also the underlying, conditioning circumstances. As a consequence, they underestimated the complexity of underdevelopment and proposed inappropriate strategies. Around 1970, the dependency view quickly proved to possess more qualities than the idea that underdevelopment was essentially an isolated problem of lost ground, caused *inter alia* by lack of capital. Soon, many academics were prepared to discard the modernization strategy and the superficial explanations of underdevelopment on which it was based.

Most supporters of dependency theory incorporated Marxist concepts into their arguments and this, too, helps to explain its success because Marxist scholarship in Latin America had acquired a degree of respectability in academic circles (Stansfield 1974).

Stansfield has given additional reasons for the success of the dependency view. Many social scientists in Latin America come from the upper and upper-middle classes. "They are, in consequence, and despite their claims to a special out-group or nonclass status, tied by class and kinship to the traditional sources of political and economic leadership. It is clear, therefore, that dependency-style explanations of their countries' problems, which play down the culpability of local élites and cite international forces as beyond local control, are in class terms more palatable than analyses which might place the blame for underdevelopment on their own bourgeois antecedents and families. It is not being suggested that 'dependencistas' are conveniently and dishonestly excusing the role of the local bourgeois élites, but rather that they are opting for an explanation which stresses international economic forces and minimizes internal domestic conflicts between and within classes" (Stansfield 1974, p. 9).

This reasoning may also explain why those who were aware of Lacoste's view, probably felt less attracted to it. After all, Lacoste strongly emphasized the negative role of the elite. Although he did discuss the role of the international capitalist system, he regarded it as having at best only secondary importance (see preceding chapter). To this we can add that in his publications of the early 1960s, Lacoste paid scarcely any attention to the important economic and political influence which the U.S. had exercised in Latin America.

This hegemony by the U.S. gave rise to growing feelings of discontent in Latin America following the end of World War II. Dependency theory provided the opportunity to give vent to these feelings and especially to the disappointment about the failed development policy of import-substitution industrialization. It is not for naught that a rather strong anti-American undertone can be detected in many dependency writings.

Stansfield has also pointed out that during the 1960s and early 1970s the Latin American countries were characterized by a veritable epidemic of authoritarianism. "Dependency-style analysis, therefore, has certain special advantages for the beleaguered social scientist, for it allows him to discuss the major economic, social and political problems facing his country without necessarily involving him in a criticism of the government of the day" (Stansfield 1974, p. 9).

In addition to the reasons just given, dependency theory owes its success to a number of inherent qualities. For example, its advocates emphasized the importance of historical analysis and based their conclusions on studies of the historical processes which had 'shaped' large parts of Latin America. They were also quite successful in demonstrating the interrelatedness of economic, social and political phenomena – much more so than had been done previously. At the same time, they brought out clearly that complexes of phenomena at the local, regional, national and global levels interact with one another. In doing so, *dependencistas* contributed significantly to a better understanding of the occurrence of disparities – not only in Latin America, but also elsewhere in the world. Many people regarded as particularly useful that dependency theory made it clear that power structures at the national level are closely related to, and manipulated by, power structures at the world level. In brief, the twin problems of underdevelopment and social injustice could be explained much more satisfactorily in terms of dependency relations than had been possible with other theories, all which suffered from placing too much emphasis either on economic or on ecological causes of underdevelopment.

C. A CRITIQUE OF THE THEORIES OF IMPERIALISM AND DEPENDENCY

Dependency theory has not only enjoyed considerable popularity in academic circles and beyond, but it has also had to face heavy criticism. In this section we will examine this criticism, much of which applies equally to modern (neo-Marxist) theories of imperialism.

A vague view, insufficiently supported by empirical evidence

An often-heard criticism is that the *dependencistas* have failed to construct their theoretical statements on a solid foundation of hard factual information. As a result, their writings are characterized not only by a certain degree of speculation, but also by theoretical and conceptual vagueness. Even as early as 1973, it was noted that the dependency view fell short of being a conceptually and logically complete theory in the strictly social-scientific sense of the word. Rather, it was a collection of divergent propositions which partly contradicted each other. Theoretical weaknesses and terminological inadequacies are particularly glaring with respect to the central concept of *dependencia*. "A theoretically definitive definition does not exist [and] there is absolutely no agreement as to the approximate scope of the concept or its level of abstraction" (Evers & Von Wogau 1973, p. 442). O'Brien also noted that one looks in vain in dependency writings for the essential characteristics of dependency. Instead, one often finds the following circular argument: "dependent countries are those which lack the capacity for autonomous growth and they lack this because their structures are dependent ones" (O'Brien 1974, p. 38). He goes on to point out that all countries form part of a wider system and are more or less dependent on others. In his view, dependency theory does not make clear why certain countries are underdeveloped while others are not. "The failure to enumerate and analyse the essential characteristics of dependency leads to confusion when it comes to [formulating] policy" (O'Brien 1974, p. 39).

254

According to critics, dependency's vagueness is due to the fact that not enough empirical work has been carried out for the explicit purpose of testing and adjusting the theory. Authors have fallen back on repetition, ultimately leading to a fair amount of rigidity in dependency thinking.

It has also been pointed out that the theory is not particularly original, built as it is on ideas formulated earlier by theories of imperialism. Baran, for example, indicated as early as 1957 that underdevelopment is the result of unfavorable contacts with the capitalist countries and the consequent draining away of surpluses. He also pointed to the emergence of structures which are attuned to the interests of the dominant countries – a theme later elaborated on by Frank. Nor is dependency's historical approach original. Lacoste uses the same approach. Even before the Second World War, reference had been made to the disadvantageous effects of colonial and neo-colonial relations (e.g., by Boeke).

Insufficient attention for the Third World's own responsibility and for its pre-colonial history

Dependency theorists start their analyses at the world level and regard the structures at the regional and national levels as being conditioned by international power relations. Although attention is paid to the presence of powerful elites within the various Latin American countries, they are looked upon mainly as bridgeheads of foreign interest groups. The fundamental causes of underdevelopment are sought not so much in the conduct of the national elites, as in the international capitalist system. Inherent in dependency theory, therefore, is the danger that it can be misused in the sense noted by O'Brien: "In the hands of some Latin American writers the theory of dependency is used as a *deus ex machina* explanation for everything which seems to be wrong with Latin American society" (O'Brien 1974, p. 24).

By its very nature, dependency has a tendency to place the causes of underdevelopment outside the Third World, without first considering its own shortcomings. It relieves, so to speak, the national elites and the national governments of a great deal of responsibility by regarding them as minor accomplices of a powerful international system. In this way, it fails to emphasize that the national elites and governments could have done more for the progress of their countries and the well-being of the mass of the population. They by no means have to be willing instruments of foreign capital.

Lacoste has stated that former colonial rule has more than once been pointed at by present elites of Third World countries as the reason for underdevelopment. Their purpose was to divert attention away from the internal situation and their own responsibility in the present state of affairs. Dependency theory could be misused in similar fashion by others looking for scapegoats.

Although it is undeniable that Latin America has been highly dependent ever since the beginning of the 16th century, the same cannot be said of all other parts of the Third World. There are regions which have had very little contact with the West, such as Ethiopia and Afghanistan. In these cases, dependency theory cannot possibly provide an explanation for the problem of underdevelopment. If the theory were applied nonetheless, it would hide more than it would reveal – covering up the real causes of underdevelopment or ignoring the possibility that underdevelopment already existed prior to the rise of capitalism and, thus, long before there could have been (colonial) dependence on capitalist core countries.

Since dependency is defined in terms of *capitalist* relations, little or no consideration is given to the influence of pre-colonial structures on the process of underdevelopment. In other words, the long autonomous history of large parts of the Third World is ignored, so that, for example, the same significance is attributed to some 100 years of African colonial history in the explanation of contemporary underdevelopment as to nearly five centuries of colonial and neo-colonial rule in Latin America. Another consequence is that insufficient attention is paid to the possibility that pre-colonial circumstances may have facilitated the rise of a colonial situation. Or, to put it differently, dependency theorists fail to raise the question whether underdevelopment might be a cause, rather than a result, of dependency.

As far as Latin America is concerned, it is safe to state that pre-colonial conditions have played a relatively insignificant role in the origin of its current underdevelopment, but the same obviously does not apply to all other parts of the Third World. A striking example of the latter case is Ethiopia, which has always been an inaccessible and highly isolated region. Prior to 1880, it had no contacts with the West, and it was able to maintain its political independence until late 1935. Foreign influence, whether capitalist or not, never was the most essential ingredient in Ethiopia's underdevelopment.

Another instructive example is furnished by China. Dietvorst rightly states that the fact of its underdevelopment cannot be simply disposed of with reference to the fatal influence of Western imperialism (after 1842) or to an unfavorable natural environment. The causes must mainly be sought in the nature of the Chinese culture, which existed for centuries prior to European penetration (Dietvorst 1975, p. 11). This does not mean that Western imperialism had no deleterious effects. Stover has pointed out that the village culture had been able to maintain its own elite over many centuries, but that the rural population was incapable of surrendering additional surplus product to this elite when the latter made common cause with foreign businessmen involved in world trade. This extra burden to support foreign trade was too heavy for the peasants, who, as a consequence of traditional structures, already lived close to the subsistence minimum (Stover 1976, p. 89).

256

The Chinese historians Zhang Zhilian and Luo Rong-qu of the University of Peking, hold a similar view. They recently wrote: "We would be the last to exonerate the inequities of colonialism and imperialism which are writ large in history, but it would be much too simple to impute the decline and backwardness of the Third World to a single external cause. In so doing, we would be covering up the conservatism of the feudal economy characterized by the combination of peasant agriculture and handicraft, the reactionary nature of feudal bureaucratism and despotism, and the stupidity of a closed-door foreign policy . . . as we probe deeper into the history of China's contacts with the West and explore the factors which have obstructed the progress of modernization, we become aware that the roots of China's stagnation lay more in the economic structure and mental make-up characteristic of pre-capitalist modes of life than in imperialist encroachments. The latter constituted no more than the external causes, which only became operative through internal ones. Attention is therefore being directed toward the research and analysis of the indigenous structures – political, economic, social, ideological – under the feudal regime, which persisted longer in China than in any other country of the world. It was basically the refusal to adapt to new conditions and the stubbornness with which they clung to the old that incapacitated our forebears to resist effectively the aggressions of colonialism and imperialism, and to absorb the truly progressive elements of modern capitalism in order to make a genuine industrial 'take-off' " (Zhang Zhilian & Luo Rong-qu 1980, pp. 110-113).

It is obvious that the old social structures – including the caste system in India – should not be lost sight of. The danger of this happening arises as soon as dependency theory is accepted as *the* explanation of underdevelopment – a tendency which has manifested itself all too strongly during the past two decades.

The *dependencistas* have tried to refute the above criticism by pointing out that many countries were not *under*developed but *un*developed before their contact with the First World. Apart from the unfortunate use of words, it must be noted that a low level of development is not a very favorable starting point for achieving a high development level in the short run, and that it facilitates sliding into underdevelopment when one comes into contact with considerably stronger societies or with more vigorous modes of production.

Capitalist determinism: its implications

According to Frank and many other dependency theorists, underdevelopment is the consequence of capitalism. That they reach this view with respect to Latin America is, to some extent, inevitable. Both during the colonial and post-colonial periods, this region has had very tight links with capitalist countries whose economic and political activities were characterized by expansion. Nor, indeed, is such a conclusion entirely

257

incomprehensible for the Third World as a whole, since during the past 150 years or so it has been chiefly the countries with a market economy which have tried to incorporate an increasingly large part of the Third World into their domain. In this process, the forms in which imperialism and dependency found expression were conditioned by the possibilities for the abuse of power which the capitalist system offered to individuals, organizations and states. The Soviet Union, which became communist in 1917, had already expanded into large parts of Asia before that date and so had grown into a state of such an extent and with such a wealth of natural resources that it could begin to lead a highly closed, self-sufficient existence far more easily than could the majority of capitalist countries.

It is nevertheless mistaken, in our view, to regard capitalism as the sole cause of the problems which now characterize the countries of the Third World. It is inaccurate to state that the *system* causes underdevelopment. According to Frank, capitalism leads to "simultaneous generation of underdevelopment in some [areas] and of economic development in others" (Frank 1969a, p. 4). Evidently, it is the particular *circumstances* and/or the *individuals* who put the capitalist system into practice that determine where development will occur and where underdevelopment will. Pronouncements such as "capitalism is the cause of underdevelopment" are at best highly suspect.

Dependency theorists have by no means always made clear which circumstances lead to underdevelopment or, conversely, what attitudes the representatives of the capitalist system need to possess in order to be able to promote development. Lacoste is much more explicit on this point by emphasizing that capitalism has led to underdevelopment especially where small ruling elites could take advantage of it to further their own interests. This presupposes the absence of a properly functioning democratic system. Where democracy does not function properly, so Lacoste maintains, the capitalist system can become distorted to the extent that it is likely to foster a situation of underdevelopment.

Ray also objects to the fact that the dependency school – particularly Bodenheimer and Dos Santos – claims that dependency, and thus underdevelopment, is caused by the economics of capitalism. He points out that if it is assumed that the U.S. is a capitalist country and that it has imposed a structure of economic dependence on Latin America, this does not necessarily prove that this dependence has been caused by capitalism. In fact, throughout history large and powerful states have imposed economic dependence on their smaller and weaker neighbors. The economic imperialism of powerful, pre-capitalist countries is, according to Ray, well enough known. It also occurs among post-capitalist powers. "Although it is ignored by the dependency theorists, Soviet economic imperialism has been no less a reality than the capitalist variety. Indeed there is a striking similarity between the economic dependence which has been imposed upon Latin America by the U.S. and the economic dependence which has been

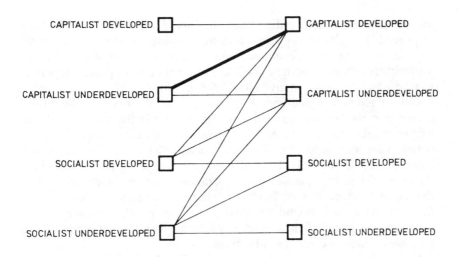

Fig. 19. Four types of countries with ten possible relationships.

imposed on Eastern Europe by the Soviet Union" (Ray 1973, p. 8). A more recent example of Soviet imperialism, of course, is the invasion of Afghanistan, which took place in 1980.

Dependency theorists can also be taken to task for the fact that dependence on a socialist country, e.g., the dependence of Cuba, Ethiopia and Guinea on the Soviet Union, is usually not referred to as an example of dependence and is rarely considered as having disadvantageous consequences.

Various authors, including Ray, have reached the conclusion that the *dependencistas* would do well to study also the dependency relationships that exist within the communist world. Reitsma (1982) has criticized the division of the world into three regions: the First, Second and Third Worlds, and has suggested that not only the capitalist countries but also the non-capitalist countries should be divided into developed and underdeveloped. If this were done, there would be ten possible types of relations (Fig. 19). He notes that the *dependencistas* have limited their discussions almost completely to only one of these types of relations, viz., the one which exists between capitalist developed countries, on the one hand, and capitalist underdeveloped countries, on the other (see heavy line in Fig. 19). He agrees with Ray that greater attention to all relationship patterns would lead to the conclusion that the common denominator of imperialism and *dependencia* is not capitalism, but a disparity of power.

According to Ray, unequal power relations gave rise to a *non*-Marxist theory of imperialism, formulated long ago by historians. He adds the following comment: "It is not claimed here that the non-Marxist theory of imperialism has been verified, nor that the Marxist theory has been disproved. It is simply suggested that the non-Marxist theory potentially explains *all* instances of economic imperialism, while the Marxist theory intrinsically refuses to address itself to instances of noncapitalist imperialism, of which there are many" (Ray 1973, p. 10).

Galjart tends to agree with Ray; witness his observation that "if we accept that the basic determinant of dependence is the use of power in exchange relations, it follows that dependence may occur in the relations between socialist states, too. In such societies power is redistributed and concentrated in the hands of a small number of people, but it is not absent" (Galjart 1974, p. 15). Despite the socialization of the means of production – that is, state ownership of farmland, natural resources, factories, etc. – these countries are bound to have a class of privileged bureaucrats, managers and party officials, many of whom will use their influence for the purpose of gaining economic advantage.

However that may be, the fact remains that developed socialist states possess power and that there is, according to Galjart, no reason to assume that this power will not play a part in international transactions. He cites Amin, who has claimed that in their trade relations with the underdeveloped countries, the developed socialist states behave exactly as the developed capitalist states do. He also quotes Karol, who has indicated that during the past twenty years there have been repeated complaints by socialist as well as capitalist Third World countries about the trading practices of the Soviet Union and other East European countries.

In order to place into perspective the thesis that dependency (and the underdevelopment which allegedly stems from it) is wholly the product of capitalism, we like to refer to the analysis which Slicher van Bath (1974b) has made of the situation in colonial Latin America. According to some authors, including Frank, this region had a capitalist system imposed upon it immediately after its conquest. Others maintain that this did not happen until after 1800. Slicher van Bath concludes that it is difficult to call Latin America truly capitalist before 1800 because there were few large enterprises, capital investment was limited, there was no credit system, there was a great deal of unfree labor (not only in the form of slavery, but also because the rural population was tied to the large landowners), there were few wage laborers, and there was hardly any labor market. Moreover, the price mechanism functioned poorly, partly because many people were forced to buy from stores owned by the mines and by large landowners. Thus, there were no market relations in which the law of supply and demand could function. Agriculture was for the most part oriented towards self-sufficiency, so that local and regional trade were limited.

The conclusion whether or not colonial Latin America was capitalistic, of course, depends on one's definition of capitalism. Opinions about this differ. Slicher van Bath's definition of capitalism leads him to conclude that a true capitalist structure did not yet exist. If one accepts this and acknowledges at the same time that the colonial period also played a part in the emergence of underdevelopment, one can only conclude that it is incorrect to attribute underdevelopment exclusively to the effects of capitalism.

The fact that capitalism is regarded by Marxist theorists as *the* cause of underdevelopment has various important consequences. One of the first is that they pay little or no attention to the problem of underdevelopment in Third World countries with a socialist or communist system. In spite of the fact that these states show similar symptoms of underdevelopment as do their capitalist counterparts, the above-mentioned theorists usually do not consider them to be underdeveloped.

Another consequence is that no real significance is attached to all kinds of circumstances which are not unique to the capitalist system, but which many people believe can, and in fact do, hamper a country in its development. Apart from the survival of ancient (pre-capitalist) religions, value systems, power structures, and class or caste relationships, one must include obstacles arising from the natural environment, such as low agricultural productivity and greatly fluctuating harvests.

The present weakness of agriculture in many Third World countries is often attributed to the failure of colonial powers to encourage native agriculture as much as they stimulated the production of export crops. Von Albertini (1980) believes it highly questionable that such attempts – if they had been undertaken – would have been very successful considering the serious natural obstacles and the great production risks arising from them in various regions, the low level of development, and, perhaps most importantly, the attitude of the peasants. In regards to Africa, Hyden (1980) convincingly argues that this latter factor continues to play a crucial role now that the countries have achieved independence.

Quite another obstacle on the path to development can be the very small size of a country; the smaller it is, the greater the chance that it lacks essential natural resources and has a far too small domestic market.

Other countries are faced with the problem of excessive internal divisiveness resulting from differences in ethnicity, religion, language and life style, and often leading to long-lasting 'tribal' jealousies, suspicions and outright animosities.

Then there are Third World countries whose development is held back by their unfavorable location. In this respect, special mention may be made of the more than twenty land-locked countries which lack their own outlet to the sea and are handicapped by the fact that they do not have a seaport. Considering that they cannot compete effectively with countries which do possess these locational advantages, it is not surprising that they are among the least-developed countries in the world. While Afghanistan and Nepal belong to the most backward countries in Asia, so Burundi and Niger rank among the poorest countries on the African continent. Essentially the same observation can be made about Bolivia and Paraguay with regard to South America.

A final consequence of the negative role attributed to capitalist penetration is that the Marxist-inspired dependency and imperialism theorists have little or no appreciation for the positive effects of contacts with the West and of the integration into the world economy. Examples include the provision for infrastructural improvements, the transfer of modern knowledge, the establishment of modern education and modern health care, the reduction in internal divisiveness and political unrest, and the creation of larger political units. Instead, the pre-colonial situation is often highly idealized, even though it was frequently characterized by low productivity, famines, epidemics, slave trade, exploitation of the peasantry by the elite, inefficient administration, and various other abuses and shortcomings.

On the basis of the above, Reitsma (1982) has come to the conclusion that dependency theory often gives the impression of being an anti-capitalist theory, rather than one which provides an adequate explanation for the problem of underdevelopment.

The notion that the theory has turned out to be less useful than its early advocates had suggested becomes apparent when we realize that some very dependent Third World countries enjoy a relatively high per capita GNP and a comparatively fast rate of economic growth. Warren has come to precisely the same conclusion. He claims that "the more trade or investment dependent they are, the more prosperous they tend to be. The cross-sectional relationship between trade dependence and per capita income in the Third World is positive; the wealthier countries are those most dependent on foreign investment" (Warren 1982, pp. 183-4).

Independence: an unattainable or nearly unattainable situation

In this concluding section of our lengthy critique, we like to devote attention to another weakness of the dependency theory, a point made by Ray (1973). In his opinion, the dependency model (at least as it has been outlined by Bodenheimer and Dos Santos) repeatedly suggests that dependence and non-dependence form a dichotomous variable, thus assuming that non-dependence is a potentially attainable alternative after the causes of dependence have been removed.

Ray finds this suggestion of a dichotomous variable one of the most fundamental misconceptions. It is clearly misleading to pretend that there are only two types of countries: dependent and non-dependent; exploited and non-exploited; underdeveloped and developed. In reality, there are many gradations of dependence and dominance.

What he finds lacking in Bodenheimer and Dos Santos is a precise definition of what they mean by non-dependence and autonomous development. They equate dependence with integration into the capitalist world market and suggest that independence can be achieved by breaking off all relations with the capitalist countries and opting for socialism. This position implicitly assumes that economic relations between countries outside the capitalist world market are of a different kind.

In Ray's view, the latter assumption is simply wrong because even in the socialist bloc a country can only sell goods if another country is willing to be a customer. If an underdeveloped country wishes to export, it will have to structure its economy so as to meet the requirements of the international market, irrespective of whether it is a socialist or a capitalist country. In either case it becomes dependent and does so in the meaning given to that word by many *dependencistas*.

There is yet another reason, according to Ray, why it is impossible for a country to be independent if it carries on trade within the socialist bloc. The bloc follows the principle of the division of labor on the basis of comparative advantages – a principle which has been "formally accepted by the socialist bloc." The Soviet Union has "endorsed and encouraged what is explicitly called the international socialist division of labour" (Ray 1973, p. 16). It is no coincidence, therefore, that socialist Cuba has abandoned the idea of rapid industrialization and economic diversification. It has even specialized more strongly in sugar production than before. Despite many positive changes in its economy, Cuba is still as dependent as it was previously, and perhaps more so. Sloan (1977, p. 33) has pointed out that this means that Cuba's economy stands and falls with the possibility of exporting sugar to, and importing industrial goods from, the Eastern bloc, or obtaining technicians, advisers and financial support from there. Cuba's national debt is also growing and the country is troubled by balance of payments problems. Various socialist authors, including Dumont, have noted that the emphasis on sugar curbs the country's development.

Ray is convinced that it is impossible for Third World countries to attain a state of non-dependence for the simple reason that a more or less dependent status is a fact of life. Even the developed countries depend upon imports of raw materials and energy sources (oil). They also export on a large scale and often make use of foreign investments for the further development of their own economies. Ray considers that the most realistic policy would be to aim for a form of dependence which guarantees progress, rather than trying to achieve non-dependence. This seems a sensible conclusion, especially for small states whose size and resources preclude them from being self-sufficient. As long as this is not fully realized by development theorists, they are likely to come up with inappropriate development strategies.

Finally, attention may be focused on the fact that Third World countries are not only dependent on First and/or Second World countries, but also on one another. What is more, some of them are, at least in some respects, more dependent on one or more neighboring countries in the periphery than they are on core countries. For example, Nepal is highly dependent on India; Mozambique, Zimbabwe and Zambia on South Africa; Burkina Faso on Ivory Coast and Ghana; and Paraguay on Brazil. What we have, then, is a complex network of differing core-periphery relations. Aside from being worldwide, this network is hierarchical in character, and may be said to comprise a number of 'constellations' (Reitsma 1983a, 1983b). A particular country, say India, occupies a dependent position *vis-à-vis* the U.S., Britain and Japan, but maintains at the same time a position of

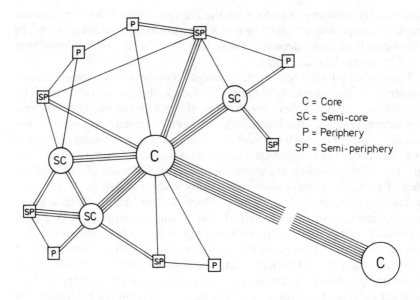

Fig. 20. Hypothetical constellation of differentiated core-periphery relations.

dominance with respect to Nepal and Bhutan. Likewise, Taiwan may be characterized as a 'satellite' (to use Frank's terminology) of the U.S. and Japan, while being a 'metropolis' with regard to various Southeast Asian countries from which it imports raw materials and to which it exports manufactured goods and capital. Although highly simplified, Figure 20 is an attempt to illustrate one such constellation of core-periphery relations. In this model, an effort is made to indicate that there are gradations of dependence and dominance by dividing the countries of the world into four categories: core, semi-core, semi-periphery and periphery.

The abridged case studies presented in the next four chapters afford the reader a chance to find out more precisely to what extent imperialism and dependency theories, or, for that matter, the views of Lacoste, can or cannot help to explain processes of underdevelopment in concrete situations.

PART FIVE
FOUR CASE STUDIES

Chapter 17   Ethiopia

Ethiopia is located in northeast Africa, only a few degrees north of the Equator. It is surrounded by Sudan, Kenya and Somalia. Northern Ethiopia borders on the Red Sea, which forms an important connection between the Indian Ocean and the Mediterranean Sea (by way of the Gulf of Suez and the Suez Canal). Ethiopia's foreign trade moves largely through the port of Djibouti, which is located in a tiny country on the Gulf of Aden, also called Djibouti.

Ethiopia's area exceeds that of Texas by some 50 percent, while its population of about 32 million is a little more than double the number of Texans.* The large majority of the Ethiopian people live in abject poverty, a condition which is primarily attributable to unfavorable internal circumstances, rather than to foreign exploitation.

Since the causes of Ethiopia's underdevelopment must be sought in its past, we will use the historical approach in this case study. Due to a paucity of reliable information, little attention is given to the period since the 1974-revolution.

The physical environment

Most of Ethiopia consists of mountains, high tablelands and deep valleys with steep slopes. While extensive areas are more than 1,200 m (4,000 feet) above sea level, some areas are below sea level. The Great Rift Valley – à long, steep-walled trough or faulted valley which extends some 4,500 miles from Syria and Israel in the north to Malawi and Mozambique in the south and which contains the Jordan Valley, Dead Sea, Red Sea and many of the elongated lakes in East Africa – divides Ethiopia into almost equal halves (Fig. 21). Because of the extremely rugged topography and unnavigable rivers, much of the country is, and always has been, highly inaccessible, especially during the rainy season. Internal communication in this most mountainous country of all Africa is beset with problems comparable to those found in Tibet or the Andean region (Fig. 22).

For many centuries, the difficult topography made it possible for Ethiopia to exist in almost perfect isolation. Whereas neighboring regions became dominated by Islamic cultures, Ethiopia was able to maintain itself as a bastion of Christianity. This cultural-religious difference – characterized by a long history of mutual animosity – further strengthened Ethiopia's isolated existence. Understandably, Ethiopia has developed its own unique cultural identity, making it very different from any other

---

* According to recent estimates, Ethiopia may well have some 42 million inhabitants, which is 30 percent more than the figure given in most sources.

Fig. 21. Ethiopia's major topographic features.

country on the African continent. This identity does not mean that Ethiopia is a homogeneous country, on the contrary, there is considerable cultural diversity within the state. As a matter of fact, Ethiopia is at the same time a plural society and a multinational state. We will see below that these internal differences and regional contrasts are an important reason why Ethiopia belongs to the group of least-developed countries.

Climatically, Ethiopia can be divided into three broad zones: the *kolla,* *woina dega* and *dega.* The *kolla,* found at elevations below 1,700 m (5,000 ft), has an average temperature of 26° C (78° F). This hot and for the most part dry zone occurs mainly in the north and east, but includes also southernmost Ethiopia (Fig. 23). Crop farming is possible only in places where there is water for irrigation. Most of the *kolla* has always been used for nomadic herding. Apart from the aridity and often intense heat –

268

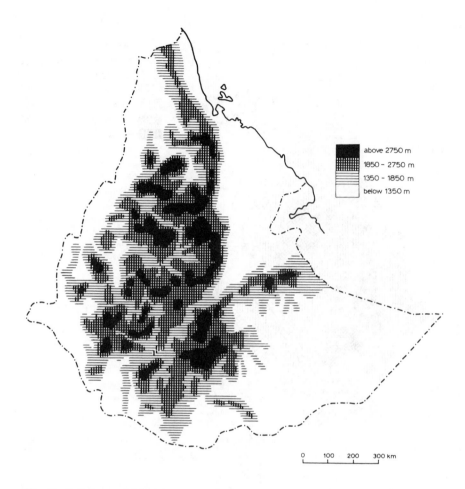

Fig. 22. Relief map of Ethiopia. *Source*: Koninklijk Instituut voor de Tropen, 1971.

temperatures of 40°-50° C (100°-120° F) are not uncommon – some of the lower-lying areas have long been ravaged by malaria, discouraging permanent settlement (Gourou 1966).*

The *woina dega*, between elevations of 1,700 m (5,000 ft) and 2,500 m (8,000 ft), includes the larger part of Ethiopia's high plateau regions. Average temperature is about 22° C (72° F) and annual amounts of precipitation average around 100 cm (40 inches). Owing to their volcanic origin, some of the soils are quite fertile. This area is Ethiopia's agricultural heartland, supporting appreciably higher population densities than the other zones. The nearly subtropical climate favors the production of a wide variety of crops, and offers excellent possibilities for livestock ranching.

* References at end of chapter.

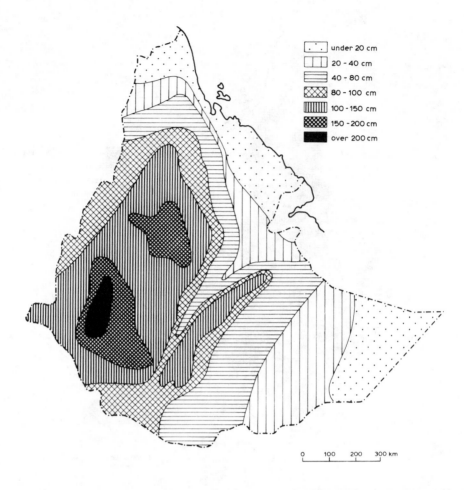

Fig. 23. Ethiopia, distribution of precipitation. *Source*: Koninklijk Instituut voor de Tropen, 1971.

The third climatic zone, the *dega,* is found at altitudes above 2,500 m (8,000 ft). Its mild temperatures and relatively abundant precipitation make this area suitable for livestock production as well as crop farming.

All in all, much of Ethiopia has considerable agricultural potential. Soil erosion, however, is a serious and widespread problem, caused by a combination of factors: cultivation of steep slopes, cutting down of trees for firewood, overgrazing and the burning of natural pastures during the dry season. Although originally about half of Ethiopia was forested, today no more than 7 percent has a forest cover. The higher areas could easily be reforested, e.g., with eucalyptus trees, but thus far the government has not carried out any large-scale reforestation projects. Insufficiently protected by a vegetation cover and root systems that hold the soil in place, over 1

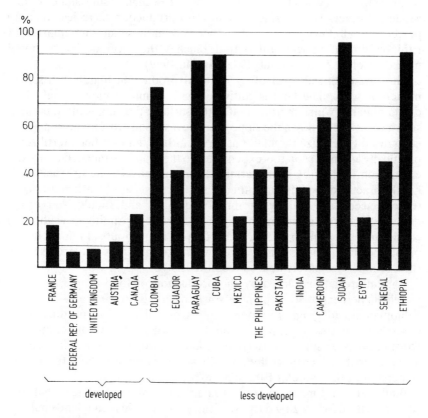

Fig. 24. Agricultural exports as percent of total merchandise exports, 1980; selected developed and less-developed countries.
Source: World Bank, *World Development Report 1983*.

billion tons of irreplaceable topsoil are each year washed down the slopes and transported to Sudan and Egypt, particularly by the Blue Nile.

The agricultural sector

The majority of the Ethiopian people – some 80 percent – are employed in agriculture. Over 90 percent of the exports of the country consist of agricultural products, chiefly coffee; well over half its GDP is derived from the agricultural sector (Fig. 24; see also Fig. 9 on page 95).

The fact that so many people are farmers or livestock herders is partly attributable to the shortage of non-agricultural employment, and partly also to the extremely backward methods of agricultural production that require large inputs of manual labor. Three out of every four farmers work no more than a few hectares on which they grow mainly subsistence crops. Modern farmers specializing in cash crop production have less than 10 percent of all farm units. Altogether, no more than one quarter of Ethiopia's total agricultural output reaches the local or international market (Cohen & Weintraub 1975, Kurian 1979).

The low technical level of agricultural production manifests itself in numerous ways. The land is cultivated with primitive plows – pulled by draft animals – which merely scratch the surface; plowing is often done in such a way (up and down the slope) that it causes soil erosion; most manure is not used to fertilize the land but serves as fuel; and artificial fertilizer is practically unknown or too expensive for the small farmers. Due to soil exhaustion, at least $1/7$ of all farmland remains uncultivated; irrigation is hardly practiced; weeds and other pests (locusts!) are insufficiently controlled; seeds are usually of inferior quality; and finally, harvesting methods, transportation and storage are downright primitive, resulting in considerable loss and spoilage. Thus, despite large inputs of human labor, output per farmer is very low. Even when drought does not strike, many rural families are barely able to feed themselves.

Agriculture is dominated by the production of food crops. Approximately 80 percent of all cropland is sown to cereals, in particular to *tef*, the Ethiopian bread grain. Of some importance also is the production of oilseeds and pulses (e.g., peas, beans and lentils). The major commercial crops are coffee, sugar, tobacco and *khat* (a stimulant, not unlike coca). The principal cash crop, coffee, usually accounts for anywhere from 50 to 80 percent of the value of Ethiopia's exports.

While cropland makes up only 10 percent of all land, at least half the country is used for grazing purposes. Since much of this rangeland could be converted to cropland, Ethiopia has the potential to become a large producer of grains and other crops. It has been estimated that the country could feed as many as 100 million people. Clearly, we are dealing here with a country whose most basic natural resource, tillable land, is grossly underutilized (Cohen & Weintraub 1975).

Underutilization characterizes not only subsistence farming, but also commercial agriculture. The production of coffee, for example, is quite primitive. Well over half the coffee trees are wild trees, rather than high-yielding, domesticated varieties. Because of traditional methods of cultivation and processing, output per acre is very low. Despite efforts by the National Coffee Board to raise the quality of the coffee beans and to improve methods of processing, Ethiopian coffee does not compare favorably with coffee from many other countries. Possibilities for the production of cotton, jute, tobacco and sugar are equally underutilized. Although Ethiopia could produce more than it needs and become an exporter, it is a net importer of these commodities.

Livestock production is no less backward; the quality of the animals as well as their products tends to be low. Fodder crops are generally not

272

37. Pastoral nomadism in semiarid Ethiopia. Although there are some 24 million sheep, the country produces hardly any wool. (S. van der Land)

grown, certainly not by the nomads, so that cattle, sheep, goats, etc. must survive on the usually sparse and relatively unnutricious vegetation of the natural pastures. Improved pastures hardly exist. Poverty and ignorance are the main reasons that the animals are not well taken care of. Little is done to control sicknesses and parasites (e.g., ticks) or to improve the quality of the livestock through selective breeding. Dictated by tradition, social and cultural aspects of livestock raising outweigh economic considerations. A herd of animals, especially cattle, constitutes a social asset rather than an economic investment: the larger the herd, the greater the owner's social prestige. Accordingly, livestock breeding is influenced more by ritual and taboos than by profitability considerations. The fact that more emphasis is placed on quantity than on quality helps explain the problem of overgrazing and soil erosion. Ethiopia, incidentally, has the largest livestock resources in Africa: 1 million camels, 7 million horses, mules and donkeys, 18 million goats, 24 million sheep, and 27 million cattle (Legum 1976, p. B 209).

Notwithstanding the above, livestock raising has considerable economic importance. Besides the fact that mules, horses and donkeys are invaluable as pack animals in this highly inaccessible country, and that cattle are used as draft animals, some 10 percent of Ethiopia's total exports consist of hides

– the second most important earner of foreign exchange after coffee. Livestock also produce large quantities of manure, which is the leading and sometimes only source of fuel in many rural communities.

In recent decades, agricultural output has grown more slowly than has the number of people. The result is that Ethiopia's food supply situation has deteriorated and famine has become even more common than previously.

Several factors appear to be responsible for the low productivity in the agricultural sector. One of these could possibly be that the rather favorable natural conditions in large parts of Ethiopia do not form enough of a challenge for the farming population. In a sense, life may be too easy, so that farmers need not make that extra effort to produce enough food to survive. For example, there is no long unproductive winter season that requires them to plan ahead and store supplies of food. Even with a minimum amount of labor and primitive methods of production, most farmers could presumably produce enough to live on. This is essentially the reverse of the *challenge-response thesis* of the British historian Arnold Toynbee. According to this theory, a civilization grows and flourishes when its response to a challenge (e.g., a harsh winter) is successful, which subsequently stimulates a further series of challenges. Overcoming these challenges may eventually lead to greater productivity, surpluses, division of labor, urbanization and higher levels of organization.

Another factor which has not had a favorable effect on agricultural productivity is Ethiopia's long history of wars and internal feuds. The resulting insecurity has meant that farmers often could not be sure whether they would reap the benefits of their labor. Thus, they were not motivated to produce more than they needed for their immediate survival.

A more important factor, it seems to us, is the highly uneven distribution of landownership which has characterized Ethiopia for many centuries. As a major cause of poverty among the tenant farmers, it has seriously limited the purchasing power of the majority of the people. At the same time, the feudal-type land tenure system and accompanying lack of concern for the well-being and rights of the peasantry have contributed to keeping the peasantry ignorant. This combination of poverty and ignorance made it virtually impossible for the rural masses to raise the level of agricultural productivity. In the following section we will discuss this problem in more detail.

Ownership relations prior to the 1974 revolution

In parts of northern Ethiopia, much of the land belonged to villages or extended families whose members were related to the individual(s) who had originally cleared it and/or claimed it as his (their) property. All persons who belonged to such a village community or extended family were entitled to use a portion of the collectively owned land. Once every five years or so the communal land was redivided by a council of elders. Each person who received a plot, cultivated it individually. The right to use a

274

piece of land is known as *rest* or *rist*. If he wished to do so, the rest holder (*restenya*) could give or sell his *rest* to another member of the community. However, he could not sell the land itself because he was not the owner. Prior to 1974, about one-third of Ethiopia's population lived in areas with this system of kinship and village tenures (Cohen & Weintraub 1975).

All members of the community theoretically had the same rights and could claim the same amount of farmland. In practice, however, some individuals received more than others, either because of closer kinship ties or because of social status. It also happened that certain individuals were entitled to use more land because they belonged to more than one communal group.

Although communal landownership has some advantages, it also has a number of drawbacks. Periodic repartitioning meant that a farmer would lose 'his' particular piece of land. This, of course, discouraged him from taking good care of it, let alone making permanent improvements. An additional disadvantage was that a farmer could not easily obtain agricultural credit because he could not use his *rest* as collateral – a common problem in countries where farmland is communally owned.

Due to population growth, an increasingly large number of persons came to share the communal land, resulting in a decline in average farm size. Around 1970, nearly half the farmers in northern Ethiopia had less than 0.5 ha (1 acre) of land at their disposal, and frequently their land was fragmented in several tiny, scattered plots – a situation which does not favor rational farming (Bondestam 1974).

In 1970, over two-thirds of all farmland was privately owned, concentrated largely in south-central Ethiopia. Much of this land was not the property of the small farmers who cultivated it, but was owned by a small number of 'landed families,' e.g., members of the royal family, dignitaries and high government officials. The Church, too, possessed a great deal of land. In contrast to the village and kinship communities in the north, these privileged groups of large landowners usually paid little or no property tax. Custers (1977) has estimated that in Ethiopia as a whole no more than one-tenth of one percent of the population owned about 70 percent of all farmland. In the southeastern province of Harar, just two landlords owned 71 percent of the land!

About half of Ethiopia's farmers were tenants in 1974. Few cultivated more than 5 ha (12 acres). Depending on the inputs provided by the landlord (tools, seed, draft animals, etc.), the tenant had to surrender anywhere from 30 to 65 percent of his crop to the landlord. Sometimes he had to pay an additional 10 percent of his net income to the landowner. But this was not all, for most landlords demanded that their tenants perform certain tasks for them. The landlords, furthermore, could easily take advantage of the fact that tenancy agreements were not written contracts.

Since there were no laws to protect the rights of the tenants, they were completely at the mercy of the landowners, who could evict them if and when they chose. Most tenancy contracts were for only one year; continuation rights were unknown. Each year the tenant faced the risk of losing his land. In order to improve his chance of being permitted to stay on, he might offer the landlord gifts or perform some extra tasks for him. Because no amelioration rights existed, tenants were generally unwilling to go through the trouble of removing stones from the fields or in some other way improve the quality of the farmland.

These unfavorable tenancy conditions explain why most peasants were not inclined, or able, to increase the level of agricultural productivity. As a consequence, agriculture remained as backward as it always had been. Because of the exorbitantly high interest rates charged by moneylenders, farmers generally decided against taking out a loan. The result was that they did not, and could not, break out of the vicious circle of poverty and low productivity.

Recent decline in rural living standards

Although the quality of life in the rural areas has traditionally been very low for the majority of the people, it has deteriorated appreciably since the 1950s. Due to accelerated population growth – made possible by modern medications – pressure on the land has increased and land prices have gone up. Tenure conditions, too, have deteriorated, while the number of landless families has risen steadily.

One of the reasons that living conditions have worsened is that the former government decided that modernization of agriculture should take place on a small number of large, commercial farms. It was believed that they would best be able to produce for the national market and for export. Large-scale production with modern machines was promoted, particularly in south-central Ethiopia where nearly all the land was held by large landowners and where soils were relatively fertile. Many tenancy contracts were terminated for the purpose of creating larger farm units. Some landlords started to do the farming themselves, but most decided to lease large pieces of land to a small number of relatively well-educated tenants who were able and willing to purchase modern agricultural implements and/or hire agricultural workers. The consequence was that the poorer and usually illiterate tenants lost their land. Some managed to find work as seasonal laborers, but many others were not so fortunate.

These developments have aggravated the problem of social disparities. While the majority of the rural population now lives in abject poverty, a small proportion has been able to improve its standard of living. Although there are indications that the trend toward greater inequality in the rural areas has been arrested since the 1974 revolution, it is as yet not clear whether the rural poor are better-off than prior to the revolution.

There are some 2 million nomads in Ethiopia. Their existence has been threatened by governmental efforts to develop irrigation projects. For example, until the early 1960s the Awash Valley in northeastern Ethiopia was the exclusive domain of the Danakil nomads, whose herds grazed the relatively lush vegetation on the banks of the river. In 1962, the Awash Valley Authority was established and nine years later one-third of all irrigable land was used for large-scale production of cotton and sugar cane.

About half the irrigated land in the Awash Valley was leased on a long-term basis to foreign companies specializing in the irrigated production of tropical and subtropical cash crops. A Dutch company grows sugar cane and a British company has large cotton farms. Thousands of hectares have been leased to an Italian banana-growing enterprise and to a Japanese concern interested in producing alfalfa for export to Japan. Within a few years after these projects were completed, impressive profits were being realized and all investments had been recovered. Although there is a paucity of reliable information, it is virtually certain that the profits which left Ethiopia prior to 1974 far exceeded the foreign investments that had come in.

The Danakil, who had lived in the area since the 16th century, were forced to move to less suitable grazing areas which soon became seriously overgrazed. Not only did their herds have to be reduced in size, but every time there is a long period of drought, many of the people and livestock fall victim to hunger and starvation.

Since the government focused all its attention on the large-scale production of commercial crops, the rest of the agricultural sector was neglected. Nothing was done to help the small farmers; for example, no land reform took place because emperor Haile Selassie, the Church and the large landlowners were against it. Tenancy relations were not improved either. The peasants themselves were too dependent, vulnerable and unorganized – and because of centuries of exploitation also too apathetic – to have any influence on the government or to stand up for their rights. In fact, they had no rights.

The secondary sector

A few years ago, manufacturing was responsible for only 10 percent of Ethiopia's GDP, while employing less than 7 percent of the economically active population. Value added by manufacturing amounted to only $13 per capita per year, compared to $2,866 in the United States.

Most industrial enterprises are small handicraft-type operations. Cottage industry is also fairly common. In 1975, there were fewer than 500 modern factories and of these only 84 had more than 100 employees. Manufacturing was characteristically dominated by the processing of agricultural raw materials (food crops, tobacco, sugar cane, etc.) and by the production of simple consumer goods, such as shoes, textile, foodstuffs and beverages.

Prior to 1936, the year in which Ethiopia became occupied by Italy, there were no factories at all. The first industrial plants were built by the Italians; others have been added since World War II. For many years, and to a large extent still today, factories were (are) run by foreigners; every one of the larger and more modern plants has been built with the help of foreign know-how and capital.

The major concentration of industrial enterprises is found in Addis Ababa and its immediate surroundings. There are also quite a few factories located along the railroad line linking the capital city to Djibouti. Other centers of industrial activity are the northern cities of Asmara and Massawa (in Eritrea) and Dire Dawa and Harar in the east. Ethiopia's only oil refinery is located at Assab on the Red Sea.

Several circumstances are responsible for the low degree of industrialization. Among these are: (1) the limited purchasing power of the population, (2) Ethiopia's inaccessibility, (3) the lack of investment capital (the 'fortunate few' have always spent their wealth consumptively rather than productively), (4) the absence of modern technological expertise, (5) the traditional value system in which manual labor was (and is) despised, and (6) the lack of natural resources (natural gas was not discovered until 1973). Although Ethiopia possesses a considerable amount of potential hydroelectricity, only about 1 percent was developed in 1970.

These same constraints exist at present, so that rapid industrialization is only possible if capital, technicians, managers and equipment can be attracted from abroad. This fact explains why in 1974 nearly half of all industry was foreign-owned. Since the revolution, several industries have been nationalized, but most apparently still are in foreign hands. Besides, the new regime looks rather favorably upon foreign investment, so that Ethiopia's external dependence has far from disappeared. Today, a large percentage of the top managers in industry are non-Ethiopians.

Since the secondary sector is still very limited in size, many manufactured goods need to be imported, which has a negative effect on the balance of payments. Another weakness is that numerous enterprises are unable to produce economically and cannot compete with foreign producers. One bottleneck is the lack of industrial experience. Another is the smallness of the domestic market which severely restricts the possibilities for mass production. Because of these problems, various manufacturing activities must be subsidized by the government. Such protectionist measures are not only costly, but tend to foster considerable inefficiency.

The secondary sector employs about 100,000 persons. Since their incomes are higher than those of agricultural laborers and most farmers, industrialization has contributed to Ethiopia's problem of spatial inequality. Increasingly, a relatively prosperous industrial middle class in urban centers contrasts with the impoverished masses in the rural areas. At the same time, the combination of industrialization and rural-to-urban migration has resulted in sharp disparities within the cities, particularly in Addis Ababa.

The tertiary sector

A few years ago, the tertiary sector employed 12 percent of the labor force and contributed 33 percent to Ethiopia's GDP. In both these respects it was more important than the secondary sector. Nevertheless, it is still quite small in size, especially when compared to the primary sector which employs approximately 80 percent of the economically active population.

The politically dominant Amharas (and other Coptic Christians) have never shown much interest in commercial and financial activities. Because in 1668 Moslems were forbidden by law to own or farm land in the Christian parts of the Ethiopian Empire, many of them have found employment as merchants. Still today, Moslems from Yemen and other Arabic countries – together with Italians, Greeks, Armenians and Indians – dominate this sector. A few years ago, Addis Ababa's wholesale trade was almost completely in the hands of foreigners; the same was true of the trade in coffee. The banking and financing sectors were likewise controlled by non-Amharas.

The tertiary sector has experienced a rapid rate of growth since the Second World War. Much of this increase has occurred in the urban *informal* sector, but also the number of government officials has multiplied. Ethiopia's informal sector, however, is not yet as large as that of Third World countries which are more highly urbanized, this despite the fact that wealthy Ethiopians have always had many slaves and now employ large numbers of servants. At present, only 15 percent of the country's population is classified as urban.

International trade

Since there is virtually no mining and very little manufacturing, Ethiopia exports exclusively agricultural commodities: coffee, oilseeds, pulses and hides. Compared to other Third World countries, foreign trade is extremely limited. On a per capita basis, the value of all exports amounted to a mere $12 in 1982 – a clear indication that Ethiopia is one of the least-developed countries in the world. It also illustrates that it is at best only marginally integrated into the global economic system.

Before 1974, nearly half its exports consisted of coffee shipments to the U.S. This one-sided trade relationship meant that Ethiopia was highly vulnerable, or, as some proponents of the *dependencia* theory would have it, very dependent. Despite an increase in exports to communist countries since 1974, total exports remain small and continue to be characterized by a notable lack of diversity.

Until the late 1950s, the value of imports was roughly in balance with the value of exports. However, as a result of the government's decision in 1958 to stimulate economic development, imports of (expensive) manufactured products and fuel have soared, so that Ethiopia has had a negative trade balance almost every year since then. During 1976-1978, for example, imports exceeded exports by respectively 23 percent, 25 percent and 43 percent (Legum 1981, p. B 223). Prior to 1974, the U.S. and other Western countries, together with international organizations, helped Ethiopia out by giving economic assistance to the tune of some $600 million worth of loans and grants. After 1974, the pattern of dependency relations underwent a sudden change. As the U.S. terminated its aid program (including military assistance), the USSR, China and Eastern Europe became the major aid donors. In 1977, Cuba began to provide economic and military aid, bringing in about 11,000 troops and military advisers. By early 1978, the Russians had poured in an estimated $1 billion worth of military supplies, an amount far in excess of the total value of arms received by Ethiopia in the previous 25 years.

Both before and after the revolution, much foreign aid – if we can call it 'aid' – had strings attached to it. The donor countries, rather than the Ethiopians, decided which industrial goods Ethiopia should buy from them, while only taking on the development projects that they were interested in, rather than those that Ethiopia needed most.

One of the consequences of Ethiopia's drive toward agricultural modernization and industrialization was a sharp rise in its foreign debt, which in 1977 stood at $471 million or 14 percent of its GNP. Four years later, its foreign debt amounted to $792 million or 19 percent of GNP. Repayment of loans plus interest payments nearly equaled the amount coming in through new loans. In other words, Ethiopia faced the predicament of having to borrow in order to be able to pay off old debts. Since it is likely to remain an exporter of (cheap) agricultural products and an importer of (often increasingly expensive) industrial goods, there is little reason to expect that it will soon break out of this vicious circle.

Urbanization

Ethiopia is one of the world's least urbanized countries. At the time of the revolution, only ten out of every hundred people lived in an urban settlement. Apart from Addis Ababa (1 million inhabitants) and Asmara (300,000), there are no large cities. The third largest city, Dire Dawa, has fewer than 100,000 inhabitants. With over one-third of the urban population concentrated in Addis Ababa, Ethiopia qualifies as a country that is characterized by *primacy*. Although Asmara, the capital of peripherally located Eritrea, has importance as an industrial center, the centrally located national capital dominates the country in every respect. Besides, Addis Ababa was for many years one of the leading and most influential cities in all Africa.

Since the bulk of rural-to-urban migrants – pushed out of the rural areas by agricultural modernization, high birth rates and recurrent droughts – trek to Addis Ababa and Asmara, these two cities expand more rapidly than other urban centers. As a consequence, the pattern of urban places deviates more and more from the presumably favorable Christaller-type pattern (see page 147).That is, the distribution of urban centers is becoming increasingly uneven or unbalanced. This imbalance is accentuated by the fact that much wealth is concentrated in Addis Ababa and Asmara, resulting in a large demand for all kinds of formal and informal service activities. The consequence is that Ethiopia's tertiary sector is concentrated almost entirely in these two central places. Knowing this, it should not surprise us that they are the major 'magnets' attracting rural migrants looking for work.

In view of the fact that the secondary sector grows at a slower rate than does the urban population, we can expect the urban tertiary sector to experience considerable expansion in the coming years. In particular the number of jobs in the informal sector is likely to grow. If, however, the informal sector is unable to absorb the influx of rural migrants – a common problem in Third World countries – it must be feared that the number of urban people who cannot find work will grow as well.

Infrastructure

Ethiopia is still highly inaccessible and if we disregard air transportation, its isolation *vis-à-vis* neighboring countries is nearly as great as it was five or ten centuries ago. Even though it is about as large as the American Middle West and has 32 million inhabitants, there are only a few thousand miles of hard-surface roads. Many places can only be reached on foot or horseback, and then only during the dry season. Ethiopia has but two railroad lines: a narrow-gauge line connecting Addis Ababa with the foreign port of Djibouti and a short line in Eritrea, giving Asmara access to the port of Massawa. The former railroad was built in 1917 and the latter dates back to the period of Italian occupation (1936-1941). No new railroads have been built since World War II.

The absence of a network of overland transportation routes makes it impossible to make full use of available natural resources. Not only are extensive areas of potential cropland underutilized, but also mining, fishing and forestry are less developed than they could be if Ethiopia possessed adequate infrastructural facilities. The same is true of the production of hydroelectricity. Although the country is well endowed with waterpower, virtually none of it has been developed. Without cheap electricity Ethiopia will be unable to make much economic progress or promote a more even distribution of industrial development and urban growth. At present, the country depends on imports of expensive oil, so that modern economic development is feasible only in places with access to one of the three port cities on the Red Sea: Massawa, Assab (site of the only oil refinery) or Djibouti.

The people and their quality of life

There are few countries that have a lower per capita GNP than Ethiopia, which in 1981 was about $140. At least 80 percent of the population lives a self-sufficient existence outside the modern money economy. Unemployment and underemployment are widespread in urban as well as rural areas.

How impoverished most people are becomes apparent when we look at the diet of the 'average' Ethiopian. Per capita caloric intake falls about 24 percent short of the minimum requirements. Actually, vitamin deficiencies are even greater since most people rarely eat fresh vegetables and fruit. Partly because taboos restrict the consumption of meat, diets are also deficient in animal protein. Undernourishment is further caused by the large number of days on which people have to fast. According to Ullendorf (1973), the Ethiopian Orthodox Church prescribes no fewer than 180 such days a year! Fasting does not mean that people must abstain from food altogether, but that they can eat only one meal a day, without any meat, animal fat, eggs or dairy products.

People are not only malnourished, but most of them do not have clean drinking water and live in primitive huts or shanties which do not protect them against the elements. The consequence is that few people are truly healthy. In 1976, there were only 350 physicians, mostly foreigners. Although medical services have been improved and expanded in recent years, especially in the larger cities, inadequate transportation facilities and long distances make them inaccessible to most rural Ethiopians. Thus, many peasant families still depend on the advice of a medicine man, witch doctor or quack. And because there is no telephone service in much of the country, there is no way to call for a doctor or a nurse.

Average life expectancy is only 46 years. This is so low not because few people live to be more than 46 years old, but because many children die before the age of five. Infant mortality rates exceed 20 percent in some rural areas.

While death rates are high, birth rates are even higher, as evidenced by Ethiopia's rapid rate of population growth: about 2.4 percent per year. Although there has not been a population census prior to 1984, it is almost certain that in spite of recurring famine Ethiopia's population has doubled during the past 30 years.

The rapid increase in the number of people exacerbates old problems and creates new ones. In an underdeveloped country like Ethiopia it causes more unemployment, greater deprivation, growing food shortages, increased pressure on agricultural land (resulting in more overgrazing and erosion), deteriorating tenure conditions and, last but not least, a more youthful population. Almost every second Ethiopian is a child. While all these children contribute little to the country's GNP, they do need to be clothed and fed and, if Ethiopia ever hopes to overcome the problems of underdevelopment, also educated and kept in good health. Schooling alone would require enormous investments.

Compulsory education does not exist in Ethiopia and 85 percent of the adult population is illiterate. Due to the rapid increase in population, the number of people who can neither read nor write has grown relentlessly during the past few decades. In 1980, only 43 percent of the children 6 years and older visited elementary school: 56 percent of the boys and 30 percent of the girls. Few finish elementary school and even fewer (11 percent in 1980) go on to junior high school. The high schools are concentrated in the larger cities and a substantial proportion of the teachers are foreigners. Only about 10,000 Ethiopians attend the universities of Addis Ababa and Asmara and probably no more than 3,000 study abroad. In contrast to the urban places, where some 70 percent of the children go to school, in rural areas often only 10 percent of the children receive an education (Kurian 1979).

Many reasons can be listed for the high illiteracy rate, including (1) lack of money for school buildings, school materials and teacher training; (2) shortage of teachers and, more generally, of literate people; (3) insufficient teacher training facilities; (4) disinterest among teachers to work in rural areas; (5) absence of transportation, so that many children are unable to attend school; (6) the need among poor people to put children to work, herd livestock, haul water or collect firewood; (7) the fact that most people do not realize the importance of an education; (8) linguistic diversity (altogether some 70 languages and over 200 dialects are spoken); (9) the complicated Amharic script (with 282 characters); and (10) the opposition among religious leaders and landlords to education and other related social changes.

Ethnic, political and social disparities

From time immemorial, the Ethiopian people have been very diverse. Most important are the politically dominant *Amharas* (Fig. 25). In the 4th century A.D. they made Christianity the official religion and their language (Amharic) the official language. They are closely related to the *Tigreans* with whom they share their mixed Hamitic-Semitic descent. Together, these two groups account for about one-third of the total population.

Although the Hamitic *Gallas* make up 40 percent of the population, they are less influential than the Amharas. The reason appears to be that they are divided among some 200 tribes, many of whom have been at loggerheads with each other in the course of time.

Other ethnic groups are the Hamitic *Danakil,* a small group of mostly Moslem nomads who inhabit the hot Danakil Valley between the Red Sea and the Ethiopian Highland; the Hamitic *Somalis* in southern and southeastern Ethiopia who, because of their religion (Islam), language and nomadic way of life, do not feel at home in Christian-dominated Ethiopia; the racially different *Shankallas* along the western boundary; the *Sidamos*; and the *Falashas* or Abessinian Jews. In addition, there are several small, mainly urban, minorities of Arabs, Indians, Yemeni, Armenians and Europeans.

Without having listed every ethnic group, it is evident that Ethiopia is a heterogeneous society. About 40 percent of the people are Christians (mostly in the north-central portion of the country), another 40 percent are

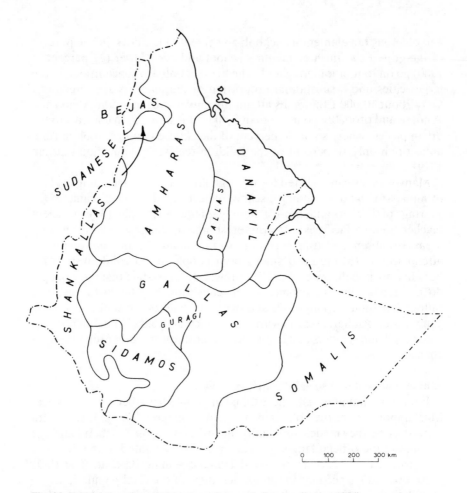

Fig. 25. Ethiopia's major ethnic groups. *Source*: J. Brummelkamp, 1956b.

Moslems (largely in the eastern half of Ethiopia), and the remaining 20 percent are for the most part animists (in the southwest). Notwithstanding fairly successful attempts at 'Amharization,' the Ethiopian people clearly do not constitute a cohesive nation. Instead, the country is torn with internal strife. Many Somalis in the Ogaden region in southeastern Ethiopia would like nothing better than to secede from Ethiopia and join the neighboring country of Somalia. In recent years, Ethiopia and Somalia have fought several wars over the Ogaden.

A similar problem exists in Eritrea. For the past 20 years or so, various liberation fronts have fought wars of independence against Ethiopia, and it looks like the Eritrean struggle for freedom will drag on for many more years.

In addition to the large-scale conflicts in the Ogaden and Eritrea, there are several smaller insurgent movements in Ethiopia. If we add to this that the country of Djibouti (with its important port for Ethiopia) is far from stable, it is clear that conditions do not favor development. Aside from the fact that armed struggles are very costly, they cause destruction, divide the people and require an enormous input of human resources that could otherwise be used more productively.

Ethiopia also has its social disparities. Some ethnic groups have more privileges and enjoy a higher status than do others. The Amharas form the top of the social pyramid. They look down upon, or even despise, most of the other groups. Some segments of the population have a low status on account of their professions – a situation which resembles the caste system in India.

These traditional social differences have become more pronounced since the 1950s. Generally speaking, Ethiopia's attempts at agricultural modernization and industrialization have enabled the rich to add to their wealth, while the poor have become progressively marginalized. Social inequality is most striking in Addis Ababa; in 1974 top government officials earned forty times as much as the lowest-paid officials. Although there is reason to believe that disparities have become less extreme since the revolution, opulent wealth and luxurious mansions still exist side by side with extreme deprivation and leaky shanties. According to various sources, about 90 percent of the capital's inhabitants live in shantytowns – the highest percentage in the world.

The political situation

Prior to the 1974 revolution, all power was vested in the emperor. He was the commander in chief of the armed forces, secular head of the Ethiopian Orthodox Church and, until 1958, also the supreme judge. In effect, he was the government.

In 1931, Haile Selassie 'granted' the Ethiopian people a constitution, thereby creating a parliament. In practice, however, the emperor did not relinquish any of his power. While all seats in the House of Representatives were taken by large landowners, Haile Selassie himself appointed all members of the Senate. Until 1955, Parliament was little more than an advisory council. Democracy did not exist; political parties were unknown and labor unions had no real influence. Besides the emperor, only his family, the national and provincial elite and the Church had political power.

Since the 1974 coup, not much has changed. Now all power is vested in the *Dergue,* a military council which is presided over by Lt. Col. Mengistu Haile Mariam. In 1977, Mengistu declared Ethiopia a socialist state – Parliament was dissolved and the constitution abolished. Political parties are still not allowed, freedom of expression is not tolerated and an unknown number of political opponents are locked up. Human rights are no more respected than they were before 1974.

The development of Ethiopia's underdevelopment

Ethiopia's underdevelopment cannot be explained in terms of colonial exploitation or neo-colonial dependence. With the exception of a short period of Italian occupation (1936-1941), Ethiopia has never been some other country's colonial 'possession.' Instead, it has always had very little contact with Western countries, less so than almost any other Third World country.

Since the 7th century, Islam has spread to areas surrounding the Christian state of Ethiopia, thereby isolating it. Access to coastal areas became increasingly difficult and foreign trade declined. In the 16th century, the Portuguese helped the Ethiopians to fight off the Moslem attacks, but their influence was only temporary. Feelings of insecurity and xenophobia drove the Ethiopians further inland, where they found refuge on the almost impenetrable plateaus northwest of the Great Rift Valley. For the next 300 years they lived there in 'splendid isolation,' bereft of outside cultural influences.

When the African continent was partitioned by European powers during the second half of the 19th century – the so-called 'scramble for Africa' – Ethiopia managed to keep the Europeans at bay and maintain its independence. Twice within a decade the Ethiopians defeated the Italians, and under emperor Menelik II they took advantage of the rivalry between Italy, France and Britain and conquered the Somali-inhabited Ogaden. Their only territorial setback was that they lost control over Eritrea, which was occupied by Italy.

Notwithstanding the fact that the French built a railroad between Addis Ababa and Djibouti (completed in 1917), European influence was practically nil during the first few decades of the 20th century. This changed after Italy (under Mussolini) invaded Ethiopia late 1935. Within a few years, the Italians built a network of roads with a total length of 7,000 km (4,500 miles), which still forms the backbone of Ethiopia's road system. This road network greatly facilitated internal communication, yet Italy failed to establish effective control. After a few years of stubborn resistance, the Ethiopians were able with British help to liberate their country. Thus, Italy was unable to exploit Ethiopia or introduce lasting social change. It is for this reason that it is more appropriate to refer to the Italian interlude as a period of occupation than a period of colonial domination. Perhaps the most important consequence of the Italian occupation was that Ethiopia's leaders came to realize that, compared to Europe, their country was far behind in terms of economic and military development.

After the liberation in 1941, relations with the industrialized West intensified. During World War II, the British helped to modernize Ethiopia's armed forces and administrative system. After the war, British influence was replaced by contacts with other developed countries, particularly the U.S.

Closer relations with industrialized countries were encouraged by Haile Selassie, who wanted to bring his country into the 20th century by promoting economic modernization. For this he needed foreign capital, capital goods and advanced technical know-how. Meantime, the wealthy elite displayed a rapidly growing interest in sophisticated consumer goods, that is, in imported manufactured products, such as refrigerators and cars. While imports and foreign investments rose, Ethiopia was offered considerable economic assistance in the form of loans and grants. Both Western and Soviet-bloc countries provided capital, technicians and modern agricultural and industrial equipment. Although these developments enabled Ethiopia to raise levels of productivity, they saddled it at the same time with a growing foreign debt.

External influence was not limited to the economic sector; militarily and politically, too, Ethiopia became dependent on foreign powers. Because of its strategic location *vis-à-vis* the oil-rich Middle East, the Red Sea and East Africa, the U.S. decided to strengthen its military position in Ethiopia. In exchange for development aid it obtained permission to establish military bases as well as a large communications base for collecting intelligence. The U.S.-Ethiopian relationship came to an abrupt halt in 1974, and at present all military aid comes from Warsaw Pact countries and Cuba.

Although Ethiopia's relations with economically advanced countries have not always been beneficial, and in some respects even harmful, it would be a mistake to conclude that its present underdevelopment has been caused by those same relations. Not only is Ethiopia's neo-colonial dependence too recent to have been able to drag the country down to one of the bottom rungs on the international development ladder, but its external dependence is also limited in scope when compared to that of numerous other Third World countries. Foreign investment in industry and agriculture is quite small and Ethiopia's per capita foreign debt is not excessive. Clearly, then, its underdevelopment already existed *before* Italian, British, American and other foreign influences began to have an impact on the country. It is not Ethiopia's current external dependence but its recent and ancient past that supplies us with the clues as to why it is one of the poorest countries in the world.

Highlights of Ethiopia's history prior to 1856

Already a few hundred years before the birth of Christ, the Amharas had an advanced civilization, characterized among others by a well-organized state system. During the first seven centuries A.D., their state expanded in various directions, and at one time it even included part of the Arabian peninsula. Trade relations with neighboring regions were of considerable importance.

Between the 7th and 11th centuries, a new religion – Islam – spread throughout northern Africa. Moslems invaded the Western shores of the Red Sea and their settlements became so numerous that Ethiopia lost control over these areas. Eventually, the Ethiopians were forced to seek refuge in the inaccessible highlands of northern Ethiopia. Contacts with

Europe, Asia and other parts of Africa were lost and trade declined. Cut off from outside impulses, Ethiopia experienced several hundred years of stagnation and disintegration.

Between 1300 and 1500, Ethiopia enjoyed a period of rejuvenation and territorial expansion, but from 1528 until 1542 it was repeatedly attacked and plundered. Much of the country was laid to rubble and hundreds of thousands of people were murdered or carried off as slaves.

Seriously weakened by these events, the Amharas were unable to stop the influx of Gallas, who, in turn, were being pushed out of the Horn of Africa by Somali invaders. The inmigration of Gallas lasted some 300 years and today they remain the dominant ethnic group in south-central Ethiopia. The arrival of Gallas, who spoke a different language and adopted Islam, caused a considerable increase in cultural diversity in the Ethiopian empire. Also, they were reluctant to be dominated by the Christian Amharas.

Ethiopia has never really recuperated from the destructive Moslem invasions and the large-scale Galla infiltration. It remained weak and internally divided (Bartnicki & Mantel-Niećko 1978). By the middle of the 19th century, the central government lost control over much of the state territory with the result that taxes collected in the provinces rarely reached the capital. In addition to religious conflicts, there was an occasional civil war, resulting in more destruction and disintegration. Because regional sentiments often were stronger than national loyalties, there were periods in which there was hardly any communication between the different parts of the empire.

Political, social and economic conditions in ancient Ethiopia

Due to communications problems, the emperor had to entrust part of his authority to provincial governors, and in order to win their loyalty he gave them land, slaves, honorary titles and various privileges. The governors, in their turn, appointed local administrators whom they gave land as well as other sources of income.

Local and regional rulers tried to enrich themselves by exacting as much tax from the peasants as possible. At the same time, they successfully kept the influence of the central government at bay and eventually the empire fell apart into a number of more or less autonomous suzerainties (feudal principalities). Occasionally, two or more suzerains would go to war with one another, usually in an attempt to conquer territory, and thus tax-paying peasants, so as to enhance their wealth and power. The fact that the emperor was unable to intervene in many of these conflicts serves as evidence that he had no effective control over the provincial governors.

It goes without saying that some emperors were better and more power-ful rulers than were others, and that there were periods in which the country was reasonably well organized and relatively stable. But after the Moslem attacks in the 16th century, *centrifugal* forces that tore the country apart were stronger than the *centripetal* forces which tend to cement a country together into a cohesive and well-integrated unit. Between 1769 and 1856, Ethiopia was a disorganized, strife-torn and weak country.

The clergy was exceedingly large, and far more numerous than desired. Since they did not pay taxes and were not subjected to other financial or economic obligations, they formed a parasitic top layer in Ethiopian society. The Church in feudal Ethiopia was as powerful as was the church in feudal Europe. Lavish land grants by the nobility and other prominent individuals guaranteed the clergy adequate income. Prior to World War II, some 20 percent of all agricultural land was owned by the Church. Part of it was cultivated by the clergy, but most of the land was leased to sharecroppers. In general, the Church exploited the rural population as much as did the landlords, tax collectors and other administrators.

Sharecroppers and other farmers were not only exploited by the elite, but often suffered crop failure and were victimized by bandits or marauding soldiers. They were also required to provide food and shelter for traveling officials, serve in the governor's army and help feed armies that happened to pass through their area. Many tenant farmers were exposed to more uncertainty and endured more hardship than most slaves.

There were hardly any urban settlements in ancient Ethiopia and the few that did exist were small in size. Invariably, they had a religious function and served as places of residence for local and regional administrators. Industrial activities and commerce were not important since the overwhelming majority of the population was largely self-sufficient and did not have the money to purchase more than a few simple household goods. Only the elite needed, and could afford, manufactured products.

From the 10th century until the end of the 19th century, there was very little foreign trade, the major reason being that Ethiopia did not produce surpluses that could be exported. Other reasons were the country's inaccessibility and the fact that the coastal areas were controlled by hostile Islamic groups who either forced traders to pay duties or who attacked and robbed them. Considering that there had been a great deal of foreign trade in earlier centuries, it is clear that Ethiopia had experienced a long history of decline and progressive underdevelopment.

Prior to about 1900, there was also hardly any domestic trade, inhibited as it was by local wars, difficult terrain, and internal divisiveness. The Amharan rulers, furthermore, thwarted commercial activities by exploiting the merchants; there were so many tollhouses in Ethiopia that traders simply could not afford to ship goods over long distances.

Aside from these 'legal' plunderers there were numerous common thieves and robbers. For centuries, only heavily armed caravans could safely reach their destinations. During all that time, the regional governors made no effort whatsoever to build roads and bridges, the explanation being that such infrastructural improvements would have made it easier for the central government to control the more or less autonomous provinces.

At the same time, the central government had good reason to fear that a network of roads would make the country vulnerable to outside invaders. After all, Ethiopia owed its survival as an independent state to its isolation and inaccessibility. The reverse side of the coin was that the absence of a network of roads did not allow Ethiopia to develop into a strong, cohesive and well-organized political entity. And there were not enough traders to act as a state-wide integrative (centripetal) force.

In summary, Ethiopia was an agrarian society of small, self-sufficient farmers who had to produce at least as much for landlords, administrators, the military and the clergy as they did for themselves. The surpluses produced by the peasants enabled the elite to live in splendor. Because surpluses were consumed, no investments were made to create new economic activities, build roads or stimulate trade. Instead, many thousands of churches and monasteries were built – today there still are some 17,000 in Ethiopia – and much effort was wasted on internal warfare. All this, together with the strong cultural bias against manual labor, the country's isolation and its difficult topography, favored stagnation more than it did progress. For about a thousand years, Ethiopia was a static and essentially feudal society of powerful lords and downtrodden peasants which was anything but conducive to urban and industrial development.

The period 1855-1930

Around the middle of the 19th century, Ethiopia came under immense pressure. Not only did Egypt have expansionist aspirations, but Europeans were showing growing interest in Africa. As a result of these developments, Ethiopia's rulers became convinced that, in order to safeguard their country's viability as an independent state, it was necessary to modernize and develop Ethiopia into a well-organized and militarily strong country. To accomplish this, the central government first had to re-establish its control over the entire state area.

In 1855, Lij Kassa, who had risen to ruler of the Amharic district of Kuara, defeated his rivals and had himself crowned as emperor Theodore III. Magdala became the new capital. Theodore's plans to abolish slave trade and tollhouses, establish relations with Europe, and build a standing army were opposed and frustrated by the provincial rulers and the clergy. Although the emperor failed and in 1868 took his own life, his ideas and efforts were successful in the sense that they 'woke up' Ethiopia. His successor, emperor John IV, adopted many of his ideas, realizing that a policy of modernization was the only way Ethiopia could avoid being overrun by foreign powers and be reduced to colonial status.

The latter half of the 19th century was marked by an extension of European political and commercial interests into strategically located Ethiopia, particularly after the opening of the Suez Canal in 1869, which made the Red Sea into an important connection between Europe and southern Asia. John's most immediate concern was Egypt's intention to

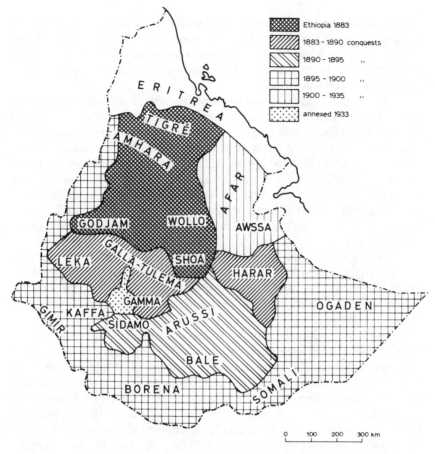

Fig. 26. Ethiopia's territorial expansion since 1833 (Eritrea became an autonomous province in 1952, but lost its autonomy in 1962).
Source: A. Bartnicki & J. Mantel-Niećko, 1978.

expand to the sources of the Nile and conquer Ethiopia. After some initial setbacks, his armies won decisive victories over the Egyptians in 1875 and 1876. Shortly thereafter, Ethiopia was threatened by Italy, which occupied the city of Massawa in 1884 and claimed Eritrea as its colony. Again John's armies rose to the occasion and virtually annihilated the Italians. The next threat came from fanatic Mahdists (in Sudan), whose plundering troops attacked Ethiopia from the west. Once more Ethiopia successfully drove off the invaders (1888-1889), although John IV lost his life in one of the battles.

While John was preoccupied fighting the Mahdists, his rival Menelik, ruler of Shoa, saw a golden opportunity to enlarge his power. Instead of joining the war against the Mahdist marauders, Menelik pursued his own ambitions. After having conquered extensive areas south of Shoa, he negotiated in 1887 a secret deal with Italy. The Italians promised him money and arms while recognizing him as the 'King of Kings' if he would help them fight John, recognize their claim to Eritrea, and approve their plans to conquer Somaliland.

As it turned out, Menelik did not need the agreement with Italy in order to become the next emperor. Since John had been killed in the war against the Mahdists, he succeeded him in 1889 as Menelik II without having had to fight his predecessor. Almost immediately thereafter he signed a treaty with Italy. According to the Italian version of the treaty, Ethiopia was to be an Italian protectorate, but the Amharic interpretation was different on that point. When Menelik abrogated the treaty, Italian protests led to war with Ethiopia, in which the Italians were soundly defeated (1896). Although Italy could keep Eritrea, it had to recognize Ethiopia's independence.

As mentioned earlier, prior to becoming emperor Menelik had conquered large areas just south of the Ethiopian heartland. After 1890, his armies brought several other territories under control of the state of Ethiopia (see Fig. 26) and by 1900 its boundaries were essentially the same as they are today.

Through the conquests Menelik wanted to make sure that the outlying areas would not fall into European hands. His expansionism also served economic purposes. In order to be able to maintain standing armies and modernize his country, Menelik needed control over more human and natural resources than were available in the old Ethiopian heartland. To the southwest there were rich agricultural regions and the Somalis and Gallas possessed millions of cattle. More importantly, however, Menelik could use an increase in the number of taxpayers. Finally, the conquests served Menelik's own purposes; they enabled him to make Shoa province, which had always occupied a peripheral location within the old Ethiopian empire, the geographical center of the state.

Whereas the Shoa elite supported Menelik's expansionist adventures, elsewhere in the country there was considerable resistance. Dissatisfaction in the provinces mounted due to brutal exploitation by local and regional rulers, all of whom had been appointed or approved by Menelik. Since governors and other officials did not know for how long they would stay in office, they enriched themselves in the quickest possible way. Sometimes, entire villages were plundered and their inhabitants sold as slaves. Rural people everywhere were subjected to compulsory labor, either as agricultural workers or as personal servants. The newly conquered areas were treated particularly harshly. Much land was taken away from the local farmers and sold to settlers from the north or to members of the upper class. Land that could not be sold became state property.

The consequence of this flagrant mismanagement and exploitation was widespread chaos, insecurity, destruction and declining productivity.

Understandably, before long the administration had become very unpopular. To make matters worse, the territorial conquests had transformed Ethiopia into a multinational state with distinct regional differences in culture and ethnic loyalty. Moreover, in this 'house divided' the Christian Amharas and Tigreans were no longer a numerically dominant group.

Despite the fact that the emperor himself made serious attempts to develop Ethiopia – during his reign foreign trade was stimulated, several telegraph connections were constructed, the tax system was modernized, a modern bank was established, the first printing establishment came into being, the first Western-type school was built, and the first modern hospital was founded – Menelik was unable to realize most of his plans. Apart from his unpopularity among the common people, his sympathy for Islam was not tolerated by the Christian elite. After several attempts to dethrone him, he decided to step down. His successor, emperor Haile Selassie, avoided some of the mistakes Menelik had made and was therefore more successful in his efforts to modernize Ethiopia.

The Haile Selassie era (1930-1974)

The new emperor continued Menelik's policy of modernization, but was careful not to move too fast lest he might upset the secular and religious elite. He also did not want to transform Ethiopia into a mirror image of a Western society. Instead, he did his best to preserve typically Ethiopian values and pursue a policy of gradual development.

One of his first concerns was to integrate the various parts of his empire into a more cohesive and better-organized state. To accomplish this, he fostered centralization at the expense of regionalism. More than ever before, the central government became represented in the provinces by carefully selected civil servants whose salaries were paid by Addis Ababa, which had been reinstated as the national capital. The collection of taxes was also done by people who received their income directly from the central government.

There were a great many other changes, e.g., the drafting of a constitution (1931), campaigns against slavery and slave trade (in 1925, one out of every four people was a slave), and attempts to lower the illiteracy rate, improve the judicial system, reduce the power of the Church, and instill feelings of nationalism in the various ethnic groups. In order to strengthen the economy, the physical infrastructure was improved, a few modern factories were built, and commercial agriculture was stimulated.

In all these efforts to create a politically and economically viable state and to 'catch up with the 20th century,' Haile Selassie pursued a policy of self-reliant development, using foreign advisors as sparingly as possible.

Skeptics have pointed out that Haile Selassie's policy of modernization was aimed more at strengthening the power of the central government (and thus his own power) than at improving the quality of life for the masses. It is true that, by Western standards at least, not much was accomplished. For example, the constitution was little more than a façade because all power remained vested in the autocratic ruler. Democratic institutions were altogether absent and the common people had virtually no rights. The majority of the Ethiopians stayed as impoverished as before, and the bulk of the agricultural land remained in the hands of large landowners. Intentions to implement land reforms were discussed but not worked out, let alone carried out. Modernization of the agricultural sector frequently had detrimental consequences for the small tenants and landless laborers as many peasants were robbed of their means of subsistence and the rural masses became increasingly marginalized.

Some 4 million ha (10 million acres) of crown land were granted or sold to a relatively small number of military officers, veterans, loyal officials and others who had contributed to Haile Selassie's efforts to transform Ethiopia into a highly centralized (unitary) state. By contrast, the landless and unemployed received less than 1 million ha. Whereas the latter were in desperate need of land, many of the former made no use of it and simply hung on to it for speculative purposes. Nomads, whose traditional grazing areas had been preempted by the administration and/or developed into cropland, were seldom given assistance in finding new pasture lands.

In the five-year plans for the period 1958-1973, considerable emphasis was placed on the development of infrastructural works, manufacturing and energy production. Agriculture was more or less neglected, especially the 'peasant sector.' The few attempts to modernize agriculture were focused almost exclusively on the large-scale production of commercial crops. Since the social infrastructure was largely ignored, rural Ethiopia kept many of its traditional, feudal characteristics, including the centuries' old rich-poor disparities.

Haile Selassie was nonetheless quite highly respected outside Ethiopia, particularly in Africa. He played a role in the founding of the Organization of African Unity (OAU) and mediated several international (African) conflicts. The fact that Addis Ababa was chosen as the site for the headquarters of the OAU and the Economic Commission for Africa was in no small measure due to the prestige he enjoyed outside his own country.

Ethiopia since the 1974 revolution

Following a few years of drought and starvation in parts of Ethiopia, a military mutiny in February 1974 forced the cabinet's resignation. A general strike in March and widespread military and civil unrest eventually led to military rule. Selassie's supporters were arrested and the emperor himself was stripped off his power. The royal family was publicly denounced for having enriched themselves at the people's expense and for having kept the peasant masses in feudal bondage. The military rulers also accused the Selassie administration of having covered up the fact that in 1973 over 100,000 persons had starved to death in the drought-stricken areas. A television showing in September of the famine disaster further turned the public against Haile Selassie and spurred demands for his punishment. The following day the 82-year-old emperor was deposed, ending 50 years of absolute rule.

In 1975, Ethiopia's new governing socialist military council, the *Dergue,* faced drought and virtual civil war. Half its forces were fighting the separatist Eritrean Liberation Front (ELF), which stepped up its 13-year-old struggle for an independent Eritrea. Around Addis Ababa the government was challenged by a counterrevolutionary group which wanted to topple the Dergue because of its harsh and arbitrary methods of maintaining discipline.

In January 1975, the Dergue nationalized all banks, key financial institutions and insurance companies. A month later, 78 manufacturing and trading businesses were nationalized and the government acquired a majority shareholding in 29 other enterprises. The result was a marked decline in economic activity.

In March, the junta issued a Land Reform Proclamation, which brought all rural land under government control. The main purpose of the proclamation was to channel peasant farmers into collective farms that were to be managed by locally formed Peasant Associations. The Act thus brought to an end the essentially feudal system of land tenure; private ownership of land was prohibited. In northern Ethiopia, where communal forms of land tenure had been in existence for centuries, there was widespread opposition to the Land Reform Proclamation.

Five months later all urban land was nationalized. In Addis Ababa, government moves to control the profits of middlemen in business nearly wiped out the local trade in foodstuffs, so that by the end of the year Addis Ababa was a starving capital. According to relief workers, the death toll was about 200 a day. Other cities, too, suffered serious food shortages.

By early 1977, Ethiopia's future had become completely unpredictable. What had begun as a well-intentioned effort to mobilize the poverty-stricken people into a campaign for national unity and economic salvation had instead become a deadly struggle between a new ruling group of revolutionaries – as authoritarian as any imperial regime – and a diverse agglomeration of disaffected elements: urban revolutionaries, determined secessionists, peasant armies, ethnocentric and regional nationalists, middle-class elites, and remnants of feudal interest groups (Legum 1977, p. B 178). Some were embittered by the Dergue's failure to sustain the promises of the revolution, others by its nationalization program; but most by the policies which resulted in mass killings, arrests without trials, urban food shortages and administrative chaos. Compulsory economic reforms created unrest, undermined business confidence and discouraged foreign investment.

Gripped with wars (Eritrea and Ogaden) and several regional rebellions, e.g., a nine-year-old armed rebellion in Tigre (just south of Eritrea), the transportation system has remained in a state of disarray during much of the

295

1970s and early 1980s. For years, the country has been on the verge of economic collapse. Due to a host of factors – war destruction, ruthless implementation of land reforms, drought, locusts, elimination of 'profiteering' merchants, removal of some 250,000 men from productive life by military conscription, and rapid population growth – Ethiopia has been haunted by one famine after another. It seems ironic that in a country in which 80 percent of the people are engaged in agriculture, where the agricultural sector contributes approximately half the GDP, where agricultural products account for about 90 percent of the export earnings, and where a large share of all industry is devoted to food processing, most people are going hungry much of the time. A few years ago, 4.2 million persons (or 15 percent of all Ethiopians) received emergency food aid. Because of a shortage of roads and bridges, the poor quality of the few roads that do exist, and widespread insecurity due to armed struggles in large parts of Ethiopia, many food shipments cannot reach their destinations or arrive too late. Such circumstances go a long way to explain why the number of Ethiopians facing starvation has not declined in recent years. In 1984, their number was estimated at about $6\frac{1}{2}$ million. Instead of doing everything it could to help the hungry people, the government spent over $100 million to celebrate the tenth anniversary of the revolution.

Conclusion

Ethiopia's underdevelopment has not been caused by a long history of colonial exploitation, nor by presently existing neo-colonial relations with capitalist core countries. Neither capitalism nor economic imperialism can explain the symptoms of the country's underdevelopment: widespread poverty, hunger, unemployment, high illiteracy rate, high infant mortality rate, low productivity, lack of industrialization, and a very small and one-sided foreign trade.

The low quality of life in present-day Ethiopia is much more a consequence of unfavorable *internal* conditions than it is of harmful *exterior* influences and foreign investments. Throughout the country's long history, a small minority of influential persons enriched themselves by exploiting the rural masses, while doing very little to improve the peasants' living conditions or enabling them to raise their productivity. To this day, Ethiopia's new socialist regime does not appear to have reaped more success with its development strategy than have its predecessors with theirs. Although the problem of socioeconomic inequality may have been alleviated somewhat, poverty and misery are as rampant as ever. Burdened with a set of unfavorable physical and human circumstances – difficult terrain, recurring droughts, semi-landlocked location, severe soil erosion, cultural diversity, absence of a democratic tradition, internal strife, secessionist Eritrea, hostile relations with Somalia, and rapid population growth – Ethiopia's prospects for reducing human suffering do not seem very promising. If the government continues to spend a large proportion of its GNP on the purchase of military hardware, rather than on efforts to improve the rural infrastructure and the production of food crops, it is virtually certain that future generations will be no better off than were the many generations that preceded them.

Selected readings

Bartnicki, A. & J. Mantel-Niećko (1978), *Geschichte Äthiopiens – von den Anfängen bis zur Gegenwart.* Berlin: Akademie Verlag.
Bondestam, L. (1974), Underdevelopment and Economic Growth in Ethiopia. *Kroniek van Afrika* 1, pp. 20-36.
Brietzke, P. (1976), Land Reform in Revolutionary Ethiopia. *Journal of Modern African Studies* 14, pp. 637-660.
Brummelkamp, J. (1956a), *Ethiopië's ontwikkeling in de twintigste eeuw van middeleeuwse tot moderne staat.* Meppel: J.A. Boom en Zn.
Brummelkamp, J. (1956b), *Ethiopië, eiland in een continent.* Meppel: J.A. Boom en Zn.
Cohen, J.M. & D. Weintraub (1975), *Land and Peasants in Imperial Ethiopia – The Social Background to a Revolution.* Assen: Van Gorcum.
Cohen, J.M. & P.H. Koehn (1978), *Rural and Urban Land Reform in Ethiopia.* Land Tenure Center Reprint 135. Madison, Wis.: Land Tenure Center.
Custers, P. (1977), *Ethiopië – internationaal slagveld.* Rotterdam: Ordeman.
Derix, J. & R. de Swart (1972), *De laatste kinderen van Job – Tijdingen uit het dorp Ado in Zuid-Ethiopië.* Amsterdam: Stichting Ontwikkelingshulp vanuit Geuzenveld-Amsterdam & Nederlandse congregatie der paters Lazaristen.
Doresse, J. (1970), *Histoire de l'Ethiopie.* Que Sais-Je? no. 1393. Paris: Presses Universitaires de France.
Ellis, G. (1976), The Feudal Paradigm as a Hindrance to Understanding Ethiopia. *Journal of Modern African Studies* 14, pp. 275-295.
Engelhard, K. (1970), Addis Abeba – Probleme seiner Entwicklung, *Erdkunde* 24, pp. 207-219.
Gilkes, P. (1975), *The Dying Lion – Feudalism and Modernization in Ethiopia.* London: Friedmann.
Gourou, P. (1966), L'Ethiopie. *Les Cahiers d'Outre Mer* 19 (75), pp. 209-234.
Koninklijk Instituut voor de Tropen (1971), *Ethiopië.* Landendocumentatie nr. 140. Amsterdam: KIT.
Kurian, G.T. (1979) *Encyclopedia of the Third World.* London: Mansell.
Legum, C., ed. (annual), *Africa Contemporary Record – Annual Survey and Documents.* London: Rex Collings (until 1977); London and New York: Africana Publishing Company (since 1977).
Lentjes, W.A.J. (1980), Milieuproblemen in berggebieden van de Derde Wereld. *In:* J.M.G. Kleinpenning, ed., *Milieuproblemen in de Derde Wereld – Een sociaal-geografische inleiding,* pp. 121-160. Assen: Van Gorcum.
Markakis, J. (1974), *Ethiopia; Anatomy of a Traditional Polity.* Oxford: Clarendon Press.
Prost-Tournier, J.M. (1974), Premières données sur la géographie urbaine de l'Ethiopie. *Revue de Géographie de Lyon* 49, pp. 5-36.
Ullendorf, E. (1973), *The Ethiopians – An Introduction to Country and People.* London: Oxford University Press.
World Bank (annual), *World Development Report.* Washington: World Bank.

Chapter 18   India

The Republic of India occupies the major part of the Indian subcontinent, a large land mass separated from Asia proper by the Himalaya Mountains. India can be divided into five broad physical regions: the Himalayan borderlands, the alluvial plains of the Ganges and Brahmaputra rivers, the Thar desert, the Deccan tableland, and the peninsular coastal regions. The rich alluvial plains in the north, reaching from the Arabian Sea in the west to the Bay of Bengal in the east, form the heartland of India. Here we find more productive irrigated land, more villages, and more industry than anywhere else in the country. Half of India's large cities are on these plains, including Calcutta, Kanpur and Delhi (with the federal capital city of New Delhi), each of which has well over 1 million inhabitants. Other large cities are Bombay (on the west coast), Hyderabad and Bangalore (on the Deccan plateau), and Madras (on the east coast).

In order to keep the length of this case study within bounds, we will limit our explanation of the origin of India's underdevelopment to its major causes. As far as the past is concerned, attention is focused mainly on the period of the Mogul Empire (1526-1857). For the period since independence (1947), only a few selected topics are discussed.*

Climate

Most of India has three major seasons: a long dry season, dominated by the northeast monsoon (October-March), an inter-monsoonal period (March-June), and a rainy season, dominated by the southwest monsoon (June-September). A second inter-monsoonal period is of short duration (September-October).

From October until March, dry and cool air flows from central Asia in southwesterly direction over the Indian subcontinent. Dry, sunny weather prevails except in the coastal plains on the east side of the peninsula where the edge of the Deccan plateau, known as the Eastern Ghats, forces the relatively moist northeast monsoon to rise, causing orographic precipitation. Although occasional night frosts occur in the north, daily maximum temperatures in Delhi during the month of January average about 17° C (63° F). Further south, temperatures are higher and frost is unknown.

Between March and June, temperatures gradually rise, eventually reaching diurnal maxima of 40° C (104° F) and even 50° C (122° F) in the northern plains. Due to the lack of rainfall, the atmosphere tends to be rather dusty. Owing to its higher elevation, the Deccan plateau is somewhat cooler, yet daily maxima average about 35° C (95° F).

---

* A list of selected readings is included at the end of the chapter.

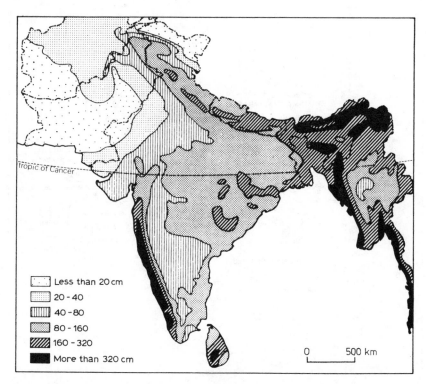

Less than 20 cm
20 - 40
40 - 80
80 - 160
160 - 320
More than 320 cm

Tropic of Cancer

0   500 km

Fig. 27. Distribution of precipitation in the Indian subcontinent. *Source:* B.J.S. Hoetjes *et al.*, 1980.

The southwest monsoon dominates the weather between June and September. This is the rainy season for most of India. The west coast (especially the Western Ghats) and northeast India, including the Bay of Bengal region, receive large amounts of precipitation during these months (Fig. 27). By contrast, the interior portions of the Deccan plateau are considerably drier, making irrigation necessary. Practically no precipitation falls in the Thar desert – the air which arrives here comes from Iran and the Arabian Peninsula and is, therefore, dry and hot. In the Gangetic plain, the amount of rainfall increases from west to east, giving the eastern portion a more productive climate. Without irrigation, the western half of the northern plains would have limited agricultural importance.

Even though it is predictable that in a given year certain parts of India will receive more precipitation than others, large annual fluctuations make it impossible to predict *how much* rain will fall in each area. Neither can one be sure *when* the so-called 'wet monsoon' will set in – in some years it begins much later than in others. Due to the variability in precipitation, there are good and bad years. A bad year is characterized by one or more of the following: (1) the wet monsoon starts later than usual, (2) produces too

299

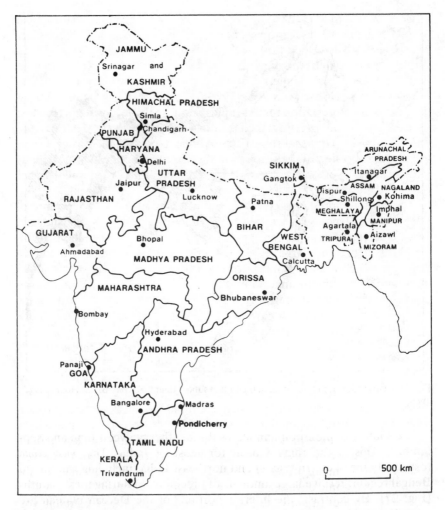

Fig. 28. India's states and their capitals.

much rain, (3) ends too soon, and/or (4) is interrupted by long dry spells in July or August. Kerala state in southwest India (Fig. 28) has the most reliable climate and always receives sufficient precipitation. This fact explains why Kerala is the most densely populated area of the entire peninsula. The north and northwest have much less reliable climates. Generally speaking, the smaller the total amount of annual precipitation, the greater the year to year variability.

The hot to very hot season (March-June) not only is a problem for agriculture, but also has a negative effect on human activity. The absence of a cold winter means that illnesses are difficult to overcome – bacteria and insects are not periodically wiped out.

Most of India has eight to nine months of dry weather, so that in areas where little or no irrigation is practiced, agricultural possibilities are seriously limited. In addition, crop failures are common in many areas, either because it rains too much or too little. Heavy downpours sometimes last for days, causing immense floods that destroy crops and livestock as well as homes, roads, railroads, bridges and other infrastructural works. Widespread deforestation fosters rapid runoff, so that even after a few days of rain, rivers may overflow their banks. Landslides, too, are not uncommon. If we add to this that some parts of India, especially the Bay of Bengal region, are occasionally battered by devastating typhoons which are usually accompanied by extensive flooding, it is clear that India gets more than her share of catastrophes.

The highly unpredictable arrival, duration, intensity, and departure of the southwest monsoon may well be India's greatest natural handicap, causing every year again intense anxiety for hundreds of millions of individuals. The rather large chance that crop failure will strike is an important reason why many small farmers are reluctant to make particular productivity-enhancing investments. Activities which are certain to increase output and/or decrease the risk of crop failure, e.g., the installation and maintenance of irrigation works, present no problem, but other inputs, including the manuring of unirrigated land, are a different matter altogether. Poor as they are, farmers cannot be blamed for being extremely cautious.

Closely associated with the above is that crop failures as well as low yields, resulting from lack of manuring and other insufficient investments, frequently lead to more or less permanent indebtedness. A large proportion of India's rural population is sooner or later forced to call upon a local moneylender or loanshark for some ready cash. Finally, the low agricultural productivity means that the agricultural sector contributes relatively little in the form of production for export and/or tax revenues to the country's economic development.

India's climates (mainly Aw, BSh and Am) generally have an unfavorable impact on the soils. In the drier regions, soils tend to have a high salt content. Elsewhere, excessive rainfall (in combination with high temperatures) is responsible for the occurrence of relatively infertile, leached soils.

Of course, the physical environment also has its advantages: (1) the warm climates make it possible to grow two or three crops a year, (2) natural conditions in much of northern India are excellent for irrigation, (3) amounts and timing of rainfall are highly reliable in some areas, (4) the north has rich alluvial soils and parts of the Deccan plateau have fertile volcanic soils, (5) only one-third of India has slopes too steep for crop farming, and (6) the country is fairly well endowed with industrial raw materials, especially iron ore and coal.

The limitations and problems of the physical environment are often underestimated, in particular by human geographers who are afraid to be accused of *environmental determinism*. They fail to realize, so it seems, that the limited possibilities of the natural environment have considerable influence in countries where the majority of the people are dependent for their livelihood directly on that same environment, while not possessing the knowledge and means to 'correct' or 'control' it. There can be little doubt that the physical environment plays a more dominant role in poor, technologically backward and overwhelmingly agricultural countries than in rich and industrially developed countries where few people are employed in agriculture. Certainly, it is a mistake to conclude that because standards of living in developed countries are relatively unaffected by environmental conditions, the same holds true for underdeveloped countries.

To be sure, we do not wish to suggest that a high level of material well-being or industrial development is unattainable in a tropical environment. Neither do we believe that the explanation for India's underdevelopment must be sought primarily or exclusively in her relatively unfavorable natural environment. We merely wish to stress that it would be unwise to ignore the limitations of a country's physical environment when trying to account for its underdevelopment.

Political organization and administration prior to British domination

If we accept the proposition that all presently existing conditions are related to the past, that they are at least in part products of past events, it follows that India's current underdevelopment is rooted in circumstances that prevailed in years gone by. The purpose of this and the following sections is to attempt to discover whether the problems of 20th century India can be traced back to developmental constraints which existed prior to the moment she became effectively controlled by the British during the second half of the 19th century.

Throughout history, India has a been a country of tillers living in thousands of villages. At the time of the Mogul Empire (early 16th century until mid-19th century), they made up about 85 percent of the population, while in earlier centuries their percentage must have been even higher. Notwithstanding fairly elaborate irrigation systems, agriculture was quite primitive. The relatively low density of population made it possible to farm only the better soils, yet productivity was mediocre or low, depending in part on the highly variable weather.

The farmers did not own the land they cultivated; all land belonged to the state. The ruling nobility, which personified the state, could determine how the land was to be used. Water courses, irrigation systems, mines and woodlands also were state property. Since the state, or rather the ruling elite, controlled the principal production factors – land and water – it had almost unlimited power. This power was used to force the agricultural producers to surrender part of their crop, pay taxes, and provide free labor power for the construction of public works. The appropriation of agricultural surpluses, etc. was justified on the basis that the state protected the

Fig. 29. The Mogul Empire; approximate maximum extent in the 17th century. *Source:* B.J.S. Hoetjes *et al.*, 1980.

people in the event of external aggression and looked after infrastructural facilities, such as irrigation works.

Administrative activities included collecting taxes, recruiting young men for the armies, training the military, administering justice, maintaining law and order, and taking care of roads, irrigation systems, etc. The majority of governors, tax collectors and other civil servants received a salary from the state. Several rulers, among them Mogul emperor Akbar (1556-1605), tried to put all administrators on the state's payroll, thus bringing them under direct control of the central government. The size of the empire, however, made this far from easy (Fig. 29). Numerous administrators, especially in the peripheral areas, did not receive a salary but were given instead control over a large territory, or *jagir,* which was farmed by local farmers. The *jagirdars* did not become the owners of this land – it remained the property of the state – which meant that their children or other relatives could not

303

inherit it. Also, the emperor could at any time abrogate an official's supervision of the land.

The *jagirdars* were not entitled to all the revenues they received; at regular intervals they had to make predetermined payments in cash or kind to the state treasurer. Since they were allowed to keep all earnings that exceeded these payments, they were inclined to exact high rents from their tenants.

This administrative system had other drawbacks. It was to the advantage of the *jagirdar* that the central authority did not have much influence in his area, so that he could renege on his obligation to hand over part of his earnings to the state treasury. Lack of effective control by the central government also gave him an opportunity to conquer and/or plunder neighboring areas and force the farming population there to pay tribute to him. Throughout India's history, regional administrators have made efforts to weaken the power of the the state and to set themselves up as independent regional rulers. Sometimes they used the regional armies of the state, which were placed under their command, to their own advantage. On a number of occasions, this rebelliousness even took the form of an attempt to seize control of the central government. Thus, political unrest and secessionist movements have been fairly common in precolonial India.

In the past, it frequently happened that large empires broke up into smaller principalities, which in turn disappeared to make room for the next large empire. Strong dynasties controlled immense territories, built roads and irrigation sytstems, had large armies, and maintained law and order. While they were in power, arts and sciences generally flourished. Sooner or later, however, such periods of internal stability and progress were followed by periods of turmoil, decline, lawlessness, growing regional autonomy, and excessive exploitation of the farming population. Internal disorder was sometimes the result of external aggression, while at other times the causal relationship was reversed, that is, internal weakness 'invited' outside aggressors to conquer or plunder large parts of the subcontinent. Northern India has been invaded several times, usually resulting in widespread destruction and instability. Add to this that many dynasties suffered from personal power struggles, jealousies, secret plots, murders and palace revolutions, and that similar conflicts also occurred at the regional level (among relatives of powerful *jagirdars*), and it becomes clear that for extended periods of time India was without the political stability and administrative efficiency that form the preconditions for cultural and economic development. Every so often the country was racked by anarchy, destruction, decline and famine.

The rural population at the time of the Mogul Empire

The self-sufficient farmers were brutally exploited by tax collectors *(zamindars)* and *jagirdars*. Since it was customary that *jagirs* were awarded for limited periods, the *jagirdars* tried to make the best of their privileged

38. Drying cow dung in India. Cow dung is a major source of fuel, both in the villages and the cities. (VDO)

position and instructed the *zamindars* to collect as much tax as possible, thus enriching themselves while they could.

The consequence was that farmers generally were left with little more than they needed for their survival. They were neither willing nor able to raise the productivity of the land they cultivated. According to Habib (1969), indebtedness among the rural population was very common, so that they were also exploited by loansharks. Those who were unable to pay off their debts ran the risk of being enslaved – a phenomenon that still occurs today in India.

Conditions were particularly unfavorable in the Moslem-dominated areas of northern India following Moslem invasions in the 11th century and later. Moslem rulers generally looked down on sedentary farmers and appropriated all agricultural surplus – the peasants were allowed to keep no more than what they needed for their 'reproduction' (a Marxist term, meaning bare subsistence). Even this, their mere survival, was uncertain because they had virtually no food supplies on which they could fall back in the event of crop failure. Periodic famines, therefore, afflicted large areas.

In addition to the lack of motivation among agricultural producers to raise productivity and improve methods of farming, most rulers did little to increase agricultural output or improve rural standards of living. Even if they did do so, e.g., by building new irrigation systems and other infrastructural works, it was for the purpose of enhancing their own influence and assuring themselves of more income. For many centuries, production per acre or per farmer showed no upward trend. Clearly, the Indian farmer was caught in a vicious circle of low productivity, poverty and lack of motivation to raise output.

Although much has been written about India's ancient civilization, few authors have emphasized that all the splendor and magnificent art work in and around the opulent palaces and lavish mausoleums could be afforded only by a tiny fraction of the population. While the wealthy elite satisfied its extravagant desires, millions of small farmers were squeezed dry by ruthless tax collectors. Without the surpluses extorted from the toiling tillers of the land, Shah Jahan (1627-1658) would not have been able to build the exquisitely beautiful Taj Mahal mausoleum in memory of his wife. Not only the famed peacock throne, covered with millions of dollars worth of gems and jewels, but also several sumptuous palaces were built in his honor. These palaces surpassed the most elegant and luxurious palaces ever built in Europe. Lamb (1966, p. 47) writes: "The interiors were hung with silks from China and carpeted with rugs from Persia. Niches in the walls contained gold and silver vases [with] flowers in the daytime and white wax candles at night. Various methods of cooling the palaces in the hot summers were evolved – by the evaporation of water from many fountains and by the use of moistened reed mats kept in motion by servants. In winter, ice was brought from the Himalayas and stored deep underground for use during the summer. In his audience hall, the Emperor sat upon his Peacock Throne made of costly jewels."

The same author has estimated that Shah Jahan's possessions must have been worth about $3.5 billion. All this wealth had been appropriated in the form of tax payments from his subjects, mostly small, poverty-stricken farmers. Even when crop failure and famine struck, famers were compelled to pay their taxes.

In summary, the surpluses which during the Mogul Empire were wrung from the rural population were not used to stimulate economic development, raise agricultural productivity or improve the material well-being of the masses. Most of it – some 70 percent – was spent on the many armies needed to maintain law and order; this law and order, in turn, made it possible for the elite to extract surpluses from the farmers. Approximately 10 percent of all tax revenues was used to finance the empire's administrative system and to support professional artists and scientists. Finally, the remainig 20 percent was consumed by the elite, who spent it on palaces, temples, mausoleums, large numbers of servants, herds of elephants and riding horses, and huge collections of gold, silver, emeralds and other valuables. For extended periods, virtually no productive investment took place in India.

Non-agricultural activities and urban centers during the Mogul Empire

The first Indian cities date back more than 2000 years. During the 17th century, there were several which were as large as the biggest cities in Europe. Most were administrative-military centers from which the surrounding rural areas were controlled. They functioned as the major points of the empire-wide tax collection system, and it was here that most of the appropriated wealth was consumed. A constant flow of 'capital' from the rural areas to the cities meant that the latter were parasitic in nature.

Industrial activities were concentrated in the cities, but few manufactured products were marketed in the rural villages. The villages were self-sufficient communities which did not maintain trade relations with other areas or nearby urban centers. For the most part, the rural areas remained outside the money economy – only in periods when farmers had to pay their taxes in cash (rather than in kind) did they sell part of their crop. Tools, implements, utensils, footwear, etc. were made locally, either at home or by artisans who traditionally belonged to a specialized caste. Traveling merchants and peddlers were virtually unknown in the rural areas, which is not surprising because the farmers usually had no money to spend. Within the villages there was a form of barter trade, with the artisans receiving part of the crop in exchange for the consumer goods they made.

Urban craftsmen produced luxury goods for the urban elite as well as arms and other equipment for the military. Industrial production also took place in factories, of which many employed large numbers of workers. The factories were the private property of rulers and high government officials, and they produced exclusively luxury goods, either for their owners or for sale to other wealthy individuals. A small proportion of the industrial output was sold in neighboring countries.

Despite the outrageously large consumption of manufactured goods by the elite and their armies, India's secondary sector was quite small. Even the well-known and thriving cotton industry was fairly limited in size because only the affluent members of society wore cotton clothes. Large-scale specialized production of manufactured goods for sale was unknown, the reason being that the large majority of the population was unable to purchase such products. There was, however, a rather significant export of cotton textiles, especially to China and Persia. Production was labor-intensive and wages were low. Due to the large supply of cheap labor, there was no need to develop technically advanced methods of production.

The predominant form of domestic trade – if we can call it that – was the distribution of agricultural surpluses among the non-agricultural population. Much of this was long-distance trade, requiring an immense network of roads, centered on the northern city of Agra, which at the time of the Mogul Empire had 500,000 inhabitants. There were some 1700 rest stops along the roads, with separate lodging accomodations for Moslems and Hindus.

There were times when merchants could do very well for themselves and in the 17th century the more successful traders amassed enormous amounts of commercial capital. It is important to point out that this capital remained commercial capital – it was not invested in non-commercial ventures, such as industrial enterprises. Neither did the merchants invest in the agricultural sector. Thus, even though there were periods in which internal trade thrived, agriculture and manufacturing underwent no change and continued to be characterized by low (pre-industrial) levels of productivity.

Spatial and social disparities at the time of the Moguls

Sharp contrasts existed between rural and urban areas. The exploited village communities with their high degree of self-sufficiency supported the predominantly parasitic cities. While a market economy functioned in the urban centers, the villagers lived in a closed economy. The concentration of wealth in the cities meant that there were striking urban-rural contrasts in culture and life style.

Even if we disregard the caste system, India was a highly stratified society. The base of the social pyramid consisted of the millions of impoverished peasants who did not have the means, knowledge and motivation to promote agricultural development. Social mobility was hardly possible and most villagers had adopted a fatalistic outlook on life, resigned as they were to the fact that they were totally powerless and unable to escape from the clutches of poverty and exploitation. Only in time of abnormally ruthless exploitation and/or widespread famine have farming communities actively rebelled against the system.

The top of the social pyramid consisted of a very small group of people with economic, political and military power. This elite was concentrated in the cities. A rural elite, as existed in feudal Europe, was unknown. The emperor and his immediate family formed the pinnacle of the hierarchy. Below him were the regional governors. Next came a layer of other high officials – the *mansabdars*. In 1647, this group counted no more than 8000 persons, some of whom were relatives of the influential regional administrators. Others were foreigners, especially Turks and Persians. Below the *mansabdars* were the many tax collectors or *zamindars*.

A large middle class did not exist, the main reason being that trade and manufacturing were relatively unimportant activities. Small industrial producers in the cities were exploited about as much as were the peasants. Required to pay a great deal of tax, most of them were also poverty-stricken. Urban centers owed their existence less to *basic* economic activities – i.e., activities which produce for export or for sale in surrounding rural areas and thus bring money into the urban community – than to the one-way flow of capital that originated in the rural areas. It is not surprising, therefore, that the urban middle class was dominated by administrators, tax collectors, soldiers and religious leaders.

Asiatic mode of production, feudalism and rent capitalism

The social order described above was based on a system of economic organization which is often referred to as the *Asiatic mode of production*, a term first used by Marx. An impression of what he meant by it can be gleaned from the box on page 217.

The Asiatic mode of production was not only typical of India, but also existed in other advanced parts of Asia, e.g., China and the Middle East. Its basic characteristics were an overwhelmingly agrarian society with largely self-sufficient rural (village) communities which did not own the physical resources (land and water) they utilized and which surrendered their agricultural products and labor power to higher authorities (rulers). The latter represented the state, which was the ultimate owner of all agricultural land and irrigation systems. The appropriation of agricultural surpluses enabled a small ruling elite to enrich itself and maintain the state as a functioning system. Another essential characteristic was the limited division of labor. Because of the largely self-sufficient rural majority, there was relatively little trade and not much industry in the cities.

One important difference between the Asiatic mode of production and other modes of production is that the producers are more or less free to determine what they produce and what production methods they use. This sets them apart from farmers and other producers in a centrally planned economy as well as from wage laborers in the capitalist mode of production.

The Asiatic mode of production has often been described as a form of *feudalism*. Authors who have labeled it such regard feudalism essentially as an overwhelmingly agrarian society dominated by a non-productive ruling class which, through control (ownership) of the agricultural land, appropriates surplus labor at the expense of rural producers. Appropriation of this surplus enables the ruling elite to maintain, or even expand, its political and economic power.

Others disagree, claiming that the term 'feudalism' should be reserved to describe the system of political and social organization that prevailed in medieval Europe. They point out that non-Western (especially Oriental) societies differed markedly from European societies. Whereas in medieval Europe nobility was inhereted, such was not the case in most non-Western societies. Bobek (e.g., 1974) has emphasized that the aristocracy in medieval Europe, although it did possess large landholdings, generally did not exploit the farming population more than it deemed necessary in order to maintain its admittedly high standard of living. In India, by contrast, anyone could join the ruling elite. Furthermore, India's leaders were much more bent on accumulating enormous wealth and were thus guilty of more excessive exploitation of the class of producers than were their European counterparts. In contrast to medieval Europe, where a personal relationship often existed between lord and peasant, in India no direct relationship existed between the ruler and the village community – the peasants usually only knew the tax collector.

309

In view of these differences, Bobek prefers to talk about *rent capitalism*. He believes that this term is more appropriate for Asia and the Middle East on account of the fact that the ruling class made accumulation of wealth (or capital) its ultimate goal. This explains the capitalism part of his term. He calls it *rent* capitalism because it differs from modern capitalism in that hardly any of the wealth was accumulated for the purpose of raising economic productivity.

The stability of the Asiatic mode of production

Middle-Eastern and Asiatic feudalism came into existence long before a somewhat different type of feudalism appeared on the European scene. Besides, it survived much longer – in India at least 4000 years, from the third millenium B.C. until well after the arrival of the British around 1600.

In order to understand this longevity it is important to realize that agriculture in India was quite primitive and not particularly productive. Combined with excessive appropriation of surpluses by the ruling class, this meant that the peasants were unable to shift from subsistence farming to commercial agriculture. Apart from the fact that they did not have the means or incentive to increase their output, the peasants were also not interested in specialization. In other words, the villages remained economically closed communities – isolated from outside influences that might have encouraged them to attempt to break out of the vicious circle of low productivity → self-sufficiency → poverty → stagnation and apathy. At the same time, the autarkic nature of the rural communities gave them the resilience to overcome periods of political turmoil, invasions and destruction, and thus survive through the ages.

The closed economy, together with poverty and stagnation, meant that there was not enough division of labor to really stimulate urban growth. Without towns that could play a role as markets where farmers could sell their products and which at the same time could be important as *central places* providing essential functions for the surrounding rural hinterlands (see the discussion of Christaller's central place theory on page 147), the villagers were unable to modernize their agricultural activities. Instead of the existence of a mutually beneficial relationship between village and town, characterized by a dynamic exchange of goods and services, urban settlements were above all the foci of a government-controlled network of tax-collecting relations which funneled agricultural surplus production to the powerful ruling elite.

In contrast to medieval Europe, where the nobility lived in the country, rather than in cities, and showed concern for the productivity and well-being of the peasantry, the Asiatic mode of production was characterized by a ruling class which resided in urban places, had no direct contact with the peasantry and looked down on farming. Subjugation of the agricultural producers was less severe in Western Europe and peasants generally enjoyed more freedom than did their Indian counterparts. Despotism or

39. Railroad construction/repairs in India. (M. Minnée)

absolutism was more pronounced in India. Whereas European peasants were able and willing to modernize and commercialize agriculture, the Indian peasantry lacked the opportunity and motivation to make such changes. In brief, an evolutionary process of growth and development in Europe contrasted with many centuries of stagnation in India.

Perhaps the most fundamental difference was the role played by the cities. In Western Europe they were not primarily parasitic centers that dominated and exploited their rural hinterlands. Instead, most of them owed their existence to small-scale manufacturing, commerce – especially long-distance trade – and to their role as marketing and service centers for agricultural umlands. After the 13th century, they developed more and more into centers of freedom and innovation in which the upcoming bourgeoisie – mainly merchants, artisans and industrial entrepreneurs – could accumulate capital, make investments, and thus expand production and trade. It was in the cities that the process of economic progress was set in motion. As their productivity and prosperity grew, they had an increasingly beneficial influence on rural living conditions and methods of agricultural production. Meanwhile, the growth of a 'free' urban middle class eventually led to the decline of the old feudalistic power structure and the rise of democratic institutions. The result was greater freedom and more rights for all citizens. Western Europe never experienced the 'Oriental despotism' that enslaved millions of people in the Middle East and Asia

311

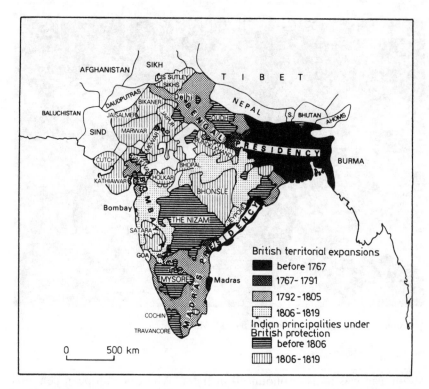

Fig. 30a. British expansion in southern Asia, prior to 1820. *Source:* B.J.S. Hoetjes *et al.*, 1980.

for many centuries, thereby obstructing almost every form of economic development (Wittfogel 1967).[1]

European penetration and British colonialism, 1600-1947

The First Europeans to arrive in India were the Portuguese. In 1498, Vasco da Gama reached the subcontinent, and a dozen years later Albuquerque conquered Goa on the west coast. It was not until 1961 – fourteen years after India had obtained independence – that the Portuguese had to relinquish control of Goa.

The British appeared in 1600, the year in which Queen Elizabeth gave the privately owned East India Company (EIC) the monopoly to trade with India. It was this trading company which conquered the subcontinent, assisted by British troops (after 1754) and the British navy (after 1861). Between 1664 and 1954, the French, too, had a few small footholds in eastern India.

[1] Although long periods of stagnation have characterized the Asiatic mode of production, Anderson (1979) has drawn attention to the fact that China has known periods of progress, innovation, industrial development, urban expansion, active trade, and rapid population growth.

312

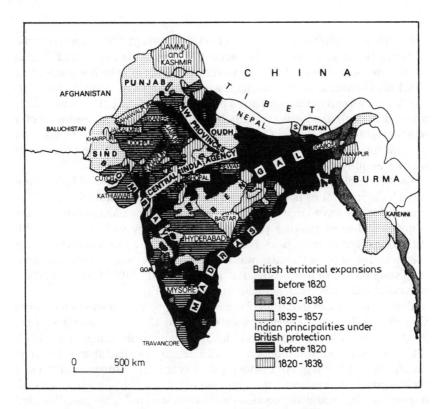

Fig. 30b. British expansion in southern Asia, 1820-1857. *Source:* B.J.S. Hoetjes *et al.*, 1980.

During the first 150 years of its existence, the EIC was not interested in territorial conquests – only in trade. To this end, agreements were arranged with local rulers. Particularly important was the trade in cotton fabrics, silk, jewels, indigo (blue dye from the indigo plant), pepper and other spices. Throughout the 17th century, the EIC remained a small operation; in 1647 it had only 23 coastal trading posts and 90 employees in India. Three of the fortified trading posts eventually developed into the cities of Bombay, Madras and Calcutta. In 1750, the British communities in each of these three 'presidency cities' still counted only a few hundred persons.

It was not until after the Mogul Empire had started to disintegrate – around the middle of the 18th century – that the EIC became interested in establishing control over the entire subcontinent. Following a brief period of conflict (1746-1757) during which the French were defeated, the EIC made a start with the conquest of India. Little by little the company extended its influence inland, especially in the northern plains. In numerous places EIC employees became *zamindars* for local rulers or granted themselves *jagirs*. Not a few of them became as autocratic as the Oriental despots with whom they collaborated or whom they replaced altogether; before long some had accumulated as much wealth as the Indian princes.

313

Largely as a result of the selfish behavior of corrupt EIC employees, the company began to experience financial problems, and in 1773 the EIC had to borrow money from the U.K. government, thereby losing some of its freedom. Government control increased further in 1784, when the Regulating Act put an end to the company's political power; the EIC was no longer allowed to declare war or sign treaties without the express approval of a newly established Board of Control. A few decades later, the EIC also lost its trade monopoly and finally, in 1853, it was no longer allowed to appoint its own employees.

By the middle of the 19th century, Britain controlled most of India, even though the number of British civil servants was very limited (Fig. 30). The army, which was not large either, was made up for the most part of Indians – only the higher ranking positions were filled by well-trained British officers. About 60 percent of India – including the entire Gangetic plains region and most coastal areas – was under direct rule, while the remainder – consisting mostly of less productive 'agencies' and 'states' further inland – was ruled indirectly by dependent maharadjas (Fig. 31).

Except for the fact that in 1912 the colonial government was moved from Calcutta to the more centrally located city of Delhi, the administrative geography of India, as depicted in Fig. 31, remained unchanged until 1947, the year India achieved independence. The only element that did change during the last 100 years of colonial rule was that the British strengthened their control of the indirectly administered areas. Slowly but surely all important administrative functions were entrusted to highly qualified civil servants. However, since many of these top officials behaved as if they belonged to some superior caste, steeped as they were in "a tradition of proud integrity and of selfless dedication to carrying the white man's burden" (Lamb 1966), they unwittingly nurtured feelings of anti-colonialism among India's intellectual elite, thereby hastening the end of the colonial era.

Consequences of British colonialism

Unlike the first 150 to 200 years, when British influence was so limited that it hardly had any effect on India, the last 150 years witnessed a succession of dramatic changes – some positive and some negative.

For the purpose of simplifying the collection of taxes, the 'permanent settlement' was introduced in many areas, e.g., Bengal, Bihar and Orissa. This meant that the nature of landownership was changed such that land became a commodity which could be sold and purchased. As a result, many of the traditional tax collectors – the *zamindars* – became large landowners and the peasants became their tenants. Thus, a new class of wealthy landlords was created and inequality in the rural areas became more pronounced. Instead of using part of their wealth to improve methods of agricultural production – as the British had hoped – the new rural elite spent it on consumption, especially on luxury goods imported from the U.K.

314

Fig. 31. India, princely states and British provinces, 1941. *Source:* R. von Albertini, *European Colonial Rule, 1880-1940,* 1982, p. 523.

Another undesirable consequence of the fact that land had become a commodity was that rich merchants and other affluent urbanites started to buy up agricultural land for investment purposes. Aside from the fact that this caused an increase in absenteeism, it drove up the price of farmland as well as the rent payments tenants had to make.

Since the permanent settlement system soon turned out to be a failure, a different approach, known as the 'ryotwari settlement,' was introduced elsewhere in India. Here, the tillers of the land (*ryots*) were declared the owners. A few decades later, however, many of them had lost their land to moneylenders, merchants and other well-to-do individuals interested in acquiring land for speculative purposes or who looked upon land as a safe investment; the *ryots* themselves had become sharecroppers or landless laborers.

315

In Punjab and some other areas, the 'Mahalwari system' was tried, whereby an entire village community became the collective owner of the land and was given the responsibility to pay the collective taxes. Despite the fact that this system was introduced for the express purpose of preventing the peasants from becoming tenants, here, too, much of the land ended up in the hands of a small number of large landowners, speculators and loansharks.

In summary, colonial rule everywhere led to radically changed land-ownership patterns, increased disparity, land speculation, usury practices and an indebted peasantry. At the same time, erosion became a more serious problem. Throughout the subcontinent forests were cut down so as to expand the total area of farmland. More positive was the construction of extensive irrigation systems. After the opening of the Ganges Canal in 1854, many other canals and dams were built, and by 1947 no less than 25 percent of India's cropland was under irrigation. Unfortunately, a comparatively small group of larger and more market-oriented farmers benefitted much more from these infrastructural improvements than did others, the result being that intra-village differences became more pronounced.

Most scholars agree that British colonialism had a devastating effect on India's secondary sector. Large numbers of artisans were put out of work as small-scale industries all over India were wiped out. Few producers could compete with mass-produced imports from the U.K. Prior to 1815, India had a thriving textile industry which produced for the domestic market as well as for export. Only thirty years later, the export had come to a standstill and approximately half of the domestic demand was supplied by modern textile mills in Manchester, England. Since Britain was the world's leading industrial power and therefore did not have to fear foreign competition, it strongly advocated free trade. This was to Britain's advantage, but for British-dominated India the absence of protectionist measures meant that a substantial part of the manufacturing sector came to a grinding halt.

As India's industrial production declined, the country became increasingly a supplier of raw materials, such as cotton, sugar, indigo, opium and tea. While raw cotton was exported to England, manufactured cotton fabrics were imported. It was not until the 1930s that the U.K. decided to provide protection for India's secondary sector, but by then Japan had replaced Britain as the major supplier of industrial imports.

Notwithstanding above-mentioned problems, India during the second half of the 19th century experienced her own industrial revolution, made possible in part by British commercial capital. The textile industry had never been completely wiped out, and by 1860 the first modern cotton mills had come into operation, producing, among others, for Chinese and Japanese markets. A growing demand for grain sacks – due to a worldwide upsurge in grain shipments – led to the rise of an important jute industry. Furthermore, steel mills were built by Indian entrepreneurs using Indian capital. In 1939, there were more than 10,000 factories in India, which

40. Road construction in northern India. (M. Minnée)

together employed nearly 2 million workers. Although this is an impressive number, we should keep in mind that this industrial labor force represented no more than 0.5 percent of the total population. On the other hand, it meant that in 1939 there were only about ten countries in the world which had more industry than India. What is more, it was mostly Indian, rather than British, initiative which was responsible for developing the country into an industrial power.

The British not only 'permitted' India's industrialization, but stimulated it indirectly by setting up a modern tertiary sector. Much of their colonial activity was centered on the development of international trade, shipping, banking and insurance. They also played an important role in providing India with a modern infrastructure. In addition to the construction of canals, dams and several large seaports, they established a telegraph system and built a network of railroad lines. In 1947, India had the best railroad system in all Asia.

Other positive effects of Britain's colonial rule were the principle of equality under the law (even though the British left the caste system intact), and the creation of a high degree of administrative unification. An undesirable side effect of the unification, however, was that it resulted in increased rivalry between Moslems and Hindus due to the fact that the British gave high-caste Hindus *(Brahmans)* important administrative jobs.

Another negative consequence of Britain's activities was the increase in regional inequality. Most conspicuous became the contrast between the indirectly ruled interior regions – which were largely bypassed by the process of modernization – and the coastal regions with their modern seaports, commercial and industrial activities, educational facilities and rapidly growing cities. Finally, mention should be made of the fact that English has become a major *lingua franca* – a valuable asset for a country with more than 800 different languages and dialects. Familiarity with the English language also makes it easier for Indian politicians, businessmen, scientists, educators and others to communicate with the rest of the world community.

At the end of this section we conclude that the legacy of colonial domination is neither all negative nor all positive. It would clearly be incorrect to attribute India's underdevelopment solely to the allegedly paralyzing effects of many years of colonial exploitation by Britain. It is equally misleading to conclude that widespread poverty in present-day India is exclusively a consequence of the penetration of capitalism during the colonial era. Whether there would have been less poverty and less inequality in 1947 if India had never been a colony, is a mute question. But in view of the unfavorable social, economic and political conditions which prevailed in precolonial India – in the days of Oriental despotism, the Asiatic mode of production, or rent capitalism – it is not inconceivable that India might now be worse-off than it is if the British had never set foot on her shores. Granted, the U.K. could have done more for India, e.g., it could have made larger investments. Prior to World War I, only about 10 percent of British foreign investment ended up in India, most of it going to North America. Britain also could have contributed more to India's industrialization or to the development of a highly productive plantation-type agriculture. Had this taken place, there can be little doubt that there would still be critics who would blame the British and/or capitalism for many of the problems that India would surely have.

The caste system, Hinduism, Islam

The caste system. Although virtually all societies are divided into two or more social classes, India is exceptional in that: (1) social mobility does not exist; one stays in the caste to which one belongs by birth, that is, education or wealth (income) cannot alter one's social standing, (2) in no other society are (were) relations between classes so meticuously defined as in India, and (3) there probably has never been another society in which behavior has been determined so rigidly and for so long a period of time as in India.

It has been assumed that the caste system was introduced by Aryan-speaking peoples who invaded India 3500 to 4000 years ago, although some scholars believe that it already existed in northeastern India prior to Aryan domination. Basically, the Indian caste system is made up of four original groups: the *Brahmans* or priests and teachers, the *Kahatriyas* or warriors

41. Informal sector activity: chopping kindling in India. (M. Minnée)

and civil servants, the *Vaishyas* or traders, and the *Shudras* or farmers and artisans. These are only the four main groups *(varnas)*. In everyday life the system is far more complex as each *varna* is subdivided into a large number of precisely circumscribed *jatis*. Altogether, there are over 3000 castes.

Lowest of all are the 'outcasts' or 'untouchables,' also referred to as 'scheduled castes,' 'pariahs' or 'Harijans' (children of God). Until reforms were instituted ('untouchability' was abolished by the 1950 constitution), they were barred from participation in administrative or religious affairs, even though they numbered at least 60 million.

Each caste has its own life style, dietary customs, and social manners; its own hereditary rules, religious rituals and traditions; and its own marriage regulations. Every caste has at least one hereditary occupation, although this does not mean that all members have that occupation. Quite a few castes are found only in one small part of the country, but migration and urbanization have resulted in more complicated geographical patterns. Finally, the caste system is characterized by a hierarchy in which the Brahmans occupy the top positions.

Despite the fact that the caste system has been officially outlawed and that discrimination is no longer allowed, unofficially life in Hindu India continues to be influenced – quite strongly even – by this age-old system of social divisions. Still today, not everyone is born equal, and some groups have more rights and opportunities than others. India has often been called

319

the largest democracy in the world, but deeply rooted caste-based behavior patterns make Indian society decidedly less democratic than many other societies.

What effect has the caste system had on the development of the country? First of all, it has contributed significantly to the problem of inequality – to social as well as to economic and political inequality. By legalizing inequality, it sanctioned discrimination and exploitation of the weaker groups in society – not unlike *apartheid* in South Africa. Secondly, since certain occupations were open only to members of particular castes, the system severely restricted occupational mobility. More generally, the inflexibility of the system has meant that a great deal of talent was wasted. As in segregated South Africa, human resources are grossly underutilized. In both countries, institutionalized inequality and discrimination constitute powerful disincentives for millions of citizens and represent insurmountable barriers to development and progress. For thousands of years, the social contradictions of the caste system have bred, and kept intact, a large measure of apathy among the many millions of people who found themselves near the bottom of the social pyramid.

Hinduism. The large majority (85 percent) of the people of India practice Hinduism – a religious, cultural and social system which rests less on faith than it does on birth and conduct. Unlike most of the major world religions, it has no known founder and no fixed creeds. Strong emphasis is placed on the spiritual aspects of life. Human existence is seen as a sequence of lives which are characterized by timelessness and, so, are meaningless. One of the most fundamental principles of Hinduism is that of repeated reincarnation, eventually leading to eternal salvation. As a consequence, discrimination, exploitation, maltreatment and other social and political abuses that occur in everyday life receive little attention.

Economically speaking, more attention is paid to sharing than to producing. Through contemplation, that is, concentration on spiritual things as a form of private devotion, one comes to the realization that one is not really a person but merely part of an illusionary world and that one must enter into, and become one with, the Absolute in order to find eternal peace. Redemption has nothing to do with one's earthly and temporary condition, which is but an illusionary sense-world *(maya)* concealing the Absolute. Since the world and everything social, economic and political that forms part of it is an illusion, it serves no purpose to look for salvation by satisfying one's desires. Instead, one should try to disassociate oneself from the world and earthly life.

It is not surprising that such a philosophy breeds resignation and that people find it easy to accept their fate and put up with deprivation, sickness, humiliation and subjugation. This resignation or indolence helps to explain why millions of people live and die on the streets without making an effort to raise their material well-being. It also helps us understand the lack of concern and compassion for the deprived masses on the part of former rulers and present-day politicians. Hinduism does not exactly inspire people to try to create a better world or stimulate economic development. One's condition is one's fate – the consequence of earlier acts *(karma)*. Earthly life is either punishment or reward for the life one has lived before. Since fate cannot be modified, it is best to accept one's condition. Only through resignation, contemplation and compliance with the rules of caste and Hinduism can one hope to be rewarded with a better life after death, for example, by being admitted to a higher caste through reincarnation. In effect, Hinduism preaches social inequality and furthers acceptance of social injustice.

Although we would not go so far as to claim that Hinduism, in combination with the caste system, is *the* cause of underdevelopment, it does appear justified to conclude that it has been an important contributing factor.

Islam and its conflict with Hinduism. A similar conclusion applies to Islam, that is to say, if we judge the Indian situation on the basis of our admittedly biased, Western, Euro-centric, Christian-Judaean values. According to the teachings of Mohammed (570-632), everyone's life is predestined by Allah, who develops everything according to certain laws. Man must serve Allah and is cautioned always to seek His guidance and accept willingly whatever comes from His hands. Only by submission to Allah can inward peace be achieved. Worldly motives should fade away and the love of Allah should be man's only objective. Since the Koran discourages adherents to take their future into their own hands, Moslems as a rule have a rather fatalistic outlook on life.

Around 1000 AD, Moslems invaded India, bringing Islam and Hinduism into close contact. Since Hinduism had always been quite tolerant toward other religions, it had assimilated elements from them. Other cultural groups with their own faiths had simply been allowed to occupy their own niche in the large and increasingly complex social and religious order that was Hindu society. Islam with its outspoken dogmas did not fit into this structure. For Moslems, there is no God but Allah, and the Koran is the book of books which contains a message for all humanity and for all ages. In other words, there is room neither for other gods nor for other faiths. Since Islam preaches the brotherhood of all believers, it also rejects the hierarchical structure of Hindu society, and thus, the caste system. If we add to this that during the first few centuries after Islam had come into existence Moslems were extremely active in their efforts to convert others to their belief, it is not surprising that comparatively aggressive and intolerant Islam came into conflict with other religions. Wars fought for the purpose of spreading Islam were considered holy wars by the Moslems.

There have been many clashes between Moslems and Hindus, often causing widespread destruction. Particularly detrimental were the long periods of unrest and insecurity in large parts of the subcontinent. It goes

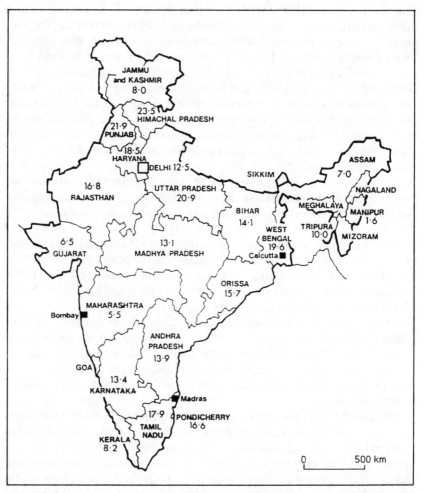

Fig. 32. Harijans as percent of total population, by state, circa 1975. *Source: India nieuwsbrief 7, 1980.*

without saying that this turmoil did not foster development. Unfortunately, British rule tended to increase the rivalry between Moslems and Hindus, thus contributing to the partition of the subcontinent in 1947 into Moslem Pakistan (including Bangladesh) and Hindu India. Partition involved the largest short-term migration in history, with millions of Moslems moving out of India and millions of Hindus (and Sikhs) migrating into the country. Apart from the fact that this massive displacement upset the lives of the migrants and resulted in immense housing and employment problems, it was accompanied by bitter riots which claimed the lives of at least one million people. Ever since that traumatic experience, relations between India and Pakistan have been dominated by hostility and distrust, and

322

several times since 1947 the two countries have become entangled in armed conflict. Naturally, the cause of development is not served by such wasteful encounters. What both countries need is not confrontation, but peaceful cooperation.

Development strategies since independence

Since 1947, India has made various efforts to accelerate the process of development. In the sections below we discuss and evaluate three such efforts, i.e., (1) the attempt to improve the position of the untouchables, (2) measures taken to reduce the rate of population growth, and (3) policies aimed at agricultural development.

Efforts to eliminate the problem of untouchability

The untouchables constitute one of the least developed and most deprived groups in Indian society. Their present number is estimated at approximately 120 million. Although they are found throughout the entire country (Fig. 32), their share of the population varies from more than 20 percent in some states to less than 10 percent in others, with a national average of about 15 percent. From time immemorial, they personify uncleanliness, to be avoided by everyone who hopes to be freed from the cycly of life, death and reincarnation. They have the lowest-paid jobs and do the least desirable work. In the rural areas they are mostly seasonal farmhands or day laborers – until recently they were not allowed to own, or even rent, land. The large majority are illiterate.

Untouchables have always been the innocent victims of extreme discrimination. To give some examples: they were not allowed to walk on certain streets and roads unless they removed their footprints with a broom; on some streets and paths they had to warn other pedestrians in order to enable them to avoid their unclean shadow; even the sound of their voice was considered unclean; in many parts of India they were not allowed to have an umbrella, walk on shoes, milk cows, possess pet animals, or wear bracelets, earrings, necklaces and other ornaments.

During the period of British rule, the caste system became increasingly criticized and the first steps were taken to create more opportunity for the most disadvantaged groups. After India gained full sovereignty, this policy of 'positive discrimination' was continued and expanded, and owing to Mahatma Gandhi's undefatigable efforts to promote social justice for the whole of India, untouchability was outlawed and a detailed listing of democratic rights was incorporated into the new constitution. The policy of positive discrimination or preferential treatment also aims to improve the lot of other disadvantaged groups, such as the 'tribes' (mostly living in isolated, mountainous areas) and the 'other backward classes' (poverty-stricken members of the Shudra castes).

In order to help the untouchables – or Harijans, as Gandhi used to call them – the government decided to set aside for them a number of top positions (e.g., in the federal government, state governments and universities) and numerous other white-collar and blue-collar jobs, awarded scholarships for study at universities and colleges, and created special credit facilities. Some programs provide aid to people who already have some education and expertise, while others are meant to help the very poorest members of society. Although most Harijans are illiterate and destitute, some have managed to do quite well for themselves and may be earning far more than the average citizen. Thus, they do not form a homogeneous group. On the contrary, the untouchables have their own social hierarchy, comprising some 400 sub-castes.

What has the policy accomplished thus far? In spite of the fact that many individual Harijans are now much better-off than they were before the program, the group as a whole has made little or no progress. The disappointing results can be attributed to the following: (1) although discrimination is no longer allowed, it is still widely practiced; (2) most Harijans accept their lowly status and lack the motivation and determination (as well as the means) to help themselves – they are mentally unprepared to take advantage of the opportunities specifically created on their behalf; (3) due to the government's limited financial resources, the program has been quite small; (4) the business community has done much less for the Harijans than the government had hoped – few industries, for instance, have reserved jobs for them; (5) as mentioned earlier, there are other disadvantaged individuals (some 80 million) with whom the Harijans must share the limited means that the government has made available; (6) most Harijans are so far behind in terms of schooling and experience that they cannot take advantage of the program – for example, there have not been any eligible candidates for certain scholarships; (7) politically, the Harijans have no power.

The last-mentioned point may well be the most important one. Partly because of their attitude of resignation and partly because of their high illiteracy rate, they are not organized at the national level or at the regional or local level. Being unorganized, they are unable to fight for their rights or demand certain changes and concessions. They do not have their own political party, and no strong Harijan leaders have emerged who champion the cause of the untouchables. Thus far, the few Harijan representatives in the federal government have failed to advance sufficiently the interests of the group they supposedly represent.

In recent years, there has been a surge in violent outbursts aimed against the Harijans. During a virtual caste war in Uttar Pradesh in 1980, they were murdered by groups of thugs, sometimes assisted by corrupt policemen. The rise in inter-caste hostility and violence appears to be related to the following: (1) many younger Harijans are well aware that they have constitutional rights and do not accept being humiliated or punished, (2) Harijans are becoming increasingly frustrated that social change and society's tolerance towards them lag behind their expectations, (3) the number of Harijans who are unwilling to take on poorly paid menial tasks is growing, and (4) higher-caste Hindus feel threatened by the growing emancipation of the Harijans and have resorted to Ku Klux Klan-type practices to intimidate them and 'show them their place.'

Although there is reason to fear that bloody confrontations will continue, and perhaps even escalate, the increase in tension clearly demonstrates that the traditionally rigid social order is undergoing change and that eventually the static caste system will be replaced by a more dynamic, and hopefully more flexible, class system which allows social mobility.

India's demographic policy

Concerned about the rapid rate of population growth, India launched her first birth control campaign in the late 1940s. Initially, only 0.3 percent of the national budget was earmarked for this purpose, but by the mid-1970s this had been raised to 3 percent. Whereas in the beginning only conventional methods were advocated, later years saw the promotion of more radical measures, including sterilization and abortion.

All in all, the population control campaign has been less successful than demographers and politicians had hoped. Between 1951 and 1981, India's population jumped from 361 million to 690 million. Notwithstanding a drop in the annual growth rate from 2.3 percent in the 1960s to 2.1 percent in the following decade, India's population presently increases at the rate of more than 1 million a month, or some 45,000 a day.

It may well be that today's growth rate is not appreciably lower than it would have been had there been no family planning campaign. No matter whether we are dealing with developed or underdeveloped countries, population policies have a reputation of having little effect on people's reproductive behavior. This is true as much of policies aimed at reducing the birth rate as it is of policies designed to raise the number of births. The fact that India's present rate of population growth is about the same as it was a generation ago is nothing exceptional. Although it is not difficult to find fault with India's population control program (see below), it would be incorrect to see that as the reason why it has failed. Even if India had poured much more money into the organization and implementation of her birth control campaign, and no mistakes had been made, it is doubtful that birth rates would have declined more than they have.

Efforts to lower the birth rate in a country like India are frustrated by a host of complications. (1) The overwhelming majority of the people are unable to read, have no calendar, cannot afford to buy contraceptives, and have no medicine cabinet in which pills, etc. can be kept safely. (2) Aside from the high illiteracy rate, other factors make it difficult to get the necessary information to the people, e.g., poor transportation and communication, and a general absence of clinics, community centers and drugstores. Especially in the more remote parts of the country there may be no electricity, no radio stations and/or television transmitters. Although a few individuals may have a transistor radio, there are many villages without one single television set. Besides, batteries are often difficult to get or too expensive for the villagers. (3) Then there is the problem of linguistic diversity. In order to reach 95 percent of the Indian population, information must be disseminated in at least fifteen different languages – a costly operation. (4) Poor people, particularly in the rural areas, prefer to have many children in order to make sure that someone will look after them when they are too old to take care of themselves or to have them contribute to the family budget by putting them to work. (5) Many people do not grasp the negative consequences of rapid population growth, are unaccustomed to thinking about the distant future or in terms of the 'national well-being,' and tend to be suspicious of strangers who try to convince them that they should have only two or three children. (6) Because it is considered important, almost essential, to have at least one son, a couple with four daughters is likely to decide to have at least one more child in the hope that it will be a boy.

In the case of India, family planning programs have been poorly organized, especially in the years 1975-1977, when the campaign became rather aggressive. In January, 1976, prime minister Indira Gandhi declared that the government was going to take some "strong steps which may not be liked by all." These strong steps attracted international attention when it became known that government employees and residents of New Delhi would be penalized if they did not limit their families to two children. A few months later, a new birth-control program was announced which included raising the legal marriage age and paying people for having themselves sterilized. A few states went so far as to introduce legislation for compulsory sterilization of those who had more than two children. Perhaps the worst aspect of the entire campaign was that medical workers received extra pay if they sterilized more than a certain number of people a day. This soon led to bizarre situations, e.g., old men and widowers as well as divorced and unmarried men were sterilized – some more than once. Mobile medical teams even held up buses and sterilized all adult male passengers. In one year, probably some 10 million sterilizations took place, many involuntarily.

The consequence of these practices was that people developed a fear of the sterilization teams, and to some degree also of other medical workers. This, in turn, had a negative impact on the adoption of more acceptable methods of birth control, such as the use of the pill, condoms and intra-uterine devices (IUDs). Meanwhile, so many medical workers were involved in the sterilization campaign that conventional forms of health care were temporarily neglected.

The aggressive sterilization scheme of 1976-1977 was so disliked that family planning in general has become rather unpopular. Just when people were finally becoming accustomed to the idea that birth control was a good thing, they lost confidence in the government's efforts to reduce the rate of population growth. Since the Indian population is unlikely to forget the excesses of the sterilization drive, it may take some time before that confidence is restored. Since the poorer and socially weaker segments of society were the chief victims of the sterilization scandals, they cannot be expected to soon overcome their skepticism regarding present and future policies of population control.

Promotion of agricultural development

The secondary sector is not able to provide sufficient employment. Although India has a great deal of industry, in which virtually all branches – including high-technology industries – are represented, only a small proportion of the economically active population is employed in industry. This 'underindustrialization' is not caused by foreign-dominated transnational concerns which purposely obstruct industrial expansion in India. On the contrary, because Indian law prescribes that every enterprise must be controlled for more than 50 percent by Indian interests, foreigners frequently prefer to invest in other Third World countries. In fact, many Indian industrialists (including multinationals) have invested abroad, especially in South and Southeast Asia, but also in East Africa. Nevertheless, there are foreign enterprises in India, with the result that there is an outflow of profit from India. In addition to this profit extraction, some of these industries use advanced labor-saving technology, so that they employ relatively few Indian laborers.

A greater constraint than foreign domination and external dependence is India's very limited market potential. Widespread poverty in rural as well as urban areas means that India lacks the purchasing power to support a high degree of industrialization. How small the domestic market is becomes apparent when we learn that India, with a population of 690 million in 1981, has the same GNP as the Netherlands (population: 14 million). Since per capita income in India is nearly fifty times lower than in the Netherlands, the industrial sector is faced with the problem of a market that is readily saturated. This fact tends to lead to industrial overcapacity and/or uneconomical use of investments.

Due to the fact that India has an overabundance of unskilled and skilled people looking for work, industrial wages are low and work conditions often abominable, e.g., poor safety measures and exposure to intense air pollution. The large supply of workers willing to accept such unfavorable conditions makes it impossible for labor unions to successfully fight for bigger pay checks and/or improved work conditions. Large numbers of highly qualified people – including physicians and scientists – have left India for higher-paying jobs elsewhere in the world. Since the country has invested heavily in the education of these individuals, this *brain drain* represents a serious loss to underdeveloped India.

Since 1948, India has made a series of efforts to upgrade the agricultural sector. One of these was the introduction of high-yielding seed varieties

(HYVs), which were supposed to lead to a *Green Revolution*. Initial successes caused Indira Gandhi to predict that India would become a major exporter of food crops, especially cereals. Indeed, total grain production has experienced such an impressive increase that India can feed all her people and sell some grain to other countries, *unless* the wet monsoon does not arrive on time, does not last long enough or lasts too long. However, even when the weather cooperates, many millions of Indians go hungry, either because they are too poor to buy enough food or because supplies cannot be shipped fast enough to the large urban markets.

A well-known problem of HYVs is that they require a number of relatively expensive inputs, such as ample amounts of fertilizer, irrigation water, herbicides and insecticides. Usually, only the larger and richer farmers can afford these inputs. Furthermore, large farmers can obtain credit more easily than can small farmers, while tenants hardly ever qualify for a loan. Large farmers have other advantages; they tend to be better informed about the requirements of modern agriculture and have larger fields or less-fragmented farms, making it easier for them to mechanize. Thus, large farmers have benefited more from the adoption of HYVs than have small farmers with the result that rural disparities have become more pronounced. Inequality has also increased because large farmers have bought up land from small farmers so as to be better able to install irrigation systems and/or make more economical use of modern farm machinery. Some landowners no longer rent land to tenants, but do all the farming themselves.

All in all, the Green Revolution has had a number of unfavorable social effects, including an increase in unemployment among landless farm laborers. At the same time, regional differences have become greater because areas with a favorable mix of human and physical conditions – productive climate, good irrigation possibilities, fertile soils, small local relief, large farms, relatively well-educated farmers, etc. – are much better suited for the production of 'miracle rice' or 'miracle wheat' than are other parts of the country. One of the consequences of these processes of polarization has been the rise in political unrest (Frankel 1971).

India has also launched a number of land reforms in order to create a more even distribution of landownership and to improve land tenure conditions. If we view these efforts chronologically, three stages can be recognized: (1) the period 1948-1954, when the numbers of *zamindars* and other intermediaries were drastically reduced; (2) the period since 1953, when numerous states took steps to improve the tenancy system; and (3) the period since 1956, in which laws were enacted to limit the maximum size of farm units.

The first-stage reform was carried out mainly in the large and densely populated state of Uttar Pradesh. The chief objective was to wipe out once and for all the many parasitic *zamindars* and other intermediaries. Farmers who cultivated land that previously had belonged to *zamindars* and others

42. Cold shower on the bank of a river. (M. Minnée)

were given two options: they could either buy the land and thus become owners, or they could stay on as tenants. No matter what they chose to do, they were allowed a considerable tax reduction. Taxes could no longer be paid to the *zamindars*, but were henceforth collected directly by the government. Other obligations which the farmers had toward tax collectors and other middlemen were abrogated as well, causing some 2.6 million persons to lose their traditional rights. This way, the government hoped to enable small agricultural producers to raise their standard of living and improve their agricultural methods.

The second stage consisted of efforts fo fix the maximum amount of rent payments, provide social security for tenants, promote the purchase of land by tenants, and counter the growing tendency among large landowners to farm all their land themselves. Apart from the fact that some of the measures were implemented in a highly arbitrary manner, resulting in substantial differences from one state to the next, the reforms caused considerable dissatisfaction among large landowners. In all kinds of ways – legal and illegal – they tried to foil or circumvent the government's efforts to protect the small farmers and tenants. So successful were they that the large majority of India's rural population remained victims of the traditional pattern of social injustice. Few peasants acquired the land they cultivated.

The results of the third stage, aimed at the redistribution of agricultural land, were no less disappointing. Partly because the program was poorly executed, owners found numerous ways to hang on to their land. Again, implementation differed from state to state – a clear indication that the reform was carried out in an arbitrary and haphazard manner. Altogether, only a minute proportion of all farmland changed hands.

Helping the poor help themselves

Since the early 1970s, the Netherlands has provided funds and technological know-how for innumerable small 'adapted technology' projects in the Third World.* One of these involved the construction of small and simple, American-type windmills in Ghazipur, India. In 1975, the Dutch development agency TOOL got together with the Organization of the Rural Poor (ORP) in Ghazipur, an organization which gives assistance to poor peasants in northern India. TOOL and ORP decided to help raise agricultural output by increasing the supply of irrigation water through the use of windmills. The richer farmers had motorized water pumps, but because the small farmers could not afford these devices, they bought their water from the richer farmers. Being dependent on the owners of water pumps, the poor farmers were charged too much. The windmills, so it seemed, could put an end to this undesirable situation.

Following a feasibility study, the actual project was started in 1978. A workshop was built near Ghazipur for the construction of the windmills. Some of the villagers were taught how to build, maintain and repair the mills, while the first mills – developed by TOOL – were installed free of charge. In the following years, the windmills were tested and adapted to local conditions.

The project was terminated in 1981. By that time, fifteen mills had been installed, twelve of which had been donated free for testing purposes. Only three windmills had been purchased by local farmers, none of whom belonged to the group of small, marginal farmers which TOOL and ORP tried to help. As it turned out, practically none of the very poor farmers was interested in buying a windmill – a great disappointment for the organizers of the project.

What had gone wrong? In an effort to answer this question, a follow-up study was carried out. The researchers came to the conclusion that three obstacles were responsible for the fact that the project fell short of its objectives.

First of all, there happens to be little wind at the time the farmers need to irrigate their land. There is more than enough wind in summer, but because of the intense heat, agricultural activities come to a virtual standstill during that part of the year. In order to make the windmill pay for itself, farmers would have to change their age-old agricultural calendar. This would mean a drastic change in their entire way of life. Apart from the fact that there are powerful psychological reasons which make such a cultural adaption difficult, it may well be risky to replace the traditional agricultural calendar by a new one. Whereas a rich farmer might be able to take this risk, a poor farmer cannot do so as it might mean his death.

A second obstacle is the smallness of most farms and the high degree of land fragmentation. Nearly 70 percent of the rural population around Ghazipur has less than 1.25 ha (about 3 acres), the ideal area to be irrigated by one windmill. Among the farmers there is no tradition of doing things cooperatively. Efforts to get farmers to share the cost of a windmill failed, partly because of the problem of how to divide the pumped up water fairly among the participating farmers.

A third problem is that small farmers are unable to obtain a cheap loan. The State Bank of India does not provide credit to farmers with less than 1 ha of land. Without a loan most small farmers cannot possibly purchase a windmill. But even farmers who can get a loan are reluctant to invest in a windmill for the simple reason that they know that they will have to pay back the borrowed amount. This means that they must find a way to earn more than they have been doing, but this is not an easy task. Possibilities to sell part of their crop are extremely limited for small farmers in rural India.

Although the development and introduction of small-scale adapted technology may appear to be, and often is, the most sensible and promising approach to helping Third World inhabitants help themselves, it need not always be the panacea that it may appear to be. This example – together with disappointing results from many other areas – demonstrates that adapted technology alone is unlikely to solve problems of poverty and low productivity. Like any innovation, adapted technology must be attuned to the 'total' (social, economic, cultural, political and physical) environment in which it is to be used in order to be successful and make a lasting contribution to the well-being of the people involved.

* Adapted technology is the same as appropriate technology or intermediate technology.

Source: G. Van der Bijl (1983).

Summarizing the above, we conclude that government policies to eliminate discrimination against the Harijans, to slow down the rate of population growth, and to promote agricultural production while at the same time trying to improve the quality of life for the rural masses, have not produced the hoped for results.

We could have given other examples of development strategies and reforms that have had disappointing results. But instead of presenting a lengthy discussion of all aspects of social, political and economic change – or the lack of it – in post-colonial India, involving analysis of a complex variety of interacting internal and external factors, we believe that the examples discussed illustrate that the process of development is an exceedingly difficult one. Development does not come overnight. It is a process which requires a great deal of time as it involves changes in attitudes and deep-rooted behavior patterns. People who stand to lose from change, will fight it and protect their vested interests. Since they are precisely those who pull the strings, both in the political and economic realm, they constitute a powerful reactionary force that can effectively slow down, or even halt, progress-oriented change. Stubborn resistance among the elite is an all too familiar phenomenon elsewhere, particularly in South and Central America.

Resistance to change tends to be most successful in so-called 'soft states,' a term first used by Myrdal (1968). A soft state is a country whose government is not capable of instituting radical reform policies or which fails to see to it that such policies are carried out properly and completely. It would seem that the immense problems of a country like India cannot be solved adequately or rapidly, if at all, by such a soft state.

Conclusion

India may be said to be characterized by fragmentary modernization or uneven development. Medical science is highly developed and the country has 120 universities and 4300 other institutions of higher learning. India has several large airlines, an extensive railroad system, numerous modern factories, a large oil-processing industry, a huge merchant marine, several nuclear power plants, labs for nuclear research, an institute for space research, rocket launching installations, and a factory for the production of rockets and parts for satellites. In addition, India has her own multinational corporations, exports sophisticated industrial goods as well as entire prefabricated industrial cities (e.g., to Kuwait and other Gulf states), and provides foreign aid, especially to Nepal and Bangladesh.

In spite of all these attributes of development, India has a weak economic structure and ranks as one of the poorest countries in the world. Per capita GNP in 1981 amounted to $260 – an indication that the economy as a whole is characterized by low levels of productivity. The occupational structure – 70 percent in the primary sector, 12 percent in the secondary sector, and 18 percent in the tertiary sector – is typical of an underdeveloped country.

Notwithstanding extensive irrigation, agricultural reforms and the introduction of HYVs (Green Revolution), average per acre yields for the country as a whole are extremely low. Most Indian farmers are too poor to replace traditional methods of farming with more modern methods. Despite land redistribution programs, most of the farmland is still in the hands of a relatively small group of large landowners. Two-thirds of all farms are smaller than 2 ha (5 acres), while one out of every four rural families has no land at all. Due to the large and growing demand for land, tenure conditions are again almost as unfavorable as they were prior to the land reforms. Agricultural mechanization and population growth cause the number of landless families to increase, while the overabundance of idle manpower keeps rural wages at an extremely low level.

Aside from the fact that the secondary sector employs only 12 percent of the economically active population, it too is characterized by low productivity and low wages. Value added by manufacturing in 1980 amounted to $16 billion, as compared with $437 billion for the US (with only one-third as many inhabitants). Another indication that India has a poorly developed secondary sector is that per capita gross industrial output is about eighty times smaller than that of the US – $54 vs. $4,280 in 1981. An important reason for the low productivity in India is that approximately one-third of all manufacturing takes place in workshops and other relatively primitive, small establishments. The low wages do not particularly encourage investments in expensive, labor-saving equipment. In other words, production in India is less mechanized and less automated, or more labor-intensive, than it is in the US. In the southern state of Tamil Nadu, factories producing matches and fireworks employ 45,000 children, some of whom are less than six years old. This fact may seem surprising in a country where millions of adults are underemployed or unemployed.

In spite of the relative smallness of the secondary sector, India has a large number of big cities – in 1980 there were 36 with more than 500,000 inhabitants each. About 22 percent of the population lives in urban places, most of which are growing at a rapid rate. Since manufacturing does not provide enough employment, most economically active urbanites have found work in the tertiary sector, particularly in the informal portion thereof.

India's weak economic structure becomes apparent further when we consider the size of its foreign trade. Since the US is a large country with a highly diverse economy which produces a very considerable share of what Americans consume, its per capita foreign trade is quite limited – much smaller, for instance, than that of Belgium or Denmark. It is nevertheless about 75 times larger than that of India. India's exports are limited due to the low productivity and output of her primary and secondary sectors; her imports are small because of the very low wages and purchasing power of the vast majority of the population.

Final evidence that India is an underdeveloped country is provided by the following bits of information: life expectancy at birth is 52 years; the infant mortality rate is 12.5 percent; nearly half the people are 15 years old or younger; and only one-third of all adults can read and write. To this we can add that there are at least 5 million 'serfs.' Although servitude is outlawed in India, it frequently happens that very poor people are unable to pay off a loan. Instead of paying back money, they work for their creditor. Because of outrageously high interest rates – up to 10 percent per two weeks – they never manage to pay off their debt, which explains why they are referred to as 'debt serfs.' It sometimes happens that a ten-dollar loan keeps an entire family in servitude for a generation or longer.

India's underdevelopment is not merely the consequence of external domination and dependence. It is true that the country has been a colony for many years, that today there is a significant, albeit not excessive, amount of foreign investment (and profit extraction), and that it has a considerable foreign debt. But it is equally true that India's present underdevelopment is related to the unfavorable political, social and economic conditions that prevailed in pre-colonial times, to the caste system, to the nearly 1000-year-long conflict between Hinduism and Islam, to a host of powerful centrifugal forces (including the conflict between Sikhs and Hindus and various demands for a greater measure of regional autonomy), and to India's present 'soft state' status. The extreme poverty of large segments of India's population is first and foremost a consequence of many centuries of stagnation and ruthless exploitation of the peasant masses by a small and extravagantly rich, urban-based elite which spent practically all its wealth in non-productive ways.

Like development, underdevelopment is too complex a phenomenon or process to be explained by one single theory. This observation becomes clear when it is realized that the causes of underdevelopment differ from country to country. In addition to the interaction of physical and human factors, there is the interplay of endogenous and exogenous factors. In some places or during certain periods, unfavorable endogenous conditions may outweigh the negative effects of exogenous relations; in other places or at other times, exogenous factors may be more harmful than endogenous circumstances. Rarely can the development of underdevelopment be explained fully either in terms of internal or external factors. This case study of India provides sufficient evidence to support this conclusion.

Selected readings

Anderson, P. (1979), The 'Asiatic Mode of Production.' *In:* P. Anderson, *Lineages of the Absolute State*, pp. 462-549. London: Verso.

Asche, H. (1977), Koloniale Siedlungs- und Raumstrukturelle Entwicklung in Indien im 17. und 18. Jahrhundert. *In:* Gesellschaft zur Förderung regionalwissenschaftliche Erkenntnisse. *Studien über die Dritte Welt*, pp. 133-266. Göttingen: Geographische Hochschulmanuskripte.

Bobek, H. (1974), Zum Konzept des Rentenkapitalismus. *Tijdschrift voor Economische en Sociale Geografie* 65, pp. 73-78.

Camps, A. (1977), *De weg, de paden en de wegen. De Christelijke theologie en de concrete godsdiensten.* Baarn: Bosch & Keuning.

De Bruijne, G.A. (1977), India. *In:* G.A. de Bruijne, G.A. Hoekveld & P.L. Ploeger, *Geografische Verkenningen* Vol. 3, pp. 127-236. Bussum: Romen.

Fahrenfort, J.J. (1965), *India/Pakistan.* Meppel: J.A. Boom & Zoon.

Frankel, F. (1971), *India's Green Revolution: Economic Gains and Political Costs.* Princeton, N.J.: Princeton University Press.

Gourou, P. (1966), *The Tropical World – Its Social and Economic Conditions and its Future Status.* London: Longmans.

Habib, I. (1969), Potentialities of Capitalistic Development in the Economy of Mughal India. *Journal of Economic History* 29, pp. 32-79.

Hoetjes, B.J.S., D.H.A. Kolff & D. Kooiman (1980), *India.* Haarlem: Romen.

King, R. (1977), *Land Reform – A World Survey.* London: Bell.

Kleinpenning, J.M.G. (1980), *Drie Maal Derde Wereld.* Assen: Van Gorcum.

Kleinpenning, J.M.G. (1981), *Profiel van de Derde Wereld.* Assen: Van Gorcum.

Lamb, B.P. (1966), *India – A World in Transition.* New York: F.A. Praeger.

Landelijke Werkgroep India (1979-1983), *India Nieuwsbrief.* Utrecht: L.W.I.

Leng, G. (1974), Rentenkapitalismus oder Feudalismus? Kritische Untersuchungen über einen (sozial)geographischen Begriff. *Geographische Zeitschrift* 62, pp. 119-137.

Myrdal, G. (1968), *Asian Drama: An Inquiry into the Poverty of Nations.* New York: Pantheon.

Rothermund, D. (1976), *Grundzüge der Indischen Geschichte.* Darmstadt: Wissenschaftliche Buchgesellschaft.

Schenk, H. (1978), *Bevolkingsontwikkeling en Bevolkingspolitiek in India.* Amsterdam: Planologisch en Demografisch Instituut, University of Amsterdam.

Sen, A. (1982), *The State, Industrialization and Class Formations in India. A Neo-Marxist Perspective on Colonialism, Underdevelopment and Development.* London: Routledge & Kegan Paul.

Streefland, P. (1982), Geloofsovergang en emancipatie in Zuid-Azië. *Internationale Spectator* 36, pp. 142-145.

Van der Bijl, G. (1983), Aangepaste technologie geen wondermiddel voor 'armsten.' *Aspecten* 16, pp. 240-242.

Van der Mark, D.F.W. (1976). *India.* (Landendocumentatie 5). Amsterdam: Koninklijk Instituut voor de Tropen.

Viljoen, S. (1976), *Economische systemen in de wereldgeschiedenis.* (2 vols.). Utrecht: Het Spectrum.

Von Albertini, R. (1982), British India. *In:* R. von Albertini with A. Wirz, *European Colonial Rule, 1880-1940; The Impact of the West on India, Southeast Asia, and Africa*, pp. 3-115. (Translated by J.G. Williamson). Westport, Conn. and London: Greenwood Press.

Wittfogel, K. (1967), *Oriental Despotism. A Comparative Study of Total Power.* New Haven and London: Yale University Press.

World Bank (annual), *World Development Report.* Washington: World Bank.

Chapter 19   Cuba

A. CUBA PRIOR TO THE 1959 REVOLUTION

From Spanish colony to American neo-colony

In 1511, Cuba became part of the Spanish empire. It did not become a particularly profitable colony, however. Epidemics virtually wiped out the Indian population, so that there were no native people who could be exploited. For many years, the island only had strategic significance. The presence of an excellent natural harbor led to the founding of Havana in 1515, which soon became one of Spain's major naval bases in the Western Hemisphere. From Havana, the Spaniards were able to control the entrance to the Gulf of Mexico and protect their interests in Mexico. Until the beginning of the 19th century, it remained the only important urban settlement in Cuba.

After 1763, sugar cane production acquired some significance in the Havana region. As was common in other parts of Latin America, production took place on large estates or *haciendas*. In order to have cheap labor available, slaves were 'imported' from Africa – altogether about one million of them. By 1817, there were more Africans than Europeans living in Cuba.

In addition to sugar, farmers grew coffee and tobacco. In fact, tobacco was once Cuba's leading export crop, and during the entire colonial period it was the most important cash crop for many small white farmers.

The most densely populated areas and most intensive agricultural land uses were concentrated in the western part of the island (the provinces of Pinar del Rio, Havana and Matanzas), which constituted the early economic core area. The rest of Cuba was sparsely populated and remained undeveloped or became used for livestock production on immense ranches or *estancias*, many of which were some 10,000 ha (or about 25,000 acres) in size.

The 19th century witnessed a considerable increase in the production of sugar cane. Owing to the economic opportunities created by this development, Cuba's population reached 1.1 million by 1850.

The Spanish did little to develop the colony. They built hardly any roads, and the few roads that did exist by the end of last century were of poor quality. Agriculture was rather primitive and lacked diversity as half of all cropland was used for growing sugar cane. Living conditions were downright miserable for the majority of the people. As a result of this neglect, Cuba became the scene of increasing political and social unrest, culminating after 1867 in a series of independence struggles. These conflicts seriously disrupted the economy and caused considerable material damage.

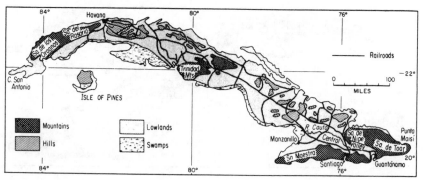

Fig. 33. Cuba, landforms and railroads.
Source: R.C. West & J.P. Augelli, *Middle America: Its Lands and Peoples*, 1966, p. 112.

They also resulted in numerous deaths, especially among poor Blacks, many of whom died in Spanish concentration camps. It was not until 1886 that slavery finally was abolished.

Another rebellion took place in 1898, and for the first time the U.S. showed interest in Cuba. It supported the insurrection and soon found itself fighting a war against Spain.

One reason the U.S. became involved was that it sympathized with Cuba's desire to throw off the Spanish colonial yoke, particularly so because Spain was unable or unwilling to advance Cuba's development. Another reason was that some $40 million worth of American capital was invested in Cuba, mostly in the production of sugar cane.

Since only about one quarter of Cuba consists of mountainous terrain (Figure 33), large parts of the country are well suited to mechanized crop production. Most soils are rather fertile and easy to cultivate, and climatic conditions also favor agricultural development (Figure 34). All parts of the island receive adequate amounts of precipitation (40 inches or more). A relatively dry season (during the Northern Hemisphere winter) greatly facilitates the harvesting of the sugar crop. Finally, the short distances to the coast and the availability of many harbors make Cuba an ideal place for the production of export crops, especially if they can be sold on the large and nearby U.S. market. Considering all these advantages, it is not surprising that Cuba appealed to many American investors.

Even though Cuba did not become an official U.S. colony – but an independent republic (1902) – the U.S. became tremendously influential during the first few decades of the present century. The consequence was that Cuba's independence existed more in theory than in practice. Witness, for example, the following:
– the U.S. helped Cuba draft its constitution;
– Cuba was not free to let its foreign debt become too large;
– Cuba had to continue the health programs started by the U.S. Army during the war;

337

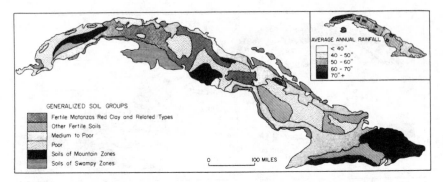

Fig. 34. Cuba, soil groups and rainfall.
Source: R.C. West & J.P. Augelli, *Middle America: Its Lands and Peoples,* 1966, p. 112.

– the U.S. obtained a naval base at Guantanamo Bay (in southeastern Cuba) and Cuba was not entitled to allow similar privileges to other countries;
– the U.S. reserved the right to intervene in Cuba's internal affairs, a situation which lasted until 1934 and which made Cuba into a virtual protectorate of the U.S.; and
– Cuba became increasingly dominated by the U.S., not only economically, but also culturally. This growing dependence became a source of irritation for many Cubans.

The spectacular rise of the sugar economy

Americans quickly came to realize that agriculturally underutilized Cuba was perfectly suited to supply the rapidly expanding U.S. market with cheap sugar. Investments totaling over \$1 billion were poured in, making Cuba the leading exporter of sugar to the U.S. In only two decades, sugar production jumped from 1 million tons to 4 million tons. By 1922, Cuba accounted for about 20 percent of the world's total output. Sugar was not only Cuba's leading crop, but also its number one export.

With the eastward expansion of cane production from Havana and Matanzas into the provinces of Las Villas, Camaguey and Oriente, extensive livestock farming was pushed into areas unfit for large-scale sugar cultivation. In fact, sugar became the dominant crop in all of Cuba except in the marshy areas along the coast, the mountainous areas, and the westernmost part of the island. In the last-mentioned area, heavy precipitation, poor soils and the presence of many small farms combined to preclude the development of cane production.

With American know-how, the entire sugar industry was modernized, e.g., ox-wagons were replaced by narrow-gauge railroads for transporting the cane to the mill. Once the cane is cut, it quickly loses part of its sugar content. Thus, the sooner it can be transported to the mill and processed,

338

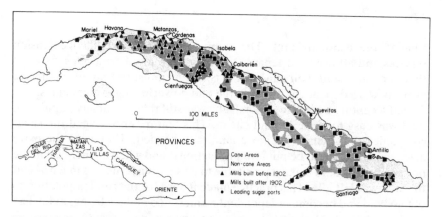

Fig. 35. Cuba, cane areas and sugar mills.
Source: R.C. West & J.P. Augelli, *Middle America: Its Lands and Peoples*, 1966, p. 116.

the more sugar it will yield. Modernization resulted in such large cost reductions that sugar producers in other countries (e.g., Brazil and various Caribbean islands) found it increasingly difficult to compete with Cuba.

Production costs were further lowered by enlarging the scale of the processing operations. Whereas in 1880 the average sugar mill processed about 650 ha (1600 acres) of cane, by 1958 this had gone up to 15,000 ha (38,000 acres). Many small, rather primitive mills (*ingenios*) were replaced by a limited number of large, modern mills (Fig. 35). This development explains why a phenomenal increase in sugar output was accompanied by a decline in the total number of sugar mills. At the same time, the cane-growing *latifundios* and plantations were enlarged, eliminating many of the smaller farms.

The consequence of the scale changes was that more and more economic power became concentrated in relatively few large enterprises. Eventually, 161 sugar mills controlled 2.5 million hectares (6 million acres) of agricultural land, or 22 percent of the entire island! This 'sugar imperium' was largely run by a few giant producers. In 1958, almost half of all cane-producing land belonged to just six companies, which together operated 36 sugar mills. Among the eleven largest companies there were no fewer than eight which were American- or Canadian-owned.

On the eve of the revolution, three-quarters of all sugar mills were Cuban-owned. Most of these mills were considerably smaller than those owned by North American enterprises. They were also less modern and less productive. Nevertheless, it is important to point out that, contrary to what is commonly believed, the sugar economy was not entirely foreign-owned. Far from it. Over half of the total sugar output was controlled by Cuban interests.

In 1958, sugar companies farmed only about two-thirds of the 2.5 million hectares they owned. The remaining 0.8 million ha (2 million acres) were leased to tenants or *colonos*, who were bound by contract to deliver all their

339

cane to the company mill. The companies usually provided extension services and allowed the tenants to borrow money. Farmers who owned their land also sold their cane to the company mills, so that all small cane growers were dependent on the large and powerful sugar companies.

Half a century ago or so, when Cuba was still rather sparsely populated, land was easy to come by and cheap. This feature encouraged the sugar companies to purchase far more land than needed. They kept the extra acreage in reserve, to be put into production if and when an increase in the price of sugar would make it profitable to do so. Sometimes, as much as half the land was left idle. This practice made it hard for the rural population to obtain land and become independent farmers. To make a living, many had no choice but to sell their labor power by becoming agricultural workers. Because the demand for work exceeded the supply, rural wages were low – a circumstance which greatly favored the sugar companies.

Other agricultural activities

Land not devoted to sugar cane production was for the most part used for raising livestock. In 1958, some 40 percent of Cuba consisted of pasture; meat and milk together accounted for one-quarter of the value of all agricultural output.

Livestock farming was carried out almost exclusively by large landowners. Their *haciendas* covered 4 million ha (10 million acres). The quality of the cattle as well as the pastures left much to be desired. Both the non-intensive use of the land and the usually low level of productivity can in part be explained by the fact that raising livestock was seldom the only, or major, activity. Many *hacienda* owners combined it with the production of sugar cane. Moreover, since the more fertile areas were planted to sugar, livestock farming was found in areas where soils were of mediocre fertility or where the land was unfit for growing crops.

Compared to sugar and livestock, other agricultural products were of minor importance. This was true also of tobacco, which accounted for no more than 5 percent of the value of Cuba's exports. Being a labor-intensive crop, tobacco was grown almost entirely on small farms.

Most small farms were only partially commercialized. Production was largely or completely for home consumption. Small subsistence farms were particularly common in a number of mountainous areas, some of which were quite densely populated. The marginal physical conditions, together with the lack of capital and the smallness of the farms, made it impossible for the peasants to grow much more than they needed to feed their often large families. Due to the highly uneven and inequitable distribution of arable land, much potential human labor was wasted, causing widespread poverty among the peasant population. Prior to the 1959 revolution, there was little if any hope that living conditions might get better. On the contrary, growing population densities, soil exhaustion and erosion made the future look increasingly gloomy.

Lack of agricultural diversity

Although Cuba was excellently suited for crop production, in 1958 only about one-quarter of the island was used for growing crops, mostly sugar cane. In fact, the entire economy was based on sugar. This one commodity earned Cuba three times as much foreign exchange as all other exports combined. Very few countries were as dependent on just one product as was Cuba. Altogether, some 2.5 million persons (40 percent of the total population) depended for their livelihood on the production and processing of sugar cane.

Owing to this overdependence on sugar, Cuba's economy was extremely vulnerable. Even a slight drop in the world-market price of sugar could have disastrous consequences. A related problem was that Cuba was unable to produce enough food to feed its own people. In the late 1950s, it had to import 30 percent of its food requirements; these foodstuffs made up 23 percent of total imports.

Social problems

On the eve of the revolution, Cuba was faced with serious social problems, especially in the rural areas. The overwhelming majority of the farms were small (less than 25 ha), and operated by tenants or sharecroppers. Since sharecroppers had to surrender anywhere from 25 to 55 percent of their crop to the landlord, most were barely able to survive. Life was no less precarious for the rural squatters or *precaristas*, that is, farmers who had no title to the land they occupied and cultivated, and from which they could be evicted.

Life was even more problematic for the rural landless. Most of them could find work for only part of the year. In areas where sugar was the dominant crop, there was very little demand for workers outside the busy harvest season (November-December). Elsewhere, employment opportunities were not much better, if at all. For Cuba as a whole, more than half the landless laborers had work for less than four months out of the year. Only 6 percent was employed for at least nine months. About 70 percent of the 810,000 people employed in agriculture were landless laborers, some 470,000 of whom found temporary employment in the sugar sector. These figures are a clear indication that rural life was degraded by massive unemployment and abject poverty.

According to Auroi (1975, p. 37), the rural proletariat spent almost three-quarters of its income on food. Most landless families lived in *bohios* – primitive, windowless huts made of wood, clay and palm leaves. Practically all *bohios* were without electricity or running water. If we add to this that because of inadequate diets most people were malnourished, we can understand why many persons were in bad health. In sharp contrast to post-revolution Cuba, the government did next to nothing to improve rural living conditions or provide educational and health care (including birth control) services.

The miserable living conditions were the major reason that many people migrated to the cities. Since large numbers of migrants could not find permanent work there either, urban centers also displayed the symptoms of underdevelopment. Grinding poverty was all too common, especially in the squatter settlements. Because people had to earn some money somehow, the informal tertiary sector employed a larger percentage of the urban population than in most other Third World countries. Havana, which had developed into the unchallenged economic and politico-administrative primate city, attracted the largest number of migrants. Partly as a result of this in-migration, Greater Havana in 1953 had more than 1.2 million inhabitants, that is, 21 percent of Cuba's total population and about half of its urban population.

Cuba's external dependence

U.S. influence extended beyond the sugar sector. To make possible the spectacular rise in cane production, a host of modern infrastructural improvements had been made, mostly financed by American investors. U.S. interests owned half of all railroads and 90 percent of the public utilities. Mining operations – nickel, manganese, chrome and copper – were also for 90 percent in American hands. As a matter of fact, an unbelievable 18 percent of all U.S. investments in Latin America were concentrated in the little island of Cuba.

The tourist industry, too, was dominated by the U.S. Not only did Americans own many hotels, casinos, nightclubs and other facilities, but most of the tourists themselves were Americans. Before the fall of the Batista regime, the tourist industry earned Cuba around $100 million a year. At the same time, it provided many Cubans with jobs, most of which would not have been available had it not been for U.S. investments.

Cuba's foreign trade formed another unmistakable indication of the island's close ties with the American economy; three-quarters of its imports came from the U.S. and an even larger percentage of its exports had the U.S. as their destination. The latter consisted for nearly 100 percent of primary products: agricultural commodities and some minerals. About 65 percent of Cuba's massive sugar exports were marketed in the U.S.

The import of American (industrial) goods plus the American-dominated tourist industry tended to make life in Cuba relatively expensive. Many wealthy Cubans had adopted an American lifestyle, spending a large portion of their income on luxury goods, all of which had to be imported. Thus, much of Cuba's hard-earned foreign exchange was spent rather wastefully on expensive consumer goods. Equally harmful was that wealthy Cubans often preferred to invest abroad, e.g., in the U.S., rather than in their own capital-poor country. All in all, very little Cuban capital was invested in the island's economy and most of the profit made by foreign enterprises left the country. Around 1958, there were no signs that the economy would fare better in the coming years.

342

Industrialization and underdevelopment

As we have already seen, the sugar industry did not provide much permanent employment and neither did the large cattle ranches. In the industrial sector, too, demand for labor was very limited. There simply was not much industry due to lack of capital, technological know-how and purchasing power. For the most part, it was not refined sugar that was exported to the U.S., but raw sugar; candy and similar products were subsequently exported by the U.S. to Cuba.

One reason for Cuba's low level of industrialization was its proximity to the highly industrialized U.S. Another was the preferential treatment it received from the U.S. concerning the export of sugar. A trade agreement between the two countries allowed Cuba to sell its sugar on the American market for a price well above that on the international market, sometimes more than 50 percent higher. This agreement obviously worked to Cuba's advantage. As part of the same deal, Cuba was obliged to reciprocate favors by giving preferential treatment to the U.S. with regard to the import of mostly manufactured goods. Artificially low import duties on American products meant that nearly 600 U.S.-made goods – together accounting for more than 80 percent of all U.S. exports to Cuba – could effectively compete on the Cuban market with similar products made in Cuba. It goes without saying that this arrangement seriously thwarted industrial development.

There was not much Cuba could do to change this situation. If it raised the duties on American imports, the U.S. would in all likelihood retaliate, e.g., by cutting back its imports of Cuban sugar. Since the relationship between the two countries was a highly unequal one – with Cuba being far more dependent on the U.S. than *vice versa* – Cuba was in an extremely weak bargaining position. Stated differently: it was next to impossible for Cuba to free itself from the U.S.-controlled neo-colonial stranglehold.

Additional aspects of underdevelopment

Before the revolution, Cuba was beset with several serious problems: (1) economic stagnation, (2) a dangerously one-sided or unbalanced economic structure, (3) a high measure of external dependence (or foreign domination), (4) massive unemployment both in rural and urban areas, and (5) extreme disparities in material well-being. To complicate matters further, Cuba's population was growing at the relatively rapid rate of about 2 percent per year.

Looking at these problems, we can hardly be surprised that there were occasional outbursts of dissatisfaction and despair. Social and political unrest, however, were not tolerated. Personal freedom, justice and human rights hardly existed; democracy was unknown. Political agitators and other suspected individuals were customarily imprisoned or even eliminated. The authoritarian regime was backed by a well-trained army. Corruption was endemic. During the 1950s, the situation became steadily more oppressive, and under Batista at least 20,000 people were put to death. Predictably, opposition grew, not only among working-class people but also among those belonging to the small middle class. Even members of the powerful elite became critical of the repression-minded government. This growing dissatisfaction eventually enabled Fidel Castro and his partisans to overthrow the Batista regime and form a new government.

The 1511-1959 period in review

Summarizing the preceding sections, we conclude that Cuba's under-development in the 1950s was the outcome of four centuries of one-sided, colonial exploitation followed by sixty years of equally one-sided neo-colonial exploitation.

Both before and after 1900, a small and selfish minority enriched itself at the expense of the rest of the people. The large majority was impoverished , had no political power, and was given no opportunity to enjoy a reasonable standard of living. The colonial era witnessed the rise of an oligarchic elite made up of slave dealers, sugar barons, ranchers and other large land-owners who looked down on manual labor. After 1900, the elite became somewhat more diversified as trade, tourism and other tertiary activities enabled a number of Cubans to amass considerable wealth. Some in-dustrialists also managed to join the ranks of 'the fortunate few.'

Many members of the elite used – or misused – their politico-administra-tive influence to enhance their position even further, thereby often resort-ing to blatantly corruptive practices. By 1950, Cuba's economic elite also controlled the political scene, and the country as a whole was totally dependent on the U.S., being subjugated to, and exploited by, American economic interests.

B. CUBA AFTER THE 1959 REVOLUTION

Land reforms

Many of Cuba's social and economic problems were direct consequences of the highly uneven distribution of agricultural land among the farming population. Because most of the land was in the hands of large private owners and companies, there were, relatively speaking, too many small farmers, sharecroppers and landless workers. Realizing this, one of the first measures taken by the Castro regime was to implement a wide-ranging land redistribution program. The following list contains the major points of the program:

1) Agricultural laborers were entitled to two *caballerias* (27 ha or 67 acres), which was considered the minimum amount of land necessary for a viable farm. The land, which was handed out free, could not be sold or subdivided.

2) Tenants with less than five *caballerias* were to receive two *caballerias* free of charge and were allowed to buy the rest.

344

3) No one could own more than five *caballerias* (166 acres). As a result, all medium and large privately owned farms disappeared.

4) Large landholdings did not necessarily have to be subdivided into smaller units. If it was economically advantageous to keep them intact, units larger than 166 acres could be maintained. However, they could no longer be privately owned.

5) Foreigners were not allowed to own land.

Dispossession of holdings took place so fast that only one year after the first land reforms were introduced, there were no large privately owned landholdings left. Some were split up into small farms. Many others were transformed into cooperative farms or 'public farms' *(granjas del pueblo)*, but since neither of these two farm types was considered a success, they were subsequently changed into state farms *(granjas estatales)*. By 1966, there were already 574 state farms, averaging 7,629 ha (18,844 acres) in size. Like the Russian state farms, after which they have been modeled, they are subjected to rigid central planning and employ wage earners to do the work.

Large sugar estates and livestock ranches, in particular, were transformed into state farms. This way, the economic advantages of large-scale production were maintained. This was of utmost importance because sugar was (and still is) Cuba's leading earner of foreign exchange, while the production of meat, milk and other animal products is essential for supplying the domestic market. In 1966, state farms occupied 58 percent of all agriculturally productive land, and of the total acreage planted to sugar cane, some 75 percent was found on state farms.

One consequence of the land reforms is that now the overwhelming majority of the rural people are landless laborers employed by the state. This situation has come about despite efforts to raise the number of privately owned family farms. Indeed, during the first seven years after the revolution, their number increased from 143,000 to 218,000. By 1966, however, so much land was in state farms that not enough was left to continue this trend, let alone give every rural family its own farm, as Castro had promised. After 1966, the government took measures to expand the state farms by eliminating some of the smaller private farms. Small farmers were encouraged to sell most of their land to the state, keeping only a small plot for subsistence purposes. Especially in the vicinity of the larger cities, where the government wanted to intensify agriculture, a certain amount of pressure was used to have farmers contribute to this process of structural change.

Although the government's efforts have not been overly successful, the number of private farms has declined: from 218,000 in 1966 to approximately 180,000 in 1975. These 180,000 farms produced a relatively large share of Cuba's total agricultural output: 21 percent of the sugar, 26 percent of the livestock, 47 percent of the fruit, 74 percent of the coffee, and 82 percent of the tobacco. But the number of private farms keeps declining. By 1983, private smallholdings numbered no more than about 35,000, and in a few decades there may not be any left. According to the 1963 land reform, farms cannot be inherited. When a farmer dies, all the land automatically becomes state property, so that eventually all farmland will belong to the state. This trend is paralleled by a shift in the employment structure. While the state sector expands, the private sector loses ground. Between 1962 and 1977, the number of people employed in the private sector decreased from 740,000 to 182,000, that is, to less than 7 percent of total employment.

The drive toward increased sugar production

In the early 1960s, the Castro regime was determined to diversify the agricultural sector. To accomplish this, production of food crops (especially rice) and industrial crops (e.g., cotton) was promoted. The campaign, however, did not last long because it led to an alarming drop in sugar output, which threatened Cuba's balance of trade.

It is important at this point to mention that in 1960 the export of Cuban sugar to the U.S. had experienced a dramatic decline. A rapid succession of events caused U.S.-Cuban relations to deteriorate to the point of outright hostility. Following the breaking off of diplomatic relations by the U.S. in 1960, there was the infamous Bay of Pigs invasion of Cuba and the nationalization by Cuba of all U.S.-owned sugar refineries in 1961. The following year was marked by the Cuban missile crisis and the decision by the U.S. to put up an economic blockade against Cuba. Exports of Cuban sugar to the U.S. as well as imports of manufactured goods from the U.S. came to a halt. Since most Western countries were unwilling to increase their trade with Cuba, lest they antagonize the U.S., Cuba could only turn to the Soviet bloc. For the modernization of its economy, Cuba desperately needed to import capital goods and the only way it could pay for these imports was to export large quantities of sugar to the USSR and Eastern Europe.

Meanwhile, largely because of the decline in Cuba's sugar output, the world price of sugar had risen, making cane growing more profitable than it had been a few years earlier. The result was that Cuba in 1963 decided to discontinue its drive toward agricultural diversification and replace it by one aimed at maximizing the production of sugar.

This change in agricultural policy was recommended by the Soviet Union. The Soviets not only questioned the wisdom of the diversification plans, but also had little confidence in Cuba's intentions to stimulate industrial development. They offered Cuba seemingly favorable trade conditions as far as the export of sugar was concerned, such as guaranteed purchases at prices higher than those paid on the international market. And in the event the world market price would go up significantly, the Soviets would pay a higher price. This agreement was anything but disadvantageous to the USSR because Cuban sugar was substantially cheaper than

Soviet-produced beet sugar. It also enabled the Soviets to take precious agricultural land out of sugar beet production and devote it to raising other crops. Considering these advantages, it is hardly surprising that the Soviet Union recommended that Cuba expand its sugar production. In exchange for their sugar, the Cubans could obtain relatively cheaply imports from the USSR. Although this trade agreement is often described as favorable to Cuba, it is interesting to point out that it is remarkably similar to the earlier U.S.-Cuban trade relationship, which has often been denounced as neocolonial, imperialistic and exploitative.

As part of their agreement with Cuba, the Soviets promised to supply specially designed harvesting machines. Cuba was most interested in these implements due to the growing shortage of experienced cane cutters and the declining output per cutter. Cuba's leaders much preferred importing these machines than having to attract guest-workers from Haiti or the Dominican Republic.

In 1965, Cuba produced 6.2 million tons of sugar, or about 60 percent more than in 1963 (see Table 6). Mechanization of the sugar harvest, however, turned out to be a disappointing experience. Some 1,000 Soviet harvesting machines were received, but they could only cut cane that stood up more or less straight, were too heavy to be used on certain soils, and were too bulky for use on somewhat rough terrain. Moreover, they consumed a great deal of fuel, were difficult to operate, and could seldom be repaired in the fields. Many of them soon were no longer operational. Towards the end of the 1960s, a few hundred lighter and better mechanized harvesters were imported from Australia to replace the abandoned Soviet machines. Today, Cuba builds its own cane harvesters.

The purchase of Soviet and Australian machinery meant that Cuba urgently needed to increase its foreign exchange earnings. Faced with this challenge, the government decided to expand the production of sugar even more so as to be able to sell also to countries not belonging to the Soviet bloc. Before long, the Castro regime was aiming for an output of 10 million tons by 1970. So much emphasis was placed on reaching this goal – especially by Fidel Castro himself – that the matter became a national prestige issue. In public speeches, newspaper articles and radio messages, the entire Cuban population was repeatedly urged to do its utmost to contribute to the realization of the plan. The people were told that it was a matter of life or death for the economy, and, allegedly, Castro declared that he would resign if the 1970 harvest would fall short of the 10-million-ton goal.

Calculations showed that it was practically impossible to produce that much. It would require a $720 million investment – an amount that exceeded the value of the entire sugar industry! However, criticisms were brushed aside as anti-socialist propaganda and the Castro regime went ahead with its ill-conceived plan. It invested an outrageously large share of the national income in the, at best moderately profitable, sugar sector.

Table 6. Cuba's sugar production, 1950-1982 (in millions of tons).

1950	5.4	1960	5.9	1970	8.5	1980	6.8
1951	5.6	1961	6.1	1971	5.9	1981	7.3
1952	7.2	1962	4.8	1972	4.3	1982	8.2
1953	5.0	1963	3.8	1973	5.3		
1954	4.8	1964	4.4	1974	5.9		
1955	4.4	1965	6.2	1975	6.3		
1956	4.6	1966	4.5	1976	6.2		
1957	5.8	1967	6.1	1977	6.5		
1958	5.8	1968	5.1	1978	7.4		
1959	6.0	1969	4.5	1979	8.0		

Source: The Cuban Economy: A Statistical Review. National Foreign Assessment Center, Washington, D.C., 1981, table 2, p. 3; various other sources.

Much land was cleared for crop production, irrigation schemes were expanded and improved, cane with a high sugar content was introduced, and different cane varieties were planted in an attempt to lengthen the harvest season so as to allow more efficient use of expensive harvesting and processing equipment. Considerable attention was paid to weed control and the eradication of plant diseases and pests. More fertilizer was used than ever before and the number of tractors was greatly increased. New state farms were created, causing a further *de*diversification of agriculture.

At the same time, campaigns were organized in an effort to rally the people and motivate them to lend their sympathy and support to the common cause. All available manpower and womanpower was mobilized in a highly regimented but well-disciplined manner, giving the entire operation a military-like character.

As the 1970 harvest season approached, it became increasingly clear that the 10 million ton goal would not be realized. As it turned out, production fell short by 1.5 million tons, which was still a major accomplishment considering it was by far the largest harvest on record (see Table 6). On the other hand, the results were artificially inflated. In a desperate attempt to come as close as possible to the planned objective, part of the 1969 crop was not harvested until 1970, while some fields with young plants were harvested a year too soon. This last-mentioned fact helps explain that in 1971 production dropped to 5.9 million tons.

Looking back at this episode in Cuban agriculture, one can only conclude that enormous sums of money and immense human resources were wasted on an unrealistically ambitious and economically unsound plan. What is more, other sectors of the economy were severely weakened in the process. Several branches of agricultural and industrial production stagnated or even declined. Education came to a near-standstill. Ensuing shortages – even sugar was rationed – caused a great deal of hardship and irritation among the Cuban people. Popular support for the regime reached its lowest level since the revolution.

The sugar debacle notwithstanding, agricultural policies were not fundamentally changed. The export of sugar, it was decided, would continue to

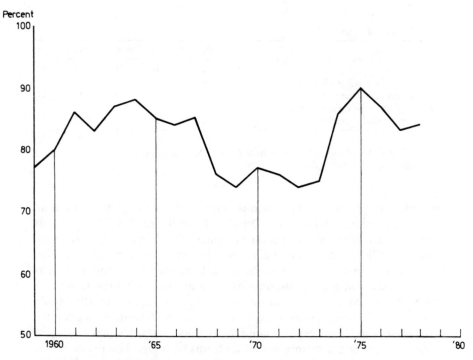

Fig. 36. Cuba, sugar exports as percent of total export value, 1959-1978.
Source: National Foreign Assessment Center (U.S.), *The Cuban Economy: A Statistical Review*, 1981, p. 30.

serve as the foundation for future economic development. This decision was partly based on the fact that the world-market price was relatively high and rising during the early 1970s. A more important factor, however, was that there were no alternative strategies available that could offer short-term solutions to Cuba's economic problems.

Once Cuba's leaders had committed themselves to giving continued priority to the export of sugar to the Soviet-bloc countries, they also decided (in 1972) that Cuba, as the first non-Eurasian state, should join COMECON – the East-bloc's Commission for Economic Cooperation, also known as CMEA (Council for Mutual Economic Assistance).

It seems worth mentioning that eventually the Soviets were successful in designing mechanical sugar cane harvesters that performed satisfactorily. In 1977, an assembly plant for these harvesting machines was built in Holguín, Cuba. Although the harvesters cut an average of 100 tons of cane a day and have replaced some 400,000 workers, it is not clear whether the number of jobless persons has increased as a result of this development. Whereas in 1971 only 1 percent of Cuba's sugar cane was harvested mechanically, by 1980 it had reached nearly 50 percent.

Since 1972, Cuba's production of sugar has grown steadily (Table 6) and in 1979 its share of the total world production amounted to more than 25

349

Table 7. Cuba's foreign trade relations, 1974-1978.

	1974	1975	1976	1977	1978
Percentage of foreign trade with USSR	41	48	53	62	69
Percentage of foreign trade with other communist countries	18	11	13	13	13
Percentage of foreign trade with non-communist countries	41	41	34	25	18
	100	100	100	100	100

Source: The Cuban Economy: A Statistical Review. National Foreign Assessment Center, Washington, D.C., 1981, p. 24.

percent. This greater production was in no small measure the result of an increase in yields, from about 45 tons per ha in the early 1970s to 55 tons during the late 1970s. With an annual output of 8 million tons, Cuba can sell about 2.5 million tons outside the Soviet bloc and thus earn 'extra' foreign currency. However, since the world-market price tends to drop as soon as Cuba's production goes up, future sugar sales are not likely to make it into a prosperous country or, for that matter, allow it to enjoy a positive trade balance. On the contrary, a comparison of recent changes in the sugar price with changes in the prices of manufactured goods reveals that Cuba has suffered a growing deterioration of its terms of trade. The result is that today Cuba must export much more sugar than a decade ago in order to be able to purchase the same amount of imports.

An additional disadvantage is that the Russian ruble is not a hard currency. As there is little demand for rubles on the international money market, they can only be converted into other hard currencies at a very low exchange rate. This means, in effect, that rubles can only be used to pay for goods imported from COMECON countries.

All in all, Cuba's economic relations with the East bloc are less advantageous than is often maintained. Cuba is not only highly dependent on the USSR, it is also a victim of unequal exchange – just as it was prior to the revolution. The Cuban leaders appear to be well aware of this dilemma, but unfortunately there is very little they can do about it. To make matters worse, Cuba's current economy depends more heavily on just one product, i.e., sugar, than it did 25 years ago. In recent years, sugar was reponsible for about 85 percent of Cuba's total export value – up from 80 percent in 1958 (Fig. 36). But that is not all. As Table 7 shows, Cuba's foreign trade has become increasingly dominated by one trade partner, viz., the USSR.

Additional changes in the rural areas
Cuba may not have been very successful in diversifying its agriculture, but it *has* managed to intensify it. Productivity has increased. Livestock production has been modernized through the use of better animal breeds, artificial insemination, and pasture improvement. In spite of these developments, Cuba continues to be an importer of agricultural products and live

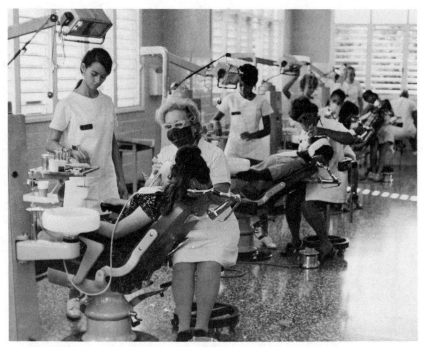

43. Dental clinic in Havana. Health care is free in socialist Cuba. (VDO)

animals. Many foodstuffs, including bread and other staples, remain rationed.

Particularly important are the various social changes that have taken place. Workers receive higher wages and enjoy drastically improved living conditions. The quality of education and health care is much higher than in almost any other Third World country. Housing, too, has improved a great deal. Between 1960 and 1976, 335 new rural settlements were built, which together house 135,000 people. Most of them contain apartment complexes, administration buildings, a party office, several stores, a cafe, a day center, a school, a medical center, a social center and often also a movie theater and a swimming pool. Many tenants have become landowners, while numerous small farmers now own more land than they used to.

By far the most remarkable achievements have been in education and health care, both in the rural areas and the cities. Since education is free, even the poorest families are able to send their children to school. Although 25 years ago only half of Cuba's rural population could read and write, today Cuba has a very high literacy rate (see Table 8). In 1964, $10 million was spent on health care, as compared to $0.5 million in 1958. Medical services also are free, which explains the generally excellent health conditions that Cubans enjoy. More generally, Table 8 clearly illustrates that on

Table 8. Quality of life indicators for Cuba and seven selected countries (values in parentheses are rank order indications).

	Cuba	Argentina	Brazil	India	Jamaica	Mexico	Philippines	U.S.A.
Adult literacy rate (ca. 1977)	96 (2)	93 (3)	76 (6)	36 (8)	90 (4)	81 (5)	75 (7)	99 (1)
Secondary school enrollment as % of age group (ca. 1979)	71 (2)	56 (5)	32 (7)	27 (8)	58 (4)	45 (6)	63 (3)	97 (1)
Population per physician (ca. 1977)	1100 (3)	530 (1)	1700 (5)	3630 (8)	3520 (7)	1260 (4)	2810 (6)	580 (2)
Daily per capita calorie supply as % of requirement (1977)	118 (4)	126 (2)	107 (7)	91 (8)	119 (3)	114 (5)	108 (6)	135 (1)
Daily per capita protein intake in grams (ca. 1977)	70 (3)	99 (2)	64 (5)	53 (7)	56 (6)	65 (4)	45 (8)	103 (1)
Life expectancy at birth (1980)	73 (2)	70 (4)	63 (7)	52 (8)	71 (3)	65 (5)	64 (6)	74 (1)
Infant mortality rate (1980)	21 (3)	45 (4)	77 (7)	123 (8)	16 (2)	56 (6)	55 (5)	13 (1)
Crude death rate (1980)	6 (1/2)	8 (5)	9 (6/7)	14 (8)	6 (1/2)	7 (3/4)	7 (3/4)	9 (6/7)
Crude birth rate (1980)	18 (2)	21 (3)	30 (5)	36 (7)	29 (4)	37 (8)	34 (6)	16 (1)
Percentage of labor force in agriculture (1980)	23 (4)	13 (2)	30 (5)	69 (8)	21 (3)	36 (6)	46 (7)	2 (1)
Energy consumption per capita (kg. of coal equivalent) (1979)	1358 (4)	1965 (2)	1018 (6)	194 (8)	1326 (5)	1535 (3)	329 (7)	11681 (1)
Sum of ranks	30.5	33	66.5	86	42.5	55.5	64.5	17.5
Average rank	3	3	6	8	4	5	6	2

Sources: World Development Report 1981 and 1982 (World Bank), The Cuban Economy: A Statistical Review, National Foreign Assessment Center, Washington, D.C., 1981.

352

Table 9. Estimated income distribution for Cuba and seven selected countries.

Countries	Year	Lowest 20 percent	2nd quintile	3rd quintile	4th quintile	Highest 20 percent
Cuba*	1973	7.8	12.5	19.2	25.5	35.0
Cuba*	1953	2.1	4.1	11.0	22.8	60.0
Argentinia	1970	4.4	9.7	14.1	21.5	50.3
Brazil	1972	2.0	5.0	9.4	17.0	66.6
Costa Rica	1971	3.3	8.7	13.3	19.9	54.8
India	1975	7.0	9.2	13.9	20.5	49.4
Mexico	1977	2.9	7.0	12.0	20.4	57.7
Philippines	1971	5.2	9.0	12.8	19.0	54.0
U.S.A.	1972	4.5	10.7	17.3	24.7	42.8

* In the case of Cuba, pre-revolution and post-revolution data are given as a rough indicator of income redistribution carried out by the Castro regime.

Sources: World Development Report 1981 and 1982 (World Bank), The Cuban Economy: A Statistical Review. National Foreign Assessment Center, Washington, D.C., 1981.

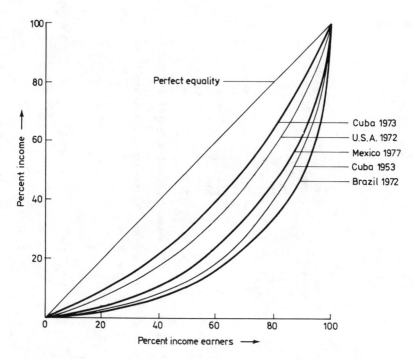

Fig. 37. Comparison of estimated income distribution in Cuba (1953 and 1973) with that in three selected countries.

Note: For an explanation of the use of Lorenz curves for depicting inequality, consult Fig. 42 and the accompanying discussion on pages 374-376.

Source: National Foreign Assessment Center (U.S.), *The Cuban Economy: A Statistical Review*, 1981, p. 51.

numerous variables Cuba compares favorably with most other Third World countries and that in some respects it resembles the rich countries more than it does the poor ones.

In 1977, the average Cuban took in 118 percent of the minimum daily calorie requirement. Because socioeconomic disparities have declined greatly since the 1950s and now are smaller than in most countries (see Table 9 and Figure 37), this value is a fairly accurate indication that the Cuban people are well fed. It is unfortunate that the same cannot be said of most other underdeveloped countries.

In spite of the replacement of many agricultural workers by modern machines, there appears to be relatively little unemployment in Cuba. The massive exodus of people who disapproved of the Castro regime has obviously had a favorable effect on the labor situation. More important, it would seem, are the many government-initiated projects that have been launched since 1959. The building of the planned rural settlements, the intensification of agriculture, and also the expansion of educational and medical facilities have created numerous new jobs. At the same time, many people have found work in Cuba's extensive administrative system or in its equally large security forces – the police and the military. Finally, tens of thousands of Cubans work in other Third World countries.[1]

If we add to above-mentioned improvements that Cubans pay very little rent, we must conclude that during the past 25 years material living conditions have been elevated greatly for the large majority of the Cuban population.

Industrial development and the cities

Shortly after the revolution, all industry was nationalized. At first, the new government took steps to stimulate industrial development. The Soviet industrialization model was adopted, giving special attention to basic industries. Soon, however, the drive toward industrialization was slowed down, and priority was given to raising the production of sugar and to developing the rural areas. This shift in policy was understandable because (1) as a highly agricultural country, most of Cuba's socioeconomic problems were found in the rural areas, (2) with a population of only 7 million in 1960, most of whom were poor, domestic demand for manufactured goods was limited, and (3) experiences with import-substitution industrialization elsewhere in Latin America had for the most part been disappointing.

Cuba's choice to emphasize agricultural and rural development did not mean that industrialization was completely neglected. But, it did mean that attention was focused on those industries which could have favorable effects on the rural areas. For example, large sums of money were devoted to the modernization of the sugar mills. Also the processing of other agricultural and non-agricultural primary products received considerable attention, as did the production of energy.

A large share of the new industries was located in small and medium-sized cities, rather than in Havana. In an effort to spread economic development evenly throughout the country, special treatment was given to Oriente province. As a consequence, urban growth has been more rapid there than in the rest of the country (Gugler 1980, p. 524).

The chief objective of the decentralization policy was to weaken Havana's economic dominance and slow down its growth. Cuba's only metropolis was deliberately neglected during the 1960s, and for a number of years its population declined. Since 1970, however, Havana has again experienced some growth, not in the last place because of the important advantages it has in attracting industries. In addition to being the capital, Havana has a large port, a comparatively well-developed infrastructure, a large pool of skilled labor, and considerable market potential. Like capital-

[1] The Cuban constitution guarantees work for everyone, so technically there is no unemployment. Although Cuba usually denies that there are people without work, according to a 1984-article in the party paper *Granma,* there were 122,000 jobless in 1981. Indications are that the number has increased since then.

ist countries, socialist Cuba cannot ignore the basic 'laws' of economic geography. Even though Havana's primacy has become less pronounced – a smaller proportion of Cuba's urban population lives in Havana now than 25 years ago – it remains the country's leading industrial center. Ignoring sugar processing, some 70 percent of all industrial activity is concentrated in the Havana conurbation.

Conclusion

While Cuba can boast impressive achievements since 1959, there have also been numerous disappointments. In an attempt to make up the balance, we separately list the major accomplishments and shortcomings of the post-revolution developments.

On the credit side of the balance we find the following:

1. Wages have increased, especially in the rural areas.
2. Unemployment has largely been eliminated.
3. Grinding poverty and hunger belong to the past; the average Cuban enjoys a much higher standard of material well-being than a generation ago.
4. Education and health care services have been greatly expanded and improved. The same is true of other welfare services, such as social security and care for the elderly. Since many social services are free, every citizen can enjoy them. Besides, the free services and low rents have reduced the cost of living, especially for large families.
5. Cuba is characterized by a high measure of social justice; the stark income disparities that scarred Cuban society prior to the revolution, no longer exist.
6. Levels of productivity have been raised.
7. The economy has become more diversified; in addition to building agricultural machinery, Cuba designs its own sugar mills, and exports computerized control systems for processing sugar.
8. An ever growing percentage of the working population is employed in the secondary and tertiary sectors of the economy. Employment in agriculture has dropped from about 45 percent in the 1950s to approximately 25 percent in the late 1970s.
9. Cuba's economy is no longer dominated by massive foreign investments and the country is no longer exploited by foreign-based multinational corporations. So, depending on one's definition of underdevelopment, one could conclude that Cuba is much less underdeveloped than it was when Batista was still in power.

On the debit side of the balance, we list the following:

1. Although land reforms have resulted in a temporary increase in privately owned family farms, their number is limited and declining.
2. Economic performance is hampered by centralized planning and bureaucratic red tape, as well as by the American trade embargo.

356

3. The heavy emphasis on sugar production keeps the economy highly one-sided. This specialization means that Cuba can only function within the framework of an international division of labor. As long as Cuba's economy remains based on the export of primary goods, it will suffer from unequal exchange and deteriorating terms of trade.

4. Cuba's trade dependence on the USSR is no smaller than was its former trade dependence on the U.S. Having joined COMECON, it is unlikely that this situation will improve in the near future.

5. Massive loans and grants have made Cuba totally dependent on the Soviet bloc as far as finances are concerned. Between 1960 and 1975, about half of all Soviet foreign aid went to Cuba. According to some sources, Cuba presently receives some $2.5 million in aid *per day*. Others estimate that the Soviet Union pours as much as $8 million a day into Cuba (e.g., *Newsweek,* June 28, 1982, p. 60). However this may be, it is clear that Soviet influence has penetrated every sector of the Cuban economy.

6. Few countries have a larger per capita foreign debt than Cuba. Several years ago its total foreign debt was estimated at $6 billion – an enormous amount for a country with only 10 million inhabitants.

7. Since many of Cuba's social and economic achievements have been financed by the USSR, they may be said to be highly artificial; they are likely to disappear the minute the Soviets discontinue their support.

8. Politically and militarily Cuba is also dependent on the Soviet-dominated East bloc.

9. Extreme wealth and extreme poverty may have been eradicated, but Cuba is anything but an egalitarian society. High-ranking officials, top managers and specialists earn about five times more than minimum-wage earners. Members of the new elite, furthermore, enjoy special privileges – only they can purchase certain luxury goods.

10. Because fresh meat, fruit, vegetables, and various other foodstuffs often are in short supply, rationing is used to ensure fair distribution. Even so, long lines of waiting people are all too common. Due to the shortages and rations, Cubans often complain that they cannot do much with their hard-earned money, just as they complain about the low quality of many goods, poor service in restaurants, housing shortages, and the poor quality of public transportation. (These problems go a long way in explaining why approximately 1 million people have left Cuba since 1959. This exodus had its advantages and disadvantages. On the one hand, Cuba got rid of people who were opposed to the new regime – including Castro's sister Juanita – and the out-migration has also helped to alleviate the unemployment problem. On the other hand, the economy was dealt a severe blow by the loss of thousands of skilled people.)

11. The Cubans have paid dearly for the gains in material well-being. Although Castro had promised democracy and respect for human

rights, Cuba is without political freedom, without a free press, and has only one political party. There are alleged to be thousands of political prisoners, and open dissent is virtually impossible on account of the presence of an extensive security apparatus. To this we can add that the Cuban people are exposed to a great deal of propaganda and political indoctrination, especially in the schools.

12. The aid which Cuba gives to other underdeveloped countries and to liberation movements (e.g., in Africa) places such a heavy burden on its economy that it makes the country extra dependent on Soviet support.

Considering the above, we conclude that Cuba has made great strides in improving internal social conditions. As far as that goes, we are hard put to continue referring to Cuba as an underdeveloped country. Economic conditions, by contrast, have not progressed nearly as much. Economically and commercially, Cuba is as dependent as it was before the 1959-revolution. Its exports have become rather more than less one-sided. Politically and militarily, too, Cuba occupies an unmistakably peripheral position *vis-à-vis* the Soviet core.

Comparing Cuba's development with that of Taiwan (see next chapter), it becomes apparent that the Caribbean island-state has not fared as well as its Asian counterpart.

Selected readings

Acselrad, H. (1979), L'économie cubaine des années soixante-dix. *Problèmes d'Amérique Latine,* number LIII (October 31, 1979), pp. 7-30.

Auroi, C. (1975), *La nouvelle agriculture cubaine.* Paris: Editions Anthropos.

Barkin, D. (1979), La transformación del espacio en Cuba post-revolucionaria. *Boletín de Estudios Latinoamericanos y del Caribe,* 27, pp. 77-97.

Blume, H. (1968), Agrarlandschaft und Agrarreform in Kuba. *Geographische Zeitschrift,* 56, pp. 1-18.

Boekraad, E. (1978), Cuba's weg naar een evenwichtige ruimtelijke struktuur. *Zone,* 8, pp. 92-105.

Constantini, O. (1981), Eindrücke einer Kubareise. *Zeitschrift für Wirtschaftsgeographie,* 25, pp. 177-181.

Graham, E, with I. Floering (1984), *The Modern Plantation in the Third World.* London and Sydney: Croom Helm.

Gugler, J. (1980), A Minimum of Urbanism and a Maximum of Ruralism. The Cuban Experience. *International Journal of Urban and Regional Research,* 4, pp. 516-536.

Hall, D. R. (1981), External Relations and Current Development Patterns in Cuba. *Geography,* 66, pp. 237-241.

Hall, D. R. (1981). Town and Country Planning in Cuba. *Town and Country Planning,* 50, pp. 81-84.

James, P. E. (1950 and 1969), *Latin America.* New York: The Odyssey Press.

King, R. (1977), *Land Reform. A World Survey.* London: Bell.

Kruijer, G. J. (1968), *Cuba, voorbeeld en uitdaging.* Amsterdam: Van Gennep.

Kruijer, G. J. (1970), Cuba. Het mobilisatiesysteem als nieuwe maatschappijvorm. *Intermediair,* 6 (33), pp. 1, 3, 5 and 7.

Kruijer, G. J. (1970), Crisis in Cuba. Op weg naar democratisering? *Intermediair,* 6 (46), pp. 1, 3, 5, 7 and 9.

Kurian, G. T. (1979), *Encyclopedia of the Third World.* London: Mansell.

Lamore, J. (1970), *Cuba.* Que Sais-Je? nr. 1395. Paris: Presses Universitaires de France.

National Foreign Assessment Center (1981), *The Cuban Economy: A Statistical Review.* Washington, D.C.: N.F.A.C.

Nelson, L. (1970). *Rural Cuba.* New York: Octagon Books.

Newsweek (1982), June 28.

Poncet, J. (1976), Les transformations de l'espace de Cuba et la nouvelle géographie administrative. *L'Espace Géographique,* 4, pp. 255-262.

Van Ginneken, J. (1979), Cuba en de suiker. De oude en de nieuwe afhankelijkheid. *Intermediair,* 15 (50), pp. 27, 29, 31 and 33.

West, R. C. & J. P. Augelli (1966), *Middle America. Its Lands and Peoples.* Englewood Cliffs, N.J.: Prentice Hall.

World Bank (annual), *World Development Report.* Washington, D.C.: World Bank.

Chapter 20 Taiwan

A. DEVELOPMENTS PRIOR TO 1895

The physical setting

Taiwan is a relatively small island located some 200 kilometers off the coast of southeastern China.*

A west-to-east cross section through the island displays a 45-km wide coastal plain in the west, gradually increasing elevations toward the east, and three parallel mountain ranges running north-south over the entire length of the island (Fig. 38). The eastern side of Taiwan is dominated by steep slopes and a very narrow coastal plain. The mountainous character of much of the island explains why over half of it is still forested and virtually uninhabited. Since Taiwan's humid subtropical climate is well suited to agriculture, nearly the entire western coastal plain is capable of supporting intensive crop production.

Formosa as a colony

Early in the 17th century, the Portuguese, Spanish and Dutch showed interest in the island of Taiwan. The Portuguese gave it the name Formosa (actually Ilha Formosa or beautiful island), but failed to make it into one of their colonies. The Dutch were more successful. They occupied south-western Formosa from 1624 until 1662 and developed very profitable overseas trade relations. In an effort to make Formosa more productive, they encouraged Chinese farmers to settle on the island because their agriculture was far more advanced than the shifting cultivation practiced by the indigenous peoples. The Dutch not only moved the Chinese to For-mosa, but supplied them with seed, draft animals and agricultural imple-ments. They also allowed the Chinese settlers to borrow money and helped them to build irrigation systems. As a result of these developments, For-mosa became an early exporter of rice and sugar.

Around the middle of the 17th century, a civil war raged in China, and in 1661 thousands of Chinese sought refuge on the island of Formosa. With the support of the Chinese farmers already there, they drove off the Dutch in 1662.

Formosa as a Chinese settlement frontier

After 1662, more Chinese migrants arrived on Formosa. Certain groups of them – especially government officials and soldiers – were given large

* Taiwan's area (36,000 km²) is about one-third as large as that of Cuba (114,500 km²). Included in Taiwan are some small islands, e.g., the Pescadores. Our discussion is limited to the main island.

360

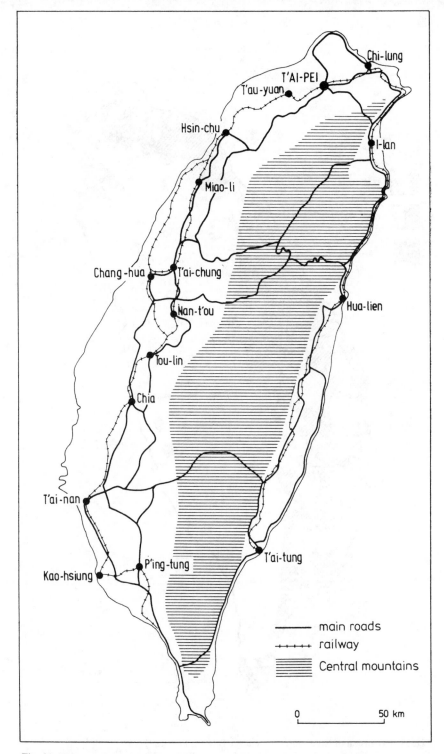

Fig. 38. Taiwan, general reference map.

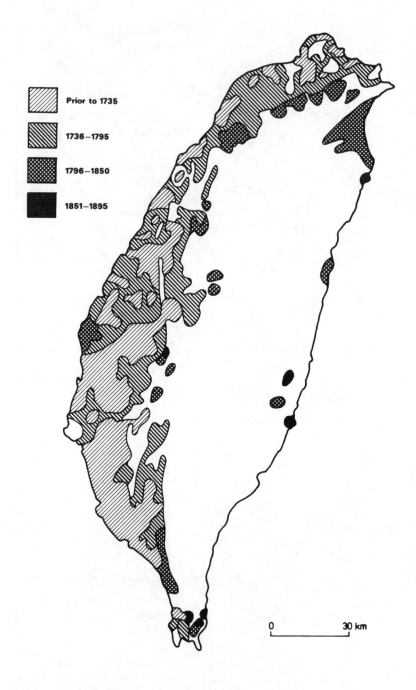

Prior to 1735

1736–1795

1796–1850

1851–1895

0   30 km

Fig. 39. Expansion of Chinese settlement on Taiwan, 1735-1895.
Source: R.G. Knapp (ed.), *China's Island Frontier*, 1980, p. 37.

362

tracts of land which they were allowed to lease to farmers. Other individuals, too, were given permission to own land and were encouraged to put it into agricultural production. By 1680, there were some 100,000 Chinese people living in southwestern Formosa, mostly small farmers who were exploited by a small elite.

In 1683, Formosa was conquered by the mainland Manchu dynasty and the following year it was officially incorporated into the Chinese empire. For the next two centuries an isolationist policy kept Taiwan out of touch with the rest of the world. During this period (1684-1895), migration from mainland China continued at a slow but steady pace, so that the western half of the island became increasingly Chinese in culture. The number of Chinese settlers reached the 2 million mark around 1800 and approximated 3 million by 1895. By that time, nearly the entire western coastal plain had been transformed into one large intensively cultivated agricultural region. The eastern half of the island, however, remained largely unaffected by Chinese colonization (Fig. 39).

The Chinese influx meant that the indigenous peoples were progressively pushed into the mountainous areas. Since these areas had little agricultural potential, the Chinese did not become interested in settling them until after 1875, when the western plains had become completely occupied. Invasion of these areas led to a number of conflicts, but by and large the indigenous peoples were assimilated and successfully adopted the language and culture of the Chinese. Only in some highly inaccessible areas did acculturation not take place.

Colonization meant that production of rice and other food crops experienced a dramatic increase. Thanks to irrigation, productivity reached a high level, allowing Taiwan to export agricultural surpluses. Particularly important was the export of rice to southeastern China, where the province of Fukien suffered repeated rice shortages. Although the production of sugar cane – introduced and promoted by the Dutch – did not disappear, it was emphasized much less than it had been prior to 1662.

The Chinese colonization of Taiwan went hand in hand with an increase in social differentiation. Much uncleared land was handed out to influential people and military personnel. They could become proprietors if they were able to make the land fit for cultivation within a given period of time. Many would-be landowners were not capable of doing this by themselves, for making the land cultivatable meant more than clearing it; irrigation systems had to be built as well. Faced with this problem, many hired small farmers and rural laborers to do the work. Thus, the stage was set for social stratification.

On the one hand, there was a small group of aspiring landowners, on the other, there was a much larger group who prepared the land for agricultural production and who, afterwards, stayed on the land and cultivated it. Out of this arrangement, two types of owners evolved: those who owned the subsoil and those who owned the surface. The latter group consisted of the people who had cleared the land and developed the irrigation facilities. The owners of the subsoil had to pay property tax, but received financial compensation from the 'surface owners' for the actual use of the land. The rights of the two groups were separated so clearly that it was possible to transfer titles to subsoil and surface separately.

In some instances, matters were further complicated by the fact that the person who had been contracted to do the clearing activities, in turn, hired someone else to do the work. This third person was allowed to stay on as a tenant – usually as a sharecropper who had to 'pay' about half the crop to the owner of the surface. Whereas most sharecroppers farmed only about one hectare (2.5 acres), those who had title to the surface or subsoil normally owned considerably larger tracts.

Social differentiation also resulted from the fact that only a limited number of individuals had the financial means needed for clearing the land and putting in the irrigation systems. They invested large sums of money in land development projects, thus further enriching themselves. Not a few eventually became large absentee landowners. Small tenant farmers who needed to borrow some money, tended to turn to their rich landlords for a loan. Since they were charged high interest rates – while at the same time having to surrender a large share of their harvest for rent – many of them spent much of their productive life paying off their debts.

By the end of the 19th century, Taiwan was still almost without urban centers. There was virtually no manufacturing, and tertiary activities were also very limited. Taiwan was overwhelmingly a land of small farmers. Due to a near-absence of roads, the countryside was very inaccessible. In fact, the inhabited part of Taiwan – that is, the western one-third – consisted of a large number of small, highly self-sufficient trade areas between which there was practically no exchange of goods. Farmers raised chiefly food crops for home consumption. Agricultural surpluses were for the most part siphoned off to the mainland – largely in the form of rent payments and taxes.

Rice was by far the most important crop. Around 1850, tea production acquired importance and a few decades later tea was Taiwan's leading export. As in Cuba, sugar cane was processed in a large number of small and rather primitive mills. Sugar exports were mostly destined for Japan.

Prior to 1895, there was no modern industrial development in Taiwan, only small-scale, artisan-type workshops. There was not one power plant on the island and hardly any mining. Most people lived on the edge of poverty, but famines occurred very rarely. A small minority of landlords and top officials was very wealthy.

B. THE JAPANESE COLONIAL INTERLUDE, 1895-1945

The establishment of Japanese rule

Soon after the Meiji Restoration (1868), Japan began to look longingly in the direction of agriculturally productive Taiwan. Inspired by Western powers, Japan decided to become a modern industrial and military power. While surging ahead, it also became interested in establishing a colonial empire – if only to protect itself against the imperialistic expansionism of other powers – and during its war with China (1894-1895) Japan conquered Taiwan and annexed it.

The arrival of the Japanese signaled the beginning of a new era for Taiwan because the Japanese were set on transforming the island into a highly developed and economically integrated part of their own country. Looking back, there can be no doubt that they succeeded. In fact, their accomplishments were so impressive that Taiwan became the envy of Western colonial powers. Although reluctant to admit it, many Westerners looked upon Taiwan as a model colony.

Changes in the agricultural sector

Almost from the very beginning, the Japanese went to work to make formerly unproductive land suitable for agriculture. The area in field crops was increased by nearly 40 percent – from 625,000 ha in 1904 to 858,000 ha in 1938. By that time, there was practically no unutilized land left that could be developed into farmland. Figure 40 shows that the areas which came into production during the Japanese period form two long belts: one on the western slopes of the island's mountainous backbone and the other in easternmost Taiwan. To stimulate development in the latter zone, Chinese farmers from western Taiwan as well as immigrants from Japan were attracted. By 1935, some 70,000 Chinese and 20,000 Japanese farmers had settled in the area.

During the Japanese period, Taiwan's total rice acreage grew by about 40 percent, the area under irrigation by some 140 percent and per hectare yields by more than 50 percent. Total rice output more than doubled, while rice exports – almost entirely to Japan – jumped from 86,000 tons to 621,000 tons.

The Japanese did more than make Taiwan into an important rice producer. Like the Americans in Cuba, they promoted the production of sugar cane. As a consequence, sugar output leaped from 18,000 tons in 1902 to more than 1,000,000 tons in the late 1930s and early 1940s, when approximately 20 percent of Taiwan's total cropland acreage was planted in cane.

The Japanese replaced the 1400 small, primitive sugar mills by a relatively small number of large, modern mills, the first one of which was built as early as 1901. (This modernization of the sugar processing industry clearly resembled similar developments initiated by Americans in Cuba.) When the Japanese evacuated Taiwan in 1945, they left behind 42 modern

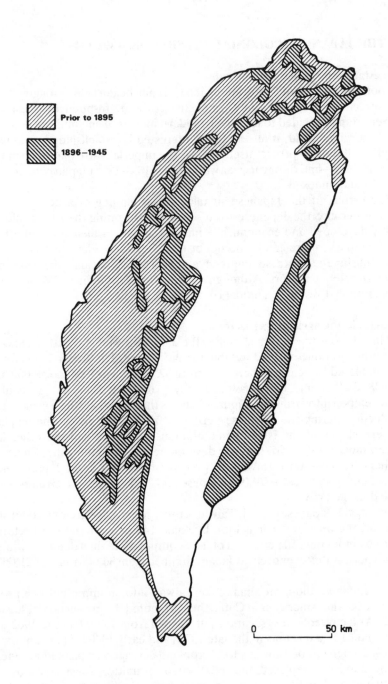

Fig. 40. Expansion of Taiwan's cultivated area during the Japanese period.
Source: R.G. Knapp (ed.), *China's Island Frontier*, 1980, p. 49.

sugar mills as well as 15 alcohol distilleries and 3,000 kilometers of narrow-gauge railroads for hauling sugar cane to the mills (Fig. 41).

Shortly after the Japanese had conquered Taiwan, they started a comprehensive landownership registration. Everyone who could not prove to be the rightful owner lost his land. The dispossessed land became the property of the state and was subsequently sold to individuals and enterprises. Much of it was bought up by Japanese investors interested in planting it to sugar cane. Wherever they could, sugar companies bought additional land from farmers, so that eventually most of the cane acreage was concentrated in a limited number of hands – again, a situation not unlike that which existed in Cuba. But in contrast to Cuba, the companies in Taiwan leased most of their land to tenants, rather than grow sugar cane themselves. All told, there were some 130,000 small cane producers – tenants as well as individual farmers, most of whom were very poor.

The greatly increased per hectare yields mentioned above were a direct consequence of the determined efforts by the colonial rulers to modernize Taiwan's agriculture. They promoted irrigation, introduced new crop varieties, and propagated the use of insecticides, pesticides and artificial fertilizers. Throughout the entire island, agricultural extension services were set up in order to help farmers adopt modern farming methods. It was also made easier for agricultural producers to obtain credit. Multiple cropping was encouraged so as to allow more intensive use of farmland. All in all, output per farmer increased about 100 percent between 1895 and 1945 – an impressive accomplishment considering that in 1945 there were many more farmers than there had been in 1895.

Although the Japanese modernized agriculture and greatly improved the physical infrastructure, they did little to 'correct' the skewed distribution of landownership. In 1939, 43 percent of the landowners had less than 0.5 ha each, and together they possessed a mere 10 percent of all farmland. What is more, fully one-third of all those who practiced agriculture for a living were landless tenants. Sharecroppers usually surrendered about half their crop as rent – in exceptionally fertile areas even as much as 70 percent. The upshot was that the gains in productivity favored the large landowners more than they did the tenant farmers. In fact, tenants were required to make certain minimum payments, regardless of how small their harvest was. To make matters worse, tenancy contracts were for extremely short periods – on average less than twelve months. Considering these adverse circumstances, it is hardly surprising that many small farmers were in debt with moneylenders, usually their own landlords, who charged exorbitant interest rates.

Industrial and infrastructural developments

The Japanese period also witnessed the rise of a modern, albeit limited, industrial sector. Only 25 years after Taiwan became a Japanese colony, there were nearly 3,000 factories, and by 1941 – just twenty years later –

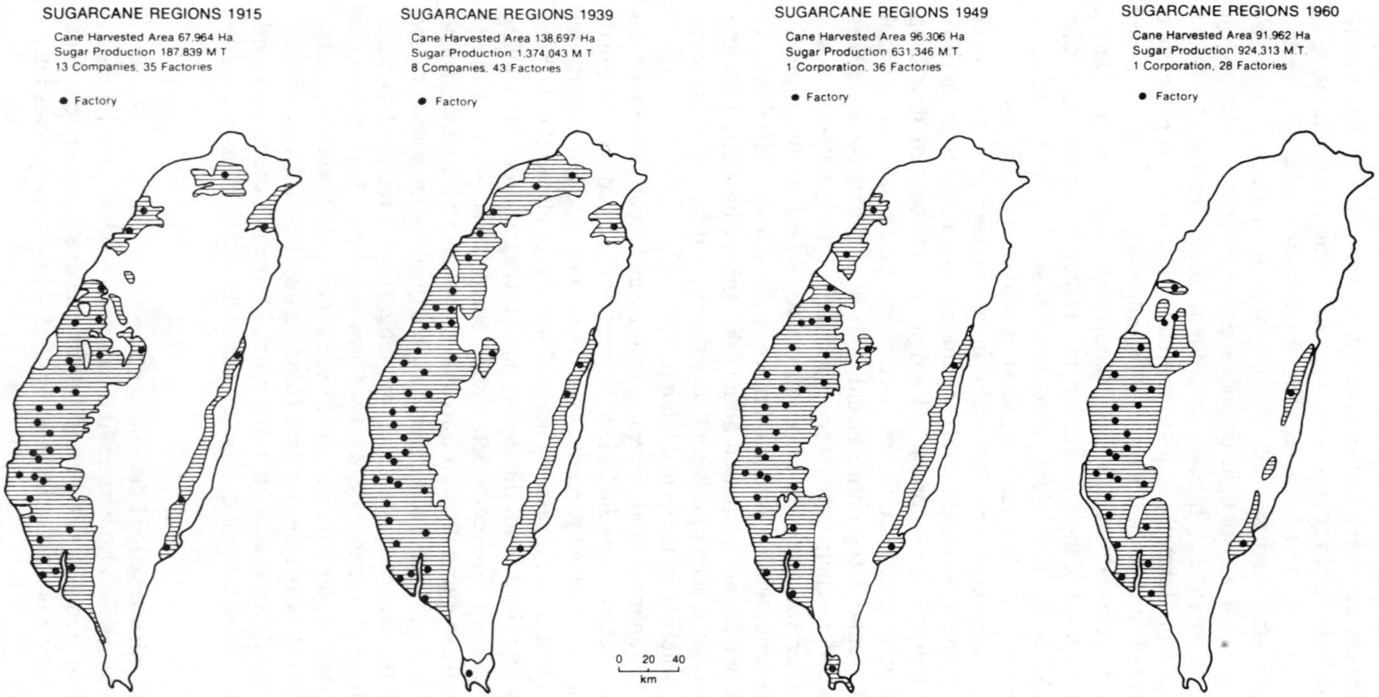

SUGARCANE REGIONS 1915

Cane Harvested Area 67.964 Ha
Sugar Production 187.839 M.T.
13 Companies. 35 Factories

● Factory

SUGARCANE REGIONS 1939

Cane Harvested Area 138.697 Ha
Sugar Production 1.374.043 M.T.
8 Companies. 43 Factories

● Factory

0   20   40
   km

SUGARCANE REGIONS 1949

Cane Harvested Area 96.306 Ha
Sugar Production 631.346 M.T.
1 Corporation. 36 Factories

● Factory

SUGARCANE REGIONS 1960

Cane Harvested Area 91.962 Ha
Sugar Production 924.313 M.T.
1 Corporation. 28 Factories

● Factory

Fig. 41. Expansion and contraction of Taiwan's sugarcane area, 1915-1960. *Source:* R.G. Knapp (ed.), *China's Island Frontier*, 1980, pp. 244-245.

their number had reached 8,683. Notwithstanding the fact that most of them were very small and employed only a few workers, they served to give Taiwan a more diversified economy than it had known. Most important was the production of foodstuffs, especially sugar. Other sectors were less developed for Taiwan's industry was complementary to that of Japan, serving Japan's needs more than it did those of Taiwan. In exchange for exports of agricultural commodities and foodstuffs, Taiwan imported manufactured consumer and capital goods from Japan.

Apart from being highly one-sided, Taiwan's industrial sector was dominated by Japanese interests. In particular the larger and more modern factories were in Japanese hands, as were most mining operations.

For the sake of increasing the productivity of the colonial economy, the Japanese rulers considerably expanded and improved Taiwan's physical infrastructure. For example, modern ports were built enabling Taiwan to greatly increase its foreign trade. The bulk of this trade was with Japan. By means of tariff barriers, preferential trade agreements (not unlike those between Cuba and the US) and Japanese monopolies concerning the supply of manufactured goods, Taiwan's economy was firmly integrated with that of Japan. Thus, Taiwan was forced into a subservient and totally dependent role.

The production of energy, too, received much attention. By 1940, Taiwan had 150 power plants, that is, 150 more than prior to the Japanese invasion. Large sums of money were invested in road and railroad construction. Whereas in 1895 Taiwan had few roads and much of the island was all but inaccessible, by 1945 it had a moderately dense network of roads and railroads. Agricultural regions were opened up, allowing farmers to produce for distant markets, and all major urban centers were linked to each other. Even the mountainous interior was opened up, making it possible to exploit untapped resources (mining and forestry) and develop hydroelectric power plants. At the time of World War II, Taiwan had 1452 kilometers of railroads, of which the north-south line along the west coast – built before 1905 and linking the busy port of Kaohsiung in the southwest with the capital of Taipei in the north – was the most important one.

Aside from the fact that the better connections enabled agricultural producers to shift from diversified subsistence farming to a more highly specialized and commercialized type of agriculture, they had a favorable effect on transforming Taiwan into a politically and culturally cohesive entity. Improved communications between all parts of the country, in other words, laid the foundation for the emergence of a relatively uniform nation-state. Meanwhile, Japan's successful efforts to modernize Taiwan caused the economy to grow by leaps and bounds. Agricultural output increased by 133 percent, net domestic product (NDP) by 178 percent, industrial output by 267 percent and exports (chiefly sugar and rice) by 361 percent.

Some social and demographic developments

The Japanese also upgraded education. They increased the number of elementary schools and introduced the first secondary schools, trade schools and institutions of higher education.

When the Japanese first arrived in Taiwan, many adults were addicted to taking opium. They cracked down hard, and a generation later there were virtually no addicts left.

Due to greatly improved health care services and medical facilities, as well as better hygienic conditions, Taiwan's gross death rate was lowered from 2.5 percent in 1925 to 1.8 percent in 1943. The birth rate, meanwhile, remained high (about 4.5 percent), so that the population experienced a rapid rate of growth. During the 50-year period 1895-1945, the number of people more than doubled, reaching well over 6 million by the end of the Second World War.

Conclusion

Even though the Japanese ruled Taiwan for only five decades, they profoundly changed life on the island, and their accomplishments compare favorably with those of the various European colonial powers in their overseas dependencies. They invested a great deal of capital, manpower, technological expertise and administrative talent in Taiwan, and although their motives were decidedly self-serving, they can hardly be accused of having exploited the Taiwanese people. Despite the large increase in population, standards of material well-being in 1945 were no lower than they had been in 1895 – probably a little higher. In that sense, Taiwan was not underdeveloped by Japan.

In another sense, however, it can be argued that the Japanese did underdevelop their colony. The only reason they modernized Taiwan's agriculture and raised the production of rice and sugar was that Japan itself did not produce enough food to feed its own people. (It was not so much that Japanese farmers were unable to grow sufficient food, but the people were encouraged to work in factories, including war industries, while millions served in the armed forces.) At the same time, the Japanese made balanced economic development in Taiwan rather impossible by promoting only certain sectors. And by monopolizing Taiwan's foreign trade, they forced Taiwan to be little more than an appendage to Japan's powerful economy and war effort.

Notwithstanding its subservient and dependent position, Taiwan in 1945 was not plagued by a dualistic structure, that is, by an economy consisting of two entirely different sectors functioning almost totally independently of each other. Most European colonies, and especially the so-called planta-tion economies (e.g., Cuba, Jamaica, Ceylon and the 'banana republics' in Central America), did have such a dual economy, with a traditional sub-sistence sector existing side by side with a modern foreign-controlled, export-oriented sector – not unlike the present informal/formal dichotomy so typical of the urban tertiary sector in many Third World countries. In Taiwan things were different: its major exports were produced by small farmers; there were virtually no modern economic 'enclaves' owned and managed by foreigners; there were important linkages between industry and agriculture; and there was no large, informal tertiary sector. Instead of having transformed Taiwan into an underdeveloped and impoverished country, the Japanese may be said to have laid the necessary foundation from which post-war Taiwan was able to 'take off' on the long and arduous road toward industrial development and economic maturity.

C. TAIWAN'S POST-WAR DEVELOPMENT

The situation after World War II

After the Japanese left Taiwan, the island was again considered to be part of China. But in 1949, after mainland China had become a communist country, all ties were severed. As a *de facto* independent and sovereign state, Taiwan (now known as Nationalist China) became a permanent member of the U.N. Security Council, representing all of China.

In the first few years after the war, Taiwan was faced with some serious problems. It had suffered considerable war damage, e.g., 34 of the 42 modern sugar mills were partly or wholly destroyed. The departure of the Japanese meant the loss of invaluable know-how. To add insult to injury, 1.2 million refugees from the mainland arrived, not including some 500,000 military belonging to the nationalist army of Chiang Kai-shek that had been defeated in 1949 by Mao Tse-tung's armies. Today, the 'mainlanders' and their descendants account for about 15 percent of Taiwan's population.

The loss of Japanese expertise was partly compensated by the influx of highly qualified managers, entrepreneurs and government officials from the mainland. Moreover, Taiwan became a chief recipient of U.S. reconstruction aid. But most importantly, the Taiwanese themselves have displayed great resourcefulness in the manner in which they have tackled the reconstruction of their country. By 1951, most of the war damage was repaired and the physical and institutional infrastructure was in better shape than ever before. Two years later, production was back at the pre-war level. Since then, the economy has continued to soar, allowing the exploding population to enjoy a steadily rising standard of living.

Taiwan's economic miracle was in no small part made possible by some fundamental changes in the agricultural sector. Foremost among these was the land reform discussed below.

Changes in the agricultural sector

The massive increase in the number of people – from 6 million in 1940 to 12 million in 1964 – necessitated an unprecedented expansion in agricultural output. Since no new land could be taken into cultivation, per hectare yields had to be raised. To make this possible, tenancy conditions were improved; an operation which required some drastic reforms.

The reforms were carried out between 1948 and 1953, partly under the supervision of the nationalist army. The structural changes which the military and political leaders (as well as their American advisors) deemed necessary, were hardly opposed by the landlords. They well knew that if Taiwan were to become a communist country or were conquered by mainland China, far more radical land reforms would take place. The presence of the military strong-arm, of course, also played a role. Another important reason why there was little opposition to the reforms was that the Taiwan-born landowners had little or no political influence after the main-land-born nationalists had seized power in 1949 and had instituted martial law. The new leaders allowed no political freedom.

The first measure taken consisted of a substantial reduction in rent payments. For each individual field, a careful estimate was made of its capacity. Once these 'standard yields' were known, rents were set at 37.5 percent of this predetermined output. Whereas previously the amount to be paid had varied from year to year, depending on the harvest, now the rent became a fixed amount. To make sure tenants would not pay too much in the event of crop failure, it was decided that they did not have to pay any rent at all if, because of no fault of their own, output was less than 70 percent of the predetermined standard yield.

Another major change was that the minimum duration of tenancy contracts was set at six years. Even at the end of this 6-year period it was far from easy for the owner of the land to terminate the contract. For instance, he would have to prove that he needed to farm the land himself or that the tenant had other sources of income large enough to support him and his family. Finally, subletting of land by tenants was forbidden, as were oral contracts.

The various reforms were put into effect within a very short period of time; all tenancy agreements were renegotiated and recorded in just a few months. Soon after the reforms had been announced, many landowners decided to sell all or most of their land, not only because the leasing of land would become less profitable, but also because they were afraid that more drastic reforms might follow. The result was that land values declined, making it possible for many a tenant to become the owner of the land he cultivated.

In addition to the measures just described, much publicly owned land was put up for sale. Shortly after the war, some land that had belonged to Japanese individuals and enterprises had been sold to Taiwanese farmers. Most of it, however, had been transferred to public corporations, such as the Taiwan Sugar Corporation. In 1949, these transfers were discontinued and farmers were given an opportunity to purchase land held by the state and the provinces. At the same time, the Taiwan Sugar Corporation was forced to sell large tracts of land. At the auctions, small farmers and landless tenants were served first and since many of them were interested in purchasing a parcel, there usually was not much left for other buyers.

In order to help small farmers and tenants to acquire land, interest-free government loans were made available. The loans could be paid back over a period of ten years; payments were scheduled in such a way that annual dues amounted to approximately 32.5 percent of the standard yield. In other words, payments were less than the 37.5 percent share which tenants had to pay for rent. Besides, after the loan had been paid off at the end of the tenth year, the new owner would no longer have to make any rent payments. The size of the parcels sold depended on their potential productivity, but few were larger than one hectare. Altogether, some 70,000 ha (170,000 acres) of farmland were sold to 140,000 families.

The most radical reform was launched in 1953. Its purpose was to eliminate tenancy as much as possible. It was reasoned that productivity could be raised most effectively if all agricultural producers owned the land they worked. Limits were set on the number of hectares a family could cultivate. Private ownership was restricted to a maximum of three hectares of irrigated rice land or six hectares of non-irrigated land of average fertility. If the quality of the soil was low, the limits were set at 6 and 12 ha, respectively, and if it was exceptionally good, the maximum acreage a farmer could own was less than the limits of 3 and 6 ha for land of average quality.

All excess acreage had to be sold to the government for a price equivalent to $2\frac{1}{2}$ times the value of the standard annual yield. Tenants who wished to purchase this land from the government were charged the same price, which they could pay over a period of ten years, either in rice or in money. Since their installments were smaller than the 37.5 percent rent payments discussed earlier, it is easy to see that this arrangement was advantageous to them. Equally advantageous was that they could obtain cheap government loans for making their land more productive. All told, this part of the agricultural reforms resulted in the distribution of 140,000 ha (350,000 acres) of land among 200,000 small farmers.

Because the land reform programs were so well organized, it took Taiwan only eleven years (1948-1959) to change from a country in which nearly half of all agriculural land was farmed by tenants to one in which practically all of it (86 percent) was the property of those who cultivated it.

A most important consequence of the reform was that the incomes of landlords and moneylenders declined sharply. Whereas just prior to World War II about 25 percent of all agriculture-derived earnings ended up in their pockets, by 1959 this amounted to no more than 6 percent. This change, together with the increase in per hectare yields and the lowered tenancy payments, meant that farmers' incomes had gone up considerably. By 1960, rural standards of living were much higher than they had been at the time the first reforms were introduced. Also the income distribution had become more even; the poor-rich disparities and social injustice that had characterized rural life in Taiwan for so long were drastically reduced. In 1953, Taiwan had a *Gini coefficient* of income distribution of more than 50, indicating a substantial amount of inequality. Ten years later it had dropped to 32, and by 1973 the Gini coefficient stood at 29. This latter figure tells us that there is less inequality than in most *developed* societies. In fact it is comparable to the low levels found in East European socialist countries.

How a country's Gini coefficient of income distribution can be calculated, and how this widely used measure of inequality relates to the perhaps even more commonly used Lorenz curve depicting the very same phenomenon, is explained in the box below.

Measures of inequelity

The Gini coefficient is calculated as follows: $G = \frac{1}{2} \Sigma |X - Y|$
where X and Y are two sets of percentage frequencies. The vertical lines indicate that the differences between the values are summed regardless of their + or − signs. G=0 in case the two frequency distributions are identical, and G approaches 100 when the distributions are as different as they possibly can be.

Table 10a shows income distribution data for a hypothetical country in 1945. In the column on the left, all households are divided into four income classes. The second column (X) lists the percentages of all households belonging to the various income classes. The third column (Y) shows what percentage of the country's total income is earned by each income class. Also shown are the differences between the X and Y percentages in each row; the sum of these differences (96.0); and the Gini coefficient (48.0). The latter value (G=48) indicates that in 1945 income was distributed very unevenly in our imaginary country.

A comparison with table 10b reveals that between 1945 and 1985 a large redistribution of income took place; the high degree of inequality has given way to a considerably more equal income distribution, as indicated by G=20 in 1985.

The X and Y values can be used to calculate the Lorenz curve (see Fig. 37 in the preceding chapter). All we need to do is to calculate the cumulative percentages for X and Y (as is done for 1945 and 1985 in table 10c) and then plot these against each other. Figure 42 shows that between 1945 and 1985 the curve moved closer to the diagonal. In other words, a low Gini coefficient corresponds with a flatter curve than does a high Gini coefficient. If there were perfect income equality, G would be zero and the Lorenz curve would coincide with the diagonal line representing equal distribution.

Table 10a. Income distribution in a hypothetical country in 1945.

Income class in 1945	Percent of households X	Percent of income Y	Difference X−Y
Households with annual income of less than $1000	63.0	15.0	48.0
Households with annual income of $1000-2000	5.0	5.0	0.0
Households with annual income of $2000-4000	9.0	10.0	−1.0
Households with annual income of over $ 4000	23.0	70.0	−47.0
	——— +	——— +	——— +
	100.0	100.0	96.0

Sum of differences:
$\Sigma|X - Y| = 96$

Gini coefficient:
$\frac{1}{2} \Sigma|X - Y| = 48$

Table 10b. Income distribution in 1985.

Income class in 1985	Percent of households X	Percent of income Y	Difference X–Y
under $2000	32.0	15.0	17.0
$2000-4000	21.0	18.0	3.0
$4000-8000	38.0	45.0	–7.0
over $8000	9.0	22.0	–13.0
	———— +	———— +	———— +
	100.0	100.0	40.0

Sum of differences:
$\Sigma|X - Y| = 40$

Gini coefficient:
$\frac{1}{2}\Sigma|X - Y| = 20$

Table 10c. Cumulative percentages for households (X) and income (Y), 1945 and 1985.

1945 cumulative percentage		1985 cumulative percentage	
X	Y	X	Y
63	15	32	15
68	20	53	33
77	30	91	78
100	100	100	100

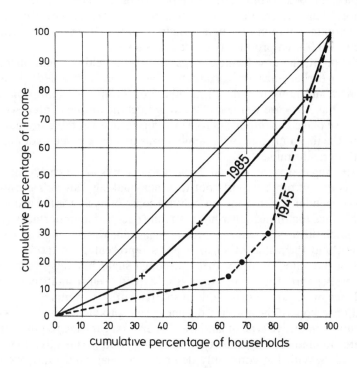

Fig. 42. Two Lorenz curves of income distribution (1945: G = 48; 1985: G = 20).

Important as the reforms were, they did not solve the problem of Taiwan's growing pressure on farmland. A rapid increase in the rural population caused average farm size to decline from 1.3 ha in 1950 to a mere 1 ha in the course of the 1960s. This necessitated further agricultural intensification, something Taiwan managed to do. Between 1952 and 1964, total agricultural output increased 60 percent. With better farming methods, new seed varieties, improved implements (e.g., small tractors replacing the water buffalo) and the application of more artificial fertilizer and pesticides, farmers were able to grow more on less land. Wherever feasible, irrigation was expanded, so that at present well over half of all cropland is irrigated. Through the use of high-quality animal breeds and imported feed, farmers were also able to raise the productivity of livestock husbandry.

Since the early 1950s, efforts have been made to make agriculture more diversified. Especially the production of labor-intensive crops, such as vegetables, has been promoted. Farmers have further been encouraged to raise more than one crop a year on their land. Today, two or even three crops are quite common on irrigated land. Of the 509,000 ha of irrigated rice land, 360,000 ha produce two rice crops a year.

At this point, the new farmers' organizations should be mentioned. In contrast to earlier such organizations, which were controlled by large landowners and non-farmers, all members of the new organizations are farmers. Thus, they are well qualified to protect the farmers' interests and as such have played an important role in securing an acceptable standard of living for the tiny and vulnerable family farms that have come to dominate Taiwan's agricultural sector.

In 1950, sugar exports earned Taiwan four times as much foreign exchange as did all other exports put together, making Taiwan's economy about as dependent on just one agricultural commodity as was the economy of Cuba. Since that time, sugar has gradually declined in importance (Fig. 41). By 1980, the total acreage planted to sugar cane was only half of what it had been, and the value of sugar exports represented no more than 5 percent of the value of all exports. Although sugar remains the leading agricultural export, Taiwan has successfully freed itself from its near-total dependence on sugar exports – this in sharp contrast to Cuba.

A major reason for the absolute decline in cane production is that it is not a particularly intensive type of land use. Whereas sugar cane requires up to 18 months to mature, irrigated vegetable production permits five to seven crops a year. With the constantly deteriorating man-land ratio, we can expect a further reduction in the amount of land devoted to cane production. The phenomenal rise in industrial exports is likely to reduce the relative importance of sugar (and other agricultural) exports even more. In fact, Taiwan is no longer an agricultural country – its economy is about as diversified as is that of most so-called developed countries. Despite an increase in the number of farmers, the proportion of the labor force employed in agriculture has declined from approximately 50 percent in 1957 to less than 20 percent in the early 1980s – a truly remarkable accomplishment.

Taiwan's post-war industrial development
Notwithstanding Japan's efforts to stimulate industrial development, Taiwan did not have all that much industry in 1946. For the most part, only the production of foodstuffs and simple consumer goods had some significance. Considering that Taiwan is not richly endowed with natural resources, possibilities for further industrialization seemed very limited. On the other hand, it possessed a relatively good physical infrastructure as well as a fairly well-educated population. Besides, the low standard of living meant that labor was cheap. Additional favorable circumstances included the massive aid Taiwan received from the U.S. and the influx of many skilled people from the mainland. Finally, the perception that there

44. Mechanization and other modern inputs enable Taiwanese farmers to reap high yields per acre. (Kuang Hua Film Syndicate)

was an imminent communist threat played an important role convincing the Taiwanese that it was imperative that the economy be strengthened. Both Taiwan's leaders and American advisors realized that this could only be done through industrial development.

Taiwan's government has made a significant, albeit largely indirect, contribution to the country's post-war industrialization. In brief, it (1) improved the infrastructure; (2) provided various public utilities; (3) developed a number of capital-intensive industries, such as steel mills; and most importantly, it (4) created a favorable investment climate for private enterprise by offering tax holidays, extending industrial loans, and providing fully serviced industrial parks and special 'export processing zones' for the development of export-oriented industries. As a result, not only Taiwanese investors, but also foreign enterprises – mainly from the U.S., Japan and Western Europe – decided that it was worth their while to invest large sums of money in industrial ventures.

Until about 1960, the emphasis had been on import-substitution industrialization, that is, on the production of relatively simple and mostly non-durable consumer goods for the Taiwanese market. Examples of such goods were foodstuffs, textiles, apparel, footwear, wood products, paper and cement. When the domestic market was becoming saturated about 1960, the government did not simply decide to pursue the import-substitution approach to its logical conclusion by encouraging the production of more sophisticated (durable) consumer goods (e.g., washing machines) and capital goods (e.g., trucks and industrial machinery) for the domestic market. Well aware that Taiwan's low wages gave the country a competitive edge on the international market, it decided to promote production for export instead – a shift in economic policy similar to the one which had occurred in pre-war Japan. At first, only inexpensive goods, such as shoes, clothing and household tools, were exported. But little by little these were replaced by more sophisticated products, such as electric appliances. Thanks to the high productivity of Taiwan's cheap and well-disciplined factory workers, industrial production in Taiwan has been more profitable than in most other countries. As a consequence, it has continued to attract foreign investors and experienced sustained economic growth.

In the wake of these developments there was an unavoidable rise in wages; by 1980 they had climbed so much that it had become increasingly questionable whether Taiwan could still be considered an underdeveloped country. Clearly, it no longer occupied a peripheral position in the international economic system and it became customary to refer to it as a *semi-peripheral* country or a NIC (Newly Industrializing Country). In view of continued economic growth since 1980, it may now be more appropriate to classify it as a *semi-core* country, indicating that Taiwan has more in common with such core countries as Japan and the Netherlands than with peripheral countries like El Salvador, Haiti and Ethiopia.

More important than the question whether Taiwan belongs to the semi-periphery or the semi-core is the fact that during the 1970s and early 1980s it developed into an important producer and exporter of high-technology products. In the past ten years or so, enormous sums of money have been spent both by the government and private enterprise on industrial research and on the development of an ultramodern electronics industry. In spite of the current worldwide crisis, Taiwan continues its ambitious drive to become a highly industrialized state by 1990. Signs of this determination can be seen at the Hsinchu industrial park, located about 70 km southwest of Taipei. There, the government hopes to build a 'silicon plateau,' which would rival California's Silicon Valley. According to the plans, some 30,000 people will be employed at 150 to 200 factories by 1990. As of late 1982, there already were 22 plants producing such hi-tech products as microchips and computer terminals. Plans for another 40 or so plants had been approved before the end of 1982; more will surely follow. Also research institutes and technical universities will be built in the Hsinchu industrial park.

Since the mid-1970s, Taiwan has also paid considerable attention to the development of heavy industry. Today it has petro-chemical industries producing fertilizer, sulphur, artificial fibers, etc., and a state-owned steel mill which supplies approximately one-third of Taiwan's iron and steel requirements. Ship building is a growing industry and before long Taiwan is likely to have a thriving automobile industry. Finally, Taiwan has become the world's leading producer of scrap iron.

45. Air-conditioned dormitory of a textile mill. (Kuang Hua Film Syndicate)

Various concomitant developments

Taiwan's economic miracle has been accompanied by a relative decline in farm population and a very rapid absolute increase in non-farm population. In these respects, developments in Taiwan are no different than those in most other countries. In one respect, however, Taiwan is rather unique. Since the government wanted to prevent too much new industrial activity from becoming concentrated in one or two large cities, many new enterprises were located in smaller towns – some even in rural areas. Owing to this decentralization policy, a large proportion of the newly created jobs is within easy commuting distance for rural people. This enables them to combine agricultural pursuits with non-agricultural activities. Apart from increasing the income of many farm families, this arrangement has made farmers less dependent on agriculture alone; a desirable situation in a country where most farms are miniscule and crops are occasionally wiped out by typhoons.

In spite of political problems (especially the uncertainty of Taiwan's future as a separate and sovereign state and growing demands for a share of political power by native Taiwanese, who comprise about 85 percent of the island's population) and the worldwide recession of the late 1970s and early 1980s, Taiwan's per capita GNP continues to grow. After having experienced a very substantial increase in the past 36 years – from $50 in 1946 to $2570 in 1982 – it might reach $5,000 by 1990.

46. Busy street in prosperous downtown Taipei. (Kuang Hua Film Syndicate)

In 1980, manufacturing contributed nearly seven times as much to the country's GDP as did agriculture; only 15 years earlier these two sectors had contributed the same amount. Additional evidence of Taiwan's economic transformation is provided by the changed composition of its exports. Whereas in 1952 agricultural goods were responsible for 92 percent (by value) of all exports, with manufactured goods accounting for only 8 percent, by 1980 the picture was reversed as manufactures contributed 92 percent and agricultural products the remaining 8 percent.

Being a small country, the value of Taiwan's per capita foreign trade is much greater than that of the U.S. Since trade is so important, it is no exaggeration to state that Taiwan's economic well-being is totally dependent on its industrial exports. This dependence on foreign markets puts the country in a vulnerable position; even a temporary interruption in its foreign trade would endanger Taiwan's economy and prosperity. The present economic crisis, therefore, casts an ominous shadow over Taiwan's ambition to become a leading producer of high-technology products. If the current economic stagnation lasts until the late 1980s, as it well may, it is unlikely that Taiwan's per capita GNP will reach the $5,000 mark by 1990.

Finally, attention may be drawn to the fact that even though Taiwan has financed a large proportion of its economic development, it has become an exporter of capital, be it at a limited scale. Various Taiwanese companies have established branch plants abroad, especially in low-wage countries in

47. Modern urban development on the edge of Taipei. (Kuang Hua Film Syndicate)

Southeast Asia. Moreover, Taiwan's foreign debt is relatively small, so that its financial obligations consume only a small proportion of its GNP.

The quality of life

Considering its rapid rate of economic growth, it should not surprise us that Taiwan has very little unemployment – only 1.1 percent in 1980. This fact alone goes some way in explaining the continuing rise in living standards. As a matter of fact, grinding poverty – so common in ex-colonial areas – has long since been eliminated. In 1953, Taiwan's income distribution differed little from that of Cuba in the same year (see Fig. 37), but just as the Lorenz curve for Cuba has moved closer to the line representing 'perfect equality,' so has the one for Taiwan. In both countries, efforts to help the poor were, and still are, accompanied by measures (e.g., land reforms) to curtail the rise of a small wealthy elite. In Taiwan, several very large industrial enterprises are owned by the state, thus ensuring that profits benifit society as a whole, rather than a few individuals.

Other developments concern the lowering of birth and death rates. Between 1953 and 1981, the crude birth rate dropped from 4.6 percent to 2.2 percent and the crude death rate from .95 percent to .45 percent. In 1979, the infant mortality rate was just under 1 percent, which compares favorably with a 1.4 percent rate for the U.S. This exceptionally low infant mortality rate tells us a great deal about the quality of life in Taiwan. It

383

indicates, among other things, that the population is highly literate, that there are excellent medical facilities, that there is clean drinking water, good transportation and communication, that people are well housed and that hygienic standards are high. Even though Taiwan's per capita GNP is three or four times lower than that of countries in Western Europe, it resembles those countries much more than it resembles countries like Pakistan, Peru and Tanzania. Clearly, Taiwan has made too much progress to be considered underdeveloped any longer, and it is too prosperous to be called a poor country.

The political situation

Politics in post-war Taiwan have been dominated by the arrival in 1949 of nearly 2 million nationalist mainlanders and by the constant fear of a communist Chinese invasion.

The nationalist Kuomintang (KMT), led by Chiang Kai-shek, grabbed the power in 1949 and has maintained a tight grip ever since. A state of martial law has lasted now for 35 years; the Army keeps the only political party – the KMT – in power, and the native Taiwanese out. Only party members are able to join the ranks of top officials. The minority government does not allow its opponents to form political parties and frequently bans magazines and other publications that delve into sensitive topics. Political activities on campuses are forbidden and there are alleged to be several hundred political prisoners. Harsh sentences are meted out to anti-KMT activists.

Many Taiwanese are bothered by the KMT's claim that it is the sole legitimate government of all China and would like it to declare Taiwan an independent country. They are afraid that reunification with the mainland will result in a considerable drop in their standard of living.

Despite these sentiments, there are few serious tensions, and there is widespread appreciation for the KMT-led economic recovery. Besides, education, communication and growing cultural uniformity – today nearly everyone speaks Mandarin – have blurred the differences between the Taiwanese, on the one hand, and the mainlanders and their descendants, on the other. The question is whether relations between the two groups will remain peaceful. A major economic setback, for example, could well kindle political unrest and result in demands for political change.

Conclusion

Since World War II, virtually all symptoms of underdevelopment, such as widespread and permanent unemployment, malnutrition, inadequate housing, poor health conditions, illiteracy, wide income disparities, internal colonialism, low productivity and extremely low wages, have disappeared in Taiwan. Although the country is highly dependent on foreign trade, it is no longer an important exporter of primary goods or a victim of agriculture's deteriorating terms of trade. In contrast to underdeveloped countries, Taiwan has not neglected the agricultural sector. Today only a small proportion of its population (about 16 percent) is employed in agriculture – many on a part-time basis. While its economy is much more diversified than that of a typical Third World country, Taiwan is making a major effort to diversify even further and strengthen its competitive position in the world market place.

Although a great deal of foreign capital is invested in Taiwan, a substantial portion of the economy is controlled by Taiwanese interests, so that it would be incorrect to conclude that its economy is at the mercy of foreign capital. Per capita GNP is almost twice that of Cuba and growing. Taiwan enjoys a favorable balance of trade and is not burdened with a huge foreign debt. Furthermore, it does not have a large (mostly unproductive) informal tertiary sector, nor an 'abnormal' urban hierarchy that is dominated by one exceedingly large primate city.

Taiwan illustrates that socialism is not a *sine qua non* for genuine development. Like Japan, Taiwan has traveled the capitalist road to progress, and has done it very successfully. Although Taiwan is less than one-third as large as Cuba, possesses more mountainous terrain, and has twice as many inhabitants, it resembles the industrialized countries in many more respects than does its Caribbean counterpart. At the same time, it appears to be less dependent and thus less vulnerable than Cuba, although it must be admitted that this conclusion depends in no small measure on one's definition of dependence. And in sharp contrast to Cuba, Taiwan has not been the recipient of foreign economic aid since the 1960s.

Taiwan's success story does not mean that it provides a suitable development model for other countries. In several respects, Taiwan was, and remains, a unique case. Meanwhile, times have changed. In all likelihood, Taiwan's success, together with somewhat similar developments in Hong Kong, Singapore and South Korea, has made it more difficult for other countries to do what Taiwan has done.

Nevertheless, Taiwan's experience can teach a very valuable lesson to all Third World countries that have aspirations of becoming developed. It demonstrates that successful development requires carefully planned and well-implemented agricultural reforms; incentives to raise productivity in all sectors of the economy; promotion of decentralized, labor-intensive industrial development; timely adjustments to changing market conditions; determined, government-supported efforts to broaden the economic base through diversification; adequate provisions with regard to infrastructure, health care, schooling, housing and family planning; and legislative measures favoring an equitable income distribution. Without exception, all these recommendations come under the heading of 'internal conditions.' Remembering that Taiwan is a unique case, its experience seems to suggest that in the final analysis internal conditions can overcome the negative effects caused by 'external obstacles.'

Dependency theory and Taiwan

In their excellent study on Taiwan, Barrett & Whyte (1982) provide evidence that Taiwan's accomplishments contradict the major predictions from dependency theory. These predictions include:

(1) Dependent countries suffer from direct exploitation as foreign firms repatriate profits overseas, rather than invest them in the domestic economy.

(2) Foreign economic interests 'dump' outmoded equipment and technology on poor countries, making it impossible for them to compete effectively in the world market or to catch up with the rich countries.

(3) Dependence on foreign interests and foreign economic penetration keep the state weak and prevent it from fostering rapid and balanced economic growth.

(4) Dependency leads to susceptibility to price manipulations, which, in turn, result in deteriorating terms of trade (or unequal exchange), trade deficits, growing indebtedness and a shortage of investment capital.

(5) Dependency causes economic growth to be confined to small enclaves, resulting in limited multiplier effects, unbalanced development and economic dualism.

(6) Dependence on foreign aid and credit reduces capital formation and thus inhibits economic growth.

(7) Dependency leads to a highly unequal distribution of income.

(8) Foreign interests obstruct governmental efforts to foster equality.

(9) Dependency places labor in a weak position relative to employers, thereby fostering inequality.

(10) Imports of industrial goods wipe out domestic industries and traditional handicrafts, causing widespread unemployment and deprivation.

(11) Foreign firms keep important parts of their organizational structures and crucial (hi-tech) industrial processes overseas, or bring in their own managerial and technical personnel. As a result, a broad middle class cannot develop.

Barrett & Whyte show that not one of these eleven arguments of dependency theorists applies to Taiwan. Despite its dependence on foreign economic aid (until the 1960s), on foreign investment and foreign trade, Taiwan has experienced an extraordinarily rapid rate of economic growth and impressive improvements in income distribution. The authors correctly conclude that this finding "forces us to question the degree of determinism implied in discussions of dependency" (p. 1085), and that "dependency does not inevitably and uniformly lead to economic stagnation and rising inequality" but instead "may provide clear benefits" (p. 1087).

Selected readings

Barrett, R. E. & M. K. Whyte (1982), Dependency Theory and Taiwan: Analysis of a Deviant Case. *American Journal of Sociology*, 87 (5), pp. 1064-1089.

Casetti, E. & L. Li Wen (1979), The Family Planning Program in Taiwan. Did it Make any Difference? *Geographical Analysis*, 11 (4), pp. 394-403.

China (Taiwan). *Länderkurzbericht 1981*. Wiesbaden, Statistisches Bundesamt. Statistik des Auslandes. Kohlhammer Verlag.

Chinn, D. L. (1977), Distributional Equality and Economic Growth: The Case of Taiwan. *Economic Development and Cultural Change*, 26 (1), pp. 65-79.

Dirkx, J. C. B. (1979), Taiwan. Een Chinees eiland door toedoen van de . . . Hollanders. *Intermediair*, 15 (11), pp. 19, 21, 23, 25.

Fei, J. C. H., G. Ranis & S. W. Y. Kuo (1979), *Growth with Equity: The Taiwan Case*. New York: Oxford University Press.

Galenson, W., ed. (1979), *Economic Growth and Structural Change in Taiwan. The Postwar Experience of the Republic of China*. Ithaca, N. Y.: Cornell University Press.

Hanrath, J. J. (1963), Taiwan, In: Boerman, W. E., J. J. Hanrath & H. J. Keuning, eds., *De wereld waarin wij wonen en werken*, Vol. VI, pp. 248-252. Zeist: Uitgeversmaatschappij De Haan.

Ho, S. P. S. (1979), Decentralized Industrialization and Rural Development: Evidence from Taiwan. *Economic Development and Cultural Change*, 28 (1), pp. 77-96.

Hsieh, Chiao-min (1964), *Taiwan – Ilha Formosa. A Geography in Perspective*. London: Butterworths.

King, R. (1977), *Land Reform. A World Survey*. London: Bell.

Knapp, R. G. ed. (1980), *China's Island Frontier. Studies in the Historical Geography of Taiwan*. Honolulu: The University Press of Hawaii.

Koo, A. Y. C. (1968), *The Role of Land Reform in Economic Development: A Case Study of Taiwan*. New York: Praeger.

Michael, R. (1980), Regionalplanung in Taiwanesischen Stadtregionen. *Raumforschung und Raumordnung*, 38 (1-2), pp. 41-52.

Newsweek (1982), Taiwan's Time of Trouble. Nov. 1, pp. 26-29.

Selya, R. M. (1974), *The Industrialization of Taiwan. Some Geographic Considerations*. Jerusalem: Jerusalem Academic Press.

Shinkichi, E. (1980), Asianism and the Duality of Japanese Colonialism, 1879-1945. In: Blussé, L., H. L. Wesseling & G. D. Winius, eds, *History and Underdevelopment. Essays on Underdevelopment and European Expansion in Asia and Africa*, pp. 114-127. Leiden: Centre for the History of European Expansion.

Thompson, W. S. (1959), *Population and Progress in the Far East*. Chicago: The University of Chicago Press.

Timmermann, O. (1962), Taiwan, ein Entwicklungsland in Südostasien. *Westfälische Geographische Studien*, 15, pp. 107-124.

Wu, Rong-I. (1978), Taiwan's Export Boom: Causes and Prospects. *Mondes en Développement*, 10, pp. 315-335.

Yang, M. M. C. (1970), *Socio-Economic Results of Land Reform in Taiwan*. Honolulu: East-West Center Press.

Epilogue

Choice of case studies

There are over a hundred Third World countries. Instead of writing one or two pages about each of them or devoting five to ten pages to maybe twenty countries, it seemed much more meaningful to select only a few cases and discuss these in considerable detail. Apart from the fact that brief descriptions can be found in any encyclopedia, including Kurian's *Encyclopedia of the Third World*, they do not enable us to test the various theories of development and underdevelopment (Chapters 14-16). Also, short descriptions do not permit us to pay adequate attention to historical causes of underdevelopment. As pointed out earlier, we agree with Bobek, Lacoste and most *dependencistas* that historical analysis is necessary if we want to come up with a satisfactory explanation of the origin of underdevelopment. Not only in Ethiopia and India, but in many other countries, underdevelopment has its roots in the distant past, predating the rise of colonialism, capitalism and neo-colonial (or imperialist) dependency relations.

The four countries selected for detailed analysis vary in size, number of inhabitants, population density, per capita GNP, physical environment, culture, political ideology, past and present external relationships, and numerous other respects. Readers may well disagree with our choice of countries, pointing out that Ethiopia is not representative of Africa, that India is not typical of southern Asia, that Cuba does not resemble Latin America, and that Taiwan has more in common with a core country like Japan than with Laos or Nepal.

To be sure, it would have been preferable if we had chosen countries which are representative of the larger geographical regions to which they belong. This, however, is easier said than done. Which country best represents Africa: Algeria or Swaziland, Nigeria or Zambia, Liberia or Tanzania? The problem is that no one country is typical of all Africa. Africa is too diverse that we can identify a particular combination of features as being typically African. This means that generalizations concerning the entire African continent are likely to be of limited value – often even misleading.

Precisely the same argument applies to Latin America, the Middle East and other large regions. Neither Brazil nor Surinam is representative of South America, much less of Latin America. Aware that it is impossible to find representative cases, we have selected four very different countries, hoping that *together* they may be representative of the Third World as a whole. To the extent that the four case studies do indeed expose us to a wide variety of circumstances responsible for currently existing problems of

388

underdevelopment, they not only allow us to test the various theories of underdevelopment, but also afford us an excellent opportunity to make a meaningful contribution to an understanding of the exceedingly complex and spatially varying phenomenon that is underdevelopment.

Ethiopia was chosen because it is one of the very poorest countries on earth, does not have a colonial past, is presently not dependent on capitalist core countries, and because its relative vitality around the beginning of the 20th century gave it a better chance to develop into a modern and economically advanced state than most other African countries.

India was selected for the following reasons: for thousands of years it has been dominated by the Asiatic mode of production; it has a colonial past which many authors consider to be the major cause of its present under-development; the sheer size of the country and its population; its experience with the Green Revolution; the role that religion and the caste system have played in the process of underdevelopment; and the fact that India's development is relatively autonomous, that is, not too dependent on foreign investments, loans or aid. In brief, India is ideally suited for testing some of the theories discussed in earlier chapters.

The two main reasons for including a case study of Cuba are that it travels the socialist road to development and is often cited as one of the few countries which have made considerable progress in a short period of time. Moreover, Cuba can shed light on the relevance of dependency theory because its former dependence on the leading capitalist country has been replaced by dependence on the dominant socialist country.

Taiwan was chosen because it is the foremost example of a country which has been successful in its attempts to catch up with the developed countries. It seems particularly instructive to compare its capitalist development strategy with Cuba's socialist approach. An important consideration also was that Taiwan's colonial past has laid the foundation not for under-development but for development by providing some of the preconditions for economic takeoff. Finally, it seemed worthwhile to find out what lessons other Third World countries might learn from Taiwan's accomplishments.

In an attempt to discover what the case studies teach us about processes of development and underdevelopment, we propose to assess the role which each of a number of factors has played (and sometimes still plays) in the four countries. First we discuss several *internal* factors, such as physical environment and the role of the elite. The major *external* factors to be discussed are colonialism and neo-colonialism.

The physical environment

When trying to account for Ethiopia's low level of development, one cannot ignore the disadvantages of its mountainous terrain, nor the prob-lems that result from recurrent droughts. In addition to frequent crop failure, Ethiopia is faced with widespread soil erosion and almost insurmountable problems of communication and transportation. Because of their inaccessibility, some provinces play virtually no role in the national economy; their water power potential and other natural resources remain largely undeveloped. At the same time, isolation keeps intact the age-old cultural differences and interregional animosities which tear apart multinational Ethiopia. As long as there are no strong nationalistic sentiments which act as a centripetal force cementing together all parts of the country into a unified and cohesive whole, there is not likely to be much economic integration. At the risk of being accused of environmental determinism, we believe that Ethiopia's difficult terrain, steep slopes and many canyon-like valleys constitute powerful divisive elements which help to explain the country's economic backwardness.

Although it may not seem unreasonable to relate India's underdevelopment to such natural factors as the unpredictability of the wet monsoons, the repeated droughts and floods, and the poor soil quality in parts of the country, we should not underestimate the potential of India's natural environment. Irrigation can be practiced in much of India and the long growing season makes it possible to raise more than one crop a year. As a matter of fact, one could argue that owing to the natural productivity of the environment, a small minority was able to exploit the farmers century after century, thus causing long-term stagnation and abject poverty among the majority of the people.

A similar environmentalism-in-reverse may be said to apply to Cuba. Possessing inherent advantages for the large-scale production of sugar for export, Cuba became a victim of external exploitation – first as a colony of Spain and later as a neo-colony of the U.S. Had Cuba's natural conditions been less amenable to cane production, the country's economy might well have become more diversified than it presently is.

Despite the fact that much of Taiwan is mountainous and unfit for agriculture, its physical environment has important advantages. Not only are irrigation and multiple cropping possible, but the island is rich in forest resources and hydroelectic potential. Furthermore, its long coastline gives it easy access to overseas trade partners. The agricultural possibilities have played a particularly important role in Taiwan's post-war development from a poverty-stricken peripheral country into an increasingly prosperous NIC with typical core attributes.

In conclusion, even though it is difficult to assess nature's role in human processes of development and underdevelopment, it is clear that we should not overlook this factor. Part of the problem of determining how and to what degree natural conditions have affected human activities is that they play a passive role. Nature does not determine; e.g., Cuba was not predetermined to develop a sugar-based economy. This means that environmental conditions should not be studied in isolation but looked at in relation to the manner in which, and the purpose for which, local inhabitants and/or foreigners have utilized the possibilities offered them by these

390

same environmental conditions. The physical environment by itself cannot explain differences in development; only in combination with political, cultural, demographic, social and other human factors can it help us account for spatial patterns of development and underdevelopment.

The cultural environment

Are differences in development attributable to differences in culture and value systems? Does Max Weber's thesis concerning the *Protestant ethic* have validity? Would Brazil be more prosperous than the U.S. if the former had been settled by the British and the latter by the. Portuguese?

Notwithstanding the problem that 'culture' means different things to different people (cf. Kroeber & Kluckhohn 1963), it seems possible to draw some tentative conclusions from the case studies. Both in Ethiopia and India there are several cultural features which result in a glaring underutilization of human and non-human resources. Since we need not repeat everything that has been said in the case studies, suffice it to list only the major cultural obstacles to development. These include various religious and non-religious taboos, the belief that life is an illusion, fasting regulations, disdain for manual work, rigid caste systems, limited social mobility, institutionalized discrimination, untouchability, emphasis on the social rather than the economic value of livestock, and restrictions on commercial and financial activities. To these we can add that both countries suffer from a lack of cultural homogeneity, resulting in out-group enmity and even open hostility.

When we compare Ethiopia and India with Cuba and Taiwan, it is apparent that the latter two countries are relatively unhampered by all kinds of culture-induced impediments, including fatalistic attitudes. Both Cuba and Taiwan stress education, equal opportunity, social welfare, and progress. Particularly striking, it seems to us, is the entrepreneurial spirit or *Wirtschaftsgeist* among the hard-working Taiwanese. It is worth noting that because Taiwan's economic miracle has much in common with those of South Korea and Japan, many observers have concluded that Buddhism apparently is more conducive to economic development than are most other religions.

Since tradition, folkways, religious beliefs and other cultural phenomena are rooted in the past and are known to be extraordinarily resistant to change, we can easily appreciate that the past has had a formidable impact on the present and that it will surely have a strong influence on the future. This is an important observation because it means that countries whose economic development is presently inhibited by cultural factors will almost certainly continue to experience the negative effects of those same features. The danger is that they will fall further behind the more dynamic countries whose development is relatively unhindered – perhaps even stimulated – by cultural elements. Thus, the gap separating the rich and poor countries threatens to become wider, leading to ever greater disparities at the global level.

Rapid population growth

Although Ethiopia and India have lower population growth rates than the Third World as a whole, both experience the negative consequences of fairly rapid increases in numbers of inhabitants. Huge investments are needed just to feed, clothe and educate the many children. The larger the number of infants per family, the smaller the amount of money available for each individual. The prevalence of large families not only means more poverty, but more malnourishment, more health problems, more crowding in the often tiny dwellings, fewer savings, less education, and a smaller market potential. Rapid population growth also results in a large demand for new jobs. As soon as fewer employment opportunities become available than are needed, unemployment is bound to increase. Growing pressure on agricultural land is another problem. In Ethiopia as well as India, increased demand for farmland has led to fragmentation of farms, shorter fallow periods, declining soil fertility, soil erosion, rural marginalization, and widespread rural underemployment. Rural deprivation, in turn, has resulted in massive migration to the cities, growing urban unemployment, alarming expansion of the informal tertiary sector, and mushrooming urban slums.

Cuba and Taiwan have successfully lowered the birth rate. At the same time, living conditions have improved substantially in both countries. Although many demographers believe that birth rates cannot decline much until *after* standards of living have gone up, it goes without saying that per capita income cannot increase as long as the rate of population growth equals or excels the rate of economic growth. The lesson that can be learned from Cuba and Taiwan is that the governments of Third World countries should not wait for birth rates to come down by themselves, but should encourage people to limit the number of children and take whatever measures are needed to enable the population to practice birth control. The faster the rate of population growth, the greater the chance that human resources remain underutilized and the greater also the likelihood that the man-environment relationship will become permanently disturbed.

The role of the indigenous elite

All four countries provide evidence that a small, powerful elite can have detrimental effects on a country's development. Throughout history, the weak have had to surrender part of the surplus they produced to the privileged few. Because the rich seldom used their accumulated wealth to raise levels of productivity, they may be held responsible for the fact that up to the present day much of humankind has lived in grinding poverty, barely able to satisfy even the most basic needs of life. Virtually everywhere we find the Taj Mahals, symbolizing the role elites have played in the development of underdevelopment. It would appear that the story of humankind is essentially the story of people exploiting people, resulting in extreme disparities in wealth.

The case studies confirm Lacoste's thesis that the egotistical and parasitic behavior of elites must be seen as a major cause of underdevelopment, in the past as well as in more recent times. There is even reason to conclude that it is *the* cause of stagnation and deprivation, certainly when we consider colonial and neo-colonial elites as variants of the 'traditional' indigenous elites. To the victims of this exploitative behavior it makes little difference whether the surpluses they produce are appropriated by their own (national) elite or by a foreign (international) elite – in both instances they are being subjugated and impoverished. As Lacoste, Galtung and others have noted, the elites in peripheral countries often enjoy harmony-of-interest relations with the elites in core countries, better enabling them to enrich themselves at the expense of the masses of Third World inhabitants.

In Cuba and Taiwan, the negative role of the elite may be said to have been eliminated. On the other hand, in India and probably also in Ethiopia it continues to be a powerful obstacle to development in that it causes or maintains extreme socio-economic polarization.

Colonialism

With the exception of five years of Italian occupation, Ethiopia never was a colonial possession. Today, it is one of the world's poorest countries. After fifty years of colonial rule by the Japanese, Taiwan is presently well on its way to become a prosperous and developed country. Both Cuba and India were colonial dependencies for a very long period of time, but present living conditions of the 'average' inhabitant are far better in the former than the latter country.

During the 1960s and 1970s, colonialism was often cited as a major cause of underdevelopment. Countries like India and Indonesia were alleged to have been plundered and 'destroyed' by ruthless colonial exploitation. Since the late 1970s, however, more and more scholars have come to realize that there is ample reason to question this view. They have felt a growing need to come up with a more carefully balanced appraisal of the role of colonialism, one which does not only stress the negative effects.

When trying to assess the role colonialism has played in Ethiopia, India, Cuba and Taiwan, we conclude that its effects have been negative for Cuba, partly negative and partly positive for India, and moderately to strongly positive for Ethiopia and Taiwan.

In Cuba, it has resulted in a weak economic structure, monoculture, a highly skewed distribution of landownership, uneven development, excessive income disparities, and external dependence. Most importantly, perhaps, colonialism lay the foundation for a period of neo-colonial exploitation.

Since the consequences of colonialism for India have been discussed in considerable detail in the case study, they need not be repeated here. It may be more relevant to point out that there is reason to believe that probably owing to colonialism India has become a more dynamic country than it was prior to becoming a British colony. Centuries of economic stagnation and luxury consumption by a parasitic elite have been replaced by growing emphasis on productive investments, modernization, introduction of democratic institutions, and attempts to create a more egalitarian society. To be sure, India still has a long way to go and abject poverty remains an all too common problem, but it would be a serious mistake to attribute India's underdevelopment solely to colonialism. It might even be more correct to conclude that widespread poverty occurs not so much because of colonialism, but in spite of it.

Because most of Ethiopia has known only a few years of colonial domination, there is not much we can say about the effects of colonialism on this country. However, considering that many of Ethiopia's roads and other infrastructural improvements came into existence during the years of colonial rule and that the Italian 'interlude' may be said to have had a favorable 'shock effect' on Ethiopia, we are inclined to assess the impact of colonialism as moderately positive.

While it lasted, colonialism had some undesirable consequences for Taiwan. Its economy lacked diversity and became totally dependent on that of Japan. On the other hand, the rapid modernization of Taiwan by the Japanese resulted in a large number of important infrastructural improvements and impressive increases in agricultural and industrial productivity. Notwithstanding the fact that prior to 1945 these developments served the interests of Japan rather than those of Taiwan, since World War II they have formed the foundation for Taiwan's development into one of the world's fastest growing economies.

Neo-colonialism and external dependence

Neither before nor after 1974 has Ethiopia been very dependent on foreign investments. Its foreign trade is negligible and the country is not a major recipient of economic assistance. In brief, it would be hard to defend the proposition that Ethiopia's underdevelopment is the result of neo-colonial relationships with capitalist core countries. Not external but internal factors are responsible for the fact that most Ethiopians live in poverty and misery.

Compared to other low-income countries, India's per capita foreign debt is quite small, relatively little foreign capital is invested in her economy, and the country has experienced a respectable rate of economic growth in recent years. Because India's foreign trade is not characterized by exports of raw materials and imports of manufactured goods, she is not a major victim of unequal exchange and deteriorating terms of trade (although India has suffered greatly from the enormous increase in oil prices since 1973). It would therefore be difficult to conclude that India's underdevelopment is a consequence of neo-colonial exploitation or asymmetrical dependency relations with the First World.

Cuba has been exposed to a considerably longer period of neo-colonial exploitation than India. Between 1900 and 1960, its economy was completely dominated by foreign interests. The all-important sugar industry was largely in U.S. hands, as were the tourist industry and various other sectors of the economy. A large proportion of all profits left Cuba, causing a shortage of domestically available capital. While thousands of farmers possessed only a few acres, foreign enterprises kept large tracts of arable land out of production.

Since the 1959 revolution, Cuba has maintained a close relationship with the Soviet Union. Although this new relationship is not normally described as neo-colonialist, the structure of the Cuban economy has undergone relatively little change; it remains a highly dependent plantation economy based on exports of raw materials in exchange for foodstuffs and manufactured products. Some economic diversification has taken place, yet Cuba continues to have a typical Third World economy that can easily fall victim to deteriorating terms of trade.

Critics of the capitalist mode of production like to point out that Taiwan has become extremely vulnerable due to its dependence on foreign investments, foreign know-how, and the rapidly growing export of manufactured goods to foreign markets. Another global economic crisis, they believe, will almost certainly have disastrous repercussions for Taiwan. It is true that Taiwan's economy is firmly integrated with the world economy and that it is highly dependent on its ability to sell its products abroad. But this makes Taiwan no different from Japan, Sweden or Switzerland. If anything, Taiwan's relatively low wages give it a competitive edge over other developed countries. Thus, there appears to be no reason for the pessimistic views mentioned above. Far from it. Taiwan demonstrates that, for small countries at least, modern dependency relations, foreign trade and integration into the capitalist world system are much less obstacles to development than they are indispensable conditions for sustained economic growth and prosperity.

Geography and underdevelopment

Regional studies remain the hallmark of geography. Case studies of individual Third World countries or of regions such as the Sahel, carried out for the express purpose of trying to find out what combination of factors can be held responsible for their present underdevelopment, may well be the best way in which geographers can contribute to development research. It is no coincidence, therefore, that four such case studies – albeit in abridged form – are included in this book. What can we learn from them?

First, they serve the purpose of testing the various theories, leading to the following conclusions: (1) no one theory can explain underdevelopment everywhere; (2) each theory contains elements which help account for the occurrence of processes of underdevelopment; and (3) several theories (or parts thereof) can be used simultaneously to explain underdevelopment in a given country or region. Second, they clearly bring out the complex nature of underdevelopment. Although human factors have played a dominant role in all four countries, the case studies show that non-human factors need to be considered when trying to account for presently existing problems of underdevelopment. Third, the historical approach used in these regional studies reveals, among others, that a particular event – e.g., colonial domination – can be a major cause of underdevelopment in one place, while laying the foundation for future development in another, or, that it can have both detrimental and beneficial effects at the same time. We could add more such conclusions, the important point being that even a small number of case studies suffices to underscore that processes of development and underdevelopment differ markedly from place to place. It is no exaggeration that the 'story' of underdevelopment is unique for almost every Third World country.

This spatial differentiation in underdevelopment experiences makes it abundantly clear that a theory capable of explaining underdevelopment in one country may be totally unsuited for explaining underdevelopment in some other country. By the same token, a specific development strategy (e.g., export-oriented industrialization) cannot be expected to have the same chance of being successful in different countries. Although these conclusions are self-evident, it still happens that concepts, theories and development models developed for a particular country or within a specific contextual framework are being applied to other countries or regions as if the subject matter were the same the world over. As pointed out in an earlier chapter, it makes little sense to apply China's development strategy to Tanzania; the two countries have practically nothing in common. In similar vein, Kenya or Senegal might be ill-advised to try to imitate Taiwan's strategy. Fully aware of these divergences, geographers have sounded warnings against the danger of transferring theoretical frameworks and strategies from one region to another. Ever since the early 1960s, they have emphasized that each country is unique, not only in terms of development potential, but also with regard to the origin and nature of underdevelopment. Even neighboring countries like Tanzania and Zambia differ so much in so many respects that each should be studied separately.

There has in recent years been much talk about 'adapted technology,' and there can be little doubt that this is a good thing. But more important than adapted technology is the idea of 'adapted development strategy': the development of an overall, long-term plan designed specifically for a particular country and in which small-scale, local projects form integrated parts of broader schemes at the regional and national levels – possibly with extensions to development schemes in one or more neighboring countries. In the absence of such integration, development will in all likelihood be a piecemeal and haphazard exercise in futility that may do more harm than good. If, for example, lack of coordination leads to highly uneven development, to excessive migration to the cities, and/or to increased urban-rural disparities, the ultimate result could well be more, rather than less, underdevelopment.

If we accept the proposition that the principal purpose of science is to solve problems, geographers should make a concerted effort to develop the study of spatial differentiation of development, material well-being, and social injustice into an applied science. To accomplish this task, geographers must not only search for "likenesses hidden under apparent divergences" (Pirsig), but also uncover differences hidden under apparent resemblances.

Bibliography*

* The references listed at the end of the four case studies (Chapters 17-20) are not included.

AMIN, S. (1973), *Le développement inégal. Essai sur les formations sociales du capitalisme périphérique*. Paris: Les Editions de Minuit.

AMIN, S. (1973), Underdevelopment and Dependence in Black Africa. *Social and Economic Studies*, 22, pp. 177-197.

AMIN, S. (1976), *L'impérialisme et le développement inégal*. Paris: Les Editions de Minuit.

AMIN, S., G. ARRIGHI, A. G. FRANK & I. WALLERSTEIN (1982), *Dynamics of Global Crisis*. New York: Monthly Review Press.

ANDREAE, B. (1964), *Betriebsformen in der Landwirtschaft. Entstehung und Wandlung von Bodennutzungs-, Viehhaltungs- und Betriebssystemen in Europa und Ubersee sowie neue Methoden ihrer Abgrenzung. Systematischer Teil einer Agrarbetriebslehre*. Stuttgart: Verlag Eugen Ulmer.

ARDANT, G. (1959), *Le monde en friche*. Paris: Presses Universitaires de France.

BAIROCH, P. (1975), *The Economic Development of the Third World since 1900*. London: Methuen & Co Ltd.

BAIROCH, P. (1980), Le bilan économique du colonialisme: mythes et réalités. In: L. Blussé, H. L. Wesseling & G. D. Winius (eds.), *History and Underdevelopment. Essays on Underdevelopment and European Expansion in Asia and Africa*, pp. 29-42. Leiden: Centre for the History of European Expansion.

BARAN, P. (1957), *The Political Economy of Growth*. New York: Monthly Review Press.

BARKE, M. & G. O'HARE (1984), *The Third World. Diversity, Change and Interdependence*. Edinburgh: Oliver & Boyd.

BARRATT BROWN, M. (1976), *The Economics of Imperialism*. Harmondsworth: Penguin Books Ltd.

BECKFORD, G. L. (1972), *Persistent Poverty — Underdevelopment in Plantation Economies of the Third World*. New York: Oxford University Press.

BERGER, P. L., B. BERGER & H. KELLNER (1974), *The Homeless Mind*. Harmondsworth: Penguin Books Ltd.

BERNSTEIN, H. (ed.) (1973), *Underdevelopment and Development. The Third World Today. Selected Readings*. Harmondsworth: Penguin Books Ltd.

BERRY, B. J. L. (1961), City Size, Distribution and Economic Development. *Economic Development and Cultural Change*, 9, pp. 573-588.

BERTHOLET, C. J. L. (1975), *De strijd om een adequaat ontwikkelingsparadigma voor de Derde Wereld*. Eindhoven.

BEYHAUT, G. (1965), *Süd- und Mittelamerika. II. Von der Unabhängigkeit bis zur Krise der Gegenwart*. Frankfurt am Main: Fischer Bücherei K.G.

BLUSSÉ, L., H. L. WESSELING & G. D. WINIUS (eds.) (1980), *History and Underdevelopment. Essays on Underdevelopment and European Expansion in Asia and Africa*. Leiden: Centre for the History of European Expansion.

BOBEK, H. (1959), Die Hauptstufen der Gesellschafts- und Wirtschaftsentfaltung in geographischer Sicht. *Die Erde*, 90, pp. 259-298.

BOBEK, H. (1962a), Zur Problematik der unterentwickelten Länder. *Mitteilungen der österreichischen geographischen Gesellschaft*, 104. Heft I/II, pp. 1-24.

BOBEK, H. (1962b), *Iran. Probleme eines unterentwickelten Landes alter Kultur*. Frankfurt am Main: Verlag Moritz Diesterweg.

BOBEK, H. (1974), Zum Konzept des Rentenkapitalismus. *Tijdschrift voor Economische en Sociale Geografie*, 65, pp. 73-78.

BODENHEIMER, S. (1971), Dependency and Imperialism. The Roots of Latin American Underdevelopment. *Politics and Society*, 1, pp. 327-357.

BOEKE, J. H. (1953), *Economics and Economic Policy of Dual Societies*. Haarlem: H. D. Tjeenk Willink.

BREESE, G. (1966), *Urbanization in Newly Developing Countries*. Englewood Cliffs, N.J.: Prentice Hall Inc.

BREESE, G. (ed.) (1969), *The City in Newly Developing Countries. Readings on Urbanism and Urbanization*. Englewood Cliffs, N.J.: Prentice Hall Inc.

BRETT, E. A. (1973), *Colonialism and Underdevelopment in East Africa. The Politics of Economic Change, 1919-1939*. London: Heinemann.

BROMLEY, R. & CHR. GERRY (eds.) (1979), *Casual Work and Poverty in Third World Cities*. Chicester: John Wiley and Sons.

BROOKFIELD, H. (1975), *Interdependent Development. Perspectives on Development*. London: Methuen & Co Ltd.

BROWNING, H. (1958), Recent Trends in Latin American Urbanization. *Annals of the American Academy of Political and Social Sciences*, 316, pp. 111-120.

BRUNSCHWIG, H. (1980), L'Afrique noire atlantique et l'Europe. In: L. Blussé, H. L. Wesseling & G. D. Winius (eds.), *History and Underdevelopment. Essays on Underdevelopment and European Expansion in Asia and Africa*, pp. 129-137. Leiden: Centre for the History of European Expansion.

BRUTZKUS, E. (1973), Centralized versus Decentralized Patterns of Urbanization in Developing Countries. *Tijdschrift voor Economische en Sociale Geografie*, 64, pp. 11-23.

CARDOSO, F. H. (1977), Current Theses on Latin American Development and Dependency. A Critique. *Boletín de Estudios Latinoamericanos y del Caribe*, 22, pp. 53-64.

CAZES, G. & J. DOMINGO (1975), *Les critères du sous-développement. Géopolitique du Tiers Monde*. Montreuil: Bréal.

CHATTERJEE, S. P. (ed.) (1968), *Developing Countries of the World*. Calcutta: National Committee for Geography.

CHIROT, D. (1977), *Social Change in the Twentieth Century*. New York: Harcourt Brace Jovanovich, Inc.

CHIROT, D. (1981), Changing Fashions in the Study of the Social Causes of Economic and Political Change. In: Short, Jr., J. F. (ed.), *The State of Sociology — Problems and Prospects*, pp. 259-282. Beverly Hills and London: Sage Publications.

CHIROT, D. & T. D. HALL (1982), World-System Theory. *Annual Review of Sociology*, 8, pp. 81-106.

CHISHOLM, M. (1982), *Modern World Development*. Totowa, N. J.: Barnes & Noble.

CHRISTALLER, W. (1966), *Central Places in Southern Germany* (translated by C. Baskin). Englewood Cliffs, N.J.: Prentice Hall, Inc.

CLARKE, J. I. (1977), *Population Geography and the Developing Countries*. Oxford: Pergamon Press.

CLARKE, J. I. *et al.* (1975), *An Advanced Geography of Africa*. Amersham, Bucks.: Hulton Education Publications Ltd.

COCKCROFT, J. D., A. G. FRANK & D. L. JOHNSON (1972), *Dependence and Underdevelopment. Latin America's Political Economy*. Garden City, N.Y.: Anchor Books.

COPPENS, H. (1976), Ontwikkelingstheorie in beweging. Benaderingswijzen van het ontwikkelingsvraagstuk. *Intermediair*, 12, 12 November, pp. 23, 25, 27, 29 and 35.

COPPENS, H. (1979), Imperialisme. Een nieuwe benadering. *Intermediair*, 15, 11 May, pp. 35, 37, 39, 41, 43 and 45; 18 May, pp. 53, 55, 57, 59 and 61.

DADZIE, K. K. S. (1980), Economic Development. *Scientific American* 243, 3, pp. 59-65.

DAVIDSON, B. (1964), *Which Way Africa?* Harmondsworth: Penguin Books Ltd.

DICKENSON, J. P. *et al.* (1983), *A Geography of the Third World*. London: Methuen & Co Ltd.

DIETVORST, A. G. J. (1975), *De Volksrepubliek China*. Bussum: Unieboek.

DOS SANTOS, TH. (1970), The Structure of Dependence. *American Economic Review*, 60, pp. 231-236.

DOS SANTOS, TH. (1973), The Crisis of Development and the Problem of Dependence in Latin America. In: H. Bernstein (ed.), *Underdevelopment and Development. The Third World Today. Selected Readings*, pp. 57-81. Harmondsworth: Penguin Books Ltd.

DRAKE, C. (1981), Socio-cultural Aspects of National Integration in Indonesia. *Tijdschrift voor Economische en Sociale Geografie*, 72, pp. 334-346.

DUMONT, R. & B. ROSIER (1970), *The Hungry Future*. London: Methuen & Co Ltd.

DUMONT, R. & M. F. MOTTIN (1983), *Stranglehold on Africa* (translated by V. Menkes). London: André Deutsch Ltd.

DWYER, D. J. (ed.) (1974), *The City in the Third World. Geographical Readings*. London: The Macmillan Press Ltd.

EHRLICH, W. (1971), *Die Bevölkerungsbombe*. München: Carl Hanser Verlag.

EMMANUEL, A. (1969), *L'échange inégal*. Paris: Maspero.

ESSER, KL. (1979), *Lateinamerika. Industrialisierungsstrategien und Entwicklung*. Frankfurt am Main: Edition Suhrkamp.

ETTEMA, W. A. (1979), Geographers and Development. *Tijdschrift voor Economische en Sociale Geografie*, 70, pp. 66-75.

ETTEMA, W. A. (1983), The Centre-Periphery Perspective in Development Geograpphy. *Tijdschrift voor Economische en Sociale Geografie*, 74, pp. 107-119.

EVERS, T. & P. VON WOGAU (1973), 'Dependencia'. Lateinamerikanische Beiträge zur Theorie der Unterentwicklung. *Das Argument*, 15, pp. 404-454.

FALCON, W. P. (1970), The Green Revolution. Generations of Problems. *American Journal of Agricultural Economics*, 52, pp. 698-710.

F.A.O. (1971), Nature and Objectives of Agrarian Reform; Urgency of Reform. In: F.A.O., *Report of the Special Committee on Agrarian Reform*, pp. 4-10. Rome: Food and Agricultural Organization.

F.A.O. (1979), *Agriculture Toward 2000*. Rome: Food and Agricultural Organization.

FEDER, E. (1974), Notes on the New Penetration of the Agriculture of Developing Countries by Industrial Nations. *Boletín de Estudios Latinoamericanos y del Caribe*, 16, pp. 67-74.

FRANK, A. G. (1964), On the Mechanism of Imperialism: The Case of Brazil. *Monthly Review*, 16, pp. 284-297.

FRANK, A. G. (1966), The Development of Underdevelopment. *Monthly Review*, 18, pp. 17-31.

FRANK, A. G. (1968), *Development and Underdevelopment in Latin America*. New York: Monthly Review Press.

FRANK, A. G. (1969a), *Latin America. Underdevelopment or Revolution. Essays on the Development of Underdevelopment and the Immediate Enemy*. New York: Monthly Review Press.

FRANK, A. G. (1969b), *Capitalism and Underdevelopment in Latin America. Historical Studies of Chile and Brazil*. New York: Monthly Review Press.

FRANK, A. G. (1978), *Dependent Accumulation and Underdevelopment*. London: The Macmillan Press Ltd.

FRANK, A. G. (1982), Crisis of Ideology and Ideology of Crisis. In: S. Amin et al., *Dynamics of Global Crisis*, pp. 109-165. New York: Monthly Review Press.

FRANKEL, F. R. (1971), *India's Green Revolution*. Berkeley: University of California Press.

FRIEDMAN, E. (1982), Introduction. In: E. Friedman (ed.), *Ascent and Decline in the World System*, pp. 9-23. Beverly Hills and London: Sage Publications.

FRIEDMANN, J. (1973), *Urbanization, Planning, and National Development*. London: Sage Publications.

FURTADO, C. (1973), *A Hegemonia dos Estados Unidos e o Subdesenvolvimento da América Latina*. Rio de Janeiro: Civilização Brasileira.

GALJART, B. F. (1974), Dependence. Some Implications of a Definition of the Concept. In: *Dependence and Latin America. A Workshop*, Amsterdam, 19-21 November 1973, pp. 11-22. Amsterdam: Centro de Estudios y Documentación Latinoamericanos.

GALJART, B. F. (1975), *Voorbij prietpraat en blijde boodschap. Over de taak van de ontwikkelingssociologie*. Leiden: Universitaire Pers Leiden.

GALTUNG, J. (1971), A Structural Theory of Imperialism. *Journal of Peace Research*, 8, pp. 81-117.

400

GALTUNG, J. (1981), The Politics of Self-Reliance. In: H. Muñoz (ed.), *From Dependency to Development. Strategies to Overcome Underdevelopment and Inequality*, pp. 173-196. Boulder, Colorado: Westview Press.

GEERTZ, Cl. (1963a), *Agricultural Involution. The Process of Ecological Change in Indonesia.* Berkeley: University of California Press.

GEERTZ, Cl. (1963b), *Peddlers and Princes. Social Change and Economic Modernization in Two Indonesian Towns.* Chicago: University of Chicago Press.

GEORGE, P. (1970), O Habitat Espontâneo nas Grandes Cidades e os Problemas de sua Reabsorção. In: *Conferências no Brasil*, pp. 67-76. Rio de Janeiro: Instituto Brasileiro de Geografia.

GEORGE, S. (1979), *How the Other Half Dies. The Real Reasons for World Hunger.* Harmondsworth: Penguin Books Ltd.

GILBERT, A. (1974), *Latin American Development. A Geographical Perspective.* Harmondswirth: Penguin Books Ltd.

GILBERT, A. (ed.) (1976), *Development Planning and Spatial Structure.* London: John Wiley and Sons.

GILBERT, A. & J. GUGLER (1982), *Cities, Poverty, and Development. Urbanization in the Third World.* Oxford: Oxford University Press.

GINSBURG, N. (1960), Editor's Introduction. In: N. Ginsburg (ed.), *Essays on Geography and Economic Development*, pp. vii-xx. Chicago: University of Chicago Press.

GINSBURG, N. S. (1961), *Atlas of Economic Development.* Chicago: University of Chicago Press.

GONZÁLEZ-CASANOVA, P. (1964/65), Internal Colonialism and National Development. *Studies in International Comparative Development*, 1, 4, pp. 27-37.

GOUROU, P. (1949), L'Amazonie, problèmes géographiques. *Les Cahiers d'Outre Mer*, 2, pp. 1-13.

GOUROU, P. (1966), *The Tropical World. Its Social and Economic Conditions and Its Future Status.* London: Longmans.

GRAHAM, E. & I. FLOERING (1984), *The Modern Plantation in the Third World.* London & Sydney: Croom Helm.

GRIFFIN, K. (1979), *The Political Economy of Agrarian Change.* London: The Macmillan Press Ltd.

GROSSMAN, L. (1981), The Cultural Ecology of Economic Development. *Annals of the Association of American Geographers*, 71, pp. 220-236.

GUIFFAN, J. (1969), *Surpopulation et Malnutrition.* Paris: Armand Colin.

GUILLAUME, P. (1974), *Le monde colonial, XIXe-XXe siècle.* Paris: Armand Colin.

HAGEN, E. E. (1962), *On the Theory of Social Change. How Economic Growth Begins.* Homewood, Ill.: Dorsey.

HALL, K. & B. BLAKE (1981), Collective Self-Reliance: The Case of the Caribbean Community (CARICOM). In: H. Muñoz (ed.), *From Dependency to Development. Strategies to Overcome Underdevelopment and Inequality*, pp. 197-206. Boulder, Colorado: Westview Press.

HANSEN, N. M. (1981), Development from Above: The Centre-Down Development Paradigm. In: W. B. Stöhr & D. R. F. Taylor (eds.), *Development from Above or Below?*, pp. 15-38. Chicester: John Wiley and Sons.

HARDEMAN, J. (1973), De agrarische situatie in Latijns Amerika. *Geografisch Tijdschrift*, Nieuwe Reeks, 7, pp. 191-202.

HARDIN, G. (1974), Lifeboat Ethics: A Malthusian View. *Bioscience*, 24, pp. 561-568.

HARRISON, P. (1979), *Inside the Third World.* Harmondsworth: Penguin Books Ltd.

HART, J. K. (1974), Informal Income Opportunities and Urban Employment in Ghana. *Journal of Modern African Studies*, 11, pp. 61-89.

HARTSHORNE, R. (1960), Geography and Economic Growth. In: N. S. Ginsburg (ed.), *Essays on Geography and Economic Development*, pp. 3-25. Chicago: University of Chicago Press.

HAYIT, B. (1965), *Sowjetrussischer Kolonialismus und Imperialismus in Turkestan.* Oosterhout, Netherl.: Anthropological Publications.

401

HECHTER, M. (1975), *Internal Colonialism: The Celtic Fringe in British National Development, 1536-1966*. London: Routledge and Kegan Paul.

HIGGINS, B. (1956), The Dualistic Theory of Underdeveloped Areas. *Economic Development and Cultural Change*, 4, pp. 99-116.

HINDERINK, J. (1970), *No Longer at Ease. Afrikanen in Steden. Steden in Tropisch Afrika*. Assen: Van Gorcum & Comp.

HIRSCHMAN, O. (1958), *The Strategy of Economic Development*. New Haven, Conn.: Yale: University Press.

HODDER, B. W. (1971), *Economic Development in the Tropics*. London: Methuen & Co Ltd.

HOSELITZ, B. F. (1960), Generative and Parasitic Cities. In: B. F. Hoselitz, *Sociological Aspects of Economic Growth*, pp. 185-216. New York: Free Press.

HOYLE, B. S. (ed.) (1974), *Spatial Aspects of Development*. London: John Wiley and Sons.

HURST, H. E. (1957), *The Nile. A General Account of the River and the Utilization of its Waters*. London.

HYDEN, G. (1980), *Beyond Ujamaa in Tanzania. Underdevelopment and an Uncaptured Peasantry*. Berkeley: The University of California Press.

HYDEN, G. (1983), *No Shortcuts to Progress. African Development Management in Perspective*. London: Heinemann.

INSTITUTO BRASILEIRO DE GEOGRAFIA E ESTATÍSTICA (1982), *IX Recenseamento Geral do Brasil, 1980. Sinopse Preliminar do Censo Agropecuário*, vol. 2, tomo 1, número 1: Brasil. Rio de Janeiro: IBGE.

INTERNATIONAL LABOUR OFFICE (1972), *Employment, Incomes and Equality. A Strategy for Increasing Productive Employment in Kenya*. Geneva: I.L.O.

JANSSEN, R. (1978), *'Wij hebben zelfs geen recht op de stad'. Vogelvrij wonen in Bogotá*. Amsterdam: Ekologische Uitgeverij.

JEFFERSON, M. (1939), The Law of the Primate City. *Geographical Review*, 29, pp. 227-232.

JOHNSON, J. H. (1967), *Urban Geography. An Introductory Analysis*. Oxford: Pergamon Press.

JOSHI, P. C. (1970), Land Reform in India and Pakistan. *Economic and Political Weekly*, 5, pp. A 145-162.

JUPPENLATZ, M. (1970), *Cities in Transformation. The Urban Squatter Problem of the Developing Countries*. St. Lucia, Queensland: The University of Queensland Press.

KAMARCK, A. M. (1976), *The Tropics and Economic Development. A Provocative Inquiry into the Poverty of Nations*. Baltimore: The Johns Hopkins University Press.

KISSINGER, H. A. (1983), Saving the World Economy. *Newsweek*, Jan. 24, pp. 46-49.

KLEINPENNING, J. M. G. (1968), *Geografie van de landbouw*. Utrecht: Het Spectrum.

KLEINPENNING, J. M. G. (1975), *The Integration and Colonisation of the Brazilian Portion of the Amazon Basin*. Nijmegen: Geografisch en Planologisch Instituut, Katholieke Universiteit.

KLEINPENNING, J. M. G. (1978), *Interregionale ongelijkheid in ontwikkelingslanden*. Nijmegen: Geografisch en Planologisch Instituut, Katholieke Universiteit.

KLEINPENNING, J. M. G. (ed.) (1980a), *Milieuproblemen in de Derde Wereld. Een sociaal-geografische inleiding*. Assen: Van Gorcum & Comp.

KLEINPENNING, J. M. G. (1980b), *Drie maal Derde Wereld. Een inleiding tot de verscheidenheid van de ontwikkelingslanden*. Assen: Van Gorcum & Comp.

KLEINPENNING, J. M. G. (1981), *Profiel van de Derde Wereld* (2nd ed.). Assen: Van Gorcum & Comp.

KLEINPENNING, J. M. G. (1984), Over rentekapitalisme en andere visies op onderontwikkeling: schroothoop of instrumentarium? *Geografisch Tijdschrift*, 18, pp. 89-94.

KROEBER, A. & C. KLUCKHOHN (1963), *Culture: A Critical Review of Concepts and Definitions*. Vintage Books. New York: Random House, Inc.

KUHNEN, Fr. (1982), *Man and Land. An Introduction into the Problems of Agrarian Structure and Agrarian Reform*. Saarbrücken/Fort Lauderdale: Verlag Breitenbach Publishers.

KURIAN, G. T. (1979), *Encyclopedia of the Third World*. London: Mansell.

LACOSTE, Y. (1963), *Les pays sous-développés*. Paris: Presses Universitaires de France.

LACOSTE, Y. (1965), *Géographie du sous-développement*. Paris: Presses Universitaires de France.

402

LACOSTE, Y. (1966), Remarques pour l'établissement d'une typologie générale de l'inégal développement. *Cahiers de Sociologie Économique*, pp. 122-134.

LACOSTE, Y. (1967), Le concept de sous-développement et la géographie. *Annales de Géographie*, pp. 644-670.

LACOSTE, Y. (1975), *Géographie du sous-développement*. Paris: Presses Universitaires de France.

LE COZ, J. (1974), *Les réformes agraires. De Zapata à Mao Tsé toung et la F.A.O.* Paris: Presses Universitaires de France.

LEE, E. (1981), Basic Needs Strategies: A Frustrated Response to Development from Below. In: W. B. Stöhr & D. R. F. Taylor (eds.), *Development from Above or Below?*, pp. 107-122. Chicester: John Wiley and Sons.

LENG, G. (1974), Rentenkapitalismus oder Feudalismus? Kritische Untersuchungen über einen (sozial)geographischen Begriff. *Geographische Zeitschrift*, pp. 119-137.

LENIN, V. I. (1948), *Imperialism: The Highest Stage of Capitalism*. London: Lawrence and Wishart.

LINDQVIST, S. (1979), *Land and Power in South America*. Harmondsworth: Penguin Books Ltd.

LIPTON, M. (1978), *Why Poor People Stay Poor. A Study of Urban Bias in World Development*. London: Temple Smith Ltd.

LLOYD, P. (1979), *Slums of Hope? Shanty Towns in the Third World*. Harmondsworth: Penguin Books Ltd.

LLOYD, P. (1980), *The 'Young Towns' of Lima: Aspects of Urbanization in Perú*. Cambridge: Cambridge University Press.

MABOGUNJE, A. L. (1980), *The Development Process. A Spatial Perspective*. London: Hutchinson & Co Ltd.

MANDEL, E. (1968), Die Marxsche Theorie der ursprünglichen Akkumulation und die Industrialisierung der Dritten Welt. In: *Folgen einer Theorie. Essays über das Kapital von Karl Marx*, pp. 71-93. Frankfurt am Main: Edition Suhrkamp.

MANGIN, W. (1967), Squatter Settlements. *Scientific American*, 217, October, pp. 21-29.

MANGIN, W. (1969), Latin American Squatter Settlements. A Problem and a Solution. *Ekistics*, 158, pp. 37-39.

MANSHARD, W. (1970), *Afrika südlich der Sahara*. Frankfurt am Main: Fischer Bücherei GmbH.

MCCLELLAND, D. C. (1961/1976), *The Achieving Society*. New York: Van Nostrand.

MCGEE, T. G. (1971), *The Urbanization Process in the Third World. Explanations in Search of a Theory*. London: G. Bell and Sons Ltd.

MORRIS, M. D. (1979), *Measuring the Conditions of the World's Poor. The Physical Quality of Life Index*. New York: Pergamon Press.

MOUNTJOY, A. B. (1969), *Industrialization and Underdeveloped Countries*. London: Hutchinson University Library.

MOUNTJOY, A. B. (ed.) (1971), *Developing the Underdeveloped Countries. Geographical Readings*. London: The Macmillan Press Ltd.

MOUNTJOY, A. B. (1976), Urbanisation, the Squatter and Development in the Third World. *Tijdschrift voor Economische en Sociale Geografie*, 67, pp. 130-138.

MOUNTJOY, A. B. (ed.) (1978), *The Third World. Problems and Perspectives*. London: The Macmillan Press.

MYINT, H. (1967), *The Economics of the Developing Countries*. London: Hutchinson University Library.

MYRDAL, G. (1969), *Economic Theory and Underdeveloped Regions*. London: Methuen & Co Ltd.

NATER, T. & R. VOKEY (1982), The Smoldering Slums. *Newsweek*, September 13, p. 28.

NEWSWEEK (1982), May 17, pp. 50-53.

NURKSE, R. (1953), *Problems of Capital Formation in Underdeveloped Countries*. Oxford: Blackwell.

O'BRIEN, ph. (1974), A Critique of Latin American Theories of Dependency. In: *Dependency and Latin America. A Workshop*. Amsterdam, 19-21 November 1973, pp. 22-40. Amsterdam: Centro de Estudios y Documentación Latinoamericanos.

403

ODELL, P. R. (1970), Regional Development Issues in the Developing Countries of Latin America. *Economisch-Statistische Berichten*, June, pp. 539-546.

ODELL, P. & D. A. PRESTON (1978), *Economies and Societies in Latin America. A Geographical Interpretation*. Chicester: John Wiley and Sons.

PALLOIX, C. (1971), *L'économie mondiale capitaliste*. Paris: Maspero. 2 vols.

PALTE, J. G. L. & G. J. TEMPELMAN (1978), *Indonesië*. Bussum: Romen.

PARISSE, L. (1969). Les favelas dans la ville: le cas de Rio de Janeiro. *Revista Geográfica*, 70, pp. 109-130.

PAYNE, G. K. (1977), *Urban Housing in the Third World*. London: Leonard Hill.

PEARSE, A. (1980), *Seeds of Plenty, Seeds of Want. Social and Economic Implications of the Green Revolution*. Oxford: Clarendon Press.

PERLMAN, J. E. (1976), *The Myth of Marginality. Urban Poverty and Politics in Rio de Janeiro*. Berkeley: The University of California Press.

PERROUX, F. (1969), *L'économie du XXe siècle*. Paris: Presses Universitaires de France.

PIRSIG, R. M. (1976), *Zen and the Art of Motorcycle Maintenance*. London: Transworld Publishers Ltd.

PREBISCH, R. (1970), *Transformación y desarrollo. La gran tárea de la América Latina*. Mexico: Fondo de Cultura Económica.

RAY, D. (1973), The Dependency Model of Latin American Underdevelopment. Three Basic Fallacies. *Journal of Interamerican Studies and World Affairs*, 15, pp. 4-21.

REITSMA, H. A. (1980), Africa's Land-locked Countries. A Study of Dependency Relations. *Tijdschrift voor Economische en Sociale Geografie*, 71, pp. 130-142.

REITSMA, H. A. (1982), Development Geography, Dependency Relations and the Capitalist Scapegoat. *Professional Geographer*, 34, pp. 125-130.

REITSMA, H. A. (1983a), A Constellation of Core-Periphery Relations. *Professional Geographer*, 35, pp. 84-86.

REITSMA, H. A. (1983b), A Conceptual Model of Dependency. *Professional Geographer*, 35, pp. 330-331.

REITSMA, H. A. (1984), Dependency with Development: the Case of Lesotho. *Drumlin* (Glasgow University Geographical Society), no. 29, pp. 19-25.

RIFKIN, J. (1981), *Entropy: A New World View*. Toronto: Bantam Books.

RIMMER, R. J. & D. K. FORBES (1982), Underdevelopment Theory: A Geographical Review. *Australian Geographer*, 15, pp. 197-211.

ROBERTS, B. (1978), *Cities of Peasants. The Political Economy of Urbanization in the Third World*. London: Edward Arnold.

RODNEY, W. (1972), *How Europe Underdeveloped Africa*. London: Bogle-L'Ouverture Publications, and Dar es Salaam: Tanzania Publishing House.

ROGERSON, C. M. & K. S. O. BEAVON (1982), Getting by in the 'Informal Sector' of Soweto. *Tijdschrift voor Economische en Sociale Geografie*, 73, pp. 250-265.

ROSTOW, W. W. (1960), *The Stages of Economic Growth. A Non-Communist Manifesto*. New York: Cambridge University Press.

ROXBOROUGH, I. (1979), *Theories of Underdevelopment*. London: Macmillan Press Ltd.

SANTOS, M. (1970), *Les villes du Tiers Monde*. Paris: Ed. M. Th. Genin.

SCHLIPPE, P. DE (1956), *Shifting Cultivation in Africa. The Zande System of Agriculture*. London: Routledge & Kegan Paul.

SCHUURMAN, F. J. (1980), *Van Andes naar Oriënte. Agrarische kolonisatie in Amazonia en de rol van de staat*. Amsterdam: Centro de Estudios y Documentación Latinoamericanos.

SENGHAAS, D. (ed.) (1974), *Peripherer Kapitalismus. Analysen über Abhängigkeit und Unterentwicklung*. Frankfurt am Main: Edition Suhrkamp.

SIDERI, S. (1971), Perspectives for the Third World. *Internationale Spectator*, XXV, pp. 469-498.

SIMOONS, F. S. (1961), *Eat Not This Flesh: Food Avoidances in the Old World*. Madison: University of Wisconsin Press.

SLICHER VAN BATH, B. H. (1974), Feudalismo y capitalismo en América Latina. *Boletín de Estudios Latinoamericanos y del Caribe*, 17, pp. 21-42.

SLOAN, J. W. (1977), Dependency Theory and Latin American Development. Another Key Fails to Open the Door. *Interamerican Economic Affairs*, XXXI, pp. 21-41.

SMITH, D. M. (1979), *Where the Grass is Greener: Living in an Unequal World*. Harmondsworth: Penguin Books Ltd.

SOUZA, A. R. DE & P. W. PORTER (1974), *The Underdevelopment and Modernization of the Third World*. Washington: Association of American Geographers.

STANSFIELD, D. E. (1974), Perspectives on Dependency. In: *Dependency and Latin America. A Workshop*. Amsterdam, 19-21 November 1973, pp. 3-11. Amsterdam: Centro de Estudios y Documentación Latinoamericanos.

STAVENHAGEN, R. (1968), Seven Fallacies about Latin America. In: J. Petras & M. Zeitlin (eds.), *Latin America. Reform or Revolution?*, pp. 13-31. Greenwich: Fawcett.

STÖHR, W. B. (1981), Development from Below: The Bottom-Up and Periphery-Inward Development Paradigm. In: W. B. Stöhr & D. R. F. Taylor (eds.), *Development from Above or Below?*, pp. 39-72. Chicester: John Wiley and Sons.

STOVER, L. (1974), *The Cultural Ecology of Chinese Civilization*. New York: The New American Library Inc.

SUNKEL, O. & P. PAZ (1976), *El subdesarrollo latinoamericano y la teoría del desarrollo*. Mexico: Siglo Veintiuno Editores S.A.

SZENTES, T. (1976), *The Political Economy of Underdevelopment*. Budapest: Akadémiai Kiadó.

TAMSMA, R. (1956), Enkele aspecten van de sociaal-geografische structuur van het Midden-Oosten. *Geografisch Tijdschrift*, 9, pp. 1-14 & 57-72.

TEMPELMAN, G. J. & O. VERKOREN (1975), De groene revolutie. Een greep uit recente publikaties. *Geografisch Tijdschrift*, Nieuwe Reeks, 9, pp. 329-337.

TODARO, M. P. (1977), *Economic Development in the Third World*. London/New York: Longman.

TROEF (1982), vol. 6, no 1. Special issue on drugs in the Third World.

TURNER, J. F. C. (1967), Barriers and Channels for Housing Development in Modernizing Countries. *Journal of the American Institute of Planners*, 33, pp. 167-181.

UNITED NATIONS (1982), *Statistical Yearbook/Annuaire Statistique*. New York: United Nations.

UNITED NATIONS (1982), *Demographic Yearbook/Annuaire Démographique*. New York: United Nations.

UTRECHT, E. (1971), Pogingen tot verhoging van de rijstproduktie in Indonesië. Landhervormingen en Bimasprojecten. *Geografisch Tijdschrift*, Nieuwe Reeks, 5, pp. 108-122.

VAN BINSBERGEN, W. M. J. & H. A. MEILINK (eds.) (1978), *Migration and the Transformation of Modern African Society*. Leiden: Afrika-Studiecentrum.

VAN DAM, F. (1974), Honderd Jaar Ontwikkelingsvraagstuk. *Economisch-Statistische Berichten*, 11 December, pp. 1108-1112.

VAN DAM, F. (1978), Mode in het Ontwikkelingsvraagstuk. *Economisch-Statistische Berichten*, 17 May, pp. 496-500.

VAN DAM, F. (1979), Noord-Zuid Relatie Herbezien. *Economisch-Statistische Berichten*, 31 January, pp. 108-113.

VAN DAM, F. (1979), Noord-Zuid: De Werkelijkheid van 1980-1990. *Economisch-Statistische Berichten*, 14 November, pp. 1188-1196.

VAN GINKEL, J. A., O. VERKOREN, G. MIK, G. DE RIJK & J. VELDMAN (1977), *Zicht op de Stad. Sociaal-geografische beschouwingen over steden en stedengroei*. Bussum: Unieboek.

VAN HEUR, A., A. KUIPERS & A. VOOREND (1982), The Marketing of Vegetables and Fruit in African Cities (M.A. thesis, University of Amsterdam).

VELDMAN, J., J. A. VAN GINKEL, G. DE RIJK, CHR. SMITH & O. VERKOREN (1974), *Zicht op de landbouw. De ruimtelijke verscheidenheid van de landbouw in de samenleving*. Bussum: Unieboek.

VERKOREN, O. (1979), Over de industriële struktuur in de ontwikkelingslanden. *Geografisch Tijdschrift*, Nieuwe Reeks, 13, pp. 2-15.

VON ALBERTINI, R. (1980), Colonisation and Underdevelopment: Critical Remarks on the Theory of Dependency. In: L. Blussé, H. L. Wesseling & G. D. Winius (eds.), *History and Underdevelopment. Essays on Underdevelopment and European Expansion in Asia and Africa*. Leiden: Centre for the History of European Expansion.

405

VON ALBERTINI, R. (1982), *European Colonial Rule, 1880-1940. The Impact of the West on India, Southeast Asia, and Africa*. Westport, Conn.: Greenwood Press.

WARREN, B. (1982), *Imperialism: Pioneer of Capitalism*. London: Verso Editions.

WARRINER, D. (1969), *Land Reform in Principle and Practice*. Oxford: Clarendon Press.

WESSELING, H. L. (ed.) (1978), *Expansion and Reaction. Essays on European Expansion and Reactions in Asia and Africa*. Leiden: Leiden University Press.

WEULERSSE, J. (1946), *Paysans du Syrie et du Proche-Orient*. Paris: Gallimard.

WILLIAMSON, J. G. (1965), Regional Inequality and the Process of National Development: A Description of the Patterns. *Economic Development and Cultural Change*, 13, pp. 3-45.

WITTFOGEL, K. (1957), *Oriental Despotism. A Comparative Study of Total Power*. New Haven/London: Yale University Press.

WÖHLCKE, M., P. VON WOGAU & W. MARTINS (1977), *Die neuere entwicklungstheoretische Diskussion. Einführende Darstellung und ausgewählte Bibliographie*. Frankfurt am Main: Verlag Klaus Dieter Vervuert.

WOLF, E. R. & S. W. MINTZ (1957), Haciendas and Plantations in Middle America and the Antilles. *Social and Economic Studies*, VI, pp. 380-412.

WORLD BANK (annual), *World Development Report*. Washington: The World Bank.

ZHANG ZHI-LIAN & LUO RONG-QU (1980), Reflections on Colonialism and Modernisation: the Case of China, In: L. Blussé, H. L. Wesseling & G. D. Winius (eds.), *History and Underdevelopment. Essays on Underdevelopment and European Expansion in Asia and Africa*, pp. 109-114. Leiden: Centre for the History of European Expansion.

Author Index

Subject Index

410

diseconomies 149; of agglomeration 180
disparities (global) 3, 8-9, 16, 27, 30, 52, 130-1, 240, 242, 254, 391; (internal) 11, 13, 25-6, 29, 39, 58-60, 66, 71, 74, 83-5, 93, 113, 117-8, 122, 139, 145-6, 159, 181, 190, 201, 203, 215, 219, 254, 276, 278, 285, 294, 296, 308, 343, 364, 392
distance bias 187
distribution centers 169-70; of farmland in Brazil 59; of landownership 57-77, 113, 118, 206, 228, 274-5, 340 (see also land-ownership structure); of urban places 147-9, 170, 202
diversification 132
diversity (spatial) 12, 16, 19, 22, 36, 42, 44, 84, 181, 203, 235 (see also spatial differentiation)
division of labor (see specialization; international division of labor)
Djibouti 172, 267, 278, 281, 285-6
domestic market (see home market)
dominance/domination 13, 15, 21, 36-7, 50, 70, 109, 111, 130, 151, 182, 200, 205, 218, 220, 235, 244, 247, 262
dominance-dependence relations 15, 21, 50, 104, 130, 145, 151, 182, 184, 200-7, 220, 239, 250-1 (see also core-periphery relations)
Dominica 20
Dominican Republic 347
draft animals 64, 66, 91, 96-8, 101, 272-3
drought 272, 294, 296
drugs production 56
dualism 108, 213, 242, 249, 370
dung as fuel 78, 272, 274, 305

East Africa 96, 128, 169, 183, 267, 287, 327
East African Community 18, 140, 175
East Asia 87, 169
East-West rivalry 12
ECLA 246
ecological damage 28-9, 35, 51, 79, 87, 100, 113, 117, 202, 212 (see also desertification; erosion; soil erosion)
Economic Commission for Africa 294
economic crisis (global) 5-6, 16-7, 20, 29, 382; growth 4, 11-2, 27, 35, 72, 114-5 (see also growth); weakness 30, 36-7 (see also weak economic structure)
Ecuador 56, 75-6, 95, 122, 177, 271
education 19, 24-6, 35, 49, 72, 77, 105, 107, 110, 112, 115, 127, 160, 164, 183, 185, 197, 206, 226, 229, 262, 351, 370, 378
efficiency 21, 93, 107, 144, 150 (see also equity-efficiency debate)

egalitarian society 57, 72
Egypt 9, 90, 95, 123, 271, 290
EIC 312-4
ejidos 71
ELF 295
elite 16, 21, 39, 49, 58, 70-1, 113, 121, 136-7, 145, 177, 179, 212, 218-9, **229-38**, 242-4, 248-9, 253-8, 262, 287, 289-90, 293, 306-10, 314, 332, 334, 344, 392-3
El Salvador 32, 380
employment opportunities 76, 108, 131, 134, 142, 164, 173, 186, 201-2, 206, 342, 354; problems 14, 54, 59, 62, 71, 76, 79, 93, 108, 117, 133, 161-2, 173, 244; structure 35, 52, 121, 137, 153, 161-4, 332, 346, 378
empresa rural 59
enclave economy 15, 108, 141, 143, 371
endogenous factors (see internal factors)
environmental degradation (see ecological damage)
environmental determinism 3, 212, 302, 390
environmentalism-in-reverse 390
environmental possibilities 8, 390, 396 (see also resources)
equal exchange 5
equality 11, 17
equity 15, 17, 19, 70, 150, 207; equity-efficiency debate 21, 203
erosion 51, 65, 79, 86, 113, 202 (see also soil erosion)
estancias 57, 336
Ethiopia 18, 22, 35, 42, 56, 87, 95, 117, 181-2, 218, 222, 256, 259, **267-97**, 380, **388-97**
ethnic diversity 182, 261, 283-4, 293; nationalism 182-3
Eurocentrism 3, 28, 153
evolutionary process of development 12, 15
expectations 24, 37, 182, 185, 324
explanation of underdevelopment 36, 218, 223, **239-54**, 257, 388
exploitation (see dominance-dependence relations; imperialism; internal colonialism; unequal exchange)
export 17, 124-5, 132-5, 141, 145, 152-3, 170-2, 175, 177, 233, 237, 241, 245, 249, 279, 342, 378, 382
export crops 20, 74, 80, 93, 103-10, 114, 116, 172, 237, 261, 337
export-oriented industrialization 139-43, 221, 379-80
export processing zone 379; export valorization 124
expropriation of land 69-71, 109
extension service (in agriculture) 72, 77-8, 80, 98, 109, 116, 367

413

415

416